Supervision
in
Social Work

Alfred Kadushin

Supervision
in
Social Work

Columbia University Press ■ New York

Alfred Kadushin is Professor of Social Work at the University of
Wisconsin–Madison.

Library of Congress Cataloging in Publication Data

Kadushin, Alfred.
 Supervision in social work.

 Bibliography: p.
 Includes index.
 1. Supervision of social workers.   I. Title.
HV41.K23   658.3   75-31514
ISBN 0-231-03657-4

Copyright © 1976 Columbia University Press
Printed in the United States of America
11 10 9 8 7

To the good people of Wisconsin who, over a quarter of a century, have paid me for doing what I would choose to do even if I did not have to do it for a living—teaching, researching, and writing.

preface

In teaching courses in social work supervision in a graduate school and leading supervision workshops and institutes, I became keenly aware of the need for an up-dated basic text on the subject. This book was written in an effort to meet this need. It provides an overview of the state of the art of social work supervision. It is addressed to supervisors and those preparing to do supervision, whatever their formal educational background. It is also useful to social work supervisees, students and workers, in enabling them to make more productive use of supervision.

The book is designed to help the reader understand the place of supervision in the social agency, the functions it performs, the process of supervision, and the problems with which it is currently concerned. While no book can directly further the development of skills, it provides the knowledge base which is a necessary prerequisite to learning how to do supervision. The book frees the course instructor from the burden of presenting the general background content of supervision so that more time can be devoted to consideration of clinical material and controversial points of view.

An effort has been made to remain eclectic and neutral in presenting a comprehensive, systematic review of social work supervision. While this is generally the orientation of the text, it is pro-supervision. The stance is frankly somewhat conservative, based on my conviction that social work supervision makes a significant contribution to ensuring effective and efficient service to the client. I recognize that such an orientation runs somewhat against the Zietgeist. However, this may be an advantage. A particular, clearly articulated point of view against which the reader can react, positively or negatively provides the basis for a dialogue and may help the reader define her, or his, own point of view.

I have made a studied effort to be generic in the presentation. Alas, it ends up heavily weighted in the direction of casework. In soliciting absolution I plead *ex nihilo, nihil fit*—out of nothing, nothing can be made. The experience of the profession and, consequently, the available literature is most heavily weighted in the direction of casework supervision. There is little recent material on supervision in group work and almost nothing on supervision in community organization.

Pronouns are a source of trouble throughout the text. At one time it would suffice to note that all supervisors would be designated "she" and all supervisees "he." We are beyond the point where such conventional designations are acceptable. Consequently, I have randomized the use of pronouns. "He," "she," and "her," "his" are scattered throughout the text in no particular pattern except to equalize the frequency with which they are used.

The book was written during the year that I was a Fellow at the Center for Advanced Study in the Behavioral Sciences, Palo Alto, California. My very warm thanks and sincere appreciation to the Center for the opportunity the fellowship provided. The Center not only offered financial support but also a stimulating, supportive context. During the year at the Center I was a member of a fellows seminar on organizational theory. The seminar discussions were relevant to the problems of social work supervision, and I am indebted to other members of the seminar for helping me clarify my ideas—Michael Crozier, Herbert Jacobs, Martin Krieger, James March, Eugene Pusic, Daniel Shimshoni, Judith Tendler, Julian Wolpert.

My thanks to John D. Moore, Editor in Chief of Columbia University Press, for editorial encouragement. My further thanks to Anna Tower who patiently deciphered my handwritten hieroglyphics and conscientiously typed many more pages than appear here.

To Sylvia, severest critic and most compassionate friend, my deepest love for constant help, support, and comfort, as well as to Goldie and Raphael, formerly children, now my friends.

A. K.

contents

Supervision
in
Social Work

chapter one

Introduction, History, and Definition

The quality of supervision is a significant factor in professional socialization, social-work job satisfaction, and job turnover. In a study of the process through which therapists are educated to perform their roles, Henry, Sims, and Spray (1971) obtained detailed material from some 1100 psychiatric social workers. They note that "among the various specific experiences considered important by mental health professionals, supervision stands out as the single most important experience —even among mental health professionals who have received psychotherapy, supervision is most often considered the single most important socialization experience" (pp. 150–52).

Samuel Miller (1970) studied the components of job satisfaction of beginning social workers and found that the technical incompetence of the supervisor was one of the most frequent sources of dissatisfaction. Kermish and Kushin (1969) reviewed the reasons why social workers resigned from a large county department of public welfare; of the six principal reasons, "four, at least, are directly related to and strongly influenced by the quality and nature of first line supervision. The quality of supervision was viewed by many of these former workers as a factor so important that improved assistance by the supervisor in the areas of support, encouragement and acquisition of further problem-solving skills might have caused these persons to remain" (p. 137).

A recent nationwide study of 1600 workers in 31 social welfare and rehabilitation agencies states that "the data are conclusive. High agency scores on the supervision variable were accompanied by greater satisfaction, better individual performance, less absenteeism, better agency performance and higher agency competence" (Olmstead and Christensen 1973, p. 304).

. Similar findings are noted in studies of supervision in related human-service professions. Aiken, Smits, and Lollar (1972) studied the job satisfaction of workers in state rehabilitation agencies. Employing a series of pschological and attitudinal scales with 360 counselors, they found that

the most important aspect of employment in State rehabilitation agencies, as far as counselors are concerned, is the interpersonal behavior in which the supervisor and counselor engage. How the supervisor treats the counselor seems to be far more important than working conditions or the reward system of the agency. The importance of the supervisor-counselor relationship is consistent with the attractability and the role demands of the counselor's position. . . . A major component of their role demands is the ability to establish rapport with their clients. It is not surprising that these same people look to their supervisors for help via an interpersonal modality. (p. 5)

Wide-ranging and sophisticated studies of job satisfaction by Herzberg, Mausner, and Snyderman (1959) indicate that while positive job satisfaction is related to job content (work performed, achievement, recognition, responsibility, growth), dissatisfaction is related to job context, one important aspect of which is supervision.

Supervision may be of increasing significance to the professionally trained social worker. With more explicit recognition, by both the National Association of Social Workers and the Council of Social Work Education, of the Bachelor of Social Work (B.S.W.) as a first professional degree for entry-level positions, greater emphasis is being placed on M.S.W. training as preparation for supervisory, consultative, administrative, and planning tasks. Briggs (1973) suggests that during the 1970s "the graduate trained social worker (M.S.W. and D.S.W.) will become a middle manager, team leader, supervisor or staff de-

veloper or a high level specialist-consultant-planner in social
problem areas—education for practice will reflect the shift in
roles" (p. 28). In many schools the process of redefinition of
M.S.W. training has resulted in an "emphasis on training Mas-
ters Degree students for middle level management and supervisory and administrative positions" (Lowenberg 1972, p. 31).

Recent studies of the activities of Bachelor's Degree and
Master's Degree social workers in the same agencies pointed
out that M.S.W.'s were more involved in directing than in providing service. B.S.W.'s were more likely to be providing direct
service, whereas the M.S.W.'s major professional responsibility
had become supervision of, and/or consultation with, B.S.W.
workers (Barker 1972, p. 92). This trend in changing functions
of M.S.W.-trained workers is further confirmed by a follow-up
study of recent graduates (Schultz 1970). Professionally trained
workers often assumed positions as administrators, supervisors,
or consultants within two years of graduation. A survey of Canadian M.S.W.'s showed that over half "were employed in administrative, supervisory, consultative and other non-direct service positions" (Melichercik 1973).

Leaders of the New Careers movement, which aims at increasing the numbers of nonprofessionals, preprofessionals, and
paraprofessionals employed in human-service agencies, point
repeatedly to the change in roles this movement would imply
for the trained professional. Employment of substantial
numbers of New Careerists would require that trained professionals be placed in the position of "supervisors, trainers, consultants, coordinators" (Pearl and Riessman 1965, p. 202).

An examination of the process of supervision is thus significant not only to social workers generally but to professionally
trained social workers in particular. These workers are very
likely to be faced with the responsibility of acting in the role of
supervisor early in their professional careers.

Historical Development

There are few and scattered references to social work supervision before 1920. Many of the references listed under super-

vision in the index of the Proceedings of Conferences on Charities and Correction or in older social work journals refer, in fact, to quite a different process from the supervision we talk about today. Such references are usually concerned with administrative supervision of agencies by some licensing authority or governmental board to which the agencies were accountable for public funds spent and for their service to the client. Supervision referred to the control and coordinating function of a State Board of Supervisors, a State Board of Charities, or a State Board of Control.

The first social work text that used the word "supervision" in the title, *Supervision and Education in Charity* by Jeffrey R. Brackett (1903), was concerned with supervision of welfare agencies and institutions by public boards and commissions rather than supervision of the individual social worker. Sidney Eisenberg, who has written a short history of supervision in social work, notes that Mary Richmond, "one of the most original contributors to the development of social work, made no mention of supervision in her published works" (1956a, p. 1).

With publication of *The Family* (now *Social Casework*) by the Family Welfare Organizing Association of America, beginning in 1920, there are increasingly frequent references to supervision as we know it today.

Mary Burns (1958) comments that while components of the supervisory process were described in the literature as early as 1880 and 1890, the entity with which we are concerned in this book was not clearly recognized and explicitly identified until much later. It "was not included in the index of *Family* until 1925 and not until after 1930 in the *Proceedings of the National Conference of Social Work*" (1958, p. 8).

Supervision as we know it today had its origins in the Charity Organization Society movement in the nineteenth century. A concern for the possible consequences of indiscriminate almsgiving led to organization of charity on a rational basis. Starting in Buffalo, New York, in 1878, Charity Organization societies soon were developed in most of the large eastern cities. The agencies granted financial assistance, after a rigorous investigation, but such help was regarded as only one aspect of the service offered. The more important component of help was offered by "friendly visitors," volunteers who were assigned to families to offer personal support and to influence behavior in a socially desirable direction. "Not alms, but a friend" was the watchword of the Charity Organization movement.

"Visitors" were the direct service workers, the foot soldiers, of the Charity Organization agencies. As volunteers they were generally assigned to a limited number of families (Gurteen 1882). Limited caseloads coupled with high turnover of volunteers meant that the agencies faced a continuous problem of recruiting, training, and directing new visitors. These tasks were primarily the responsibility of a limited number of "paid agents" employed by the Charity Organization societies. The paid agents are the early predecessors of the modern supervisor. Each agent-supervisor was responsible for a sizable number of visitors. The few statistics we have available testify to the fact that the principal burden of contact with the client was covered by visitors under the direction of a limited number of paid agents. Burns (1958) indicates that "by 1890 there were 78 charity organization societies with 174 paid workers and 2,017 volunteer friendly visitors" (p. 16).

Initially the paid agent shared responsibility for supervision of the visitor with the district committee. The district committee was in effect the local executive committee of the Charity Organization district office. The committee generally consisted of lay people and representatives of local charitable agencies.

When a family requested help the initial study was done by an agent who then reported the findings at a weekly district committee conference. The committee discussed the case and decided its disposition. The fact that cases were brought directly to the district committee for determination of action meant that, initially, the paid agent-supervisor had relatively little managerial autonomy. He and the visitor both were "agents" of the district committee. Gradually, however, district committees became more policy- and general-administration oriented. Responsibility for decision-making on individual cases was gradually given to the paid agent-supervisor. The visitors, and the paid workers who subsequently replaced them, discussed their cases with the agent-supervisor who was responsible for the decision and its subsequent implementation by the visitor or worker. The agent-supervisor thus became the administrative-managerial representative of the organization who was most immediately responsible for the work of the direct service worker.

The agent provided a dependable administrative point of contact for the visitor, gave continuity to the work, and acted as a channel of communication. "The agent is always to be found at certain hours and, giving all his time, naturally becomes the center of district work, receiving both from visitors and [the District] Committee information and advice to be transmitted one to the other" (Smith 1884, p. 70). As Fields says in one of the earliest social work texts, *How to Help the Poor* (1885), "The agent becomes the connecting link for the volunteer visitors who come daily for advice and assistance" (p. 18). The agent-supervisor, acting as a channel of communication, needed to be "careful to represent the Committee faithfully to the visitors and the visitors faithfully to the Committee" (Smith 1887, p. 161).

All the significant components of current supervisory procedures can be discerned in descriptions of the activities of the paid agent-supervisors. Zilpha Smith, general secretary of the Boston Associated Charities and later director of the Smith College Training School of Psychiatric Social Work, was one of the first to write on supervision and training of visitors. She exhorted the district agent to "look over the records of the visited families frequently to see if the work is satisfactory or if any suggestions can make it so" (Smith 1901b, p. 46). Here the administrative requirement of ensuring that the "work is satisfactory" is coupled with the educational task of supervision.

According to a Boston Associated Charities report of 1881, the agent was charged with the responsibility of "investigation and preparation of cases for the volunteer visitors and advising and aiding the visitors in their work. . . . The visitors . . . consult with the agent regarding the families they have befriended. Investigation by the agent precedes the appointment of a visitor in every case. This is necessary for the purpose of getting accurate and thorough knowledge; and when we know the family we can select the visitors whom we think most likely to persevere and be of greatest benefit" (Burns 1958, p. 24). Here the administrative task of differential case assignment is coupled with the educational task of "advising and aiding" in consultation with visitors.

In a report written in 1889, the Boston Associated Charities stated that "a large part of the agent's day consists of consultation with visitors . . . and there is opportunity for much tact and personal power in helping new visitors to understand what aid will benefit and what aid would harm their families, and in inspiring those who become discouraged to keep on until things look brighter again." Here the supervisor's responsibility for "consultation with visitors" in furthering the visitor's "understanding" is supplemented by the need to offer support in inspiring discouraged workers.

Since visitors were always difficult to recruit, easy to lose, and often frustrated and disappointed, they needed supportive supervision from the agent-supervisor in addition to administrative direction and training. The early literature talks about the need for the agent-supervisor to guide and inspire the visitor, to "encourage him to keep on . . . when discouraged."

(In addition to the allusions, in the early literature, to all of the current principal functions of supervision, the literature points to many currently accepted principles of desirable supervision.)It was emphasized that the agent's administrative, educational, and supportive responsibilities were most effectively implemented in the context of a positive relationship. In 1901, Smith said:

In order to make friendly visiting succeed . . . the agents must care to really help the visitor—not merely to give what the visitor asks, but, with tact and patience what he needs and to go at it simply and informally. The agent . . . must learn patiently to know and understand the new visitor. . . . Thought must be given to his problems and both direct and indirect means used to help him help himself in working them out with the poor family. (1901a, pp. 159–60)

Earlier she had noted that "the agent should be one able to guide and inspire others, ready to step in and help when necessary in what is properly visitor's work but sufficiently patient with the imperfections and delays of volunteers not to usurp the visitor's place" (1884, p. 69).

It was noted that education of visitors should emphasize principles for worker action: "The meetings of visitors rightly managed are a great power of education. In these meetings, and in talking or writing to visitors, details should not be allowed to hide principles on which the work rests. The principles should be discussed and the reasons for them given again and again as new visitors come to the meetings or new knowledge invites a change of policy" (Smith 1887, p. 160).

While group meetings of visitors were frequently the context for such instructions, individual supervision, using the visitor's case record as the text for training, was employed more and more frequently.

The amplifying effect of supervision in extending the influence of a limited number of trained and experienced workers was recognized early. "The agent's knowledge and experience was extended over a far wider field than he could have covered alone. The inexperienced worker was trained by actual service without the risk of injuring his beneficiaries in the process, and the family visited had the advantage of both the agent's professional knowledge and the visitor's more intimate and personal friendliness" Conyngton 1909, pp. 22–23).

By the turn of the century there was a gradual change in the composition of agency staffs, which affected supervision. Difficulty in depending on a staff of volunteer visitors who needed to be constantly "obtained, trained and retrained" became more evident as demands on agencies expanded. With the growth of industrialization and urbanization in late-nineteenth-century America and the large increases in immigration, the need for paid staff increased. As a consequence there was a gradual decrease in the ratio of volunteer friendly visitors to paid staff. Although such staff still initially required training by more experienced agent-supervisors, a cadre of trained workers who remained on the job for some time was being built up. The demands for supervisory education and support became somewhat less onerous. At the same time the burden of educating workers in the supervisory context was partly relieved by other resources.

From the very beginning of the Charity Organization movement, discussion groups of visitors and agents had been encouraged. Evening reading groups met to discuss current literature and to share experiences. The 1892 annual report of the Charity Organization Society of Baltimore notes that short papers, followed by discussion, were presented at meetings of visitors on the following topics: "How to Help Out-of-Work Cases," "The Treatment of Drunkards' Families," "Sanitation in the Homes of the Poor," "The Cost of Subsistence," "Deserted Wives," "Cooking and Marketing." The Boston South End District visitors and agents heard lectures on "Housing the Poor," "The Sweating System of Boston," "Trade Unions," "The Social Situation at the South End" and one, by Professor John R. Commons of the University of Wisconsin, on "Training of the Friendly Visitor."

The better-established Charity Organization societies gradually began to conduct more formal training programs which involved systematic education of those selected to be paid agents. For instance the Boston Charities Organization initiated in-service training programs for new agents in 1891. The new agents were "apprenticed" to more experienced workers, participated in group teaching sessions conducted by the general secretary of the organization, were assigned readings from the well-developed agency library. The supervising, experienced agents met periodically with the general secretary to discuss problems of educational supervision. By 1896 the Boston Organization stated in its annual report:

We have a higher standard for our agents. When the society started, there were no experts at this work; the agents and committees had to work together to acquire their training as best they could; while now, we have a well-organized system for training agents by having them work under direction, both in the Conferences and in the Central Office, before they are placed in positions of responsibility; so that there is always an agent qualified for the place should a vacancy occur. . . . We have undertaken to prepare our[agents] for their work by a system of preliminary training which we hope will make them more positively efficient and guard them from errors unavoidable among the untrained. . . . We have had hopes of being able carefully to train new volunteer visitors. . . . We have thought, thus, to develop wisely the good intentions of those who join us with the generous, if sometimes indefinite, purpose to do good.

State and national conferences offered an opportunity for the exchange of information and ideas among people working in welfare organizations and institutions. They were, in effect, a source of training. The first National Conference of Charities and Correction was held in Chicago in 1879. In 1882 Wisconsin organized the first State Conference of Charities and Correction. The published proceedings of such conferences provided material for education and training. These were supplemented by a growing body of periodical literature that spoke to the concerns of people working in the field. Texts and tracts devoted to the work of charities' agency personnel were also published. In addition to the texts referred to above, Mary Richmond, then General Secretary of the Charity Organization Society of Baltimore, published *Friendly Visiting Among the Poor: A Handbook for Charity Workers* in 1899, and Edward Devine, General Secretary of the Charity Organization Society of New York City, published *The Practice of Charity* in 1901.

The 1887 annual report of the Brooklyn Bureau of Charities states that "the nucleus of a library has been formed at the Central Office and now includes some 2,500 books, pamphlets and papers relating to the principles and methods of charitable work and cognate subjects. The collection is already worth the attention of those interested."

Gradually a body of practice wisdom was being developed, codified, and made explicit for communication through published channels. A group of practitioners interested in a particular phenomenon that ultimately became known as social work was gradually being identified and was developing a sense of conscious self-identification. The development of a knowledge base was accompanied by growing recognition that sympathy and interest alone were not sufficient to make a good worker. The 22d annual report of the Charity Organization of Baltimore (1903) comments that the "day is long passed when the only necessary qualifications for social service are good inclinations. To minister successfully to a family whose own resources have broken down requires intelligence and skill of a high order." The prerequisites associated with the emergence of a profession gradually began to become clear.

The development of a knowledge base made it possible to offer courses on social work content in colleges and universities—the beginnings of professional education—by departments of sociology and economics. These disciplines were closely allied with "social work" at that time and saw it as applied sociology. Frequently the academic courses used the Charity Organizations as social laboratories for student education. In 1894 it was reported that 21 of 146 colleges and universities contacted in a survey were giving courses in charities and correction (cited by Brackett 1904, p. 158). For instance, the University of Wisconsin offered courses in practical philanthropy in the early 1890s. Professor Richard T. Ely, who was responsible for the development of that program, arranged for a course of lectures on charities by Dr. Amos G. Warner. "Expanded and published as 'American Charities' in the Library of Economics and Politics edited by Dr. Ely, these lectures became the first standard book on the subject" (Brackett 1904, p. 162).

These various approaches to training personnel for the emerging profession culminated in the movement for development of a formal comprehensive program of specialized education. Anna L. Dawes is generally credited with making the initial suggestion for "training schools for a new profession." In a paper presented at the International Congress of Charities in Chicago in 1893, she argued that "it ought to be possible for those who take up this work to find some place for studying it as a profession." Students in such a training school could be taught "what is now the alphabet of charitable science—some knowledge of its underlying ideas, its tried and trusted methods and some acquaintance with the various devices employed for the upbuilding of the needy so that no philanthropic undertaking, from a model tenement house to a kindergarten or a sand heap, will be altogether strange." The motion was seconded by Mary Richmond, who argued for the need for a training school in applied philanthropy at the 24th National Conference of Charities in 1897. Richmond (1897a) reported that while it was true that each Charity Organization Society took some responsibility for training its visitors and its workers through the district-committee conferences and the activities of the paid agent-supervisors, such education was apt to be agency centered and parochial: "This training specializes too soon and our leaders have but the need for a more intimate and sympathetic acquaintance on the part of our agents with almshouse work, reformatory work, care of defectives and all the other branches of work represented at this [National] Conference. . . . The school that is to be most helpful to our charity organization agents, therefore, must be established on a broad basis" (p. 184).

In June 1898 a six-week summer training program was offered to 27 students by the New York Charity Organization Society. This program is regarded as the beginning of professional education in social work. The summer course was repeated for a number of years and then expanded to become the New York School of Philanthropy, the first full-time school of social work. It is now the Columbia University School of Social Work. A school for social workers was established by Simmons College and Harvard University in 1904, and in 1907 the Chicago School of Civics and Philanthropy (now the University of Chicago School of Social Service Administration) was established.

By 1910 five schools of social work had been established in the United States. Primary responsibility for training a cadre of social work professionals was vested in such schools. Agency supervision was seen as a supplementary educational resource. But since the number of schools was so limited, the greatest bulk of paid agents (later called charity workers and ultimately social workers) still received their training through apprenticeship programs in social agencies under the tutorship of more experienced agent-supervisors.

Although charged with this responsibility for educational supervision, almost none of the supervisors had any formal training in supervision since none was available. A short course in supervision was offered for the first time in 1911 under the aegis of the Charity Organization Department of the Russell Sage Foundation. The department was headed by Mary Richmond at that time.

Thus, starting with the development of the Charity Organization movement in the 1880s, supervision gradually emerged as a necessary aspect of Charity Organization work. The agent-supervisor organized, directed, and coordinated the work of visitors and paid agents and held them accountable for their performance; he advised, educated, and trained visitors and paid agents in performance of their work and supported and inspired them in their discouragements and disappointments. The three major components of current supervision were thus identifiable among the tasks assumed by the early agent-supervisor. The case record had been identified as the principal vehicle for supervision, and the individual conference as the principal context.

By the turn of the century the educational apparatus of a profession was being organized and was assuming the main responsibility for training. Supervision continued to perform an educational function but now more as a supplement to such formal training institutions. Over time, supervision achieved more visibility in the agency administrative structure, and the process itself gradually became more formalized. Time, place, content, procedures, and expectations of supervisory conferences received clearer definition. As social work became more diversified, supervision took root not only in family service agencies where it had had its origins but also in corrections, psychiatric social work agencies, medical social work agencies, and schools.

As supervision became a more identifiable process, it was subjected to explicit analysis. Between 1920 and 1945 *Family* and then *Social Casework* published some 35 articles specifically devoted to supervision. A number of books have been written that are devoted exclusively, or primarily, to social work supervision. Virginia Robinson published a pioneer work in 1936, *Supervision in Social Case Work*, followed by *The Dynamics of Supervision under Functional Controls* (1949). In 1942 Bertha Reynolds wrote *Learning and Teaching in the Practice of Social Work*, which is devoted in large measure to educational supervision. In 1945 Charlotte Towle included an extended section on social work supervision in her widely distributed pamphlet *Common Human Needs*, published by the Federal Security Agency and later reprinted by the National Association of Social Workers. Towle enlarged on that work in *The Learner in Education for the Professions*, published in 1954.

Almost all of the literature cited above derives from work in casework agencies and is casework oriented. With the development of group-service agencies, supervision was enriched by contributions from this segment of social work. Williamson's book *Supervision* (1950, revised 1961), while general in nature, was oriented toward the Y.M.C.A. worker. Two additional texts on supervision were similarly directed toward group service agencies (Lindenberg 1939; Dimock and Trecker 1949).

Supervision nonetheless continued to be strongly influenced by its origins in casework. Miller (1960), in one of the few articles written by a group worker on supervision, deplores the tendency of group work to pattern its supervisory procedures in accordance with those developed by casework. Supervision is less clearly formalized in group work agencies. Spellman (1946) noted the "odd assortment of practices which had grown up" in response to the need to perform supervisory functions but without explicit consideration of the process:

We've had the "trouble shooter method"; "let me know if anything goes wrong and you need me for any emergency—and I'll be right there." Then there is the "hit-and-run method"; "I'll see you in the hall a couple of minutes after the meeting is over and we'll check on what happened and what you want for next week." Others had worked out the "crutch philosophy"; "I'll help you get started until you can stand on your own two feet." (p. 125)

A 1972 study of Chicago group work agencies showed that "most executives confer with staff members individually when necessary without planned supervisory conferences" (Switzer 1973, p. 587). Another study of group work supervision finds some additional distinctive elements. Olyan (1972), studying social group-work supervision as compared with casework supervision, found that group work supervisors were more likely to feel that social workers were not ready to assume responsibility and needed close supervision. They gave administrative supervision greater emphasis than did casework supervisors and used observation procedures more frequently.

Supervision in community organization is even less explicitly formulated. Community organizers often work in agencies with limited staff or are members of a small specialized unit in large agencies. In either case there is no elaborate hierarchical structure which includes supervisory personnel. The nature of the work of the community organizer often tends to be diffuse and the goals amorphous. This requires a great measure of on-the-job autonomy in dealing with the demands of a nonstandardized situation.

The functional requirements of supervision in community organization—assignment of work, review and assessment of work done—may be performed by the agency administrator. These functions have to be performed, however infrequently or casually, but often no one is clearly designated as supervisor and there is no explicit recognition that supervisory tasks are being discharged. The failure to recognize supervision is intensified by the particularly negative connotations the term has for community organizers. Of all the specialized subgroups in social work, community organization feels most strongly about the need for worker autonomy. Supervision suggests a subservience that runs counter to this strong value. Hence there is a tendency to reject the idea that any supervision is associated with com-

munity organization, and there is an almost total lack of literature on the subject.

In some respects, however, the need for supervision is
even more urgent in community organization than in other
areas of social work. The community organizer inevitably represents the agency. Working in a highly politicized arena, the
worker is subject to a variety of pressures and power plays. In
dealing with community groups he may commit the agency to
activity, to policies that the agency finds difficult to defend or
support. Consequently there is a great need for the agency to
know what might have been promised, what deals are being
contemplated, what action the worker plans to take. This
requirement for accountability to agency administration is a task
of supervision.

A review of the published material tends to indicate that
the direction and concerns of social work supervision have mir-
rored, over time, some of the changes in orientation of social
work generally and casework in particular. Early in the history
of social work it was thought that the worker, or friendly visitor,
knew what was best for the client. Knowing this, the worker offered the client clear advice as to what should be done and she
arranged, independently of the client, to make resources available in the client's behalf. This was sometimes called an "executive treatment" approach (Lee 1923). Analogously the supervisor, knowing what was best, told the worker what needed to
be done.

As social work developed a greater appreciation of the need
to actively involve clients' participation in, and planning of,
their own solutions to problems, there was a complementary
change in the approach in supervision. Supervision moved from
telling the supervisees what to do to a greater encouragement of
supervisee participation in planning and an increased mutuality
in the supervisor-supervisee relationship (Glendenning 1923).

Although the impact of psychoanalytic psychology on the
actual service offered the client in the 1920s may have been ex-
aggerated (Alexander 1972), many of its ideas do seem to have
influenced the orientation of supervision during that period.

Supervision was seen as a kind of relationship therapy analogous to casework for the client. In order to be effective with clients, workers needed to be aware of, and have the help of the supervisor in resolving, their own intrapsychic conflicts (Glendenning 1923). Marcus (1927) suggested that

> the supervisor consider herself a caseworker whose case work must embrace not only the student's cases but the student herself. This demands, of course, that the supervisor investigate and treat the personal problem of the student as the latter investigates and treats those of the client. . . . If casework is an art and a philosophy and not merely a trade practiced on the handicapped and helpless, it was to be just as thoroughly a part of the caseworker's attitude toward herself. (p. 386)

In the midst of the "psychiatric deluge," however, Paige (a supervisor) writes of supervision in terms which emphasize accountability. She talks about the supervisor's holding the worker "to the meticulous adherence to the enforcement of social legislation in which minimum social standards have been crystallized" (1927, p. 307).

During the same period, Dawson (1926) explicitly stated the functions of supervision in traditional terms, as administrative—the promotion and maintenance of good standards of work, coordination of practice with policies of administration, the assurance of an efficient and smooth-working office; educational—"the educational development of each individual worker on the staff in a manner calculated to evoke her fully to realize her possibilities of usefulness"; and supportive—the maintenance of harmonious working relationships, the cultivation of esprit de corps (p. 293).

The component of supervision that has received the greatest emphasis in the literature is educational supervision. Theoreticians of social work supervision have attempted to apply a more general theory of change to the educational process in supervision. Robinson, in the first book written on casework supervision (1936) and in her subsequent work (1949), attempted to apply the Rankian-functional approach to behavioral change to the supervisor-supervisee relationship. Towle (1954), on the other hand, attempted to analyze the relationship between supervisor and supervisee in terms of Freudian ego psychology. Supervision was seen as a change-oriented process, the dynamics of which were made explicable by application of ego psychology theory.

Since there was a problem of recruiting and retaining visitors, the earlier history of social work supervision contains little on evaluation. Beginning in the 1920s, evaluation was identified as an administrative responsibility of supervision. This concern grew as a result of the rapid expansion of public welfare staff during the Great Depression. The civil-service apparatus was utilized in recruiting staff. General civil-service requirements for standardization of hiring, advancement, and termination procedures led to the development of such standards for social work positions, and social work supervisors were given the responsibility for evaluating staff in terms of such standards. Despite the importance of evaluation, as well as other administrative aspects of supervision, this component in supervision has received limited attention and discussion in the literature.

Currently, concern with deprofessionalization, de-emphasis of power and authority in human relationships, and a heightened concern with individual rights and individual autonomy have led to some derogation of supervision and to attempts at redistribution of its functions. Reflecting this pattern, there has been a reduction in concern with supervision in the social work literature and research in recent years.

The literature of social work supervision is notable for the general absence of empirical research. The material available is largely descriptive—exposition based on practice wisdom and supervisory experience. Even contributions regarded as benchmarks, such as the work by Robinson and Towle, contain little research material in support of the presentation. Briar (1966), in reviewing the practice of supervision in family service agencies over the period 1960–1965, called attention to the need for research on supervision. In a subsequent review, covering the period 1965–1970, Briar (1971) noted that "no significant studies of supervision have been offered since the last review" (p. 111). Here, as in other fields, however, doctoral theses have contributed to our knowledge (Amacher 1971; Burns 1958; Holtzman 1966; Kettner 1973; Kledaras 1971; Nelsen 1973; Olyan 1972).

Definition

The word supervision ultimately derives from the Latin *super* "over" and *videre* "to watch, to see." *Webster's Collegiate Dictionary* (4th ed., 1948) consequently defines a supervisor as "an overseer, one who watches over the work of another with responsibility for its quality." Such a definition of supervision leads to the derisive pronounciation "snooper vision." The orthodox definition stresses the administrative aspect of supervision, the concern with seeing that a job is performed at a quantitatively and qualitatively acceptable level.

The earliest explicit definitions of supervision in social work stress a different component. Robinson, in the first social work text on this subject, *Supervision in Social Casework* (1936), defined supervision as "an educational process in which a person with a certain equipment of knowledge and skill takes responsibility for training a person with less equipment" (p. 53).

A review of the social work literature shows that supervision has been defined primarily in terms of the administrative and educational components, the emphasis varying with the author. For instance the first edition of the *Encyclopedia of Social Work* (1965) defines supervision as an educational process. It is the "traditional method of transmitting knowledge of social work skills in practice from the trained to the untrained, from the experienced to the inexperienced student and worker." The second edition of the *Encyclopedia* (1971) emphasizes the administrative component: "supervision in social work is essentially an administrative process for getting the work done and maintaining organizational accountability."

On occasion both components are included in the definition. Towle (1945) defines social work supervision "as an administrative process with an educational purpose" (p. 95; similarly Burns 1958, p. 6). A standard group-work text states that "the supervisor's responsibilities are both administrative and educative in nature. . . . The ultimate objective of supervision is that through more effective effort on the part of its workers, an agency's services are improved in quality and its central purposes come nearer to fulfillment" (Wilson and Ryland 1949, p. 587).

The definition often emphasizes the objectives of supervision. Another definition that represents the group work literature states that "supervision is a cooperative educational process in which, through a relationship established by supervisor and supervisee, the supervisor helps the supervisee to accomplish his job better within an agency framework" (Jewish Community Center 1949, p. 44). A sociologist who has studied the profession highlights a quite different objective. "Supervision is the institutionalized built-in mechanism through which the attitudes and performance of social workers are controlled" (Toren 1972, p. 65).

Each of the definitions presented is only partially correct. It is true that supervision is both an administrative and an educational process. The social work supervisor has responsibility for implementing both functions in contact with supervisees. There is, however, an additional and distinctively different responsibility that needs to be included in the definition. This is the expressive-supportive-leadership function of supervision. The supervisor has the responsibility of sustaining worker morale, helping with job-related discouragements and discontents, giving supervisees a sense of worth as professionals, a sense of belonging in the agency, a sense of security in their performance.

These three major functions of supervision are complementary. All are necessary if the ultimate objective of supervision is to be achieved—a purpose above and beyond the more limited purpose of each of the three. The ultimate objective of supervision is to offer the agency's service to the client in the most efficient and effective manner possible. It is toward that goal that the supervisor administratively integrates and coordinates the supervisees' work with others in the agency, educates the workers to a more skillful performance in their tasks, and supports and sustains the workers in motivated performance of these tasks.

In attempting to formulate a definition of social work supervision, we have thus far been explicating the principal cluster of functions discharged by the supervisor—administrative, educational, and supportive. Other characteristics of the position also help to define it. The supervisor is an administrative officer, occupying a position of managerial responsibility, who is given authority to direct, regulate, and evaluate the work of others and who is accountable for the work performed.

The supervisor, then, is a member of the administrative hierarchy of the agency with delegated authority vis-à-vis his supervisees. The supervisory position is a middle-management position. The supervisor is sometimes referred to as the "highest level employee and the lowest level manager," a "subadministrator and a supra-practitioner" (Towle 1962). A member of both management and the work group, he acts as a bridge between them. He is the member of the agency administrative staff in personal contact with the direct service worker, the operating staff.

As the term will be used in this book, a social work supervisor is an agency administrative staff member to whom authority is delegated to direct, coordinate, enhance, and evaluate the on-the-job performance of the supervisees for whose work he is held accountable. In implementing this responsibility the supervisor performs administrative, educational, and supportive functions in interaction with the supervisee in the context of a positive relationship. The supervisor's ultimate objective is to deliver to agency clients the best possible service, both quantitative and qualitatively, in accordance with agency policies and procedures. Supervisors do not directly offer service to the client, but they do indirectly affect the level of service offered through their impact on the direct service supervisees. Supervision is, thus, an indirect service.

Supervisory Staff

Frequency distributions from the manpower data bank of the National Association of Social Workers showed that in February 1975 supervision was the primary job responsibility listed by 8.1 percent of the membership and a secondary job responsibility for an additional 4.5 percent. Thus nearly 8,000 of the 63,000 members in the national organization had supervisory duties.

The 1973 report on personnel in public welfare published by The National Center for Social Statistics, Department of Health, Education and Welfare, indicates that in June 1973 there were 11,100 casework supervisors employed in public welfare agencies. There was approximately one casework supervisor for every five caseworkers (U.S. Department of Health, Education and Welfare 1975, Table 8, p. 16).

A review of civil-service announcements obtained from state personnel directors throughout the country indicated that in 1973 entry-level supervisory positions frequently required a social-work master's degree plus one year of experience. In many states, one year of social work experience could be substituted for each year of graduate training. Consequently a person with a bachelor's degree and three years of social work experience could qualify for an entry-level supervisory position.

Personnel vacancy listings appearing in various social work journals were also reviewed, including *Child Welfare, Social Casework* and *N.A.S.W. News*. In general, the requirements associated with the job openings paralleled the civil-service requirements—a master's degree in social work and two or three years of casework experience. Rarely did an advertisement call for more experience. Unlike the civil-service listings, however, only a few advertisements permitted a substitution of experience for the educational requirement.

Some advertisements called for specialized kinds of experience. Psychiatric social work, adoptions, and foster care agencies for instance were likely to require that the prospective supervisor have experience in their particular field of practice.

In only one instance did the advertisement require some formal training in supervision. Most advertisements were for caseworker supervisors; there was only one for a groupwork supervisor and none for a community organization supervisor.

Some advertisements called for membership in the Academy of Certified Social Workers (A.C.S.W.) in addition to the master's degree. This, apparently, is in response to the A.C.S.W. requirement that applicants be supervised by an A.C.S.W. member for a period of time. Hence some caseworkers may be hesitant to take a position in an agency where the supervisor is not an A.C.S.W. member.

The Importance of Supervision in Social Work

We have noted that, historically, supervision has always been an important element in social work. Supervision is not, of course, unique to social work, but the function and process of supervision have achieved special importance in social work as contrasted with most other professions. This prominence might be explained by some distinctive aspects of the profession, the nature of its service delivery pattern, the problems with which it is concerned, the clientele to whom service is offered, and the characteristics of social workers.

1. Social work, as contrasted with other, more entrepreneurially oriented professions, offers service to the client group through an agency. An agency is a complex organization and therefore needs to develop some bureaucratic structure if it is to operate effectively. The work of different people, each performing some specialized task, has to be coordinated and integrated. The social agency thus requires a chain of command, a hierarchy of administrators. Since the greatest percentage of social workers perform their professional functions within an agency, they find themselves in a bureaucratic structure in contact with the supervision which a bureaucracy requires.

A very small number of social workers operate autonomously as private practitioners outside an agency. To the extent that the profession moves toward implementation of its function outside an agency setting, a concern with supervision may be de-emphasized. However, the current situation, in which social work is practiced primarily in an agency setting, is likely to prevail for some time.

Other professions that find the bulk of their practitioners working in agency settings have been concerned with supervision for similar reasons. This is true particularly for teachers and nurses. As the more traditionally entrepreneurially oriented professions become bureaucratized (as is happening currently with medicine and law), they find themselves building a bureaucratic apparatus that includes supervisory personnel and supervisory controls.

Social work, however, from its inception has been organizationally based. It knows no other tradition. Having a longer history in an organizational context, it has had a more prolonged concern with supervision. Considerable educational and training effort is expended in helping social work recruits understand and identify with organizational models and values. Social workers are evaluated in terms of their identification with, acceptance of, and adherence to agency policies and procedures.

The whole orientation of the profession gives centrality to the agency. While other professions socialize recruits in terms of a professional image that is largely modeled after the independent entrepreneur, social work has always heavily emphasized the organization-agency context as the locus of the worker's activity. Consequently, as Scott (1969) notes, "social workers, unlike members of other professions expect to enter an organization where their work will be subject to routine hierarchical supervision" (p. 92). As a result of tradition and training, the "social worker is a sophisticated and accomplished 'organization man'" (Vinter 1959, p. 242; see also Epstein 1970; Rothman 1974, p. 96).

2. A significant component of social agency activity is concerned with the distribution of services and supplies which the agency does not own. The money grants, homemaker service, foster homes, and day-care facilities, made available to agency

clients are financed by the community. By contrast, a doctor or a lawyer employs the skills which he himself "owns." The social work situation brings greater pressure from the community for explicit accountability procedures regarding agency activity. This pressure, translated into operational terms, means that ultimately there has to be some system of accountability developed within the agency regarding the service activity of the worker. This, once again, leads directly to a need for a supervisory apparatus.

One might argue that traditional accountability procedures in other professions require the professional to be self-disciplined and self-accountable, subject where necessary to peer review. However, even in the oldest and most solidly established professions there is a demand for more formal procedures of accountability once public funds are involved, procedures which are supervisory in nature.

In 1972 Congress passed legislation which provided for Professional Standards Review Organizations (P.S.R.O.) "to monitor the quality of every doctor's professional work whether it be performing open heart surgery or making a house call, if the services are being paid for by Federal [Medicaid and Medicare] programs" (*New York Times*, December 3, 1973). Neither Congress nor the American Medical Association (which ultimately approved the legislation) felt that the individual physician's self-accountability was sufficient. Given the large amount of public funds being expended for medical programs, supervision here, too, is regarded as necessary.

3. Not only the finances and resources which the agency employs to help its clients, but very frequently also the policies which the agency implements orginate elsewhere. Policy for public social-welfare agencies is often created by political bodies such as public welfare boards and commissions. The agencies are then answerable to these political entities for correct implementation of policy. This circumstance, too, creates an organizational pressure for some system of accountability for workers' activity within the agency.

Scott (1965) terms professional organizations that are controlled, in some measure, by external agencies "heteronomous organizations" and includes social agencies, schools, and libraries under such a rubric. His study of their administration confirms their greater concern with supervision and supervisory procedures.

The outside dictation of agency policy is justified not only by the fact that public funds are being used in offering the service but also by the fact that social agencies are concerned with problem situations which present a great danger to the community, situations in which the community has a strong vested interest. Crime, dependency, discrimination, and family breakdown are particularly costly financial and ideological threats to society. Response to these problems involves the embodiment of society's values, its ideological commitments in sensitive areas—family structure, legal conformity, sexual mores, the work ethic, racial conflict. The community feels impelled to indicate how such situations should be handled through its articulation of social policy. The fact that social work agencies are concerned with problems which pose not only a financial but also an ideological danger to the community again leads to external control of agency policy and internal agency control of worker autonomy.

4. The autonomy granted any member of a profession reflects the degree of autonomy granted the profession as a whole. If the community is hesitant about granting full autonomy to a profession, there will be pressure toward supervision of the individual professional. The degree of autonomy granted is a function of the extent to which there is general consensus about the profession's objectives. Where powerful segments of the community disagree about the ultimate aims of a profession's activity, there will be greater reluctance to grant autonomy to the profession since this will permit the profession to decide on its own objectives. Autonomy enables a few professionals to decide for the many in the community. There is less general consensus as to the aims of objectives of social work than there is regarding, for instance, the objectives of the health services.

Hence, there is greater community reluctance to grant social work a full measure of autonomy.

Community confidence in the competence of a professional group to effectively implement society's mandate is a necessary prerequisite for the grant of full autonomy. Whether the opinion is justified or not, it seems clear that the community has doubts about social work competence. Since society's grant of autonomy to the profession is limited as a result of these considerations, there is less protection of autonomy of any individual professional.

5. Research suggests that when a profession, such as social work, performs nonuniform tasks in an uncertain and unpredictable context, toward the achievement of diffuse and ambiguous objectives with heterogeneous populations, there is more decentralization of decision making and a greater need for worker autonomy (Dornbusch and Scott 1975, pp. 76–87; Rothman 1974, 152–57). These findings logically argue for less bureaucratic structure since they suggest difficulty in codification of procedures, formulation of standardized rules of action, and routinization of performance. They would also seemingly argue for a less elaborate supervisory apparatus. One can, however, deduce the opposite need from the same considerations. Where objectives are unclear, where there is great uncertainty as to how to proceed, where the effects of interventions are unpredictable and the risk of failure is high, workers may need, and want, the availability of an administrative representative with whom they can share responsibility for decision making, from whom they can receive direction, and to whom they can look for support. Consequently, the conditions under which the work of the profession is performed argue for the desirability of a supervisory cadre.

6. Social workers perform their functions under conditions that do not permit direct observation. The ethos of the profession encourages such protection from direct scrutiny, and practice principles further support it. We hold interviews in private and discourage observation as an intrusion on the privacy of the

encounter. We contend that direct observation of our practice would create hazards for effective worker-client interaction. We thus create an unusual situation of role performance invisibility and interdicted observability. This being the nature of our practice procedures, the client would be left without effective protection from practice which might be damaging if there were no system for supervisory review of what the worker was doing. Many other professionals perform their services publicly and their work is thus open to more general evaluation. The lawyer can be observed in the courtroom, the musician on the concert platform, the professor in the lecture hall. These situations make less imperative the need for supervisory review of performance as a protection to clients. The fact that group workers to some extent and community organizers to an even greater extent perform "in public," mitigates some of the pressure for supervision in these areas of social work.

7. Certain other professionals such as doctors and dentists do perform their functions privately, but the outcome of professional activity is more objective and observable than in the case of social work. The doctor may perform his functions in private without benefit of supervisory review, but consistently inadequate professional performance means sick or dead patients. The cause-and-effect relationship between social work activity and changes in the client's situation is much more subtle, and difficult to define. Since the damaging effects of poor practice are not so self-evident and observable, protection of the client requires a procedure for explicit periodic review of worker activity.

8. Two additional aspects of the social-work delivery system create a need for supervision: the agency provides the workers with their clientele and clients are often "captives" of the agency.

A captive clientele reduces the need for self-discipline and critical self-evaluation. The professional entrepreneur, the lawyer or doctor, pays a price for ineptitude, inefficiency, and outmoded professional skills, in a reduction in income owing to loss of clients. The social worker, operating in an agency that provides the clients, does not face the same kind of penalties which alert him to the need for examining and correcting his practice. The setting again dictates a greater need for organizational controls of practice since the context of practice does not automatically provide such controls.

Furthermore, the client's use of agency service is often involuntary, dictated by organs of social control such as schools and courts. Even without such formal directives, situational imperatives may deny the client the freedom of choice. The need for food, shelter, or medical care may determine the client's need for agency service, a service for which the agency is granted a monopoly.

The fact that the client's use of the agency is often in response to coercive factors which compel the decision, means that greater provision needs to be made to protect the client than would be the case in situations where the client could freely choose to withdraw if dissatisfied with the service.

9. Despite the fact that social workers use resources provided by the community, are required to implement policies formulated by groups outside the agency, perform their tasks in private on clients who often have no alternative options, and are concerned with outcomes which are difficult to discern and evaluate objectively, is there a real need for supervisory review and control around accountability and client protection? One might counter that the supposition that such conditions argue for the necessity of supervision is demeaning and insulting to the worker. All of these conditions might accurately characterize the social work situation yet not require supervision if we granted the social worker her professional prerogative. One would expect that the direct service professional in contact with the client would herself be concerned about protecting the client and implementing agency policy in a clearly responsible manner. Operating autonomously, she would provide, for herself, the controls of supervision. But it is here, once again, that we encounter a situation characteristic of social work which creates a pressure for the development and elaboration of a supervisory apparatus.

Kaufman (1960) identifies the significant conditions which ensure that the autonomously operating worker will be self-supervised so that agency policy will be adhered to and the needs of the client protected. These conditions include extensive professional education, a strong interest in the tasks to be performed, a commitment to the ends to which these tasks are directed, and periodic agency indoctrination reinforcing the saliency and legitimacy of these goals. The result of these conditions is to socialize the worker so that she does, as a matter of personal preference and professional conscience, those things that are professionally required. The composition of social work agency staff, now and in the past, raises questions about the degree to which these conditions are met. In the absence of these conditions there is greater pressure to develop a supervisory control system to insure that work performance is in accordance with professionally desirable norms.

The process of professional recruitment, selection, and education has implications for the kind of supervisory system a profession establishes. If the process of occupational selection is deliberate, and if the program of training is prolonged, the need for elaborate supervisory procedures is lessened.

A candidate who deliberately makes a choice of some profession after careful evaluation of alternatives is apt to feel a sense of commitment to the profession. The very process of applying for, and being selected by, a graduate professional school acts as a screen which ensures recruitment of those applicants who, in some way, share the values, assumptions, and predispositions characteristic of those performing the work. This is reinforced by the professional training experience.

The objective of professional training is not only to teach the knowledge, skills, and attitudes that would enable the recruit to do a competent job but also to socialize the student to the ways of the profession, to develop a professional conscience. It is the elaborate process of professional socialization, during a prolonged program of intensive training, which permits workers, in all professions to operate autonomously, free of external direction and control but subject to internal direction and control on the basis of competence and values incorporated during training. The supervisor is, in effect, internalized during the transformation of the lay person into a professional, and supervision does not then need to be externally imposed. Discipline becomes self-discipline; accountability is accountability to one's professionalized self. Such constraints are further maintained and collectively sustained by strong professional organizations to which the professional feels an affiliation, even if he is not formally a member, and by periodic in-service training courses, conferences, meetings, and professional journals.

All of this is quite different from the situation which characterizes job entrance for the largest percentage of social workers—currently and throughout the history of the profession. For most social workers who have ever occupied the position, entrance to the job has not been the result of a serious commitment to social work as a lifetime career but rather a decision of limited commitment, frequently made because other, more attractive, alternatives were not available. Workers often come to the job with no previous knowledge of social work, no firm identification with the profession, its objectives, standards, and values—an identification which might have been developed during a prolonged period of professional training— and with no resolute commitment to the profession.

In 1972 there were approximately 230,000 people in the United States occupying positions as "social workers" (Newman and Delaplaine 1974). Of these, approximately 65,000 were professionally qualified (from data in *N. A.S.W. News,* March 1973). Thus, only about 30 percent of all social workers in 1972 were professionally trained to do the job prior to accepting the position. This low ratio of professionally trained to total work force reflects a situation which has been typical throughout the history of the profession. In fact, the situation in 1972 was more favorable than the relative proportions which existed earlier. A 1926 study showed that only 7 percent of the workers had full professional training (Walker 1928, p. 108). In 1940, of the 69,000 social workers listed by the 1940 census only 11,000 (16 percent) were members of the American Association of Social

Workers, which enrolled most of the professionally trained social workers at that time (Hathway 1943). By 1960, some 25 percent of the 116,000 people holding social welfare positions had graduate social-work degrees (National Social Welfare Assembly 1961, p. 1).

Lacking control of job access and job entry, the profession can dictate to only a limited extent the personal and professional qualifications of the personnel responsible for offering social agency service. This situation has implications not only for the education and training that recruits bring to the position but also for their attitudes toward, and commitment to, the work they are called on to perform. In reference to the situation in the late 1960s, a study of the public welfare system notes that

For the most part [caseworkers] are quite young, are college graduates with only modest professional training, are not members of professional social work organizations, have been with the agencies only a very short time, lack field experience elsewhere and do not expect to be in public assistance very long. In short, they view their jobs as way stations and this is borne out by the very high turnover. (Handler and Hollingsworth 1971, pp. 201–2)

A sociologist's participant-observer account of social worker staff in a public assistance agency comments that "many of them chose a welfare [position] because they are presently unable to enter their chosen occupations. . . . Few intend to make it a life long career. . . . Welfare work for many becomes an easy way of making a living" (Levy 1970). They accept the job casually, work at it with detachment, and leave without regrets for the first attractive job alternative. Chatterjee (1972) found that public welfare workers manifested limited commitment to their job. Miller and Podell (1970) concluded that only about 10 percent of the caseworkers in the New York City Department of Social Services were "socialized professionals with a commitment to social work combined with a positive disposition to the department" (p. 12). High turnover rates compound the problems caused by lack of previous opportunities for socialization to the job:

Caseworker turnover reaches epidemic proportions. With an arrival staff growth rate of about 16 percent in 1971 the Atlanta Welfare Agency hired new employees to fill about 50 percent of its caseworker positions. For fiscal 1970 HEW reported an accession rate of almost 35 percent nationwide and a separation rate of almost 31 percent. In 1969 HEW reported that out of 11 cities studied the lowest caseworker turnover rate was 20 percent; five of the cities had rates higher than 40 percent. . . . In 1969 HEW reported that in 11 cities studied, more than half of the caseworkers had been on their jobs less than 2 years. The highest median age of caseworkers in any one of the cities was 31. (Galm 1972, p. 33)

The direct service staff often includes, consequently, a large percentage of new workers without experience, needing training through educational supervision and some measure of administrative supervisory control.

High turnover rates have other consequences which intensify the importance of administrative supervision. Group consensus in support of professional norms might act as a constraint on the untrained worker. The pressure of the informal group in supplementing supervisory controls operates most effectively when workers have been in the agency long enough to feel identified with the group. Rapid turnover, aborting the development of solidarity between colleagues, implies tenuous attachment and indifference to group controls.

There are, in effect, two different kinds of staff to which supervision is directed. One (often found in highly professionalized, generally voluntary agencies) is composed of people who have made a career choice of social work after considerable exploration and deliberation, who have invested effort and money in a prolonged program of professional education, and who have thereby developed some beginning competence in performing social work tasks, some identification with, and commitment to, the social work profession.

At the same time there is an even larger number of workers (more often concentrated in large public welfare agencies), holding the job title of social worker and performing social work tasks, who often have come to the job fortuitously, because an opening was available. They often have had no prior exposure to social work, have not considered it seriously as a career, have had little, if any, education or training for the job and have little, if any, identification with, and commitment to, social work. This second group is, of course, highly diversified.

Thus, there always has been and continues to be, because of abnormally high turnover rates in social agency staff, a need for agencies to induct, train, and socialize new recruits to the job, on the job. And because of tenuous commitment, or lack of prior opportunity to socialize toward a firm commitment to the mission of social work, on the part of many recruits, social work has had to assign supervisory personnel to perform the functions of administrative supervision.

10. The need for agency organizational controls embodied in supervision is made more imperative in social work by the absence of effective professional organizational controls. The professional associations in medicine and law, controlling entry into and expulsion from the profession, can effectively be delegated the responsibility of policing their members to limit abuses of professional autonomy and guarantee professionally responsible behavior. Until very recently the National Association of Social Workers did not even accept for membership the non-M.S.W. social workers who filled the majority of social work positions. While currently technically eligible, few such workers are affiliated with the professional organizations. The ability of professional social work organizations to guarantee the conduct and competence of the social worker's performance is seriously circumscribed. The absence of effective professional control groups in social work, as compared with more traditionally established professions, argues for an alternative control system such as agency supervision.

11. Bureaucratization, of which supervision is a component, results not only from the limited training of a large number of people carrying the title of social work but also from the limited knowledge base and technology available even to fully trained workers. Where the level of development of a profession's knowledge and technology is such that the professional often finds himself encountering situations in which he

cannot operate with full confidence that he knows what to do and how to do it, as is true in social work, there is a greater tendency to share decisional responsibility with a supervisor and less readiness to resist supervisory "suggestions" and rules that dictate action. A person needs to be very confident of his ability to make use of autonomy if he is going to claim it aggressively and defend it tenaciously. "Control over the work of semi-professionals is possible because they lack the weapon—knowledge—with which professionals resist control, and the motives which drive professionals to seek autonomy is strong intrinsic commitment to specialized knowledge and skills together with confidence in their ability to exercise such skills" (Simpson and Simpson 1969, pp. 198–99).

12. The distinctive nature of the problems encountered and the tasks performed by social workers makes desirable, perhaps even necessary, the availability of supportive supervision. Social workers are in constant contact with highly charged affective situations that make heavy demands for expenditure of emotional energy in behalf of the client. The problems encountered—parent-child conflict, marital conflict, illness, death, dependency, deviance—are those that a social worker struggles with in one way or another in her own life situation. The principal instrumentality for helping the client is the worker herself, so that failure to help may be sensed as a personal failure. The responsibilities are great; the solutions available are ambiguous; the possibilities for happy solutions are limited. The risks for excitation of guilt, anxiety, discouragement, and frustration are numerous. There are few professions that come close to social work in developing in the worker the need for support, encouragement, reassurance, and restoration of morale—a need met by supportive supervision.

13. Supervision in social work may have developed prominence and significance because it performs necessary and important functions in response to the distinctive characteristics of the profession. At the same time it may have been assisted toward prominence by a lack of active opposition to development of a supervisory apparatus. The personality characteristics of

people attracted to social work and the large proportion of women in the field may further help explain the prominence of supervision.

The tendency toward bureaucracy and toward administrative controls (including supervision) is characteristic of all professions that operate in the context of complex organizations. It is particularly characteristic, however, in those professions operating in the context of a complex organization with a predominantly female labor force. Approximately two-thirds of all social workers are women. Socialization to the professional identity through a prolonged period of training is only one of the factors associated with levels of commitment (Geer 1966). Intensity of commitment is also related to the priority given the professional role as against possible alternatives. Alternate socially acceptable roles such as motherhood compete with the professional role for the allegiance of many workers (Chafetz 1972; Reid 1967; Tropman 1968). As a result a sizable percentage of social workers offer the professional role a commitment of limited intensity and limited duration. Conversely, the professional who sees this role as her overriding, principal concern is likely to invest and involve herself to a greater extent in its occupational tasks. Such intensity of commitment is related to desire for autonomy and opposition to supervisory controls.

Traditional social sex roles may also play a part here. A sociologist, writing about the social work profession, declares that

the way in which the female role is defined in general may still mean that women will be more submissive in an organizational context than men and therefore more likely to allow their work to be controlled by administrators. It is difficult to know whether organizations such as social work have taken this form because of the high percentage of female employees or whether they recruit females to fit the kind of context. (Heraud 1970, p. 256)

Less unreservedly committed to the occupational role, more discontinuous in work history, less interested in long-range career goals, often responsive to the cultural norms regarding defensiveness and submissiveness on the part of the female, the women who constitute a high proportion of social agency staffs "submit more willingly to bureaucratic subordination then men and strive less for autonomy as professionals" (Simpson and Simpson 1969, p. 244). This pattern reinforces the tendency toward bureaucratization in social work agencies and the acceptability of supervision.

These last paragraphs might be regarded as sexist. They reflect the results of recent empirical studies on the sociology of professions rather than a personal point of view. Given the women's liberation movement, the changing status of women, and the devaluation of the "sacredness" of motherhood as *the* principal female role, these contentions may be less true in the future. But while such considerations may move in the direction of progressive attenuation, they currently retain some measure of explanatory potential regarding the prevalence of, and limited opposition to, social work supervision.

The concept of a professional subculture suggests that different occupations attract and produce different occupational personalities. The conjecture is that people with particular kinds of personalities are attracted to different professions; that the process of professional socialization then tends to reinforce those aspects of personality which are congruent with, and conducive to, smooth adjustment to the professional subculture.

Some of the selective personality characteristics of social workers may have relevance to the supervisor-supervisee relationship. Gockel's nationwide study of undergraduate students who major in social work indicates that they are "significantly less likely to express a desire for freedom from supervision than are those who remain out of the field. . . . They bring their acceptance of supervision (whatever its genesis) to the career decision when they decide to shift into social work" (1967, pp. 95–96). Gockel notes that this is true for both male and female social-work recruits. Morris Rosenberg (1957), in a study of occupational values, found that the highest concentrations of compliant, acceptance-seeking students were among those selecting social work and teaching as preferred careers. These students showed a willingness to be dominated, a reluctance to dominate others, and a general concern with "approval, acceptance, warmth, support" (p. 42). Strauss (1964) finds that social workers as compared with clinical psychologists function more willingly and effectively in a subordinate role vis-à-vis psychiatrists (p. 83).

Interestingly, McCune found that community organization students rated highest in independent job orientation and medical social workers rated lowest (1966, p. 123; also see Brager and Michael 1969). Supervision is least highly developed in community organization and perhaps most highly developed in medical social work.

Thus the distinctive personality characteristics of social work recruits as well as the fact that it is a female profession may help account for the lack of active opposition to the development of supervision in social work.

No single factor cited in this section can account for the significance and prominence of the process of supervision within social work. In aggregate, however, they form an impressive explanatory array.

Summary

Following a brief historical review of supervision, I noted the variety of definitions of social work supervision. For the purposes of this book, the supervisor was defined as a member of the administrative staff offering an indirect service which included administrative, educational, and supportive functions.

In explaining the prominence of supervision in social work, I noted that organizationally based workers offers resources provided by the community in implementation of community-formulated policies. Working with clients who often have no alternative options, workers who are often untrained and need frequent support offer service under conditions of privacy, with ambiguous outcomes. The predominantly female composition of the work force and some selective personality characteristics of people attracted to the profession tend to reduce opposition to supervision.

chapter two

Administrative Supervision

Supervision is a special aspect of organizational administration. When a number of people are brought together and are then provided with the necessary equipment and facilities to get a particular job done, there needs to be systematic coordination of effort if the objectives of the group are to be efficiently accomplished. The systematic, cooperative, coordinated effort of a group of people in getting a desired job efficiently accomplished, if sustained for any period of time, leads inevitably to the development of some kind of formal organization of the work. Schein (1970) defines organization as "the rational coordination of the activities of a number of people for the achievement of some common explicit purpose or goal through division of labor and function and through a hierarchy of authority and responsibility" (p. 9). More tersely, Blau and Scott (1962) define an organization as "a social unit that has been established for the explicit purpose of achieving certain goals" (p. 1). Organizations are thus "consciously planned and deliberately structured" so as to increase the probability of achieving organizational goals and objectives.

A bureaucracy is a specialized kind of organization. The term "bureaucracy" is used here not pejoratively but descriptively and neutrally, to designate a particular organizational form. A bureaucracy is, theoretically, the most rational, efficient, effective organizational format for coordinating the cooperative efforts of a sizable group of people, each of whom is engaged in a different task necessary for the achievement of common organizational objectives. A bureaucracy may be characterized as follows:

1. There is a specialization of function and task, a division of labor, among units of the organization and among different employees within each unit.
2. There is a hierarchical authority structure, different people being assigned positions of greater or lesser responsibility and power.
3. People in the hierarchy exercise authority on the basis of the position they hold.
4. People are recruited, selected, and assigned to positions in the organization on the basis of objective, impersonal, technical qualifications rather than on the basis of who they are or whom they know.
5. There is a system of regulations and procedures, universally and impersonally applied, which determine the rights and duties of people occupying each of the positions in the agency.
6. All organizational activities are deliberately and rationally planned to contribute to the attainment of organizational objectives. Bureaucracy is sometimes described as the "rational organization of collective activities."

These are the essential characteristics of the bureaucratic organizational structure in its ideal form; actual bureaucracies achieve the ideal in varying degrees. Consequently any bureaucratic organization can be more or less bureaucratic.

Most social work organizations have employees who engage in specialized tasks, and have an administrative hierarchy, a set of clearly formulated rules and procedures, clearly defined roles and statuses, all designed to achieve specific objectives. In short, not only are social agencies organizational in nature, they conform to the definition of a particular kind of organization—a bureaucracy.

Any organization, and particularly a bureaucratic organization, needs administration. The characteristics of a bureaucratic organization describe the nature of its structural arrangements. Administration refers to the process which brings the structural arrangements to life. It is a process which implements organizational objectives. Stein (1965) describes it as a "process of defining and attaining the objectives of an organization through a system of coordinated and cooperative effort" (p. 58). The management of the organization is the particular responsibility of administration within the bureaucratic structure.

The supervisor is a link in the chain of administration—the administrator who is in direct contact with the worker. As an administrator, the supervisor has responsibility for agency management, and specific, clearly defined, administrative-managerial functions are assigned to her. These functions are the essence of administrative supervision.

Tasks

What specifically are the tasks the supervisor is called upon to perform in discharging the responsibilities of administrative supervision?

work assignment and planning

Administration sets general policies and objectives. These then need to be broken down into specific duties and, ultimately, into specific tasks—a certain unit of work to be completed within a given period of time. This is a process of progressively greater refinement of general policy objectives at each descending administrative level so that they can be parceled out in small, manageable units. It is at the first-line supervisory level that agency policies and objectives get their ultimate translation into tasks to be performed by supervisees.

The supervisor's position in the organizational network makes her the most immediate representative of administration at the working group level. She is directly in charge of a group of employees responsible for maintaining a productive flow of work. Through supervisory channels of delegated responsibility, the work "flows from points of decision to points of action." The supervisor is charged with the achievement of objectives, established largely by others higher up in the hierarchy, through the efforts of others lower down in the administrative hierarchy. In less elegant terms, this key administrative responsibility of supervision is called "getting the work out," "putting the job description to work."

The supervisor has the responsibility of selecting tasks for assignment to workers. In social agencies, case or group assignment generally is made in terms of the specific strengths and weaknesses of individual workers. Consequently, in discharging this responsibility the supervisor needs to know the workers' capacities intimately. Implied here is not only a knowledge of the areas that are likely to be problematic for a certain worker, but also the level of complexity of casework demands that the worker can handle with some likelihood of success.

Selection for assignment may be made in terms of variations in job pressures carried by the different workers for whom the supervisor has responsibility. Good administration requires an attempt to equalize the demands made upon workers at the same title and salary level. The supervisor needs to consider the current total caseload carried by each worker, in terms of number of cases and also in terms of the activity likely to be demanded of the worker. The supervisor then assigns new cases so as to ensure some equitable distribution of work load.

Another criterion in assignment of tasks should be diversity. Too great a concentration on one particular kind of task, one kind of case, or one kind of problem situation denies the worker the satisfactions and competence derived from variety in job assignments. This criterion needs to be balanced against assignment in terms of workers' strengths and weaknesses. Some workers do better, and derive greater satisfaction, from highly concentrated job assignments. Others resent this practice and find it stultifying. Currently, greater consideration is being given to the question of matching worker-client characteristics in case assignment in terms of age, sex, race, and ethnicity.

Wherever possible, workers should have an opportunity to express preference for certain kinds of case situations in which they may have a particular interest. Joint discussions of case assignment might further elicit the workers' subjective reactions to work loads. While having the same number of cases as peers, a worker may nevertheless feel overloaded. Sharing her sense of resentment with the supervisor can be helpful. In addition, the supervisor has the opportunity to discuss techniques of case-load management with the worker. The total case load might be reviewed and some decision made as to those cases on which minimum effort might be expended because the situation is stable and not subject to much change. Other cases might be selected for more intensive consideration. The client in such cases may be more vulnerable, or the client and the social situation may be open to positive change in response to active intervention by the worker. At the same time the supervisor can make clear to the worker where the agency's preferred priorities lie, which cases should receive service if time and energy are limited.

A study of case assignment procedures in voluntary and public welfare agencies shows that the most frequent system, by far, is for the supervisor or other administrator to assign cases "based on knowledge of case characteristics, worker ability and experience, etc." (Haring 1974, p. 5). In only about 5 percent of the agencies did the procedure entail "division of labor by staff members among themselves either at periodic meetings or by rotating responsibility for intake" (Haring 1974, p. 4). A high percentage of the workers reacted favorably to the assignment of work by the supervisor.

A supervisee writes about her reaction to case assignments by her supervisor:

I, personally, felt that a random distribution of cases and task assignments provided me with a far greater array of experiences than would have been available had I selected cases and assignments more in accord with my own preference. Under these circumstances, I was often forced into situations that, had I been operating of my own volition, I might have tried to avoid. I think that this produced an environment for substantial personal growth. Allowing an individual to select cases or work assignments which he feels are suited to his personal preferences may lead to stagnation, rather than the development of a flexible individual who can work with a diversity of problems and people. Too often personal preference can be used as an avoidance mechanism or a "cop-out." This does not mean that individual preferences should be categorically ignored or denied, but that the supervisor should evaluate the request for certain assignments or cases critically before giving his assent, to insure that such action would primarily be in the best interests of the client and/or the agency and not just the worker.

Work assignment involves administrative questions of scheduling. Assignments are made, tasks are allocated, with some understanding of the time span in which the work needs to be completed. Work flow is organized so that deadlines can be met. Within the unit itself the supervisor is responsible for planning and scheduling that ensures the workers' ability to perform their jobs without undue stress. The scheduling of meetings, supervisory conferences, dictation time, and report due dates must be made with some appreciation of the total load imposed on the workers and the time available to do the work.

In assigning cases the supervisor faces a number of contradictory pressures that are difficult to resolve. While willing to accede to a worker's preference, the supervisor still must assign every case for service. Even if no supervisee has expressed preference for some particular kind of client, or worse, even if all supervisees have expressed dislike for that kind of client, the supervisor must nonetheless assign the client for service.

Ms. P., a medical social worker, has been assigned cases on the Pediatrics Ward. The large number of handicapped and defective children, especially children requiring institutional placement, has been disturbing to her. After three months at the hospital a case is assigned of a three-year-old spastic boy to discuss institutional possibilities with the parents who are felt to be receptive to placement. Rather reluctantly, Ms. P. tells her supervisor that she would rather not be assigned this case and mentions that a child of a friend was placed in a colony for the mentally defective a year ago. Ms. P. visited with her friend, and the institution seemed depressing.

Rather than acceding to, or rejecting the request or resorting to her positional authority to back up her assignment of the case, the supervisor engaged Ms. P. in elaborating on, and examining her feelings about the assignment. The supervisor did this with the acceptance of the fact that every worker has limits to tolerance and there are some cases that should not be assigned because the worker has strong negative feelings about the assignment. At the same time, there was a recognition that workers have to be helped in extending their limits of tolerance. To permit Ms. P. to reject every assignment with which she might feel uncomfortable would do an injustice to her capacity for growth. In addition to discussing with Ms. P. her own feelings about the situation, the supervisor reviewed the knowledge available regarding the advantages and disadvantages of institutionalization for such children. She helped Ms. P. apply this knowledge to the particular situation of the family of this particular spastic child.

There is a further conflict between the supervisor's desire to assign every case to the most competent and experienced worker and the need for equitable distribution of caseload, between the desire to give each client the best worker and the need for new, inexperienced workers to learn the job.

In assigning tasks, the supervisor is helpful if she clearly designates the objectives and outcomes to be achieved. The explicit formulation of outcomes permits management by objectives (M.B.O.). A clear statement of expected task outcomes gives the supervisee a way to measure work achievement and the supervisor a way to determine if the task has been accomplished. Management by objectives (or, more appropriately, supervision by objectives) is an effort to establish a procedure of control which is acceptable and measurable. With the participation and cooperation of the supervisee, definite objectives are formulated for achievement in each case. These objectives are stated in precise and explicit terms which lend themselves to observation and measurement. Validation of work efforts lies with establishing the extent to which such objectives are achieved in each case.

In assigning work the supervisor not only has to deal with

the problem of task selection, in terms of the criteria discussed above, but also has to decide the explicitness with which she instructs the worker about action that needs to be taken in implementing the assignment. Task assignments indicate what work needs to be accomplished. Task direction indicates how it is to be accomplished. Where work is assigned under conditions of maximum worker autonomy and discretion, the objectives of task assignment are clearly stated and the worker is permitted to initiate any action, at any time, which he feels will result in accomplishment of the objectives. Under conditions of more limited autonomy, the worker may be delegated authority to act only after obtaining prior approval or she may be told in advance what to do.

Most frequently the more adequately trained and experienced workers are given the freedom of deciding the details in implementing an assignment. The supervisor assumes little responsibility for specifying how the assignment is to be implemented. In supervising the less adequately trained and inexperienced worker, the supervisor may have to take more administrative responsibility for directing the specifics for implementation of assigned tasks.

Intrinsic job satisfaction and heightened motivation tend to be positively associated with greater autonomy in implementation of job assignments. Consequently, on a continuum of directivity, the supervisor should permit the workers as much discretion as they can safely and productively handle. Whenever possible, tasks are delegated—that is, the supervisor indicates what results need to be achieved without specifying the procedures to be employed. However, the supervisor should be ready, when necessary, to be more directive, not only assigning the task but clearly specifying how it should be done.

Often even the more experienced, trained worker may want some directive assistance in task implementation. This function—"analysis and planning of client contact with supervisees"—is rated by supervisors as one that occupies a very high percentage of their time (Kadushin 1974). In effect, such planning is like a briefing session. The assignment is explained, the objectives are clarified, the method of implementation is discussed. Delegation does not imply abdication of responsibility. It involves a readiness to help, the granting of authority to permit the worker to take necessary action, and some provision for feedback to ensure that the task has been performed.

Even maximum worker autonomy, however, is exercised within constraints that derive from the objectives of the agency, the requirements of agency survival, the tenets of the profession. Autonomy in task implementation is "an exercise of discretion toward prescribed ends, within prescribed limits."

Task delegation, as an administrative supervisory responsibility, is a complex function dependent on a number of interacting variables. These include supervisor attributes, supervisee attributes, the nature of the task delegated, and organizational climate.

Supervisors differ in the anxiety they feel about delegating tasks. Some are less willing than others to accept the risk of mistakes and failure in their supervisees, for which they might be held accountable. This unwillingness may stem from a supervisor's lack of confidence in himself or from an anxious relationship with his own supervisor. Some are less ready to encourage the development of independence on the part of their supervisees and are gratified by the continuing dependency exemplified by controlling the work decisions of supervisees. Some obtain satisfaction by vicarious involvement in direct practice. More active direction of the work of their supervisees gives them a sense of being involved in the worker-client relationship. The more authoritarian, controlling supervisor will be less ready to delegate than will the democratic-equalitarian supervisor. The supervisor who is oriented toward upward mobility and anxious to please administration is less likely to delegate responsibility than is the supervisor who is free of such internal pressures. In summary, "The ability of a supervisor to delegate effectively depends on the way he relates to his job, his subordinates, his superior and himself" (Bishop 1969, p. 112).

Supervisees who feel uncertain about their competence to

do the job will press for greater direction and more precise delegation from supervisors than will their more confident peers. Supervisees who feel a strong need for independence, who are ready to risk mistakes and who need less structure, will encourage the supervisor to delegate tasks in a general way.

Where there is pressure for precise accountability of agency activity from groups to which the agency is responsible, supervisors will feel a greater pressure to delegate tasks with exactness.

Operating in a host setting alongside professionals of other disciplines increases the hesitancy to delegate. In schools, hospitals, and psychiatric clinics, supervisors are sensitive to the fact that their supervisees are being closely observed by others. Supervisors further have to negotiate with other professionals for the position and prerogatives of social work within the host setting. This situation is more tenuous than one in a setting controlled by social workers.

In summary, the decision around task assignment and the degree of autonomy granted the worker in implementing a task are determined by such factors as: the complexity of the task, level of worker skill and interest, worker caseload in terms of nature and number of cases, vulnerability of and risk to the client, sensitive nature of the problem and likely visibility of error, readiness of supervisor and supervisee to incur risk, and administrative penalties for supervisory failure.

There is limited information on the extent to which social work supervisors actually limit supervisee discretion regarding work decisions. A study of the actions taken by public welfare social workers regarding 35 different significant decisions indicated that more than two-thirds were made "independent of higher authority" (Kettner 1973). These ranged from deciding "which cases should have priority of attention," through "which cases should be closed or referred," to "whether or not to act as client's advocate with landlord, utility company, credit agency." The worker was free to engage in such activities as acting as client advocate or advising clients to use the Welfare Rights Organization as a resource. The decisions most commonly indicated as requiring higher approval focused on assignment of workers' time and money matters. In both instances we are dealing with scarce, or limited, resources. Thus, prior supervisory approval was more often required regarding cases the worker might accept or refuse, setting up a group for clients with similar needs or problems, deciding which of the client's economic needs could be met, whether or not to offer a service when an additional cost to the agency was involved.

The overall conclusion of Kettner's (1973) research was that "while some policy clarification with regard to individual freedom to make decisions may be helpful, most public welfare employees seemed to agree that considerable leeway has already been delegated the worker in making decisions relating to work with clients" (p. 183).

Although a supervisor may delegate a task and the authority to carry it out, the supervisor retains administrative responsibility for the work assigned. Supervisors accept the fact that they are responsible for the work done by their supervisees. Seventy percent of the supervisors studied by Olyan (1972) agreed with the statement, "The supervisor is responsible for the work done by each of his supervisees" (p. 162).

Supervisors tend to phrase task assignments as suggestions or requests: "I think it would be helpful if you. . . ." "Would you please take responsibility. . . ." However, the supervisor has a right to direct and require that certain work be done. Since the supervisor is administratively responsible for seeing that the work assigned to the unit is covered, failure to exercise authority when the situation warrants may result in the supervisor's having to do the work. This happened in the following situation:

An agency was notified that a boy of 17, actively known to it, had been arrested for stealing a car, and that the hearing was to be held in the Magistrate's Court that morning. The possible consequences to the boy were fairly serious in that this was his second offense. The judge, on being called, agreed to hold off the hearing until a worker from the agency could come down and discuss the boy with him. The worker in the case was not in the office, and could not be reached. The supervisor asked another worker, who was dictating, to take this as an emergency. The worker refused, saying he could let nothing interfere with his dictation. The supervisor herself went to the court because another worker was not available. ("Casework Notebook" 1939, p. 42)

(The principal resource the supervisor has available to ensure that the work of the agency gets done is the time and skill of the supervisees.) In accepting the role of employee of an agency the supervisee implicitly agrees to place his time and skill at the disposal of the agency for some specific period during the day and week. Consequently, the supervisor has the responsibility of knowing when and if the supervisees are available for work during the agreed-upon period. In discharging this administrative function the supervisor needs to be concerned with tardiness, absences, requests for time off, sick leave, vacation schedules, projected and emergency overtime manpower needs to ensure adequate coverage of work assignments. If the supervisor does not have final authority with regard to these questions, as she should, she often has the power of decisive recommendation.

In implementing the work-assignment responsibilities of administrative supervision, the supervisor is concerned with assuring continuity of service. The worker represents the agency to the community. The supervisor represents the agency as well, though once removed. If a worker leaves the agency, the supervisor is there to step in and ensure that the agency is still responsible for offering service. Thus the worker's leaving does not result in a break in the continuity of contact, merely an interruption and possible delay. If the worker is absent or sick, the supervisor again ensures continuity of contact and work coverage.

work review and evaluation

Case assignment implies a second significant responsibility, that of case review. The supervisor is responsible for seeing that an assigned case is satisfactorily handled by the worker, that the worker actually has competently offered the service the agency is charged with offering. The supervisor has to know, in some general way, the progress of the worker's caseload and to be sensitive to indications of indifference, incompetence, or neglect in any instance. Work review is necessary to determine if the work is being accomplished as planned. It closes the loop in the processes of administrative supervision. As a consequence of determining what work has been done and how it has been done, additional tasks are assigned.

(The supervisor not only has the administrative responsibility for seeing that the work is done but, further, that it is done in accordance with agency policy and procedures.)Procedure dictates that the workers keep certain hours, meet certain deadlines, maintain certain schedules, and proceed in a particular manner in making referrals, in interacting with the client, in using office files, in working with clerical staff. The supervisor is administratively responsible for seeing that the workers adhere to such procedures within feasible limits.

The supervisor or administrator not only has to review the assignment to be assured that it is actually being accomplished, and accomplished in accordance with agency policies and procedures, but further has to make some judgment as to whether it is being accomplished at a minimally acceptable level. The supervisor then has responsibility for evaluation. Formal evaluation of the workers' performance is an administrative act. If the agency is to operate efficiently, then someone has to share clearly with the workers an objective appraisal of the things they are doing right, the things they are doing wrong, to point out the behaviors that require changing. Agency procedures regarding raises, promotions and changes in job assignment require periodic formal evaluation if such decisions are to be implemented in a rational manner. Since evaluation is a very important function of administrative supervision and is the source of much confusion and difficulty, we have reserved a more detailed discussion for chapter 6.

Review of work to ensure that it meets some acceptable qualitative and quantitative standards, that it is performed in accordance with agency policies and procedures and in line with statutory requirements, requires explicit procedures for systematic feedback. In the past, social agencies have often operated with a cavalier attitude toward management procedures that provide systematic information on day-to-day operations. We have been scornful of the variety of sophisticated techniques that business management has developed to ensure that organizational objectives are, in fact, being achieved in an acceptable and efficient manner. All of this seemed beneath us somehow. Recently this attitude on the part of social workers, and social work administrators, has been changing to a considerable extent in response to external criticism. Social work is experiencing insistent demands for quality controls and accountability. Taxpayers, state legislators, the federal government, local community and client groups are demanding precise answers to questions about agency operations.

We have, as a profession, paid a high price for our repugnance toward, and perhaps disdain for, precise, management-monitoring feedback procedures. Uncertainty about what we are actually doing has contributed to increasing reluctance to support social work programs previously funded, leading to a reduction in services and a contraction of professional job opportunities.

The image of the profession has been scarred by reports of agency mismanagement as a consequence of inadequate supervision (New York State, Office of the Comptroller 1973). The poor managerial performance of social workers has led to efforts to replace them with professionals trained in management and administration. For instance, in April 1972 the Human Resources Administration announced a "major shake-up" of New York City Welfare Centers. New directors were appointed in a sizable number of centers to "stress 'managerial talent' instead of past emphasis on social workers" (*New York Times*, April 12, 1972). The job requirement that the appointee hold an M.S.W. degree was waived in hiring management professionals for administrative positions in the agency.

The press toward greater concern with accountability is accompanied, inevitably, by a greater stress on specification and objectification of activities and outcomes. More people want to know exactly what the worker is doing, how she is doing it, to whom she is doing it, for what purpose and with what results. These are the kinds of questions that the supervisor is administratively responsible for answering as part of supervisory review of worker activity.

As a consequence, a new vocabulary is being introduced into social work which is associated with new procedures and techniques, providing more precise information of social agency operations and workers' activities: P.E.R.T. (Program Evaluation and Review Techniques), G.O.S.S. (Goal-Oriented Social Services), M.B.O. (Management by Objectives), F.J.A. (Functional Job Analysis), S.S.I.S. (Social Services Information System), C.P.I.S. (Compliance Performance Information System). There are C.A.S.S., M.I.E.S., and P.I.N.S. Different acronyms for different systems, and all asking for more systematic feedback regarding work effort. In line with these changes, departments of public welfare have been computerizing their service operations, and management-system consultants have been retained by social agencies to help them establish procedures for greater organizational effectiveness.

But any and all of these techniques and procedures, all the brave new managerial approaches, ultimately require the active cooperation of the supervisor in implementing the responsibilities of administrative supervision. The informational inputs that are basic to any review system have to be obtained through the supervisor in direct contact with the worker. Without some kind of systematically collected case-control data sheet, daily or weekly workload schedules, case progress reports, case disposition logs, records of starting and completion time for job assignments, and client complaint data, it is difficult to know systematically how much of what kind of work workers are doing, whether they have been most efficiently deployed, how to budget unit cost of services. Such information is basic for making operative the most comprehensive systems for ensuring agency accountability. Instruction regarding the rationale for the forms and how to use them is an educational task of supervision. Seeing that the forms are distributed and correctly completed within time limits is an administrative responsibility.

Because social work agencies have tended to err on the side of lax administrative supervision, there is need to emphasize the desirability of greater concern with systematic review and control of worker availability and productivity. However, there are ideological and pragmatic constraints to intensification of such administrative supervisory procedures. The ethos of the profession stresses mutual trust in the supervisor-supervisee relationship. The relevant research supports the desirability of this as a pragmatic requirement in effective agency operation. Suggestions that the supervisor, in her administrative capacity, make greater efforts to systematically review the worker's activity seem to run counter to the development of a relationship based on mutual trust.

The profession has, however, met the problem previously in the worker-client relationship and has resolved it satisfactorily. Here, too, mutual trust is required if social work is to function well. Yet we have accepted the need for checking eligibility by requiring validation of the client's statements. Similarly, in discharging the responsibilities as licensing agents in foster care, day care, institutional care, we have accepted the necessity for checking significant applicant data. In accepting and processing applications to schools of social work, we require documentation of the applicant's claims. Such procedures, which we have employed for some time, have not proved antithetical to the establishment of relationships characterized by trust. The worker is no more, and no less, worthy of acceptance than the client, the day-care-center director or the graduate-school applicant. Reviewing his work to make certain that he has done what he was assigned to do is no more reflective of suspicious distrust.

Supervisory administrative responsibility for case review may seem demeaning to the worker. It gives substance to the least flattering component of the dictionary definition of supervision: to oversee the work of others. Nevertheless, it is an inescapable function if the community and the client are to be adequately protected and if the credibility of the agency is to be maintained. Even the most autonomous of professionals employed in complex organizations are, of necessity, subject to such review. We noted earlier the pressures that led to the development of review boards for all Medicare and Medicaid decisions; the situational imperatives that called for such a procedure are real and compelling. Even before the development of government-enforced review procedures, the medical profession had developed peer controls which perform the function allocated to social work administrative supervision.

Katz (1968) reports on review committees established by hospitals and staffed by pathologists who review surgeons' decisions regarding the need for surgery. In checking for surgical errors the pathologist "while rejecting the label of policeman is, in fact, carrying out the role of policeman" (p. 134). The review committee infringes on professional autonomy in checking on surgical decisions. But if the hospital is to protect the patient and maintain its legitimacy in the community, somebody has to perform this function—unless one assumes that surgeons are totally infallible and totally ethical. If we abolished the administrative supervisory responsibility for work review, the profession in discharging its responsibility to client and community would have to establish an analogous peer review committee regarding, let us say, adoptive placement decisions or parole revocation decisions.

The problem of work review is related to the question of closeness of supervision. Close supervision implies restrictions on the workers' discretion, detailed instructions to workers regarding the implementation of the job assignment, and frequent, extensive checking of work done. The effects of close supervision are that workers tend to feel dominated, stifled, anxious, and infantilized. Loose supervision implies infrequent review of selective aspects of the supervisee's activity. The disadvantage of supervision which is too loose is the risk that assignments may be poorly or improperly completed and that problems are developing about which administration has little awareness. Workers are denied the possibility of help they might want if it were actively offered. Again, the middle ground seems to offer the most desirable approach—supervision which is loose enough that the worker feels free and trusted and not so loose that agency responsibility for accountability is disregarded.

To suggest the need for more supervisory review than we have customarily employed is not to advocate very close supervision. Requiring too much feedback and spending an excessive amount of time in checking are counterproductive. They involve an inefficient disposition of supervisory time and incur the resentment of supervisees (Kaufman 1973).

Although there is considerable evidence from business-management research that close supervision adversely affects the supervisee-supervisor relationship, there is limited research on the effects in social work. In studying the relationship between supervisors and supervisees in a public welfare agency, Blau and Scott (1962) examined authoritarian practices as an element of supervisory style. Close supervision was one of the activities which contributed to the measure of authoritarian practices. They found that authoritarian supervision decreased worker satisfaction, decreased worker independence and decreased the tendency to offer casework services as against concern with determining client eligibility. Unexpectedly, however, close supervision did not adversely affect worker productivity nor did it result in alienating the supervisee from the supervisor (Blau and Scott 1962), p. 153). However, Marcus (1961) analyzed additional material which was part of the Blau-Scott study and did find productivity adversely related to supervision that was authoritarian, procedural, and task oriented as compared with supervision that was more permissive and client oriented.

coordinating, facilitating, and sanctioning of work

The supervisor, as administrator, coordinates and integrates the work of the individual supervisee and the unit of other supervisees, with other units of the agency and with other agencies in the community's social welfare network. The supervisor not only occupies a position in the vertical hierarchy but relates horizontally to other administrative units on the same hierarchical level. The supervisor in the family service unit of a multiservice neighborhood center might help coordinate the activities of her supervisees with the homemaker unit, the employment unit, the day-care unit, the protective services unit. She might help coordinate the supervisees' activity with that of the clerical unit, seeing that typing time is available, a dictaphone provided. She might help make available psychiatric consultation and psychological test resources to the supervisees. She functions here to ensure the availability and smooth scheduling of a variety of different agency and community resources for the supervisees.

The supervisor organizes and orchestrates the activities of a number of different workers so that their joint efforts are cooperatively directed toward accomplishing some significant aspects of the mission of the agency. Coordination involves some assurance that the different workers understand the goals and objectives of the agency in the same way and accept them—or at least behave as though they accepted the same objectives. Each worker can operate in the confident expectation that others in the group are working together rather than at cross purposes.

Each worker's performance, then, has to be related to some other worker's performance. Coordination is the administrative process of implementing the relationship between activities of different workers in the agency. It is the "orderly arrangement of group effort to provide unity of action in the pursuit of common objectives" (Olmstead 1973, p. 29), of meshing disparate, but complementary, activities.

Coordination requires that the supervisor perform the administrative function of adjudicating conflicts between workers in his unit and between his unit and other units of the agency. Two workers may be competing for the same assignments, or may disagree about who should be doing what with regard to a complex problem for which they have joint responsibility. The unmarried mothers' unit may be dissatisfied about the availability of adoptive homes for which the adoptive unit is responsible; the family care worker may be getting little cooperation from the agency's employment unit or housing unit. The supervisor has the responsibility of seeing that such conflicts are satisfactorily resolved. Put positively, the supervisor has the administrative function of maintaining harmonious working relationships within the unit and between his units and other units in the agency.

Spergel (1966) gives an interesting example of such coordination in his analysis of the outreach program working with street gangs.

> Service to fighting and highly delinquent groups requires a high degree of cooperation among street workers along with representatives of other agencies, especially the police. . . . One example of a device for coordinating and controlling the area-oriented worker is the central communications system. When a critical situation arises, the worker is expected to relay information to the supervisor as soon as possible via a central control switchboard. The supervisor can then deploy other workers and involve the police, if necessary. This kind of communication system assists the supervisor to know where workers are in the field, and permits him to inform, advise, or direct them as to the most appropriate way of handling the emergent situation. (pp. 243–44)

The supervisor has the administrative responsibility of facilitating the supervisees' work. However skillful the individual workers, their effectiveness is reduced if they operate in a defectively organized unit. The supervisor is responsible for providing the supporting organizational setting that would maximize the workers' contribution. The supervisor relates effective people to effective programs through effective organization of the work context. This means that the supervisor makes sure that workers are provided with adequate facilities, supplies, staff help, and information.

Supervisors need the authority to require that facilities be made available. Strong chief unit clerks often contend with weak supervisors about the allocation of facilities and the work time of typists and file clerks. Despite the fact that the agency table of organization gives the supervisor greater authority, in-ability in effectively exercising this power may put the super-visor's workers in a disadvantaged position for access to the resources they need to do their work effectively.

The supervisor performs the additional function of acting for agency administration in authorizing and legitimizing super-visees' decisions and recommendations. This gives official agency support to the workers' actions. In doing this the super-visor acts to coordinate the claims of the worker on behalf of his client with the services the agency is ready and willing to offer.

the supervisor as a channel of communication

In discharging her administrative responsibilities the su-pervisor acts as an integral link in the chain of administrative communication. The supervisor, in the vertical line of authority, faces two ways—toward the administrators above her in the hi-erarchy and toward the workers below her. The supervisor's position is, then, one of the administrative control centers for gathering, processing and disseminating information coming both from above and below in the chain of command.

A small group cooperatively performing certain tasks can rely on face-to-face communication among all members of the group. A complex organization, in which administrators rarely see and have direct contact with workers, requires other ap-proaches if messages are to reach their proper destinations and be understood and accepted. Formal channels of com-munication need to be provided, and the nature of the work to be done and the conditions under which it is to be completed need to be precisely stated and clearly defined.

Communication permits more effective coordination of the work of the agency through linkages provided by the flow of in-formation and feedback. The volume of communication varies with the degree of diversity of a social agency because of the greater necessity for coordination in more complex organiza-tions (Hage et al. 1971). Communication as a vehicle for coor-dination is particularly necessary in organizations, such as so-cial agencies, where tasks are ambiguously defined and therefore it is difficult to explicitly codify procedures for task implementation. Rather than being able to rely on written manuals and handbooks, administrators need to make frequent efforts to clarify and check to see if messages have been understood.

A recent large-scale study found adequate and effective communication within the agency to be a very important determinant of worker satisfaction. The study of 1600 workers in 31 agencies found that "the biggest problem is that higher levels in an organization usually assume communication is adequate but lower level personnel do not agree. The great majority of personnel feel they do not have all the information they need to do their jobs effectively" (Olmstead and Christensen 1973, p. 13).

(In effectively discharging his responsibility for administrative supervision, the supervisor has to do more than act as a messenger.) Lacking direct contact with administration, supervisees look to the supervisor to represent their interests and actively press for the implementation of necessary changes. Effective administrative supervision requires active representation of supervisees' interests and viewpoints as an intermediary with administration.

Blau and Scott (1962) found that those supervisors in a public welfare agency who related to administrators in an independent manner and who regularly backed their subordinates commanded high loyalty from their supervisees (p. 155). A psychiatric social worker in a state hospital says that in one case she

judged it necessary to call in an outside consultant-advocate in an incident involving the civil rights of a patient. My supervisor supported this decision verbally and by attending the meeting which was held to discuss the patient's situation. She did this even though the hospital administration disapproved of my action. It was gratifying to see that my supervisor was open to the facts and exercised judgment based on client need rather than on official administration policy.

The act of communication is abortive unless it is accompanied by some confidence in the possibility that the message will have an effect. Supervisee satisfaction with supervision appears to be related to the level of influence the supervisor has with administration (Pelz 1952). There was dissatisfaction with the supervisor who promised much but was able to deliver little. There was high satisfaction with the supervisor who communicated worker requests and was able to get action. The lesson for administrators is that they should make a sincere effort to respond to communications from supervisees via supervisors. The lesson for supervisors is that they must honestly share with the supervisees the limits of their power, to forestall unrealistic expectations about the effects of upward communication.

Some studies have shown that workers are not confident that supervisors will take responsibility for decisions when these are questioned by higher-ups (Greenleigh Associates 1960, p. 133). The most frequent complaint about supervisors listed by supervisees in a questionnaire study of N.A.S.W. members is that the supervisor was "hesitant about confronting agency administration with the needs of his (her) supervisees" (Kadushin 1974).

Mr. E., a school social worker, was indignant at the judgmental attitude of the Board of Education's policy regarding admission of unmarried mothers to special school programs. The supervisee informed his supervisor that it had been his experience that school officials were discouraging unmarried mothers from attending school by erecting unnecessary procedures for admission to school. Mr. E. had hoped that the supervisor would either join him in talking with Board of Education officials or support him in doing so. Instead the supervisor chose to focus on Mr. E.'s "indignation" and "hostility" toward the Board of Education and was insensitive to the need for change in school policy.

This account suggests one of the principal barriers to the free flow of communication up and down administrative channels. The supervisor may be reluctant to communicate negative information to people to whom he is administratively responsible because he fears incurring hostility or displeasure. Similarly, the supervisee is reluctant to communicate negative information to the supervisor because he fears rejection, a negative evaluation, a censuring reaction. Consequently, rather than a sharing of dissatisfactions and problems in offering service, communication is carefully restricted to telling others only what they want to hear or what will reflect favorably on one's own performance. The safest procedure is to act the part of a not-too-obvious "yes man" and "play it close to the chest." Freedom to speak is felt only as freedom to agree. This pattern operates more intensely for supervisees who are motivated to obtain the approval of supervisors and who are seeking a good evaluation.

Barriers to organizational communication result from conflicting group loyalties as well as from a need for self-protection. The supervisee is reluctant to share information that may reflect discredit on fellow peers or groups of clients with whom he might feel identified. Supervisors may be reluctant to share with administration their critical, but accurate, assessment of some subsection of the agency with which they must continue to work.

Information is power. It is not true that what people don't know won't hurt them. They can very well be harmed because they have not been informed about things they need to know in order to perform effectively. This suggests an additional barrier to the free flow of communication. The supervisor may withhold information from supervisees because this increases their dependency on him.

If these barriers to the free flow of communication do not result in withholding information which should be shared, they more often result in "selective emphasis" and "selective omission" in transmission. Communication takes place but is distorted so as to meet the needs of the communicator.

One might realistically anticipate that every agency faces impediments to the free flow of communication. Even in the best of circumstances one might expect supervisees to be pragmatically self-protective in the information they selectively choose to share. But if one cannot hope to achieve best communication, one might perhaps attain better communication. And here the supervisor is a key figure. Olmstead (1973) claims that

The climate created by an individual's immediate supervisor is probably the most important influence affecting his communication. Every encounter with the supervisor teaches him something. When the supervisor gives an order, reprimands, praises, evaluates performance, deals with a mistake, holds a staff meeting or contacts [supervisees] in any other way (or fails to contact them), the [supervisees] learn something. They learn about the kinds of information that will be rewarded or punished and the means of communication which the [supervisor] views favorably or unfavorably. (p. 47)

The stronger the sense of mutual respect and trust between supervisor and supervisee, the more effective the channel of communication. In the context of a good relationship there is less of a tendency to commit sins of *suppresso veri, suggestio falsi.*

Credibility is an important prerequisite for effective communication. Supervisees need to have developed an attitude of confidence and trust in the motives and sincerity of the supervisor. This attitude is based on experience which established the fact that supervisors were truthful in their communications and that words and action went together. Supervisees are constantly engaged in "search behavior" in an effort to distinguish the reality from the rhetoric.

In general it might be said that communication in the agency flows down more easily than it flows up. Communication in the organizational hierarchy has often been described as a system where information flows up through a series of filters and comes down through a series of loudspeakers.

In a communication system free from inhibiting influences, the supervisor still has a problem of deciding what information needs to be shared and can be shared. Not all of the information that comes from administration should automatically be communicated to supervisees, and not everything shared by supervisees needs to be transmitted to administration. Applying some general principle of selectivity, such as that one should transmit only information which helps supervisees do their job more effectively, implies that the supervisor needs to have an intimate, detailed knowledge of the workers' job and agency administration. Only on the basis of such knowledge and understanding would the supervisor be able to assess the value of information she has available for possible communication.

The supervisor has the responsibility of encouraging relevant communication from supervisees, establishing a climate of receptivity and a readiness to listen. Conversely, the supervisor has to demonstrate a readiness to share relevant information with supervisees, keeping them informed, indicating a willingness to answer questions fully and to correct misconceptions. The supervisor should avoid assumptions. "Don't assume that the supervisees know; tell them. Don't assume that you know how they feel; find out. Don't assume that they understand; clarify" (U.S. Civil Service Commission 1955, p. 22).

Because the orientation of the direct service workers to task-related information is different from that of the supervisor, the supervisor needs to be sensitive to the fact that the same communication may be differently perceived by them. A message from the administrator to the supervisor may ask that the agency be more accountable to the community. This is translated by the supervisor to mean that he will need to assign tasks so that they are more objectively measurable and this message is communicated to the workers. The workers translate the supervisor's message to mean that they will have to fill out more forms with greater care than previously. The affective response to essentially the same cognitive message is apt to be different at the different levels of verbal communication because at different levels the message has different implications for action.

We have noted that the supervisor is a channel of communication in the vertical hierarchy. The supervisor also communicates horizontally—within the agency and with other agencies. The supervisor maintains communication between her unit and other units through communication with peers at the supervisory level. Downward communication, from supervisor to supervisee, is concerned with long- and short-term changes in agency policy and procedures, information about work assignments, how the workers' functions fit into the total agency operation, and feedback about workers' performance. Upward communication, from supervisee to supervisor, is concerned with reports of work completed, plans for future activity to be performed, problems encountered on the job, ideas and suggestions for agency change. Lateral communication from supervisors in one unit to supervisors in related units is concerned with problems of conflict and overlap, changes which might make for more effective coordination of joint efforts, information about impending changes which may affect coordinated activities.

the supervisor as administrative buffer

The supervisor serves as a buffer in relation to agency clients. Agency administration looks, in general, to the first-line supervisory staff to handle problems relating to service. Consequently, the supervisor performs the function of dealing with clients who want to discuss a complaint with someone other than the worker. A child welfare worker writes:

> When an irate and emotionally disturbed parent wished to visit her child in foster placement and I had denied her request, she contacted my supervisor when I was out of the office. My supervisor listened supportively, gathered the facts, upheld me in my decision but suggested that the client come to the office to discuss the situation with both my supervisor and me.
>
> The parent came in a day or so later, as agreed between the three of us as to time and date, and we had a very productive meeting. Client was able to express some of her hostility and anger at the child's removal from her home—which anger had been focused on me—however, my supervisor completely supported my position which then freed me from becoming defensive and allowed me to support the client also. The result was a better relationship with the client and more cooperation from her, which ultimately worked to her advantage in the later return of her children to her.
>
> Having reviewed the case material my supervisor had decided to support my decision. However, she also gave client respect and courtesy which eased the tensions of the interview and allowed us all to gain by it. The client did not feel we were in league against her as she could have if my supervisor had not been skillful in encouraging her feelings and right to them; nor did the client manage to manipulate my supervisor and me into opposite corners.

The supervisor also performs an administrative function in protecting the organization from potentially embarrassing deviance and heresy. Deviance involves behavioral contravention or subversion of agency regulations; heresy involves ideological opposition to the presuppositions on the basis of which the rules were formulated. The worker in an Orthodox Catholic child welfare agency who helps an unmarried pregnant girl solve her problem by obtaining an abortion is deviant in that context. If she champions the point of view that there is really nothing wrong with an out-of-wedlock pregnancy and questions the legitimacy of agency efforts to help women conform to society's traditional sexual mores, she would be heretical.

The functions of administrative supervision relating to work planning, assignment, and review derive from the organization's responsibility to implement its mission. The function of buffering derives from the agency's responsibility to ensure its existence. Every social work agency not only has a client constituency but also a donor constituency, its sources of public funding or private contributions. An agency operates in, and is tied to, an external environment whose salient aspects include clients, funding sources, regulatory agencies, and the general public as well as other agencies with which it competes for income and resources. The agency needs to maintain the good will and support of the external environment. Activities that undermine the legitimacy of the agency with its donor constituency threaten its existence. The elimination of many agencies during the past decade testifies to that fact that the threat is real.

Agency self-preservation is a legitimate objective. More than a question of opportunistic defense of selfish vested interests is involved. If agency workers have a sincere conviction in the value of the agency's mission, their concern for agency preservation is ultimately a concern with providing a needed service. The failure to obtain continued funding results in denial of this service to a client group.

Furthermore, the willingness of workers to extend themselves in working toward achievement of agency objectives depends on a conviction in the desirability of agency objectives and the procedures that have been developed to achieve them. Serious questions about the desirability of the objectives, or the efficacy of procedures, are a threat to the belief system which unites members of the organization in working together. The supervisor as guardian of the organization's cosmology performs a priestly function in helping to maintain the belief system intact. To reject significant aspects of agency policy and procedure is regarded as an act of hostility and a challenge to organizational authority. It threatens agency operation because "it suspends the rules that produce loyalty and cohesion" (Peters and Branch 1972, p. 290), without which the agency finds it difficult to operate.

Preserving stability—implementing change. It is at this juncture that conflict between the worker and the organization often become most clearly manifest. The whole philosophical debate regarding the obligation of civil disobedience to unjust laws is applicable to the problem faced by social workers in meeting agency requirements for conformity to policies and procedures which they are convinced are oppressive. Workers are encouraged to seek redress and change within the agency. There is a rich literature available on tactics that workers can employ in attempting to effect changes in agency policies and procedures in the face of resistant or inaccessible administrators (Patti 1974a, 1974b; Patti and Weissman 1972; Weissman 1973). Going outside the agency, outside of channels which include the supervisor as the first point of contact, is enjoined— although there are more frequent examples of such "whistle blowing" recently (Peters and Branch 1972; Nader, Petkas, and Blackwell 1974).

Part of the problem stems from a widely held but rarely explicit assumption—that of the "noble worker." Brager and Specht (1973) describe it as follows:

> There is a kind of neo-populist myth that correlates integrity with position on the organizational totem pole. The lower in the hierarchy, the notion goes, the more socially concerned the person will be. Implicit in this idea is the belief that the desire for social change to benefit the poor is disproportionately held by those of lower status, that indigenous workers [nonprofessionals] are "better" or "more activist" than their supervisors, and so on. Although this class-distinction-in-reverse may fill workers' needs for ingroup celebration, it is an over-simplification of reality. (p. 215)

The myth suggests that in the conflict between the agency and the worker, the worker is more likely to be right.

The conflict between worker and organization is administratively manifested first at the level of contact between worker and supervisor. Consequently, "in many organizations it seems systematically to become part of whomever is formally designated as first in command of each particular work unit to occupy the buffer zone which contains heretical confrontations between the individual and the social organizations" (Harshbarger 1973, p. 264). The function is one of "crisis absorbency" and prevention of the development of a threat to the agency's legitimacy with its supporting constituency.

This administrative function of supervision is implemented by offering workers the opportunity to discuss with the supervisor their questions and doubts about the agency's philosophy, rules, and procedures. Patient, open discussion of the workers' views in an accepting atmosphere is designed to help them understand the rationale of the agency's approach. If the workers remain unconvinced, the supervisory conference still offers a safe channel for the open expressions of their opposition. The cathartic effect of such an opportunity results, as Goffman (1952) says, "in cooling the mark out"—a reduction in the intensity of feeling of indignation, an increased readiness to conform to organizational demands. Another frequent procedure in the management of heresy is cooption, an attempt to retranslate the worker's opposition so that it can be channeled into kinds of changes that the agency can accept.

In a study of authority relationships in a public welfare department (Peabody 1964), 83 percent of the welfare department employees said that at one time or another they had received instructions from above which seemed to conflict with their own standards, often with regard to regulations for processing welfare grants. The most frequent reactions to such a conflict situation, in descending order, were "discusses with immediate supervisor and works for change but still complies"; "consciously questions but accepts as binding"; "informs immediate supervisor of views but complies or seeks to be converted" (p. 107). Welfare workers were more inclined than police officers and elementary school teachers included in the study to discuss situations of conflict with their supervisors and to work for change.

The responsibility of acting in defense of agency policy can be a source of considerable dissatisfaction for supervisors. Frequently they find themselves in disagreement with some particular agency policy, rule, or procedure. Nevertheless their role requires communication of the policy and attempts to obtain compliance with it. Forced by their position to perform such functions, supervisors feel uncomfortably hypocritical. In a survey of dissatisfactions felt by supervisors the "need to get workers' adherence to agency policy and procedure with which I strongly disagree" was among the dissatisfactions most frequently checked (Kadushin 1974).

There is a danger that too rigid "management" of deviance and heresy, the "absorption of protest and domestication of dissent" may be dysfunctional for the agency. The imperceptive supervisor would then be performing a disservice. The agency must balance contradictory needs—accepting change while maintaining stability. It would be impossible to run an efficient organization and maintain effective working relationships with other agencies if the agency were not essentially stable and predictable. However, stability can foster rigidity which becomes ossification. In ossifying, the agency risks elimination because it can no longer respond to the needs of a changing situation. Consequently, while defending the agency against deviance and heresy, the supervisor has to be open to suggestions for useful innovation. As Reich (1970) says, agency administration "is always neutral in favor of the Establishment" (p. 100). The bias needs to be explicitly recognized, but lightly held.

While the problem which generates the most indignation is agency temporization, or outright rejection, of workers' suggestions for changes, there is often a problem in the other direction. Progressive, innovative administrators often have difficulty getting supervisees to accept changes in policies and procedures (Pruger and Specht 1968). A whole host of factors understandably stand in the way of acceptance of change. Additional energy needs to be expended in overcoming habitual patterns of dealing with work problems, in unlearning and in learning new ways of working; there is anxiety about whether one can adequately meet the demands of new programs and new procedures; there is reluctance to accept an increased measure of dependency while learning new patterns; there is a struggle involved in developing a conviction in the value of the change; there is anxiety about rearranged interpersonal connections in the agency as work procedures change.

Change is best accomplished if supervisees participate from the start in planning the change, if they are informed early of the nature of the planned change, if the change is introduced slowly, preferably with some initial trial effort, if expectations are made clear and understandable, if the change is in line with perceived agency norms and objectives, if there is some assurance that the change will have the effect predicted, if the administration, including supervisors, communicate strong conviction in the desirability of the change, if there is some appreciation of, and empathy with, the difficulties that change generates for the staff, and if provision is made to reduce the costs of change to the staff. Putting himself in the supervisees' place, the supervisor has to make an effort to understand the possible costs and benefits the change implies for them.

The functional value of rules. In a less dramatic sense than as a guardian of the agency's cosmology, the supervisor, in monitoring conformance to agency rules and procedures, permits the agency to get its work done effectively. In prescribing and proscribing, in monitoring what should be done and what cannot be done, the supervisor is ensuring predictability and reliability in performance. Workers doing different things, whose work needs to be coordinated, can be assured that the work their partners are doing will be in accordance with some uniform expectations. The worker in the unit of the agency offering service to the unmarried mother interested in placing her child for adoption can discuss the characteristics of an approved adoptive home without having herself seen one. She can do this because she knows the requirements and procedures which regulate the work of her colleagues in the adoptive home–finding unit. Workers have to have confidence in the reliability with which these fellow workers will follow prescribed procedures, as a prerequisite for performing their own tasks.

The supervisor, as protector of agency rules and procedures, has the responsibility of seeing that policy is uniformly interpreted. If each worker were permitted to establish his own policies, or to idiosyncratically interpret centrally established policies, this would ultimately set client against client, and worker against worker. A liberal interpretation of policy by one client's worker is an act of discrimination against the client of a second worker. It would encourage competition among workers in an effort to tap agency resources to meet the needs of their own clients, with whom they are, understandably enough, primarily concerned.

The general social-work press toward autonomy, self-determination, and individualization tends to develop a negative attitude toward rules. Rules suggest that people are interchangeable rather than being uniquely different. The negative attitude toward formalization of prescribed behavior in rules and procedures has, of course, support in the real negative consequences which can result from their application. They do limit the autonomy of the worker, they discourage initiative, they tend to make the agency muscle-bound, less flexible and adaptable, "set in its ways." They predispose toward a routinization of worker activity. Rules can become ends in themselves rather than means for achieving organizational objectives; they restrict the freedom to individualize agency response in meeting particular needs of particular clients and encourage deception and duplicity as workers feel a need to "get around" the rules.

Social workers are generally well aware of, and sensitive to, the negative consequences of rules. It might be helpful to the supervisor who inevitably faces the responsibility of communicating and enforcing rules and uniform procedures if some conviction can be developed regarding the positive aspects of standardization.

While each rule and prescribed procedure, if taken seriously, limits worker autonomy by deciding in advance what action should be taken in a particular situation, the rules permit more efficient agency operation. When the recurrent situation to which a rule is applied is encountered, it need not be subject to an exhaustive process of review and decision making. The supervisee does not need to discuss the situation with the supervisor and can act with the assurance that the decision, congruent with the procedure, has agency sanction. This relieves anxiety and frees the supervisee's energies to deal with those unique aspects of the client's situation that cannot be codified in some formal policy statement. If everything in every case had to be decided afresh, the worker could easily be overwhelmed and immobilized. Here, as elsewhere, there is no real freedom without clearly defined laws. They provide a structure within which workers can operate with comfort, assurance, and support. Rules provide a clear codification of expectations. They communicate to the worker how he is expected to respond in a variety of recurrently encountered situations. This understanding is particularly important in social work where the various groups the social worker faces communicate contradictory, and often conflicting, expectancies. The community may expect him to respond in one way to client problems, the client a second way, the profession in still another way. The rules offer a worker the serenity of unambiguous guidelines as to how the agency expects him to respond in defining clearly the "minimum set of behaviors which are prescribed and proscribed." The rules mitigate conflicts to which workers might otherwise be exposed.

If the agency wisely formulates its rules and procedures with active worker participation and if it further provides for a periodic critical review of them, the agency, of necessity, must make a systematic analysis of professional practice. The best rules are, after all, merely a clear codification of practice wisdom, what most workers have found is the best thing to do in certain situations. The call for rules and procedures is, consequently, a call for a hard analysis of practice.

Ultimately, rules protect the client since the procedures to which all workers adhere in a uniform manner assure him of equitable service. He is assured that another client will not be given preferential treatment because his worker likes him better and that he will not be treated worse because he has antagonized the worker by his militancy. If a client meets the qualification as codified in agency procedures, the worker is under some constraint to approve his application for adoption, to authorize his request for a special assistance grant, or whatever.

Rules reduce the possibility of friction between supervisors and supervisees. They set impersonal limits to individual exceptions that the supervisee might press for. They are also a source of support and sanction to the supervisor in making decisions that threaten the relationship. Rules depersonalize decisions which might be resented as a personal affront by the supervisee: "I wish I could go along with your request, but agency regulations prevent this." More positively, the procedural norms substantiate the desirability of the decision the supervisor is making: "In these kinds of problems we have found such an approach is not particularly helpful. In fact, based on our experience, we have developed a procedure which requires that the worker not take such action."

Rules protect the worker from arbitrary, personalized decisions by the supervisor, from favoritism, and from discriminating acts based on irrelevant criteria. While rules constrain those "to whom they are applied," they constrain the "behavior of the rule applier as well." In fact, a sophisticated worker armed with a detailed knowledge of the rules can use them to control the authority and discretion of the supervisor (Mechanic 1964).

Rules reduce the possibility of supervisor-supervisee friction because they operate as remote-control devices. Supervision can occur through adherence to a universally applied rule rather than through the direct, personal intercession of the supervisor suggesting that this or that be done in this or that way. Control takes place at a distance in the absence of the supervisor. A rule is a "definition of expectation." The explicitness of a rule makes clear when a required action was not taken or when a prohibited action did take place. A rule therefore provides the supervisor with a guideline to nonperformance and objectively legitimates the application of sanctions.

Gouldner (1954) has pointed out that rules can be used as devices to create social obligations. Supervisors, by deliberately refraining on occasion from enforcing rules, can create a sense of obligation on the part of supervisees. Because the supervisor has been lenient about enforcing certain requirements, she can more freely ask the supervisee to extend himself to do some things which need to be done. Blau and Scott (1962) found that supervisors in a county welfare department actually did differentially enforce rules to attain the effect of developing loyalty and social obligation. The supervisor employing such an approach, however, needs to have a sophisticated knowledge of the work situation so that she can "judge which operating rules can be ignored without impairing efficiency" (Blau and Scott 1962, p. 143).

The relaxed supervisor can adopt a flexible attitude toward agency rules. She accepts the fact that some degree of noncompliance is, in all likelihood, inevitable. She recognizes that not all procedures are of equal importance and that some can be ignored or subverted without much risk to agency or client.

Helping the staff to understand clearly the nature and purpose of the agency's rules lessens the dangers of ritualism and overconformity. Rules, regulations, and procedures often become ends in themselves rather than a means of more effectively serving the client. If workers are encouraged to participate in the formulation of rules and procedures, if they are helped to understand and critically evaluate the situations which required formulation of the rules, they will have less of a tendency to apply them in a rigid, routine way. Supervisees will be able to apply the rules more flexibly, more appropriately, and with greater conviction. Furthermore, understanding clearly the rationale for the particular rule, the worker will be in a better position to suggest modification in those situations where the procedure seems inappropriate or self-defeating. To encourage and reward such initiative the supervisor needs to be receptive to such suggestions for change communicated by the supervisees.

Compliance, sanctions, and noncompliance. In the context of adherence to rules and procedures, we again encounter the problem of conflict between the organization and the worker, between the need for stability, predictability, and standardization of behavior and the need for change, innovation, the freedom to develop imaginative behavioral responses to novel situations.

Steggert (1970) raises this question when he asks, "How then does the [supervisor] in a bureaucratic structure resolve the conflict between the organization's legitimate need for predictability (and thus for a variety of formal controls and coordination procedures) and the human unpredictability resulting from allowing subordinates to function more autonomously (and thus engaging in more needs-satisfying behavior); how does he simultaneously maintain that part of the organizational system for which he is responsible while satisfying . . . the human side of the enterprise?" (p. 47). As Green (1966) notes,

> The problem . . . is essentially one of reconciling the professional worker's need for autonomy and the organization's need for employees to be integrated within the complex of its activities. For the social worker autonomy means maintaining professional standards, developing a creative and resourceful approach to practice and finding opportunity for professional development and research activity. For the organization integration involves maintaining administrative standards and rational coordination of activities together with development of responsibility and loyalty in the employees. (pp. 82–83)

One characteristic of bureaucratic organizations is that the prescribed behavior for any role in the agency is formulated objectively and impersonally without reference to the individual who might become the role incumbent. Consequently there is always the likelihood of differences between the job requirements and the need dispositions of the series of individuals who are at different times hired to fill the job. The individual worker's definition of the specifics of the role behavior is the result of his attempt to reconcile the demands of the job with his own particular need dispositions. The supervisor's responsibility is to help supervisees reduce the gap between organizational demands and personal idiosyncracies. Her task is to "integrate the demands of the [agency] and the demands of the staff members in such a way so that [the job] is, at once, organizationally productive and individually fulfilling" (Getzels and Guba 1957, p. 428).

The sensitive supervisor needs to be selective in efforts to achieve greater congruence between the individual's way of performing his role and the agency's definition of role performance. The supervisor will select for discussion, and possible change, only those differences which do negatively affect efficient and effective service to the client. The supervisor gives priority to concern with behaviors which are "required" and those which are "prohibited." The rationale for designating the behaviors as either required or prohibited is, we assume, that they have greatest potency for helping or hurting the client. Consequently, they have to be most carefully monitored. But between "required" and "prohibited" there are many behaviors which are less crucial and critical for the effective implementation of tasks the worker performs in offering service to clients. Consequently, the supervisor can view such modifications of prescribed role behavior with greater permissiveness and equanimity.

Another problem faced by supervisors is to decide on the relative balance between standardization and uniformity in procedure and supervisee autonomy and flexibility. Formally codified rules and procedures to which all workers have to uniformly adhere restrict the workers' autonomy in flexibly responding to the needs of the individual case situation. On the other hand, if all workers were permitted to formulate rules and procedures differently for each case situation, the result would be organizational anarchy. As Stewart (1972) says, "No organization can set order as its overriding aim nor can any put flexibility as its prime concern. All organizations need elements of both and the problem is to decide what is the appropriate balance between them" (p. 151). The general principle might be to grant supervisees as much freedom as is compatible with efficient, effective, and equitable implementation of the agency's goal. This of course is a nice, rounded statement which, admittedly, is often difficult to apply in specific situations.

The supervisor in his role as protector of agency policies, rules, and procedures may have to get supervisees to do some things in some particular way or have them stop from doing some things in some particular way. The supervisor may find himself in a position where he has to employ sanctions in requiring compliance with agency policy, rules, and procedures, where he has to take corrective action. Supervisors face situations in which workers consistently fail to get work done on time, are consistently late or absent, fail to turn in reports, or complete forms carelessly, conspicuously loaf on the job, disrupt work of others by excessive gossiping, are careless with agency cars or equipment, are inconsiderate, insulting, or disrespectful to clients, or fail to keep appointments with personnel of cooperating agencies and services.

Such a situation should not be permitted to develop unchecked. There generally are prior indications of resistance or opposition to compliance. If earlier manifestations have been ignored, if the supervisor "looks the other way," it becomes progressively more difficult to take action when action can no longer be avoided. The supervisee can rightly claim that the supervisor has been remiss in never having earlier discussed the behavior he now wants stopped. The supervisor's effectiveness in dealing with the situation is reduced by feelings of guilt and defensiveness. A supervisor writes:

In our last conference of the year, I hesitantly raised the question of B's persistent lateness to meetings and conferences. I had been aware of this failure on her part, but for a variety of reasons, had overlooked to deal with this directly. At this time, my opening this issue resulted in [B's] unburdening herself of a number of severe personal and family problems. I dealt with these as appropriately as possible, but referred back to the lateness, etc. B acknowledged her discomfort

with her behavior, but felt she had not been sure about my expectations because I had not previously made an issue of this. I agreed
about my remission and we ended with some appreciation for not having completely overlooked an important part of her development. The
timing was unfortunate, in that this problem should have been dealt
with much earlier in the year for it seemed to be symptomatically tied
to important personal blockings that were interfering with [B's] development. Perhaps my "better late than never" behavior was similar to
what she had been doing all year!

The supervisor should make provision to discuss in private
the problem that calls for a reprimand. To criticize a worker in
front of his peers makes it more difficult to help him change his
behavior. A supervisee writes that she was late in submitting a
monthly statistical report:

The supervisor meeting me in the hall loudly reprimanded me in the
presence of other workers and threatened to put my report-lateness in
his evaluation. The supervisor returned to his office without giving me
a chance to reply. The supervisor had a chance to release his anger but
he was unsuccessful in getting my report in any sooner. I was sore. He
publicly called attention to what I had done. It was nobody else's business. He never gave me a chance to explain—or even asked for an explanation.

A reprimand is also best delivered at a time when the supervisor is not upset about the incident. These two suggestions
which require delay operate in contradiction to a third suggestion that a discussion of the incident should take place as soon
as possible after it occurs. However, they can be reconciled by
noting that while a delay is desirable for cooling off and for
provision of privacy, the delay should be as short as possible.

The best approach is one which communicates concern for
the supervisee, a willingness to listen to his explanation of what
happened, a desire to understand how he sees the situation and
a readiness to help him change. The emphasis is on a change of
behavior so as to increase the agency's effectiveness of service
rather than on the apprehension and punishment of noncompliance. If the supervisor perceives noncompliance as a
threat or an act of hostility, any discussion of the incident is apt

to be emotionally charged. Regarding it as a learning opportunity for the worker or as an opportunity for improving the supervisor-supervisee relationship generates a different, more positive, attitude.

The supervisor should make some record of the incident so that if there is a recurrence, and more severe sanctions need to be employed, they can be justified by the record. There is a series of actions the supervisor might take, graded in terms of increasing severity. The first is a joint review of the situation by supervisor and supervisee. The supervisor can offer the worker a warning, followed, if behavior continues, with a verbal reprimand. This might be followed by a written reprimand which is placed in the record, a lower than average evaluation rating, suspension for a limited period, demotion, and ultimately dismissal. A supervisor details the positive use of sanctions in the following example:

A woman in her mid 50's with a college education but no work experience was hired by a public welfare agency as a caseworker. Serious problems began to manifest themselves and the worker appeared overwhelmed by the poverty she observed visiting the homes of welfare clients. She became emotionally involved with clients' problems and attempted to personally meet their needs, supplying money from her own funds, clothing from her family, even cooking and delivering meals to the sick. At the same time she showed little sensitivity to the feelings of the clients and no conception of the meaning of confidentiality. Other problems that interfered with effective social work were chronic tardiness, conducting personal business and going to the beauty shop on agency time, habitual reckless driving which resulted in a series of minor accidents, a poor relationship with other staff members and aggressive resistance to supervision.

The supervisor in this situation recognized the problems and the emotional needs of the worker and planned for more intensive supervisory help than usually given an average new worker. When no improvement was noted and the problems even became worse, the supervisor arranged for the worker to be transferred to another unit with a different supervisor. When this did not result in improvement in any of the problem areas, the decision was made to terminate employment before the end of the probationary period. At each step the supervisor had attempted to discuss the problems frankly with the worker although she seemed to have no insight into her role in them and advised her to seek employment in another type of work. The worker appealed her dismissal but the supervisor's decision was upheld. Shortly afterwards the woman took a job as a bookkeeper and held it for over ten years to the apparent satisfaction of herself and her employer.

The supervisor's early recognition of the problem, implementation of vigorous and planned efforts to deal with it, recognition of the futility of these efforts, and prompt, appropriate and firm action benefited both the employee and the agency.

Throughout this process, the supervisor is making an effort to understand and, if possible, help the supervisee understand the noncompliant behavior. Here, as always, the assumption is that behavior is purposive.

It may be that the supervisee does not know clearly what is expected of him and does not clearly understand what it is he is supposed to be doing. Noncompliance might then yield to a clarification of what is called for by agency policy. The worker may understand what is required, may be in agreement with what is required, but be unable to meet the demands of the rule or procedure. He does not know enough or is not capable enough to comply. Education and training are required, rather than criticism, to obtain compliance.

Although it had been agreed that Mr. F. would arrange for group meetings of the patients on his ward, he had consistently and adroitly avoided scheduling such meetings. Despite repeated discussion of the need for this and tentative plans, no meetings were held. Finally, in response to the supervisor's growing insistence and impatience, Mr. F. shared the fact that he knew very little about how to conduct a group meeting, despite all his early verbalized knowledge, and was very anxious about getting started with a group.

Ability to fulfill task responsibilities may also relate to the client and the client's situation rather than to any inadequacies on the part of the worker. The client may be so resistive to help, or the resources available to change the situation so limited, that the worker avoids contact with the family.

Children in foster care had been ordered by the court to be returned to the physical custody of the mother against agency recommendations. The worker, prior to this order, had been working with one of the teenage children, Sally, around school adjustment, adolescent conflicts, etc. Following the return of Sally to the mother, the worker failed to keep a scheduled appointment with Sally and did not schedule another appointment. When this was discussed in a supervisory conference, the worker indicated that with Sally's return to her own mother she felt no confidence that she could be of any help. The situation in the house was such that she did not feel that anything she could do would enable Sally to change.

Noncompliance may result from a disagreement with the policy or procedure. The worker may regard compliance as contrary to his definition of the agency's objective. This might require some discussion of the purpose of the policy in an effort to reconcile it with the worker's view of agency objectives. The worker may in fact be correct in claiming that agency objectives would best be served by ignoring the rules in this instance and amending or revising them. For instance, during the 1960s, social workers in West Coast public welfare departments were fired after they refused to conduct "midnight raids" to check on the continued eligibility of A.F.D.C. clients. They strongly felt that such procedures were a violation of clients' rights and their own professional standards.

Noncompliance may result from some incompatibility between agency policy and procedures and the worker's personal values or the values of his reference group.

Mrs. R's caseload included a black family with four children. Part of the difficulty resulted from inadequate housing and Mrs. R. was helping them to find a larger apartment. However, she avoided exploring the possibilities which might be available in a large neighborhood housing project. In discussions with the supervisor, she indicated that she felt it inadvisable for black and white families to be living together and was reluctant to help her clients move into the housing project. This was in contradiction to the nondiscriminatory policies of the agency.

A point of persistent difficulty in Mrs. L's handling of her caseload is her consistent failure to inform clients of the different kinds of services and financial help to which they might be entitled despite the fact that the procedure calls for sharing this information. She has a strong feeling that many of the clients are getting as much, or more, than they need and sharing this information is just inviting a raid on the county treasury.

Noncompliance may result from a work conflict. The worker makes a discretionary decision to do one thing and not another because she cannot do both. Thus the worker may have failed to get an important report in on time because she had to arrange an emergency placement for a child.

The worker's noncompliance may be in response to a conflict between the needs of any one client and the need for efficient, expeditious task performance in order to provide service to the client group. Unless the worker can rapidly meet the administrative demands for obtaining the information necessary to make valid decisions regarding foster care or adoptive applications, for instance, the system may become overwhelmed as new applications wait to be processed. This means that only that content which would help answer the questions required for administrative decision would be explored in interviews. Other considerations, however significant they may be to the applicant and the agency, are likely to be discouraged as extraneous to the immediate task of completing the home study. The fault then lies with excessively heavy demands on the agency rather than with the unwillingness of the worker to explore aspects of the situation which the agency wants reviewed.

Noncompliance may result from disagreement about interpretation of policy. A supervisor writes: "A worker refused to follow policy. She asked for a clearance from the supervisor in the state office. A written interpretation was provided which was in accord with my interpretation of policy. The worker insisted on acting her own way. Because of the 'semantics' of wording in the agency manual, the worker contended that she had the prerogative."

Sometimes policies, rules, and procedures are contradictory, and adherence to one requires noncompliance with another. Protecting the suicidal patient from himself, for example, may require breaking the rules of confidentiality.

Noncompliance may result from a conflict between bureaucratic demands and casework goals as perceived by the supervisee. "Ms. B had accepted a gift from a client. Her supervisor called attention to the fact that acceptance of gifts from clients was not in accordance with agency policy. Ms. B. said, in response, that she was aware of this but felt that if she had not accepted the gift the client would feel that she was rejecting her. She had accepted because this helped strengthen the relationship."

In general terms this is the classic conflict between the bureaucratic orientation and the service orientation, identified in social work by Billingsly (1964a) and Piven and Papenfort (1960), among others. Workers may decide that there are some actions which need to be taken in behalf of service to the client even though the actions conflict with agency policy. In this sense, noncompliance comes close to innovation, permitting individualization of agency policy and enabling the agency to serve the client more effectively. It illustrates the fact that noncompliance may be functional.

Noncompliance may be due to psychological considerations, as in the case of the worker who fails to turn in a sufficiently detailed record because of anxiety regarding self-exposure. Similarly, noncompliance may relate to developmental experiences. A supervisor writes:

I had a 25-year-old worker who seemed unable to follow rules. When she first came to the unit, she seemed bright, eager and intelligent. I was aware her father was a judge in a small town in another state. I did not realize how this was affecting her until several months passed. She never let me know, through "out" slips, where she might be in case of emergency. One day she was needed for an emergency, had not left an "out" slip or any word of where she might be located. I kept going to her office and asking other workers if they had seen her. Finally, she came bursting into my office where my secretary and another worker were and started blasting me. I stated, "Just a minute, young lady." The two people in my office quickly left. I pointed out to her that certain rules and regulations are necessary for running our unit efficiently and why I had been requesting "out" slips from her. What I had failed to realize was that her actions were those of an adolescent, that she still was rebellious and was projecting some of her own rebellion toward her father (an authoritarian figure in two ways—father and judge) on me and the department (the "System").

The supervisor, of course, is making a speculative inference that needs confirmation in discussions with the supervisee. If confirmed, the incident illustrates noncompliance based on personal developmental problems.

Noncompliance may also be an act of hostility toward the supervisor or the agency he represents. The worker deliberately fails to implement agency policies or procedures as an act of defiance. There is personal satisfaction in such covert manifestations of hostility.

Noncompliance may result from the fact that the supervisee is subject to a variety of pressures from the client and is dependent on the client for psychic gratification. In this sense the client has power over the supervisee which may force him to act in contravention to agency policy. Supervisees are subject to rewards from clients in terms of expressions of gratification, praise, affection, and friendship. They are subject to punishments from clients in terms of expressions of aggression, hostility, deprecation. Supervisees would like to be told that they have been helpful to the family, that they are loved for it, and that they are a wonderful people; supervisees tend to avoid taking action which might result in the client's telling them that they are "stupid bastards who never did know what it was all about and have never been of much help to anybody." Noncompliance may then follow from supervisees' being pressured by the client to do what the client wants them to do, not what the agency or their professional conscience dictates as being necessary and desirable. A supervisee in protective service writes:

The agency is reasonably clear as to the circumstances which require initiating a petition for removal of the child. Of course, only the worker knows the specifics of a particular case so a lot depends on the worker's discretion. But in this instance of a black 4-year-old boy in the home of a single-parent A.F.D.C. family, I really knew the kid was being abused. Yet whenever I even hinted at starting procedures to remove the child, which is what I should have done according to agency policy, the mother began to get hostile and abusive, accusing me of being a "meddling white racist." She knew how to manipulate me, making me feel anxious, guilty and uncertain. I could, of course, have discussed this with my supervisor but I was afraid that it would end on a firm decision to remove the child and, given the control this mother had, I did not want to have to fight with her in implementing such a decision.

Green (1966) points out that the pull toward overidentification of social workers with the client is likely to be greatest in large, highly bureaucratic organizations. The client is often a "victim" of the same bureaucracy. "Thus the social work victim unconsciously identifies with the client victim" (Green 1966, p. 75). This leads to the temptation to make an alliance with the client against agency regulations and procedures, resulting in noncompliance with agency policy.

Noncompliance may be a response to real dangers encountered on the job. The worker, often a young, white female, is obliged, in many instances, to go into apartment buildings in areas characterized by high rates of crime. Social workers have, in fact, been mugged, assaulted, and molested during the course of their work. As a result there is considerable anxiety, and visits to clients may be resisted and not scheduled (Mayer and Rosenblatt 1973a).

Supervisee noncompliance may be prompted by a desire to make the job easier, less boring, more satisfying. Noncompliance is, in such instances, a response to the worker's effort to "increase his own power and status and freedom and security while shedding uncongenial work and unwelcome responsibilities" (Jay 1967, p. 89). These are the pragmatic rewards of noncompliance. As Levy (1970) notes in discussing the activities of some workers in a county welfare department, "employees begin to identify with and work within the logic of the 'system.' This entails the playing of a highly elaborate game in which the general idea is to make one's job as easy as possible through meeting enough statistical requirements to keep administrators and supervisors off one's back, doing just enough for clients so [one] won't be bothered by them and keeping [one's] caseload as low as possible by 'transferring out' as many cases as possible and accepting as few as [one] can" (p. 172).

Noncompliance may be a deliberate act of defiance in a conscious effort to call attention to policies which need to be changed. The worker is pointing to the need for change by challenging the system (Merton 1957, p. 360).

Sometimes noncompliance is a necessary and useful expedient in dealing with conflicting and irreconcilable demands. The worker subjected to the pressure of client needs in the context of bureaucratic rules and procedures which make difficult the satisfaction of such needs, bends or breaks the rules. In such instances supervisors often tolerate or ignore nonconformity (Jacobs 1969). A supervisor writes:

> After a time you get to be self-protective. You learn how to "manage" the clients so that they impose less of a burden. I remember one case of a middle-aged woman in marital counseling. She was very dependent, talked incessantly and called me continually. Even though I recognized it was part of the service, I always "arranged" to be going out if she caught me in. She gradually got the message, "Don't call us, we'll call you."

A supervisee in corrections writes:

> There are a number of different circumstances which require revocation of parole. But that's a lot of extra work and a lot of harder work because it means a big hassle with the parolee. Okay, if something is very serious you play it according to the regulations. But if it is something ambiguous and you figure that even if something happens you can justify not having revoked parole, you figure, "To hell with the regulations, why bust your ass?"

Understanding the worker's behavior is not the same as excusing it. Even though there may be understandable reasons for noncompliant behavior, clients are still harmed as a result and the agency's objectives are not implemented. Being "therapeutic" to workers in permitting them to continue to operate contrary to agency policy may be antitherapeutic to the clients.

It needs to be noted that most workers, on most occasions, do conscientiously comply with agency policies, rules, and procedures. Noncompliance is the exception. However, the limited number of exceptions give the supervisor a maximum amount of difficulty. A disproportionate amount of time and psychic energy needs to be devoted to the few workers who frequently are noncompliant.

Achieving compliance is, then, another general administrative function of supervision. The supervisor seeks to obtain compliance with agency policies, rules, and procedures in protecting the agency and the clients from the consequences of deviance, heresy, and noncompliance. At the same time the supervisor accepts responsibility for initiating and supporting changes in those regulations that are dysfunctional to effective, efficient agency operation and are potentially harmful to the client.

"placing" the worker

The supervisor has the administrative responsibility for placing the worker in the agency. Workers need to find their place in the organizational framework. Knowing clearly to whom they report, and who reports to them enables workers to find their "particular location in the invisible geography" of the agency's human-relations network. Through the supervisor, their immediate administrative link, workers are tied into the total organizational apparatus.

The process of such placement and identification has its beginning in the worker's induction into the agency, a function for which the supervisor is administratively responsible. The supervisor prepares to induct the worker by reviewing the worker's personnel folder, informing other workers in the unit that a new worker has been hired, finding an office and a desk, selecting some reading material about the agency and its functions, and selecting a limited number of tasks to discuss with the worker for possible assignment.

On meeting the newly hired worker, the supervisor discusses the function of the unit to which the worker has been assigned, how it fits into the total agency operation, the relationship of the supervisor to the worker, and his relationship with other workers in the unit. Hopefully, questions about job specifics (pay, hours, fringe benefits) have been discussed as part of the formal job offer, but they may need further clarification.

The supervisor personally introduces the worker to peers, office personnel with whom he will be working, and administrative officers. She is aware that the man or woman on a new job, in a new organization, is likely to be lonely. The supervisor might ask one of the more experienced employees in the unit to act as sponsor for the new worker, answering routine questions and being available to help the new worker during the first week or so.

Some of the hazards of induction, and the supervisor's handling of them, are detailed in a social worker's recollection of her first day as a psychiatric social worker in a mental hospital:

From the start, the supervisor seemed to be sensitively aware of possible anxiety on my part. She had made considerable plans in advance as to what I would do my first few weeks at the hospital. The first day she arrived fifteen minutes early and met me at the door. We went to her office, she took my coat and offered me a cup of coffee. She then took me with her to get it so that I would know where the pot was for future use.

We had to go through two locked doors and as we did so, Ms. B. explained that she would see that I got a set of keys for my own by the end of the day. (She did this and I was to find that she was equally prompt with other matters as well. If I asked a question she would either answer it or be on the phone immediately to find out from someone who knew.) These two gestures served to make me feel like one of the staff and, as such, accepted and very comfortable.

As we sat drinking our coffee, Ms. B. explained her plans for me for the day. First off, she would show me around the immediate area and introduce me to the people with whom I would be in frequent contact. She noted that she would not confuse me by giving a tour of the whole grounds. She confided that this is what was done when she first came to the hospital and she ended up not remembering where anything was nor who any of the people were.

As we toured the second floor, Ms. B. introduced me as a new worker. This made me extremely uncomfortable, as such a label is generally a hindrance in working with a client. I wished that, as some of the literature suggested, a name such as "assistant caseworker" or "intern" or "trainee" had been used. I brought this up later and Ms. B. agreed that the label of "new worker" might present problems and that henceforth she would just refer to me as a social worker around patients unless asked. Unfortunately, she did not inform other staff members of this and so half of them still referred to me as the "new worker."

Ms. B. gave me some pamphlets on the functions of the hospital and the specific expectations of social workers.

Unfortunately, she then handed me great volumes of material to read, the content of which had little meaning at the time as it dealt with specifics such as addresses and special policies of agencies with which the hospital might have contact. Glancing at the indexes would have been just as useful since even the regular social workers at the hospital did not know these infrequently used specifics without referring back to the manuals. I was considerably chagrined at the assignment of this task as I knew from past experience how fruitless it would prove to be and had hoped that my supervisor would also have remembered from her past. Before I got around to reading very much of this, Ms. B. suggested that I attend a staffing by a psychiatrist other than the one on whose service I would be working. This proved to be very worthwhile as I was able to be more fully appreciative of the great variation in psychiatrists and the way in which they staffed patients.

When I returned from the staffing, my supervisor informed me of the fact that I would be sharing offices with her. This was greatly upsetting as I not only felt threatened by having someone seeing my every move but also knew it would be distracting. Sensing my discomfort, Ms. B. indicated that this was only a temporary arrangement while efforts were made to find a separate office for me. I felt somewhat relieved at that.

policy formulation and community liaison

The functions discussed thus far have focused on the supervisor's administrative responsibilities with reference to supervisees. The supervisor also has administrative responsibilities with regard to agency policy and relationships with other agencies and the community. The supervisor is an active participant in the formulation, or reformulation, of agency policy. This is an extension of the communication function. Having learned from the direct-service workers about client and community needs, having learned about the deficiencies and shortcomings of agency policy when workers have attempted to implement it, the supervisor should do more than act as an inert channel for upward communication of such information. The supervisor has the responsibility of using her knowledge of the situation to formulate suggested changes in agency policy and procedure. (The supervisor is in a strategic position to act as agency change agent. Standing between administration and the workers, she can actively influence administration to make changes and influence workers to accept them.)

The supervisor acts as the administrative liaison between her unit and other units within the agency. Similarly, she acts as the administrative liaison between her unit and other agencies in the community. She is responsible for seeing that interagency agreements are implemented and complied with. The supervisor promotes contacts with other agencies which will facilitate the work of her supervisees.

Not only is there specialization of work within the agency but there is a specialization of assignment within the total community of social work agencies. While the total network of agencies in a community may, as a group, cover all or most of the social situations requiring service, any one agency is assigned special and particular responsibility for only one aspect of the community's social service needs. Consequently, agencies have to work together, refer clients to one another, coordinate diverse services being offered a single family. To do this efficiently and effectively, they have to be able to count on the fact that their colleague agencies will operate in accordance with certain standardized procedures that can be formally communicated from one agency to another. A worker in a family agency dealing with a client who has a marital problem may need to refer the family to A.F.D.C. so that it can obtain financial assistance for which the family agency has no responsibility. In making the referral, the family-agency worker needs to know something of A.F.D.C. eligibility and intake procedure. He needs to know that the agency will operate in accordance with some predictable, standardized procedures. (Here the supervisor's function in monitoring conformance to rules within the agency ensures successful interagency cooperation.)

summary

The functions of administrative supervision relate to planning the work that is apportioned by administration to the unit; allocating the specific tasks which need to be accomplished; organizing, coordinating, and facilitating the manpower and agency resources necessary to do the job; reviewing to see that the job is adequately done, both quantitatively and qualitatively, in accordance with agency procedure; "placing" the worker; acting as a channel of communication and as an administrative buffer; helping in the formulation of agency policy; and implementing community liaison.

(The supervisor is not entirely an independent agent in determining how she will respond to problems posed by the functions of administrative supervision.) The attitude and behavior of agency administration are constraints that supervisors must acknowledge. A restrictive communication pattern on the part of administration encourages a similar pattern on the supervisory level; discouragement of worker autonomy by administration results in close supervision on the supervisory level. (Administration needs to be aware that agency interaction tends toward consistency.) Administration must set the example for the behavioral pattern it would like to see manifested in supervisor-supervisee interaction.

Rationale for Authority and Power in Administrative Supervision

If one agrees that the functions of administrative supervision must be performed if the agency is to operate effectively, it follows that the supervisor needs to be granted the authority which would permit her to perform these functions. As Studt (1959) says, authority is delegated and sanctioned when "in order to get the job done properly a person in one position in an organization is authorized to direct the role activities of a person in another position" (p. 18). Assigning supervisors the responsibility for implementing the essential functions of administrative supervision without at the same time granting them the necessary authority is the organizational equivalent of asking them to make bricks without straw. The organizational axiom is that delegation of authority is a necessary concomitant of administrative responsibility.

(The need for administrative authority in an agency derives from organizational complexity and task specialization.) If groups of individuals are to work together to accomplish desired ends, their efforts must be integrated. Some administrative officer, in this case the supervisor, has to be given authority to direct and coordinate individual activities toward the achievement of a common purpose, to review and evaluate work, and to hold workers accountable. Formal channels of authority must be established since it must be clear who has the authority to assign, direct, and evaluate work and who is being directed and evaluated.

Since compliance with directives toward the achievement of joint efforts cannot be left to chance, individual desires, or whim, some kind of authority–control system is an organizational imperative. It is designed to "minimize discretion based on subjective considerations" (Stein 1961, p. 15). Vinter says, "All organizations create means for ensuring that cooperative action is oriented toward desired objectives. To avoid a state of anarchy among participating personnel, an explicit structure of authority and responsibility is defined in every social agency. . . . This structure seeks to ensure predictable behavior of workers in conformity to policy" (1959, pp. 199–200).

Tannenbaum (1968), in his study of organizational controls, notes that

organization implies control. A social organization has an ordered arrangement of individual human interactions. Control processes help circumscribe idiosyncratic behaviors and keep them conformant with the rational plan of the organization. Organizations require a certain amount of conformity as well as the integration of diverse activities. It is the function of control to bring about conformance to organizational requirements and achievement of the ultimate purposes of the organization. The coordination and order created out of the diverse interests and potentially diffuse behaviors of members is largely a function of control. (p. 3)

The authority delegated to the supervisor ultimately derives from the community. In public agencies the collective intent is embodied in the statutes that established the agency and in accordance with which the agency operates. In private agencies, the collective intent is manifested in the support the agency obtains for its existence and continuation through voluntary Community Chest contributions. Agency objectives reflect what the community wants done, and use of supervisory authority to ensure achievement of these objectives can be seen as an act in furtherance of the collective will.

Legal authority derives its legitimacy from the fact that it, supposedly, represents the common good. The objectives of the agency similarly are supposed to represent the common good. Authority employed to achieve the common good is regarded as legitimate authority.

The legitimacy of this ultimate authority may be questioned by workers, who thereby also question the legitimacy of the supervisor's authority. They may feel that neither the statutes which establish the public agency nor the community welfare council which sponsors the voluntary agency do, in fact, represent the will of the community.

The subjective acceptance of the legitimacy of organizational authority is the significant aspect, for the agency, of developing in the supervisee a sense of commitment to agency goals. When the agency and the supervisees are committed to the same objectives, the supervisee will more freely grant the right to be controlled if this contributes to the achievement of the accepted task. The common goal becomes the common good which justifies acceptance of authority.

Supervisory Authority and Sources of Power

(Authority needs to be distinguished from power. Authority is a right which legitimizes the use of power; it is the sanctioned use of power, the expected and validated possession of power.) Authority is the right to issue directives, exercise control, require compliance. It is the right to determine the behavior of others, to make decisions which guide the action of others. In the most uncompromising sense, "authority is the right to demand obedience; those subject to authority have the duty to obey."

This right of authority is distributed to the supervisor through the agency administrative structure. The supervisory relationship is established through authority delegated the supervisor by the agency and through the supervisee's reciprocal acceptance of the supervisor's legitimate entitlement to authority.

(Power is the ability to implement the rights of authority.) The word "power" derives from the Latin *potere*, "to be able." If authority is the right to direct, command, and punish, then power is the ability to do so. The distinction is clearly seen in situations in which a person may have authority but no power to act and contrariwise in those situations in which the person has no grant of authority but nevertheless has the power to command. Extreme examples are the hijacker of a plane, who has power but no authority, and the prison warden held hostage by mutinous prisoners, who has authority but no power.

The source of the supervisor's authority is the agency administration representing community will. What are the sources of power which energize authority and make possible the implementation of the right to command? Recognizing the legitimacy of the authority invested in the supervisor, what prompts the supervisee to actually comply with the supervisor's directives?

There are a variety of descriptive systems that categorize sources of power (Etzioni 1961; Presthus 1962; Weber 1946). Among the most frequently used is the classification developed by French and Raven (1960), who have identified five distinctive bases of social power: reward power, coercive power, positional power, referent power, and expert power. We will attempt to apply their categories to the social work supervisory situation.

reward power

The supervisor has the ability to control tangible rewards for the supervisees, such as promotions, raises, more desirable work assignments, extra secretarial help, a better office, recommendations for training stipends, agency-supported attendance at conferences and workshops, a good reference on leaving the agency. Rewards can be psychic as well—approval, commendations, supervisory expressions of appreciation.

If reward power is to be effective, it needs to be individualized and clearly related to differentials in performance. If rewards become routinized, as in the case of across-the-board raises, they lose their power to stimulate improvements in worker performance. The supervisor therefore has to be knowledgeable about the quality of the performance of different workers if he is to make a fair determination of allocation of rewards. Furthermore, the supervisee needs some confidence that the supervisor does, in fact, control access to rewards, that administration has granted him the authority to make crucial decisions relating to dispensation of available rewards.

As contrasted with certain other employment situations, social agencies have limited reward power because they control only a limited range and variety of rewards. Production incentives, stock options, and so on are not available as possible rewards.

coercive power

The supervisor has the ability to control punishments for supervisees. These include demotion, dismissal, a poor "efficiency rating," a less satisfying work assignment, a negative reference on leaving the agency. There are psychic punishments as well—expressions of disapproval and criticism, snubs, and avoidance. Reward power and coercive power are overlapping, since the withholding of rewards is in effect a punishment.

Whereas in the case of reward power the supervisees are induced to comply with supervisory directives in order to achieve a reward, here compliance results from the effort to avoid punishment. The strength of coercive power depends on the extent of belief in the likelihood of application of disciplinary actions. If the supervisees have reason to believe that little serious effort will be made to apply punishments, this is not an effective source of supervisory power.

legitimate or positional power

By virtue of being invested with the title, the supervisor can claim the authority that goes with the position. We accept the authority of the office and in doing so accept as legitimate the authority of the person occupying it. The supervisee in taking a job with the agency has implicitly contracted to accept direction from those invested with agency authority. There is a sense of moral obligation and social duty related to the acceptance of positional authority. Our entire experience with social groups, social organizations, and social institutions develops a predispositional set of constraints toward the acceptance of a person's right to command by virtue of being invested with a particular title. As a result of developmental experiences with parents, teachers, and others, we acquire a generalized readiness to conform to the rules of a game in which we care to participate, to the rules of an organization in which we seek membership. We recognize that general rejection of positional authority would make social life difficult if not impossible. Consequently the supervisee feels that the supervisor has a legitimate right, considering her position, to expect that her suggestions and directions will be followed.

Positional power derives its force not only from prior reinforcing experiences in which obedience to those in positions of authority was rewarded by acceptance and approval, but also from its effect in making one's job easier. Barnard (1938) notes that the initial presumption of the acceptability of organizational authority enables workers to avoid making issues of supervisory directives without incurring a sense of personal subserviency or a loss of status with their peers.

referent power

The supervisor has power which derives from the supervisees' identification with her, a desire to be liked by the supervisor and to be like the supervisor. Referent power has its source in the positive relationship between supervisor and supervisee, in the attraction the supervisee feels toward the supervisor. It is relationship power. In effect, the supervisee says, "I want to be like the supervisor and be liked by her. Consequently, I want to believe and behave as she does" or "I am like the supervisor, so I will behave and believe like her." The supervisor is perceived as a model of the kind of social worker the supervisee would like to be.

The stronger the relationship, the stronger is the power of the supervisor to influence the behavior and attitudes of the supervisee. As a consequence of the relationship, the supervisee is strongly motivated to seek the approval and commendation of the supervisor. The supervisor becomes a person of meaning and significance whom the supervisee would like to please and to whom she feels a sense of personal loyalty. Referent power offers expressive rewards, the approval, commendation, and recognition of one's good work by the supervisor.

As a consequence of a strong interpersonal relationship, the supervisee is receptive to influence efforts on the part of the supervisor. There is gratification in responding to a self-image which is congruent with the supervisor's communicated expectation. As a result of identification, the supervisor's expectations become internationalized. Supervisees then act as their own "supervisor," behaving as they expect the supervisor would want them to act.

expert power

Expert power derives from the special knowledge and skills which the supervisor has available and the supervisees need. This is the power of professional competence. The supervisee who attributes expertise to the supervisor has trust in his decisions and judgments. The supervisor has credibility for the supervisee. One component of attribution derives from relevant credentials the supervisor can offer. The supervisor who has an M.S.W., who has passed the Academy of Certified Social Workers' written examination, is initially perceived as having more expertise than a supervisor who does not possess such credentials. Ultimately, of course, the supervisor has to prove in practice that she can live up to the promise of her credentials.

The supervisor is able to influence the kinds of behavior that supervisees will manifest because she has the knowledge which indicates the way in which it is desirable or necessary for them to behave if they are to deal satisfactorily with work problems. The supervisees may not know what to do; the supervisor in her expertise knows what should be done. The supervisees' need for guidance from the supervisor's expertise results in control over their behavior.

types of power

The five sources of power have frequently been subdivided into two groups, functional and formal power. Functional power, which includes expertise and referent power, depends on what the supervisor knows, is, and can do. Functional power resides in the person of the supervisor. Formal power is related more directly to the title the supervisor holds and the authority with which the title is invested. Formal power includes positional power and the power of rewards and punishments. The two groups of powers are complementary and support each other. The most desirable situation for effective exercise of power is one where the formal power and functional power are congruent. This is the situation when the person accorded positional authority and the power of the office to reward and punish is, by virtue of his human-relations skill and knowledge of the job, also capable of demonstrating the power of expertise and of developing referent power. Functional authority tends to legitimize and make acceptable formal authority. Difficulty arises when the person with formal authority knows less or has less work experience than the supervisee or does not gain the respect of the supervisee. The supervisee is therefore less willing to grant the person's entitlement to the power of his position and this tends to attenuate and undermine his formal authority.

Since formal power is related to the office of the supervisor and functional power is related to the person of the supervisor, the latter is apt to be a more variable source of power. There is little difference between one supervisor and another in the same agency in their positional, reward, and punishment power. There may be considerable difference, however, in their total ability to implement their authority because of differences in their expertise and relationship skills.

The supervisees' readiness to accept the supervisor as an expert and as an object of identification and emulation is contingent on their experience in the interaction. If they find, as they grow in knowledge and experience, that they are less dependent on the supervisor for help in solving their work problems, if in testing the supervisor's advice and suggestions in practice they conclude that she is not the expert she claims to be, or the expert they previously perceived her to be, expert power tends to be eroded. Similar kinds of changes may gradually take place in the power of the relationship to determine the behavior of supervisees as the relationship undergoes changes.

Formal authority is received automatically by ascription when a person is assigned to the position of supervisor. Functional authority has to be achieved by the supervisor and continuously validated. If the supervisees do not perceive the supervisor as an expert, the supervisor has no expert power; if supervisees feel no attraction to the supervisor and do not care whether or not the supervisor likes them, the supervisor has no referent power.

The different sources of power available to the supervisor to induce behavioral change in supervisees, and to control their actions, have different kinds of applicability and costs associated with their use. Further differences derive from professional ideology and the supervisor's predispositions. These result in differential readiness to employ particular sources of power.

Both reward power and coercive power relate to specific kinds of supervisee behavior that are either encouraged or discouraged. The effect of using such power is apt to be rather limited in scope. Both require the opportunity and constancy of surveillance. Only if the supervisor knows that the supervisee is doing or not doing certain things can these sources of power be applied. Supervisees feel a pressure to engage in the required behavior only if there is some chance that the supervisor will find out. The use of reward and coercion as sources of power achieves compliance.

Expert power and referent power, by contrast, are more diffuse in their effects. Once these sources of power have been established, then whatever the supervisor says, whatever the supervisor requests, is likely to be considered seriously by supervisees. The effect of such power is internalization of the supervisor's authority, which then exerts a pressure toward conformity whether or not the supervisor can witness the behavior. While reward and punishment power can achieve compliance and a change in behavior, the exertion of expert and referent power in achieving internalization of influence can achieve changes in feelings and attitudes as well.

Warren (1968) has analyzed the various sources of power as differentially related to conformity to agency norms under conditions of low-visibility performance that are characteristic of social work. Under these conditions, expert power and referent power are most effective in ensuring both attitudinal conformity (implying internalization of norms) and overt behavioral conformity.

Because the force of positional power as felt by supervisees is the result of earlier socialization, this source of power is vulnerable to problems in developmental history around relationship to authority figures. The supervisee who has had developmental experiences which result in opposition to, and hostility toward, parents and parent surrogates is more likely to resist the power of position.

Studies of worker satisfaction in a variety of contexts as related to supervisory sources of power show expert power and referent power to be positively related to supervisee satisfaction, coercive power least frequently related to satisfaction (Burke and Wilcox 1971). Coercive power frequently leads to a downward cycle—punishment resulting in resentment which incites behavior which elicits punishment. If performance is not visible, coercive power can encourage deception, false reporting, and cover-ups to avoid punishment.

Coercive and positional power may be sufficient to induce supervisees to work at a level which meets the minimal requirements of the job. This is what they have technically contracted for in accepting the job. Referent and expert power, however, can induce supervisees to exert themselves beyond this level. They want to do better to please the supervisor whose referent power makes him a person of significance for the supervisee. They get satisfaction doing a better job as they are helped to solve job problems through the supervisor's use of expert power. Reward power can also have this effect if the range of rewards available is sufficiently attractive to the supervisees and if they feel assurance that better work will, in fact, be rewarded.

The various sources of power are interrelated. Reward power increases the likelihood of developing a positive relationship. A positive relationship, once established, increases the potency of psychic rewards (praise, approval) offered by the supervisor. The use of coercive power tends to increase the difficulties of establishing a positive relationship and hence impedes development of referent power as a possible source of influence.

The exercise of power, when accepted by the supervisee, results in some change in her behavior. She acts, and refrains from acting, so that her behavior conforms to the needs of the organization in achieving its objectives. Power is used to attain some deliberate, intended effects. Where power is successfully applied, we can talk of control.

What sources of supervisory power are perceived by social workers as influencing their behavior? In a study of non-M.S.W. supervisees supervised by non-M.S.W. supervisors in a public welfare agency, positional power was most frequently mentioned, followed by expert power (Peabody 1964). Referent power was seen as a less significant source of influence. In a second study involving M.S.W. supervisors and supervisees, both groups saw expert power, professional competence, as the main source of the supervisor's influence (Kadushin 1974). The supervisors saw this as almost the exclusive source of their power. A sizable percentage of supervisees, however, saw positional power as a significant source of supervisory influence. Apparently supervisees were readier to grant supervisors the power of their position in the administrative hierarchy than supervisors were ready to accept this as a source of power. It is interesting that in neither study was referent power, relationship power, seen as a significant source of supervisory influence. As was expected, neither reward power nor coercive power was seen as a preferred source of power.

A study of some 1600 employees in 31 social welfare and rehabilitation agencies shows the same relative ranking of the sources of supervisory power. "Expert power" was listed as the principal reason which induced supervisees to "do things my immediate supervisor suggests or wants me to do," followed by positional power as the second source of supervisory influence. Referent power was given middle-range ranking. Reward power and coercive power were perceived as the least potent sources of influence (Olmstead and Christensen 1973).

Although it is clear that expert power is the kind of power most readily acknowledged and most comfortably employed between social work supervisor and supervisee, the question might be raised whether this is a viable and potent power base for the social work supervisor.

The base of reward, coercive, and positional power is the community through the agency. The base of referent power is the person of the supervisor. The base of expert power, however, is the profession. The profession provides the knowledge which makes the supervisor an expert. Consequently the potency of expert power depends on the "state of the art" of the profession. If a profession has a well-developed, highly sophisticated technology and the supervisor is well educated in what the profession has available, the gap in expertise between the supervisor and the supervisee recruit is very wide. If, however, there is little specialized knowledge available, if the technology which the supervisor possesses is limited, the gap is narrow and can be eliminated within a short period.

There is a question as to the real extent of this gap between supervisors and supervisees in social agencies. The limited empirical material available does not substantiate a gap. Supervisors' scores on the Academy of Certified Social Workers' qualifying examinations were not generally higher than those of supervisees. Research projects that required both supervisors and supervisees to perform a practice task did not demonstrate higher skill on the part of the supervisory group (Brieland 1959; Brown 1970). Rapid changes in the field with reference to what is accepted theory, techniques, and interventions tend to erode the supervisor's authority of expertise. Socialized in terms of an earlier view of social work, skilled in approaches generally used in the immediate past but somewhat outmoded in the present, the supervisor may know less than the supervisee about what is *au courant*.

Difficult as it is for the supervisor to maintain authority on the basis of expert power when there is, objectively, little real expertise, the task becomes even more difficult in an ideological climate in which possible differences in expertise are explicitly rejected. Where the ideological press is toward a declaration of equality between client and worker, teacher and student, supervisor and supervisee, where differences in roles are denied, and all become peers and colleagues, authority based on expert power is further eroded.

It must be noted, however, that the preceding paragraphs refer to the extent of the gap in expertise relating to general professional knowledge and skills. Expert power may be validated on the basis of other kinds of information. If the supervisor has more experience in the agency than the supervisee, as is usually the case, her greater expertise may relate to her knowledge of agency policy, procedures, and operations. The supervisor, in this instance, has the knowledge and skill which enable her to help the supervisee "work" the agency system, find her way in the agency system so as to get the work done. She is party to much-needed organizational intelligence.

This base of expert power is supplemented by the supervisor's strategic position in the agency communications network. Not only does she know more about agency operations because she has had more intra- and inter-agency experience, but she also possesses much-needed knowledge about agency policies and procedures because she has initial access to such information from administration.

Supervisory authority, once accepted, is reinforced for the individual supervisee by the pressure of the peer group of coworkers.

Authority requires legitimation. And while authority can be exercised in pair relations, it can originate only in a group because only a group can provide legitimation of the control exercised. What social process legitimates the control exercised by a supervisor? The supervisor's ability to help subordinates solve complex problems commands their respect, and his willingness to furnish help and do favors for them commands their allegiance. As the members of the work group share their respect for and loyalty to the supervisor, there develops a consensus among them that they should comply with his wishes and suggestions. Once established, these norms of allegiance and respect are enforced by the group because all might suffer if some members failed to repay their obligations to the supervisor. In this fashion, compliance within certain bounds becomes a group norm . . . internalized by group members and enforced by group sanctions. These values legitimate the extension of the supervisor's authority beyond the legally prescribed limits. (Blau and Scott 1962, p. 143)

It is easy to exaggerate the power of the supervisor vis-à-vis the supervisees and to underestimate their countervailing power. Although control in the relationship is asymmetrical, it is not unidirectional. While the supervisor has, clearly and admittedly, more authority and power than the supervisees, the supervisees also have some power in the relationship even though they may lack formal authority (Mechanic 1964).

The concept that power is ultimately based on dependency might be usefully applied in analyzing the countervailing power of the supervisees (Emerson 1962). The supervisees depend on the supervisor for rewards, for solutions to work problems, for necessary information, for approval and support. However, the supervisor is also dependent on the supervisees. The supervisor may have the formal power to assign, direct, and review work, but she is dependent on the supervisees' willingness and readiness to actually do the work. If supervisees fail to do the required work because of opposition or resistance, the supervisor is in trouble with administration which holds her responsible for getting the work done. Supervisees thus have the power of making life difficult for the supervisor. In discussing her present assignment a supervisee said she could

drive her supervisor frantic if she wanted to—and she sometimes did. She was responsible for processing foster home applications. If she wanted to gum up the works she just took longer to do them—always for legitimate reasons—it was difficult to schedule an interview with the father or the last time she scheduled an interview with the family they had to cancel it when she got out there because of some emergency, or there were special problems which required more detailed exploration, etc.

A supervisee writes that a supervisor newly appointed to the unit

had the tendency to "command" his supervisees to carry out specific tasks and responsibilities, refusing to discuss the reasons behind them and replying coldly, "Because I said so," when asked. Our group of supervisees resented this approach to the extent that they "boycotted" the supervisor, flatly refusing to do anything more than minimum work required and giving him the "silent treatment." Once this reaction became apparent to the supervisor, he began to be more communicative and understanding and less strictly authoritative than he had been previously.

The willingness to obey is sometimes given key consideration in defining authority. In this view, authority is not delegated from above in the hierarchy but granted from below; it is based on the consent of the governed. If this is the case, then the legitimacy of the supervisor's authority is, in fact, controlled by the supervisees and can be withdrawn by them (Barnard 1938, pp. 161–65). Although agency administration legitimates the authority of the supervisor, such authority must be endorsed by supervisees before it can be fully implemented. Both official legitimation and worker endorsement of authority are necessary (Dornbusch and Scott 1975, pp. 37–42).

In the last analysis the supervisees have the ultimate veto power. They can refuse consent to be governed by resigning from the organization. "You can't fire me, I quit." Realistically, however, the labor market situation may act as a constraint on the worker's "veto power."

The potency of the supervisor's authority is related to the worker's commitment to the job. If the worker does not care whether the agency retains him or not, if he has little concern about whether the client receives or does not receive adequate service, the supervisor has little power to influence the worker's behavior.

Workers not only have the power of not cooperating, they have the power of overcompliance or rigid compliance. Good Soldier Schweick was able to bring the army to its knees by compulsive, meticulous compliance with every order in the rule book. Supervisees can effectively sabotage the work of an agency by the literal application of all policies, rules, and procedures. This is sometimes termed "malicious obedience."

Since the supervisor lacks direct contact with clients, she depends on the supervisees for information about the clients and their reactions to agency policies and procedures. Workers can manipulate the supervisor by manipulating the information they feed to her about the client and the client group. A worker might exaggerate the difficulties which some procedure occasioned for his client and exaggerate client opposition to the procedure.

The power of the individual supervisee in controlling the work flow (how much work or what kind is done within a given period of time) and his control of information fed to the supervisor may be augmented in coalition with other supervisees. Supervisees acting as a group can develop considerable power in controlling their supervisor.

The supervisor is also dependent on the supervisees for some kinds of psychic rewards. Approbation from supervisees, expressions of commendation and appreciation from supervisees, is a source of intrinsic job satisfaction for the supervisor. It hurts the supervisor never to be told by a supervisee that she has been helpful to her, that she is a good supervisor. Supervisees can manipulate supervisors' dependence on such gratification by studied deference and apple-polishing. Blau and Scott (1962) found that one significant source of emotional support for the supervisor was the loyalty of his supervisees (p. 162). The fact that supervisees supply this need gives them a source of power over the supervisor. The threat of withdrawal of loyalty acts as a constraint on the supervisor's exercise of his authority and power.

Workers have power by virtue of the problems and losses involved in replacing them. Dismissal is a blunted weapon that is used, workers realize, with considerable hesitancy. If a worker is dismissed, the agency has to spend considerable time and energy finding a replacement and then more time and energy training the replacement.

The supervisor's power is limited not only by countervailing supervisee power, but also by the nature of the situation. The possibilities of direct control and observation of workers' behavior are very limited. Consequently, while the supervisor can "order" that certain things be done, and that they be done in a prescribed manner, there often is no way she can be certain that the directives will be carried out. Ultimately, she is dependent on the worker's report to her that work has been done in the way it should be done.

The nature of the social worker's job makes it difficult to control. Each situation encountered is nonstandardized, diffuse, uncertain, unpredictable, and highly individualized. These are the characteristics of a work situation that demands allocation of a large measure of discretion to the person in actual contact with the client—the supervisee. The relevant research shows that the less specific the task, the less standardized the job, the less likely it can be controlled (Litwak 1964). Since the problems the social work supervisee faces are not easily standardized and only he knows the situation in any great detail, he has to be given considerable discretion and power.

In smaller agencies where the supervisor cannot physically distance herself from the supervisee and where frequent interaction is inevitable, this closeness acts as a constraint on the use of supervisory authority and power. There is a tendency not to do or say anything that might lead to resentment or covert hostility if these feelings have to be lived with day after day in coffee breaks and other informal encounters.

While the supervisor uses her authority to control, she is at the same time controlled by that authority. The nature of the delegated authority sets clear limits to her jurisdiction and clearly prescribes boundaries to her authority. She is not authorized to employ certain sanctions, offer certain kinds of rewards, intrude on certain aspects of the workers' behavior. Authority is the domestication of unregulated power. It explicates the perogatives and limitations in the exercise of power (Dornbusch and Scott 1975).

Unfortunately, but inevitably, it is difficult to respond to authority, power, and control in functional terms alone. Power does have the purely pragmatic effect of ensuring a more favorable situation, a better deal, for those holding more power. Beyond that, however, power relationships are highly emotionally charged. Differences in authority and power influence how people perceive themselves as individuals and in relation to others. While authority, power, and control are functionally necessary for achieving organizational objectives, they get all mixed up with feelings of prestige, self-esteem, superiority and inferiority, dominance and submission. It may be significant to note that the words "power" and "potent" derive from the same roots. Strong currents of feeling are evoked by power relationships in any context because they reactivate memories of our first encounter with authority and control in the parent-child relationship.

These general difficulties are exacerbated in social work by the anti-authority orientation of social work ideology. Vinter (1959), speaking to this problem, says that a "strain . . . arises from juxtaposition of the non-authoritarian ideology of social work and the exercise of authority and control within the administrative context. Valuation of autonomy and self-determination for the client has pervaded the administrative structure of social welfare" (pp. 262–63).

A study by McCune (1966) of the job-interest patterns of social work students as compared with students in law, education, and business administration shows them as having a tendency to "avoid systematic-methodical methods for processing information and making decisions" (p. 134), "evidencing a dislike for forceful exertion of leadership" (p. 131), and a "dislike for the use of external controls to guide the behavior of others" (p. 111).

A more recent study calls attention to this problem (Olyan 1972). Using a standardized Leadership Opinion Questionnaire, Olyan obtained responses from 228 supervisors in three different settings. One scale included in the questionnaire concerns structure and is designed to reflect

the extent to which an individual is likely to define and structure his own role and those of his subordinates toward goal attainment. A high score on this dimension characterizes individuals who play a very active role in directing group activities through planning, communicating information, scheduling, criticizing, trying out new ideas and so forth. A low score characterizes individuals who are likely to be relatively inactive in group direction in these ways. (p. 172)

Low scores on the structure scale suggest a reluctance to exercise control and authority.

A second scale included in the questionnaire is the consideration scale, designed to measure

the extent to which an individual is likely to have job relationships with his subordinates characterized by mutual trust, respect for their ideas, consideration for their feelings, and a certain warmth between himself and them. A high score is indicative of a climate of good rapport and two-way communication. A low score indicates the individual is likely to be more impersonal in his relations with group members. (p. 172)

While the social work supervisors scored relatively high on the consideration scale as compared with 35 other occupational groups for which scores are available, they ranked lowest of all 36 occupations on the structural scale. Olyan concludes that the data "suggests that supervisors in this study group are not oriented toward goal attainment techniques such as planning, communicating information, scheduling, criticizing" (p. 178). These are the activities central to implementation of the responsibilities of administrative supervision and relate to the exercise of authority.

According to the studies which have used the Leadership Opinion Questionnaires in management research, the most desirable combination is that of a supervisor who scores high both on consideration and structure. The pattern of the social work supervisors with high scores on consideration, very low scores on structure, suggests a situation in which supervisees would not take the supervisor seriously. This pattern is conducive to a relationship in which the supervisee finds it easy to ignore the supervisor. Proficiency and goal attainment, key objectives of administrative supervision, are likely to suffer as a result.

Despite our distaste for the words and our resistance to the activities implied, authority and power are built into the supervisory relationship. Miller (1960) suggests that "it would help a great deal to give up the sentimental sham that the worker-supervisor relationship exists between equals or between professional colleagues who happen to have different functions and responsibilities. This kind of well-meaning distortion obscures the power and authority inherent in the supervisory function" (p. 76). The supervisor who has the broadest base of power, by virtue of being able to activate and use all sources of power, operates most effectively. The supervisor who is unable or unwilling to employ rewards and punishments or who cannot obtain the respect of his supervisees because of a lack of perceived expertise diminishes his potential power. This fact implies that the supervisor must accept, without defensiveness or apology, the authority and related power inherent in his position. Use of authority may sometimes be unavoidable. The supervisor can increase its effectiveness if he feels, and can communicate, a conviction in his behavior. If he acts with confidence and with an expectation that his authority will be respected, his directives are more likely to be accepted.

The question of power and authority in the supervisory relationship is just a special instance of the problem of authority in social work generally, a difficulty which has received special attention in the professional literature (Foren and Bailey 1968; Orchard 1965; Studt 1954, 1959; Yelaja 1971).

Nonauthoritative Authority

If, in order to perform functions that are necessary for achievement of organizational objectives, the supervisor must be granted, and must exercise, some measure of authority, how can this authority be most effectively manifested? The likelihood of the supervisees' accepting the supervisor's authority is increased if certain caveats are observed. They are designed to help the supervisor exercise authority without being officiously authoritative.

In general, the most desirable use of supervisory authority is oriented toward "exerting power with minimal side effects and conflicts," and seeking approaches "for the limiting of the exercise of power to the least amount which will satisfy the functional requirements of the organization and for maximizing role performance without the exercise of power" (Kahn 1964, p. 7).

There is apt to be greater voluntary compliance with supervisory authority if its sources are perceived as legitimate, the methods employed in its exercise are acceptable, the objectives of its use are understandable and approved, and it is exercised within the limits of legitimate jurisdiction.

The attitude, the sprit with which authority is employed, is significant. If it is used only when the situation demands it, when it is required to achieve objectives to which both supervisor and supervisee are jointly committed, it is more likely to be accepted. If it is exercised in a spirit of vindictiveness, in response to a desire for self-aggrandizement, a pleasure in dominance, a delight in self-gratification, it is less likely to be accepted. Supervisees can more easily understand and accept the exercise of authority if it is clear that authority is being used for the achievement of organizational goals rather than because its use is intrinsically pleasurable to the supervisor. If supervisees are committed to the achievement of the organizational goal, acceptance of authority is then congruent with their own needs and wishes.

The use of authority has to be perceived as a rational procedure designed to achieve mutually acceptable aims. If authority is employed in a manner which indicates that the supervisor is flexible and open to suggestions for changes in "commands" on the basis of relevant feedback from supervisees, it is less likely to be viewed as capricious and arbitrary. If, in exercising authority, the supervisor shares with his supervisees the reasons which prompt the directive, if he gives an opportunity for questions and discussion of the directive, the supervisees' feeling that this is a rational procedure over which they have some control is further enhanced. Through such participation the supervisees share control.

If authority is exercised in a predictable manner, the supervisees again feel they have some control over the situation. They can clearly foresee the consequences of certain actions on their part. Arbitrary exercise of authority is unpredictable and inexplicable.

Authority needs to be used with a recognition that supervisees, as adults, tend to resent the dependence, submissiveness, and contravention of individual autonomy implied in accepting authority. Authority is best exercised if it is depersonalized. Even in the best of circumstances, we are predisposed to resent and resist authority. It is, in its essence, anti-equalitarian. It suggests that one person is better than another. Depersonalizing the use of authority is designed to mitigate such feeling. The attitude suggests that the supervisor is acting as an agent of the organization rather than out of any sense of personal superiority. The supervisee is not asked to acknowledge the superiority of the supervisor as a person but merely her assignment to a particular function in the agency hierarchy.

If it is not to be resented, authority has to be impartially exercised. Impartial does not necessarily mean equal. It means that in similar situations people are treated similarly. If there is a rational and acceptable reason for unequal, preferential treatment, this is not resented. One worker can be assigned a much smaller caseload than another. If, however, the smaller caseload includes difficult, complex cases, the assignment will not be regarded as an unfair exercise of supervisory authority.

The supervisor needs a sensitive awareness that her authority is limited and job related. The administrative grant of authority relates to a specific set of duties and tasks. The legitimacy of the supervisor's authority is open to question if she seeks to extend it beyond recognized boundaries. Attempting to prescribe a dress code for supervisees or to prescribe off-the-job behavior causes difficulty because the supervisor is exceeding the limits of her legitimate authority.

The supervisor has to be careful to refrain from using authority unless some essential conditions can be met. Barnard (1938) points out that supervisory directives will tend to be resisted unless the supervisee can and does understand what needs to be done; believes that the directive is consistent with his perception of the purpose of the organization; believes it is compatible with his personal interests and beliefs; and is able to comply with it. Similarly, Kaufman (1973) notes that supervisee noncompliance results from the fact that the supervisee does not know clearly what needs to be done, cannot do it, or does not want to do it (p. 2).

The most effective use of authority is the minimal use. Persistent use of authority increases the social distance between participants in supervisory relationships and results in a greater formality in such relationships. It intensifies a sense of status difference between supervisor and supervisee and tends to inhibit free communication. The supervisor therefore should make authority explicit as infrequently as possible and only when necessary.

Supervisory authority can be more effectively implemented if agency administration observes some essential considerations. Most basically, only those who are qualified as supervisors should be appointed to the office, and appointment should be a result of fair and acceptable procedures. Only then will supervisees be likely to grant the supervisor's legitimate right to the title and to the authority associated with it.

Administration needs to delegate enough authority to enable the supervisor to perform the functions required of him, and to delegate it in a way that conforms to the principle of unity of command. This principle suggests that a supervisee be supervised by, and answerable to, one supervisor. The exercise of authority is difficult if more than one administrative person directs the supervisee with regard to the same set of activities. There is difficulty, too, if no one has responsibility for some significant set of duties that the supervisee has to perform. Both gaps and overlaps in administrative responsibility create problems.

The administration needs to make clear to both supervisors and supervisees the nature of the authority delegated to the supervisors, the limits of that authority, and the conditions under which the authority can be legitimately exercised. A supervisee writes:

A reporter of a local paper asked the supervisor for permission to attend a group session of A.F.D.C. mothers who had been meeting with me for some time. The supervisor referred the question to me. I indicated that I would like a chance to discuss it with the group. However, when the supervisor pressed for an immediate answer since a decision needed to be made without delay I said "no, I didn't think the reporter should attend the meeting." The next day the supervisor decided that agency policy dictated that the reporter should be permitted to attend because of the public relations opportunity for the agency. If I [the supervisee] had no real authority to make the final decision, the supervisor should not have asked me. It should have been clear in the beginning who has the right and responsibility for a decision of this kind.

Bureaucratic, Leadership, and Professional Control Structures

The preceding discussion of authority, power, and control in the supervisory relationship and the emphasis on the managerial responsibilities of supervision are apt to sound abrasive to most social workers. This is understandable. Social work supervision has, it seems, suffered from an opposite kind of imbalance from that which characterized supervision in business and industry. Of the two essential variables in organizational behavior—the formal organization and the human beings who compose it and do its work—business administration was, for many years, oriented toward the organization and its needs. The persistent trend in the literature of business administration over the past three decades is to educate toward a recognition and appreciation of the human problems of management. This is what Mayo, Roethlisberger, Barnard, Likert, McGregor, Argyris, and Bennis have in common in their prolific research and writings.

In contrast, social work supervision has been primarily sensitive to, and aware of, the human being rather than the organization. Here the corrective emphasis has to be in the direction of raising the level of consciousness regarding the organizational needs in the equation. Administrative supervision and its managerial functions require more explicit attention. We have tended to see the conflict between organizational imperatives and worker needs in terms of personality conflicts between supervisees and administrators. We need to see it more directly in structural-organizational terms, not as matters of individual psychopathology but as consequences of the way people need to be organized in the social system which is the agency.

Social workers have tended to see the agency primarily as a system of human relations, ignoring the fact that it is also a mechanism for achieving production, whereas the earlier proponents of scientific management saw the organization almost exclusively in terms of production. Some correction is needed in both perspectives, since both deny some essential aspect of the objective reality of the situation.

The traditional literature in social work supervision suggests an image of the supervisor which, I think, is essentially correct and desirable. The image is that of a person who establishes full and free reciprocal communication with the supervisee in an atmosphere that not only permits but encourages the expression of authentic feeling; who projects an attitude of confidence and trust toward the supervisee, resulting in optimization of supervisee autonomy and discretion; who has a problem-solving orientation toward the work of the agency, based on consensus and cooperation derived from democratic participation rather than power-centered techniques; who values a consultative-leadership relationship in supervision rather than a subordinate-superordinate relationship. Correct and desirable as this image is, it needs a dash of managerial backbone which has been absent. To call attention to this need is not to deny the importance of the other ingredients, but correcting an apparent imbalance in concerns tends to sound shrill and overstated.

The abrasiveness of the presentation may derive further from an orientation toward a hierarchical-bureaucratic control structure of administrative supervision. Although social workers may reluctantly concede the need for some sort of control structure in order to accomplish the work of the agency, they prefer control structures that are differently organized and differently oriented.

The preferred control structure is based on democratic leadership rather than hierarchy. The leader should be freely chosen by the group and deposed by the group. Supervisees should voluntarily respond to the leader's directives because they want to, not because they have to. Leadership, freely granted by supervisees, is an attribute of the person, not of some position in the organizational hierarchy.

There is no necessary, significant conflict between the supervisor as a bureaucratic-hierarchical appointee and the supervisor as freely accepted leader of the group. While remaining true to the responsibilities of administrative supervision, the democratically oriented supervisor can act in such a way that she is perceived as an acceptable leader to her supervisees: encouraging supervisee participation in decision making, sharing authority with supervisees to maximize their discretion, reviewing work infrequently and selectively. The effort is made to transform a bureaucratic relationship into a leadership relationship in which influence efforts are freely made and freely accepted.

However, administrative supervision enacted as democratic leadership in an organization faces a basic paradox—that of motivating people to do, through their own free will, the tasks which are necessary to achieve organizational objectives. Dwight Eisenhower is credited with saying that leadership is the ability to get a person to do what you want done because he wants to do it.

Realistically, there are limits to the extent to which the agency can depend on leadership rather than authority to get the work done. A genuine leadership relationship gives the worker the option of ultimate decision. He is free not to follow the leader. The supervisor does not have the luxury of offering this option to the worker who chooses to remain in the agency. The policy of the agency does have to be implemented, whether the worker agrees with it or not. Acceptance of policy cannot be thrown open to debate anew with each worker for each decision.

In discussing organizational considerations operating in welfare and rehabilitation agencies, Olmstead (1973) notes that "attempts to control entirely through suggestion and discussion . . . can result in an organization's getting so far out of control that powerful coercive measures may be required to get it back into effective operation. Although effective control in professional organizations involves the liberal use of suggestions and persuasion, authority is still a requisite" (p. 34).

Realistically, too, the supervisor is generally not freely chosen by the supervisees but by administration. It is a choice to which supervisees are asked to adjust.

A more explicitly identified alternative control structure, other than that of leadership, which is frequently contrasted with the bureaucratic control structure is the professional control structure. There is recognition that a complex organization requires the performance of certain tasks, but the basis for obtaining conformance to organizational needs, for ensuring coordination, and for limiting individual, idiosyncratic behavior lies not in hierarchically delegated authority but in professional self-discipline, in voluntary adherence to professional norms and peer governance. The essential difference between these control structures is outlined by Toren (1972):

> The distinctive control structure of the professions ... is fundamentally different from bureaucratic control exercised in administrative organizations. Professional control is characterized as being exercised from "within" by an internalized code of ethics and special knowledge acquired during a long period of training and by a group of peers which is alone qualified to make professional judgments. This type of authority differs greatly from bureaucratic authority which emanates from a hierarchical position. (p. 51)

The difference lies in the basis of legitimated authority which supports the differing control systems, one based on expertise which prompts voluntary compliance, the other based on power vested in a position which obligates compliance. The professional control structure recognizes colleagues having equal authority and power rather than supervisor and supervisee with differing amounts.

There is not only a difference in the nature of control but also in its disposition. The professional seeks maximum autonomy, maximum freedom of discretion, and the right to complete self-direction. The organization, in its concern for accountability, efficiency, and effectiveness, in its need to maintain its support so it can be assured of survival, is ready to grant this slowly and reluctantly. Only after the agency is assured of the professional's competence and his commitment to the agency, its objectives and procedures, will greater autonomy be granted. Therefore, the greatest period of strain for a professional in accommodating to the bureaucratic-hierarchical control structure comes shortly after graduation from professional school. Expecting and wanting autonomy, the professional finds himself under supervision until he has proved himself to the agency. Agencies differ, of course, in the extent to which the agency bureaucratic structure is infused with professionalism. Professionally trained workers tend to gravitate toward fields of service and toward agencies where such infusion is greatest.

The strain between the professionals' preference for self- and peer-government and the bureaucratic-hierarchical control structure encountered in working in complex organizations such as social agencies is the subject of very considerable discussion (Abrahamson 1967; Billingsley 1964a, b; Miller and Podell 1970). However, with the "bureaucratization of the professions" and the "professionalization of bureaucracies," there has been increasing accommodation between the two control systems. "Organizations are increasingly governed by professional standards and professions are increasingly subject to bureaucratic controls" (Kornhauser 1962, p. 7). The basis for accommodation efforts lie in the fact that the professional needs the organization almost as much as the organization needs the professional. Engel's (1970) research is relevant here in demonstrating that bureaucratic organization is not necessarily antithetical to professional autonomy.

Actually, the strain seems less pronounced in social work than in other professional areas. Lawler and Hage (n.d.) studied 144 social workers in 14 agencies and found that there was less conflict between the professional and the bureaucracy regarding control than had been hypothesized. The results were attributed to the nature of social work training. The findings "suggest that social work training involves substantial bureaucratic socialization. That is, such training seemingly involves significant acclimatization to the organizational setting in which

one will eventually work" (p. 20). The consequence of such
professional socialization is that (bureaucratic norms become
professional norms requiring professional adherence.)

We have noted earlier the unanimity with which supervisors would prefer that supervisees see the source of the supervisors' power in their expertise. Reliance on expertise as the
principal source of power tends to convert the administrative-
hierarchical relationship of supervisor and supervisee to a colleague relationship of consultant and consulter, fusing bureaucratic and professional control structures.

The accommodation of the two different kinds of control is
further made likely in those agencies in which the administrative apparatus is controlled by social work professionals. Here
managerial administrative personnel such as supervisors are
likely to share with supervisees an adherence to professional
values, norms, and procedures. The tendency to appoint technically qualified, professionally trained social workers to supervisory positions increases the overlap between the bureaucratic
and professional control systems.

Supervisors often make an explicit effort to fuse the bureaucratic and professional control structures. Agency procedures
are translated into terms that are congruent with professional
norms. Supervisee compliance is then in response to a demand
of the profession as well as the agency. As a consequence of
such procedures for fusion, the worker risks a double penalty
for noncompliance. He risks not only administrative displeasure
but also a violation of professional conscience since he is simultaneously subject to both bureaucratic and professional controls.

Areas of conflict between the bureaucratic control structure
and professionalism are reduced, Scott notes, in a number of
ways by supervisory staff (1969, pp. 113–23). Sometimes tasks
are redefined so that they are congruent with professionally
desirable objectives. During a period when social workers in
public welfare agencies were responsible for determination of
eligibility, supervisors defined this task as a professional service
since it provided the caseworker with an entrée to a rela-

tionship with the client and detailed knowledge of client problems for which help might be needed.

Professional reconciliation attempts to demonstrate that the policy, rule, or procedure is, in fact, in the interest of the client or the client group so that adherence does not involve a violation of professional norms. For instance, if regulations require that the deserted mother initiate legal action against the deserting father before being eligible for A.F.D.C., this is seen as an opportunity for involving the father in a service which may achieve reconciliation with the family. Similarly, some bureaucratically desirable behaviors are redefined so that they are interpreted as professionally desirable attributes. Acceptance of agency authority, disciplined conformity to agency policy, rules, and procedures, are defined as professionally desirable qualities in the supervisor's evaluation of the supervisee.

Because of these procedures that translate bureaucratic requirements into professional obligations, the distinction between bureaucratic and professional control systems seems to be less clear in social agencies than in other contexts.

Although the use of authority and power is essential to achieving organizational objectives, it is not essential that power be distributed so that it is concentrated unevenly in the hands of supervisors and administrators. It could be distributed in a wide variety of ways. The professional power structure distributes it horizontally, among colleagues; the bureaucratic power structure distributes it vertically. Authority and power may be delegated downward so that more is given to workers, work councils, or committees of workers. There is a widespread experimentation in industry with this kind of redistribution of organizational power and authority (Hunnius, Garson, and Case 1973; Jenkins 1974). Authority may be distributed to project groups and work teams. Some social agencies have reorganized service delivery along these lines; a fuller discussion of such innovations in supervision is presented in chapter 8.

Admittedly, the problem of authority becomes a matter of increasing difficulty. Barnard (1938) noted that in situations

which involve authority there is a zone of indifference, a zone
of neutrality, and a zone of unacceptability. The zone of indifference (which Simon [1957] calls the zone of acquiescence)
relates to supervisory directives that are accepted and obeyed
without conscious questioning; the zone of unacceptability includes directives that generate opposition and resistance. Currently, with the general erosion of the legitimacy of constituted
authority, with the increasing critical examination of the relative distribution of rights and entitlements in society, there has
been a general decrease in the zone of indifference and an increase in the zone of unacceptability. There is a greater tendency to be critical of authority and to question entitlement to
the exercise of power.

Much that was accepted and taken for granted is currently
being questioned. New workers want to know why agencies are
organized in a particular way, why they are asked to do what
they are asked to do. Supervisors, more frequently now than at
any time in the past, have to be ready to explain and defend the
rationality of what they ask of supervisees.

Associated with these recent currents of thought is a literature which speaks of debureaucratization of organizations and
the end of bureaucracy (Bennis 1966). Bureaucracy is regarded
as a less desirable organizational form in a period of rapid
change when a large percentage of the work force is highly
educated and professionally trained. A less hierarchical, more
humanistically oriented, highly flexible organizational form is
suggested. Whereas in the past an organizational system was
designed to "optimize conformity and stability," the organization of the future may need to "optimize diversity" to meet the
need of continuing change.

There is also talk of a job revolution and changing attitudes
toward work. The traditional work ethic is being reevaluated
and redefined (Gooding 1972; *Work in America* 1972). There is
a supposition that job and career roles are not so central to life's
goals and meaning as they were previously. Consequently the
work setting not only has to be democratized, it also needs to
be transformed. To elicit the workers' full and continuous coop-

eration with the organization requires that the work situation be made more attractive and provide greater satisfactions. There is much talk of "job enrichment" to provide greater opportunities for personal fulfillment and self-actualization. These changes, if implemented, will have significant effects on supervisory-management styles and the supervisor-supervisee relationship.

While the greater part of these debates has gone on outside of social work, in the teaching and research of business management and organizational sociology, social work has not been and is not now impervious to the impact of these ideas. Since the controversy has direct implications for orientations toward administrative supervision as a function of agency management, we do well to take note of it.

Summary

A review of the definitions of an organization and the characteristics of a bureaucracy identify social agencies as bureaucratic organizations requiring the use of administrative supervision. The functions of administrative supervision include planning and assigning work; organizing, coordinating, and facilitating manpower and agency resources available to complete the work; reviewing work performance to ensure that it is adequately done, quantitatively and qualitatively, in accordance with agency procedures; placing the worker; acting as a vertical and lateral channel of communication and as an administrative buffer; helping in the formulation of agency policy; and facilitating intra-agency coordination. In implementing the functions of administrative supervision the supervisor needs some appreciation of the utility of rules and an understanding of the factors relating to noncompliance.

Administrative supervision requires the delegation of authority and power to the supervisor, authority being defined as the legitimation of the use of power, power being defined as the ability to implement the right of authority. Five different sources of power were reviewed—expert power, referent power, positional power, reward, and coercive power. A further distinction was made between functional power, relating to the personal attributes of the supervisor, and formal power inherent in the position of supervisor.

The supervisor needs to come to terms with the delegation of authority and power. Power and authority should be used only when necessary to help achieve the objectives of the organization, in a flexible, impartial manner and with a sensitive regard for worker response.

The functions of administrative supervision can be alternatively implemented through a bureaucratic control structure based on hierarchy and position and a professional control structure based on recognition of expertise and peer governance. Social work has attempted an accommodation between these types of control structures.

chapter three

Educational
Supervision

Educational supervision is the second principal responsibility of the supervisor. Educational supervision is concerned with teaching the worker what he needs to know in order to do his job and helping him to learn it. Every job description of the supervisor's position includes a listing of this function: "instruct workers in acceptable social work techniques"; "develop staff competence through individual and group conferences"; "train and instruct staff in job performance."

I noted earlier that one of the singular aspects of social work is that a very sizable percentage of agency staff come to the job without prior training. There is also considerable turnover and lateral job movement from agency to agency. Consequently there is a constant need to train people to do the job of the social worker and to do the job in a particular agency. The responsibility for such training is assigned to staff-development personnel, which include first-line supervisors when they are engaged in educational supervision.

Some distinction needs to be made between staff development, in-service training, and educational supervision. Staff development refers to all of the procedures an agency might employ to enhance the job-related knowledge, skills, and attitudes of its total staff, and includes in-service training and educational supervision. Training sessions, lectures, workshops, institutes, informational pamphlets, discussion groups for caseworkers, administrators, clerical staff, and supervisors are staff-development activities.

In-service training is a more specific form of staff development. The term refers to planned, formal training provided to a delimited group of agency personnel who have the same job classification or the same job responsibilities. Educational supervision is a still more specific kind of staff develpment. Here training is directed to the needs of a particular worker carrying a particular case load, encountering particular problems and needing some individualized program of education.

The supervisor in discharging the responsibilities of educational supervision helps the worker implement and apply the more general learning provided through the in-service training program. He teaches "the worker what he needs to know to give specific service to specific clients" (Bell, n.d., p. 15) and helps the worker make the transition from knowing to doing. In-service training and educational supervision complement each other. The supervisor will reinforce, individualize, and demonstrate the applicability of the more general content taught in planned, formal in-service training sessions (Meyer 1966).

Educational supervision is a line, rather than a staff, function. Other staff-development activities may be the responsibility of specialized personnel whose sole concern is education of staff and who have no administrative responsibility for the staff they are training. Educational supervision, as a staff-development function, is one of a number of different responsibilities. Furthermore the supervisor does have administrative responsibility for the supervisees to whom she is offering training.

Educational supervision is a very significant part of the supervisor's activities and responsibilities. Two of the three strongest sources of satisfaction for supervisors are "satisfaction in helping the supervisee grow and develop as a professional" and "satisfaction in sharing social work knowledge and skills with supervisees." Two of the three main sources of supervisee satisfaction with supervision are related to educational supervision: "my supervisor helps me in dealing with problems in

my work with clients" and "my supervisor helps me in my development as a professional social worker." In addition both supervisors and supervisees agreed that "ensuring the professional developments of the supervisee" was one of the two most
• important objectives of supervision (Kadushin 1974).

Conversely, when supervision fails, the failures are most keenly felt in the area of educational supervision. Two major sources of dissatisfaction expressed by supervisees relate to this function: "my supervisor is not sufficiently critical of my work so that I don't know what I am doing wrong or what needs changing" and "my supervisor does not provide much real help in dealing with problems I face with my clients" (Kadushin 1974).

Relationship of Educational Supervision to Administrative Supervision

Administrative supervision and educational supervision share the same ultimate objective, to provide the best possible service to the clients. Administrative supervision provides the structure directed toward this goal; educational supervision provides the training which enables workers to achieve it. Educational supervision provides the knowledge and instrumental skills which are the workers' necessary equipment for effective practice.

Educational and administrative supervision also reinforce each other. Educational supervision is designed to increase the effectiveness of administrative supervision. As a consequence of educational supervision the tasks of administrative supervision are alternatively implemented. "Training and guided experience [take] the place of detailed and close supervision as a means of accomplishing the same control functions" (Olmstead 1973, p. 90). With more education, workers can act more autonomously and independently, reducing the burden of administrative supervision.

Attitudes of commitment and loyalty to agency values, aims, and procedures are developed through educational supervision. If the agency can, through education, indoctrinate workers with a personal conviction in doing what the agency wants done, in the way the agency wants it done, toward objectives the agency wants to achieve, the agency will be less hesitant to delegate authority for autonomous performance. Educational supervision provides administrative controls through a process of helping the worker internalize such controls.

We are using the term "indoctrinate" here in its least pejorative sense, to mean a form of consciousness raising. As Olmstead says, "Indoctrination is the process by which personnel internalize sets of principles and values that will, in part, govern their behavior. Much of professional education is, in effect, indoctrination" (1973, p. 87).

Educational supervision involves the communication of a belief system which has, as one of its tenets, the legitimation of the agency's authority structure. Such socialization has, as one of its aims, the "engineering of consent" so that ultimately the supervisee voluntarily endorses the legitimacy of the supervisor's positional authority.

Simon (1957) cogently summarizes these relationships between the functions of educational and administrative supervision:

Training influences decisions "from the inside out." That is, training prepares the organization member to reach satisfactory decisions himself without the need for the constant exercise of authority or advice. In this sense training procedures are alternatives to the exercise of authority or advice as means of control over the subordinate's decision. ... It may be possible to minimize or even dispense with certain review processes by giving the subordinates training that enables them to perform their work with less supervision. Training may supply the trainee with the facts necessary in dealing with these decisions, it may provide him with a frame of reference for his thinking; it may teach him "approved" decisions; or it may indoctrinate him with the values in terms of which his decisions are to be made. (pp. 15–16)

The role of training in administration is perhaps best understood by viewing it as one of several alternative means for communicating decisional premises to organization members. (p. 169)

Making decisions on the basis of mutually shared values, presuppositions, and knowledge increases the predictability of the workers' actions. Thinking in a way which is similar to the thinking of their fellow professionals, they are likely to come to the same conclusions independently.

Professional socialization involves the reduction of idiosyncrasy. Lay attitudes and approaches to problems are diverse; professional approaches tend to be more homogeneous. Professional socialization involves taking on a professional identity and a special outlook regarding one's work which is shared with collegues. Educational supervision is the context for role transition from lay person to professional, providing the supervisee with this sense of occupational identity.

Because administrative supervision and educational supervision provide alternative procedures for control of workers' performance, more of one requires less of the other. Hall (1968) concluded from a study of the relationship of bureaucracy and professionalism in a number of different professions, including social work, that "an equilibrium may exist between the levels of professionalization and bureaucratization in the sense that a particular level of professionalization may require a certain level of bureaucratization to maintain social control" (p. 104). Higher levels of professionalization were associated with lower levels of bureaucratization. Similarly Hage and Aiken (1967) in a study of 16 social welfare and health agencies found that "close supervision is less likely when members of an organization are professionally active . . . and when they have been professionally trained" (p. 90).

Development of knowledge and skills, as a consequence of educational supervision, permits relaxation of administrative controls. Not only will the worker feel a personal obligation to do a good job, he will have the necessary competence and capability to do so.

Educational supervision permits smoother administrative coordination and more effective communication. Having learned how the agency operates, and what the functions of other people are in the agency, the worker can coordinate his own work with others. Having learned the specialized language of the agency and the profession, the worker can communicate with colleagues with fewer risks of misunderstanding. The shared "universe of discourse" aids communication.

Studying changing interpersonal perceptions of social work supervisors and supervisees over a period of a year, MacGuffie, Janzen, and McPhee (1970) found a growing congruence in perception. Supervisor-supervisee interactions toward the end of the year were based on developed communalities in perception which tended "to minimize the chance of distorted communications and to clarify both cognitions and feelings of co-communicators" (p. 268). Education of the supervisee to the consensus of values, uniformity of perspectives, and standardization of language shared by other workers in the agency reduces the likelihood of intra-agency conflict while increasing the level of intra-agency cooperation.

As a result of educational supervision the worker is in a better position to evaluate his own performance. He learns the difference between good and poor practice and has some criteria by which he can be self-critical. Thus the administrative supervisory functions of control, coordination, communication, cooperation, and evaluation are all made easier as a consequence of educational supervision.

Conditions for Effective Teaching and Learning

The supervisor's principal responsibility in educational supervision is to teach the worker how to do the job. Our task here is to delineate what promotes effective teaching and learning. The teacher can organize content, provide a suitable atmosphere for learning, and make learning available but cannot ensure its acceptance and certainly not its use. This only the learner can do. Teaching is essentially the "art of assisting another to learn." As Robinson says, "Teaching provides the subject matter, the stimulus, the materials, sets the tasks and defines the conditions. But learning is the process of utilizing opportunity and limits in one's own way for one's own ends" (1936, p. 128). Learning is a creative personal experience.

Our interest, therefore, is in how learners learn. The supervisor needs to be aware of some of the factors that facilitate learning and know something about techniques that maximize it. In this section I outline some general principles of learning and some techniques derived from these principles that are applicable to the supervisory conference. In the absence of a comprehensive, generally accepted "integrating theory in pedagogy," there is "principally a body of maxims" (Bruner 1971, p. 31) which may, nonetheless, be highly useful.

principle
We learn best if we are highly motivated to learn. In applying this principle the supervisor can use the following techniques.

techniques
1. Explain the usefulness of the content to be taught. We owe the worker some explanation of why it might be important for him to know this material if he is to discharge his professional responsibilities effectively. Motivation increases as usefulness of the content becomes clear. The new worker may not appreciate the importance, for instance, of learning effective referral procedures. If we can show, by citing the relevant research, the sizable percentage of people who need referral service and the effects of different referral procedures on subsequent client experience, the worker may better understand the significance of this unit of learning. The adult learner is concerned with current problems that require learning for solution. In teaching-learning situations involving adults we can take advantage of this orientation by stressing the utility and applicability of what is learned.

2. Make learning meaningful in terms of the individual worker's motives and needs. However useful or sigificant the material is generally, the worker is not likely to be motivated unless one can show its usefulness and importance for a prob-

lem or situation that is meaningful to her. Showing how the supervisee could have improved on her last interview if she had had a surer grasp of the dynamics of behavior will do more to increase motivation than lectures on the general importance of such knowledge.

3. Tie areas of low motivation to areas of high motivation. The worker may be highly motivated to help the client but indifferent to the content which the supervisor is attempting to teach—for instance, recording. If the supervisor can demonstrate that recording permits the worker to be more helpful to the client, he may then be motivated to learn it.

One needs to be aware of the variety of the possible motives for learning. Motivation is "an internal process initiated by a need which leads to goal seeking." Intrinsic motives are tied to the content itself. People want to study the content because they are interested in the material itself, because there is satisfaction in meeting the challenge of the content and mastering it, because there is pleasure in solving professional problems and in acquiring knowledge.

Motives may be largely extrinsic, however. Learning the content is only a way of reaching other goals. There may be psychic rewards from the approbation of peers, the supervisor, parents, one's own professional superego. Other psychic rewards are derived from competitively learning better than sibling-peers in the agency. Learning the content may be motivated by a desire for autonomy and independence, so that one does not have to turn to the supervisor for help. There may be administrative rewards such as pay raises and promotions.

Motives for learning may result from a developing commitment to the agency, its staff, and its objectives. Having a strong conviction in the agency's objectives, the worker wants to see them achieved as effectively as possible. Motivation is strengthened by idenification with the agency and colleagues. Feeling identified with the agency, the worker wants the agency to be favorably perceived by the community; feeling loyal and close to his colleagues, he wants their good opinion. As a consequence of these considerations, the worker is motivated to learn so as to be as competent as possible.

Research on the nature of job satisfactions helps clarify the incentives that are likely to motivate on-the-job learning. The main studies on job satisfactions have been done by Herzberg and his group in a wide variety of contexts (Herzberg 1968; Herzberg, Mausner, and Snyderman 1959). Five factors were identified as the principal sources of job satisfaction for most people. Arranged in order of frequency, these are: achievement (feeling pleased with something done in which one would take pride); recognition (good work was commented on and complimented); the work itself (the work was interesting, challenging, varied); responsibility (freedom to do the work independently and autonomously); and advancement (the possibility of moving up to more responsible positions). These factors can be used to motivate learning. For instance, there is greater possibility of meeting the need for achievement if the worker learns how to do the job more effectively; learning to do the job increases the probability that the worker will be granted more responsibility, more opportunity to work independently; learning to do the job enhances the possibility of advancement.

We would do well to utilize any and all motives to optimize learning. If the worker wants a promotion or raise, or a student wants a high grade, we can explicitly tie these extrinsic motives to the need to learn the content as a requirement for achieving their goals.

Motivation increases receptivity to learning and makes energy available for learning. It thus sets the stage for learning and provides the teachable moment. But it does not in itself make for learning. The supervisor has to take advantage of the teachable situation to teach something of significance. Motivation needs to be provided with a learning opportunity and direction. The supervisor provides guidance to the learning that motivation seeks.

4. Since motivation is of such crucial significance, the supervisor needs to safeguard and stimulate motivation where it

exists, and instill motivation where it does not. Motivation indicates a readiness for learning. A worker who lacks motivation to learn certain content may have no felt need for it. He is satisfied with what he is doing, in the way he is doing it. He has no problem that requires additional learning for its solution. The worker may be right, in which case the supervisor has nothing to teach him.

If the supervisor, however, is convinced that the worker's perception of his performance is wrong and that there is much he needs to learn, she would first have to stimulate dissatisfaction with his performance. The supervisor may want to confront the worker with the gap between what he is doing and what he can do, what he is doing and what needs to be done, what he is doing and what he wants to be able to do. (Dissatisfaction with his current performance is a necessary prerequisite before the worker is ready to learn new and better ways of working with the client.)

Consequently, the supervisor makes a deliberate but compassionate effort to create some desire for, or curiosity about, the learning she has to offer. Rather than being passive in the face of lack of motivation, the supervisor acts as a catalyst for change, creating tension that needs to be resolved. The worker's equilibrium needs to be disturbed if receptivity to learning is to be stimulated.

At times the "supervisor must awaken anxiety by penetrating the rationalization and defenses that bind it. If the supervisor avoids conflict for purposes of keeping the supervisory relationship untroubled and outwardly smooth he will have abdicated his responsibility to the supervisee and will have compromised his trustworthiness" (Mueller and Kell 1972, pp. 30–31).

Motivation for learning follows the general principle that all behavior is purposive. We learn only when we want to learn, when we feel a need to learn. While this justifies stimulation of a need, such a procedure may be unnecessary. The first assumption about an apparently unmotivated supervisee might well be that we are not sensitive enough to discern the motives that he does have. It would initially be better to attempt to understand and use those motives which the learner himself brings to the situation.

principle
We learn best when we can devote most of our energies in the learning situation to learning. Energy needed to defend against rejection, anxiety, guilt, shame, fear of failure, attacks on autonomy, or uncertain expectations, is energy deflected from learning.

We can maximize the amount of energy available to learning in the following ways.

techniques
1. Clearly establish the rules of the game regarding time, place, roles, limits, expectations, obligations, and objectives. If the worker is anxious because he is uncertain of what is expected from him in the role of supervisee, he is not fully free to devote full attention to learning. The nature of the supervisory relationship should be clear. The frequency of supervisory meetings, the length of such conferences, the respective responsibilities, expectations, and obligations of supervisee and supervisor in preparation for, and in the conduct of, such conferences should be clearly established, mutually understood, and mutually accepted. Such details provide the comfort of unambiguous structure.

Clarity relates to learning objectives as well. The supervisor needs to know, and to share with the supervisee, some idea of where he hopes the learner is going, what she will know and be able to do after she has learned what the supervisor hopes to teach. Objectives give meaning to each discrete learning unit and permit us to measure progress. As Seneca said, "No wind is favorable if you do not know your destination."

2. Respect the worker's rights, within limits, to determine his or her own solutions. The structure, while supportive in its clarity, should not be so rigid that it becomes restrictive. Some flexibility needs to be permitted the supervisee so as to prevent

psychic energy from being diverted from learning to deal with rising hostility and resentment at infantilization. This is particularly true in adult education since the learner operates with considerable freedom and autonomy in other significant areas of his life. Here, however, he is partially dependent, as is every learner who needs to turn to others to teach him what he does not yet know. As a generally independent adult, he is more apt to resent this necessary dependency. The supervisor should then permit the greatest amount of independence that the learner can profitably use without danger to the client. Respect for the worker's autonomy and initiative ensures that psychic energy necessary for learning will not be dissipated in defense of autonomy.

3. Establish an atmosphere of accepting, psychological safety, a framework of security. Learning implies a risk of mistakes and a risk of failure. It implies, too, a confession of ignorance. A worker who fears censure and rejection for admitting failure or ignorance will devote psychic energy to defense against such anticipated attacks. The supervisor should be the supervisee's mentor rather than tormentor. An atmosphere of acceptance permits a freer involvement in risk-taking and a greater psychic concentration on learning rather than on self-defense.

Acceptance involves expectations. Psychological safety does not mean a permissiveness that ignores the demand for adequate performance on the part of the worker. We must make firm demands on the worker for learning what she needs to learn. But our demands are made in a friendly way, out of a desire to help rather than to hurt. They do create tension. However, such tension is necessary to motivate the supervisee to learn.

The supervisor has to be consistently helpful to the supervisee rather than consistently popular. This means challenging error, calling attention to areas of ignorance, pointing to mistakes and deficiencies in performance. The supervisor has to offer a judicious balance between stimulus and support. The supervisor is responsible for maintaining the balance between a degree of tension which motivates and challenges, and a degree of tension which immobilizes. We utilize the tension which derives not from the fear of failure but from the discrepancy between what the worker knows and what he wants to know. It involves making demands with the utmost possible respect, compassion, and understanding. It would be foolish to pretend that balancing these contradictory and vaguely defined variables is anything but the most difficult of tasks.

4. Acknowledge and use what the worker already knows and can do. This technique decreases anxiety since it indicates to the worker that he can draw on what he already knows to meet the demands of supervision. Affirmation and use of the already rich learning the worker brings to the teaching-learning situation is an advantageous aspect of adult education.

5. Move from the familiar to the unfamiliar. The unfamiliar provokes anxiety. If the supervisor can relate new material to familiar material, the new learning seems less strange, and less difficult to learn.

6. Demonstrate confidence, if warranted, in the worker's ability to learn. He himself may have doubts about his ability, doubts against which he needs to defend himself at some expenditure of psychic energy robbed from learning. Communication of a feeling of confidence in the worker's ability, where warranted, helps to allay feelings which detract from learning. Confidence in the learner's ability to learn is contagious. Communication of confidence increases motivation for, and interest in, learning.

At the same time the supervisor has to accept, and make allowances for, the fact that learning is a growth process and takes time. One must expect nonproductive plateaus where little progress is being made. There needs to be time for reflection, absorption, consolidation of learning. There is likely to be some regression in learning, much zigging and zagging. Like all growth processes, it is uneven and variable, and different kinds of content are learned at different rates of speed.

7. Know your content; be ready and willing to teach it. The supervisor not only needs the wish but also the ability to be

helpful. The worker does not know what he needs to know and this makes him anxious. His anxiety is tempered, however, by the fact that if he does not know, at least the supervisor knows the answer to some of his questions. Not only does she know but she is willing to share this knowledge with him, if necessary. If the supervisor does not know, or seems unwilling to share her knowledge, this increases tension since it suggests to the supervisee that he faces the prospect of dealing with situations for which he has no adequate response available. Lack of knowledge in a situation which requires responsible action is anxiety provoking. Knowing that someone knows and is ready to provide the helpful knowledge diminishes anxiety. It might be noted that supervisor competence rather than omniscience is all that the supervisee does, and can, expect. But the greater professional competence of the supervisor can help to meet the supervisees' legitimate dependency needs. And the supervisor has to be capable and ready to meet these needs.

principle

We learn best when learning is attended by positive satisfactions—when it is successful and rewarding. We seek to repeat what has been satisfying and avoid repeating what is painful.

techniques

1. Set conditions of learning so as to ensure high probability of success. A successful experience in one's practice rewards and reinforces the behavior associated with the successful experience.

It would be inadvisable to present the worker with a learning demand that is clearly beyond his capacity to meet it. If there is little chance of success, there is little motivation to try. The learner needs some assurance that he can succeed if he is going to risk himself in trying. On the other hand, the task needs to be sufficiently challenging to engage the worker's interest and prompt him to extend himself. If a task is too easy, one is not likely to experience a feeling of success in achieving it. Selecting a learning task that is challenging but not over-whelming is a neat trick. It is, admittedly, much easier to de-scribe than to do, particularly without any gauge by which to measure how much challenge a worker can hope to meet suc-cessfully.

2. We increase positive satisfactions in learning if we praise, where warranted, success in professional accomplish-ment. Praise is a psychic reward that reinforces the behavior that prompted the commendation. Indiscriminate praise is counterproductive, however. The supervisee is an adult capable of independent critical assessment of his own performance. If we praise performance which he recognizes as substandard, we lose credibility in his eyes and our subsequent assessments are discounted. The worker might feel he cannot trust our judg-ment. It is, therefore, important to commend only what can be defended as objectively praiseworthy. The supervisor should be specific about the behavior which has elicited approval. Not the general statement, "You really indicated your understanding of Mr. P.'s behavior," but the specific statement, "You really indi-cated your understanding of Mr. P.'s behavior when you said . . . in response to his comment about. . . ." Such specificity not only ensures that such learning is attended by positive satisfac-tions because it is being rewarded but also makes conscious and explicit the behavior which the supervisor hopes to reinforce.

Pleasure and pain, reward and punishment overlap with the question of motivation in learning. We are motivated to learn so that we can avoid the pain that comes from inability to deal successfully with problems in job performance. We are mo-tivated to learn so as to feel the pleasure of doing a job compe-tently and effectively. We are motivated to learn so that we can avoid the punishment of being dependent and can obtain the reward of acting autonomously. We are motivated to learn so that we can avoid the pain of criticism and guilt and be re-warded with praise and approbation from ourselves and from "significant others," including the supervisor. We are motivated to learn to avoid the dissatisfaction which comes from the un-certainty of not clearly knowing what we are supposed to be doing or how to do it. We are motivated to learn in order to feel the satisfaction in the security which comes from knowing, with assurance, what it's all about.

3. Praise through positive feedback. Such reinforcement is most effective if offered while the learning situation to which it applies is still fresh and vivid. This fact emphasizes the importance of regularly scheduled conferences at reasonably frequent intervals (once a week perhaps) so that the supervisor can offer his critical reaction to recently encountered experiences in which learning has been applied by the supervisees. Assessment of results is necessary if the learner is to modify his behavior in a desired direction, and feedback regarding the application of learning is necessary if the learner is to experience a feeling of success which is a reward.

4. Periodic stock-taking provided in a formal evaluation conference at less frequent intervals (every six months perhaps) further ensures learning attended by positive satisfaction because it permits a perspective on long-range progress. The supervisee can get some sense of progress in learning over time, which is rewarding.

5. We ensure the greater probability of success if we partialize learning. "A man can eat whole steer—one steak at a time." We offer learning in digestible dosages. The agenda for a particular conference should cover a limited, defined unit of learning, which is clear, acceptable, and attainable.

6. Success and positive satisfactions in learning are more likely if the material is presented in graded sequence, from the simple to the complex, from the obvious to the obscure. It is easier for a worker to understand concrete situational needs such as a home for a totally dependent, abandoned infant than it is to understand the psychological dependency needs of a middle-aged neurotic. It is easier to understand that feelings are facts than to grasp the idea of ambivalence. Grading the complexity of content is more difficult in social work than in mathematics or chemistry. Seemingly simple situations have a tendency to present unanticipated complexities. However, to the extent that we can discern the measure of comparative difficulty

of material to be taught, we should attempt to teach the simpler content first.

There are some general criteria for differentiating between simpler and more difficult social-work learning situations. The client who is motivated to use the service, has good ego strength, is not unduly defensive, and with whom the worker can, in some way, identify presents less difficulty. A situation in which cause-and-effect relationships are clear, for which remedial resources and services are available, and in which the problem is well focused, presents less difficulty. These characteristics represent treatable clients in treatable situations, ensuring greater probability of successful application of learning.

7. We ensure the greater probability of positive satisfaction in learning if we prepare the worker for failure. It may be necessary to expose the worker to situations of a complexity and difficulty for which he is as yet not fully prepared. The demands of case coverage may not always permit the assignment of cases that are within the worker's competence. In such instances it would be helpful to explicitly recognize with the worker the possibility of failure in the encounter. He is then less likely to be overwhelmed by personal guilt or shame and be more open to learning from the experience.

principle
We learn best if we are actively involved in the learning process.

techniques
1. The supervisee should be encouraged to participate in planning the agenda for the supervisory sessions. This technique ensures the supervisee's active involvement in the learning situation. In addition it increases the probability that content of primary interest and concern to the supervisee will be discussed.

Active participation in selecting the content for learning tends to heighten commitment to the task of learning. This is the content the learner herself suggested she was motivated to learn. The objectives of the learning-teaching encounter are therefore probably acceptable to her.

2. We ensure the greater active involvement of the supervisee in learning if we encourage and provide opportunity for him to question, discuss, object, express doubt. The supervisor should supplement, rather than substitute for, a supervisee's thinking. Thinking is trial acting. The worker will use what is being taught in active encounters with clients. He can, however, also be encouraged to engage with the content to be learned through discussion. This is a cognitive rather than behavioral engagement with the learning but one which nevertheless requires active participation in learning. Such involvement of the supervisee is only possible in an atmosphere of psychological safety in which the supervisee feels comfortable about questioning the supervisor and presenting his own, perhaps opposing, point of view.

3. Provide the explicit opportunity to utilize and apply the knowledge we seek to teach. If we are teaching the worker some of the principles of client advocacy, we would need to provide an assignment which involves the worker in client advocacy. The worker then, of necessity, is actively engaged in testing the learning through use. We learn to do by doing. Learning determines action, but successful action reinforces learning.

The worker may, however, engage in incompetent practice. Consequently, providing practice experience has to be followed by a critical review of what was done. Such feedback enables the worker to know specifically what might need correction and change. This review should again be followed by the opportunity to practice the corrected learning.

principle
We learn best if the content is meaningfully presented.

techniques
1. As much as possible, select for teaching the content that is of interest and concern to the supervisee. Readiness for learning is often related to some specific situation. The worker

needs to know that which will help her deal with a problem she is having with a particular client. This is the teachable moment for the presentation of the relevant content. At this point the content has meaning for the supervisee and can be most effectively taught.

2. Content is meaningfully presented if it fits into some general theoretical framework. Different supervisors adhere to different theoretical systems—psychoanalytic psychology, behaviorism, existential psychology. The choice of system is not as important as the fact that there is belief in some comprehensive, internally consistent configuration which satisfactorily explains the mysteries of human behavior (at least for its adherents). Our subject matter is people. We need some cognitive map, some cosmology, which makes sense of why people do what they do in the way they do it.

It is difficult to learn discrete, unrelated details of behavior. If, however, the supervisor is knowledgeable about some well-articulated scheme, she can relate details to principles which act as an organizing focus for details. Whatever one's opinion is regarding id-ego-superego, or drive-stimulus-response, one needs to recognize that these ideas suggest large-scale, coherent, explanatory frameworks of human behavior which meaningfully organize details regarding the human condition. The supervisor needs to have available some reasonably comprehensive explanatory framework which meaningfully organizes the content she is attempting to teach. Such ideational scaffolding provides the "unity behind the plurality of experiences" and gives a sense of connectedness to discrete learnings.

Bruner (1963) notes that "perhaps the most basic thing that can be said about human memory after a century of intensive research is that unless detail is placed into a structured pattern it is rapidly forgotten" (p. 24). "Organizing facts in terms of principle and idea from which they may be inferred is the only known way of reducing the quick rate of loss of human memory" (p. 31). Bruner further comments that "the principal problem of human memory is not storage but retrieval" and that "the key to retrieval is organization."

3. Meaningful teaching is selective teaching. Some things

are more important than others, some content requires more attention, emphasis, repetition than other content. The supervisor needs to have priorities that guide the choice of content to be taught.

4. Imaginative repetition makes learning more meaningful. If we select a number of experiences that teach the same idea in different ways, it is easier to grasp and accept. Through comparison and contrast, illustration of similarities and differences, the same content is more meaningfully presented.

Practice of skills is, after all, the opportunity to repeat in different situations the exercise of such skills. But repetition is not haphazard. It is carefully selected in terms of organizing principles. As Tyler (1971) states, "in order for educational experiences to produce a cumulative effect they must be organized so as to reinforce each other" (p. 83). The best repetition involves not sheer drill of old learning but some variation that includes new elements to capture the learner's interest.

5. Teaching that is planned in terms of continuity (reiteration of important content—deepening learning), sequence (successively building toward greater complexity—broadening learning) and integration (relating different content to each other) is apt to be teaching presented in a more meaningful context. Content has to be planfully organized and systematically presented if it is to be taught effectively.

6. Some of the techniques mentioned in relation to previously cited principles of learning are applicable here as well. The content is more meaningful if the supervisor can relate new learning to previously acquired learning, moving from the unfamiliar to the familiar, and if the content can be presented in logical progression, moving from simple to complex.

7. Learning is more meaningful if it can be made conscious and explicit. We are not always aware of what we have learned. To the extent that we can consciously articulate and label what we have learned, the learning is apt to be more meaningful and transferable. This fact calls attention to the need for periodic recapitulation and summarization of units of completed learning.

principle
We learn best if the supervisor takes into consideration the supervisee's uniqueness as a learner.

techniques
1. Individualizing the learner calls for an educational diagnosis. We study the learner so that we can understand how she learns. Educational diagnosis of a supervisee includes a statement regarding what she already knows well, what she needs to learn, what she wants to learn, and how she wants to learn it. To individualize teaching we need to know not only where the worker is but where she wants to go. With such an educational diagnosis we are in a better position to fit the learning situation to the learner rather than the learner to the learning situation. The advantage of tutorial teaching in the supervisory context is precisely that the supervisor can tailor his choice of approach and content to the learning needs of the individual supervisee.

In making an educational diagnosis of supervisees, one needs to consider the special attributes of the adult learner. Adult learners have a long attention span, can sustain learning activity and postpone gratification for long periods. A good deal of adult learning might more properly be termed relearning rather than primary learning, and the learning process therefore involves some necessary unlearning. There is more resistance to accepting the temporary dependency that learning often requires. Adult learners are, of course, often able to articulate what they want to learn and why they want to learn it. Maximum participation of the learner in the teacher-learner interaction is not only desirable but eminently feasible. The adult learner has a fund of learning and life experience that might be adapted to the current learning situation.

The eduational diagnosis of the individual adult learner is developed in ongoing contact with him. The supervisor observes the supervisee's use of supervision, the level of motivation manifested, the balance of rigidity and flexibility in learning, the level of preparation for, and participation in, conferences, the general attitude toward the content to be learned and toward the learning situation. The supervisor attempts to discern the procedures which elicit the supervisee's best response. Some people learn best in a highly structured situation, some people learn best in a loosely structured situation; some learn through listening, others through reading; some learn only through action in a practice situation, some cannot begin to act until they have learned; some learn best in an individual tutorial situation, others learn best through group interaction; some learn best through ready acceptance of teaching, some learn best through active opposition to content presented; some are ready to learn but are less ready to be taught.

Is resistance to learning manifested in submissiveness, detachment, arrogance, aggression, self-depreciation, dependence, ingratiation? What failures in performance are due to ignorance or inexperience, amenable to change through education and experience, and what problems are the result of personality difficulties? What character defects impede learning and tie up psychic energy that might otherwise be available for learning? Is content learned for self-protection or for mastery of problem situations? Is learning collected as a possession or acquired for the aggrandizement of status? Does the supervisee think his way through a problem or feel his way through it? Is he responsive to a deductive pattern of instruction, moving from the general idea to the particular situation, or does he learn more readily inductively, requiring an experience with a series of similar situations before he can truly grasp the relevant generalization? Is he a fast learner, always ready and anxious for new material, or a learner who needs to take more time in integrating learning?

In a study of social work students, Berengarten (1957) identified three distinct learning patterns. The *experimental-empathetic* learner relies heavily on repetitive experiences as the basis of learning, while combining an intuitive approach with reflective self-appraisal. The *doer* learns from being able to carry out assignments that are specifically and concretely delineated and from the reinforcement of having satisfactorily com-

(me)

pleted the tasks. The *intellectual-empathetic* learner prefers to
conceptualize, critically evaluate, and make the connection between theory and practice. According to Berengarten, a learning
program should be tailored to fit the learning needs of each of
these distinct types.

Individualization implies some understanding of what the
learner risks in learning this content, both internal risks and external risks. The internal risks relate to the meaning this learning has for his self-image and his current belief and attitudinal
system. The external risks concern his relationship with his reference group. Those who believe that the Bible is literal truth
cannot afford to learn the proof in support of the theory of evolution, and the right-wing conservative might feel out of place
with his friends if he accepted liberal ideas about social welfare.

2. It is desirable to engage the supervisee actively in an assessment of what he already knows and what he wants to learn.
This, once again, individualizes the learning needs of this particular supervisee, spares him the boredom of redundant learning, and spares the supervisor the effort of teaching what does
not need to be taught. In addition, the learner's employment
record and his record of experience at the agency give relevant
information about his educational and experiential background.

3. The educational diagnosis is for use. The supervisor, in
preparation for a conference, would need to review what the
supervisee most needs to learn at this particular time, how best
to approach teaching the content to this particular supervisee,
how the supervisee is likely to react in response to the efforts to
teach him this content, and so on.

Individualization implies that each of us has his own
unique, best way of learning. However, while it is recognized
that the supervisor may not always be capable of modulating
her approach to be neatly congruent with the needs of the
learner, she should at least be understandingly aware of the nature of the learner's educational diagnosis.

Throughout this section we have made allusions to the supervisor-supervisee relationship as having crucial significance

for learning in supervision. The teacher-learner relationship is of prime importance because teaching is mainly a problem in human relationships. The term "relationship" as used here means the nature of emotional interaction. In general, learning can take place best when the nature of such interaction is positive, when teacher and learner accept each other and are comfortably relaxed with each other. The level of participation is higher and anxiety is lower in the context of a positive relationship, facilitating learning. There are a number of additional factors which suggest the importance of a good relationship for educational supervision.

Not only must the learner be motivated to accept the content of what needs to be learned, but he must be motivated and ready to accept it from the teacher. A worker resists accepting content offered by a supervisor he does not like and respect. The relationship, if positive, is the bridge over which the material passes from teacher to learner. If the relationship is negative, communication is blocked.

A positive relationship intensifies the impact of the supervisor's educational efforts. There is considerable empirical support for the contention that the nature of the relationship is a powerful variable in determining the supervisee's openness and receptivity to the supervisor's efforts to educate toward change (Goldstein, Heller, and Sechrest 1966, pp. 73–91).

Identification with the supervisor heightens the worker's motivation to learn. As a consequence of identification, the worker wishes to be like the supervisor, to have her competence, and to learn in order to emulate her. Only if the relationship is positive will the worker identify with the supervisor.

In the following quotation the supervisee describes how she uses her supervisor, Morrie, as a source of identification. "I find myself in situations thinking 'Well now, what would Morrie do?' And I'm kind of generalizing from what he does with me. I've never seen him with a client. You know, thinking if I was feeling a certain way, how would he react? I kind of use that" (Amacher 1971, p. 36). (Perhaps identification does, at the beginning, involve a sizable component of imitation.) But as

Steinbeck says, "Only through imitation do we develop toward originality" (*Travels with Charley*).

(Establishing and maintaining a positive relationship with the supervisee is experiential teaching of essential social work content.) In her competence in developing such a relationship, the supervisor is modeling the way in which the supervisee might effectively relate to the client. Having experienced a helping process in educational supervision, the worker is then in a better position to understand what is involved in seeking and using help. As Robinson states, "Since supervision in social casework teaches a helping process, it must itself be a helping process so that the [worker] experiences in his relationship with the supervisor a process similar to the one he must learn to use with his client" (1949, p. 30).

Content in Educational Supervision

Any delineation of the content of supervisory teaching has, of necessity, to be general. An overview of supervision, such as this book, is directed toward workers in many different kinds of agencies who must learn different kinds of content to do their jobs well. However, since all social work agencies have elements in common, there are certain uniformities in what needs to be taught. The following discussion of the basic content of educational supervision is derived from material developed by Helen Harris Perlman. Perlman (1947) points out that what every social worker needs to know is concerned with people, problems, place, and process—the four P's. To this might be added a fifth P—personnel, the person of the worker offering the service.

The nuclear situation for all of social work is that of a client (individual, family, group, or community—*people*) coming, or referred, to a social agency (*place*) for help (*process*) by a social worker (*personnel*). The client comes with a *problem* in social functioning.

Supervisors in every social agency will be teaching something about each of these five content areas. However diverse the specifics of people, place, process, problems, and personnel, these will be matters for the agenda of educational supervision. Despite differences in specifics, in each instance there is a particular group of people, either an individual or collectivity, presenting a particular kind of social problem, seeking help from a social worker who is affiliated with a particular social agency and offers some particular approach to helping. And the worker, in order to perform his job effectively, would need to know about the process by which he hopes to help, about the agency through which he is offering such help, about the people with whom he will be working, about the problems which they present, and about himself as the principal instrumentality for helping.

However diverse the agency, the supervisor has to teach something about how the agency is organized and administered, how it relates to other agencies and fits into the total network of community social services, what the agency's objectives are, what kind of services it offers and under what conditions, how agency policy is formulated and can be changed, and what is the nature of the agency's statuatory authority.

However diverse the social problems with which different agencys are concerned, the supervisor will have to teach something about the "causes" of social problems, community response to particular social problems, the psychosocial nature of these problems, the impact of social problems on different groups in the community, the effect of a particular problem on people's lives, the relationship of agency services to the social problems that are of primary concern to the agency's mandate.

However diverse the clientele served, the supervisor will have to teach something of human behavior in response to the stress of social problems. While the casework supervisor might be primarily concerned with teaching how individuals and families respond to social problems and adjust to them, the group work supervisor and community organization supervisor might be more concerned with teaching how people in collectivities such as groups and communities behave in responding to social problems. In order for the supervisee to understand problematic individual and collective response to social stress, the supervisor needs to teach something of "normal" individual and collective development and behavior.

Whatever the processes employed in helping the client to a restoration of a more effective level of social functioning or ameliorating or preventing social disfunctioning, the supervisor will have to teach something of the technology of helping. This, in the end, is where everything gets put together. Knowledge about people, problem, and place is taught because ultimately it enables the worker to help more effectively. The supervisor has to teach what the worker is to do, how he is to act if he is to help individuals, groups, or communities deal effectively with their social problems. And he has to teach something of the theory that explains why the particular helping technology the agency espouses, whatever it is, is likely to effect change.

In any agency, whatever the methodology for helping, the supervisor teaches something of the sequential nature of the helping process. It is described in a variety of ways: social study, diagnosis, treatment; data gathering, data processing, intervention; obtaining information, processing information, exerting social influence. All of these descriptions, however diverse, imply a process of remedial action based on understanding derived from the facts.

The supervisor further has to teach the supervisee something about himself in developing a greater sense of self-awareness. Nathanson (1962) defines self-awareness as "the capacity of an individual to perceive his responses to other persons and situations realistically and to understand how others view him" (p. 32). Grossbard (1954) notes that "broadly speaking, self-awareness is a person's ability to recognize with a reasonable degree of accuracy how he reacts to the outside world and how the outside world reacts to him" (p. 381; see also Purvis 1972).

People are, of course, not helped by a social agency in dealing with problems of social functioning but by social workers representing the agency. Furthermore, the principal instrumentality for helping is generally the social worker herself.

There are, of course, social utilities administered by social workers which are essential resources for helping, such as homemaker service, foster care, institutions, day care, and income maintenance. Most frequently, however, the principal resource the agency makes available in the process of helping people is the skill and competence of the worker herself. It is the social worker who leads the group, organizes the community, acts as advocate, supports, sustains, clarifies, offers herself as a model for identification, rewards and shapes behavior, and so on.

In work environments where instruments, machines, or mechanical devices of one sort or another are used, they determine how the work is to be done and limit the effects of personality differences among workers. In social work, where the worker is the main instrumentality, the person of the worker determines what is done and how it is done.

Since the worker's personality and behavior are significant determinants of what happens in the worker-client interaction, the supervisee herself, her attitudes, feelings, and behavior become a necessary and inevitable subject of educational supervision. The aim is to develop a greater measure of self-awareness in the worker so that she can act in a deliberate, disciplined, consciously directed manner in the worker-client interaction so as to be optimally helpful to the client. The capacity to perceive one's behavior as objectively as possible, to have free access to one's own feelings without guilt, embarrassment, or discomfort, is a necessary, if not sufficient, prerequisite for the controlled subjectivity the helping process demands. The freedom to use feelings imaginatively and creatively for helping also requires considerable self-awareness.

Developing a high level of worker self-awareness is further necessary because the social problems that are the professional concerns of the worker also affect him personally. Here, unlike the situation in many other professions, there is considerable interpenetration between life and work. The worker may be involved, to some extent, in many of the kinds of problems encountered by the client—parent-child conflict, aging, marital conflict, deviance, illness, financial problems, death. "Living on a job that is so closely allied to life itself makes separation of work from other areas of life exceptionally difficult. Since, in social work, the work task and living are often simultaneously experienced, anxiety is greater than in many other fields of endeavor" (Babcock 1951, p. 417). A supervisor in medical social work writes:

> We got to that part in the record where one relative began talking about problems with unexpected bowel movements with the patient at home. The relative asked R a question to which she didn't know the answer. R offered to invite a doctor to the next group meeting. She read on, but I stopped her and said: "I feel that you have missed the relative's concerns. Let's go back into the experience. What were your feelings at that moment?" She began to laugh uncomfortably and spoke about the whole bowel movement business making her uncomfortable. I asked her: "What did you feel at that moment?" After a pause, she responded that at that moment she didn't really want to listen, to get too closely involved with the relatives re giving patients digitalis. I responded that I could understand and suggested that she might have felt hopeless. "Like what good is talking about these things going to do?" She agreed, describing her anxiety and a sense of being trapped by it. After having her assume the role of the relative and obtain a "feel" for the specific underlying concerns, we role played different ways in which she might have reached for the member's concerns. She particularly liked her idea of reflecting the member's concern to the group, asking whether anyone else had similar concerns or experiences. I found myself being caught in her excitement as we both threw ourselves into the role playing. R searched the record for other places where she disconnected and suggested a doctor to "explain" the reasons behind problems, e.g., bowel movements, catheter, sex. She exclaimed, "Wow, I see how I ran away—that was really scary, but I do sense how I will do it differently next time." (Gitterman 1972, p. 37, reprinted with permission of Jossey-Bass)

Education toward a greater development of self-awareness permits the worker to think objectively about these matters. It provides a greater assurance that the worker's own reactions to these professional problems will not adversely contaminate the helping relationship.

In the following brief excerpt the worker is talking to the

supervisor about a 12-year-old girl named Thelma. The young-
ster is described by the worker as provocative, snide, impudent,
and upsetting. She teases adults, including the supervisee.

> As the student talked about Thelma's behavior and described it in
> some detail in response to my questioning, she suddenly looked as
> though a thought had struck her and said, "You know, I was very much
> like her when I was her age." The student went on to describe how
> she had taunted a Junior High School teacher with certain remarks,
> daring the teacher to punish her. I felt that the worker was really work-
> ing on something and confined myself to listening and encouraging her
> to speak, with an occasional comment. (Gladstone 1967, p. 11)

Awareness of similar life experiences permits the worker to understand the client's behavior.

A somewhat different group of problems relating to educational supervision also calls for developing self-awareness. Any
systematic educational program is in essence a program of
planned change, the teacher being the change agent, the
learner being the target for change. But the pressure to change,
resulting from learning, generates ambivalence and resistance.

The particular content that needs to be learned, the attitudes that need to undergo change, sometimes results in blocks
to learning, to problems in learning. We learn only what we can
emotionally afford to learn. If the content learned is a threat to
our self-esteem, strongly discordant with attitudes and beliefs
that are essential to the maintenance of emotional equilibrium,
we refuse to learn this content. The repertoire of maneuvers
that permit us to shield ourselves from content include all the
mechanisms of defense. Educating toward self-awareness may
help the supervisee resolve some of these resistances to learning. Persistent blocks to learning are the exception rather than
the rule. However, such problems are encountered in a less intense and less pervasive form by all learners. For the reasonably mature learner the work of the ego in the service of adaptation is sufficient to counter the work of the ego in the service of
defense. Learning takes place despite resistance because of the
learner's need and desire to meet the demands of the job.

This discussion of the justifications for concern with development of self-awareness reflects the fact that it is an important content area of educational supervision. The supervisor has the responsibility of teaching the worker about himself as well as teaching the worker about people, problems, place, and process. In fact, social workers tend to perceive the education toward self-awareness as one of the unique aspects of social work supervision. In a study that asked about factors which differentiated social work supervision, "the commonest theme expressed" by the 100 social work respondents was the following: "Because the skill to be developed is the disciplined use of self in professional relationships, supervision in casework affects personality more closely than supervision in other fields which are more dependent on objective skills" (Cruser 1958, p. 23).

The requirement of a didactic psychoanalysis for certification as an analyst is an institutionalized testimonial to the importance of self-awareness in the people-helping professions. The desirability of this objective of educational supervision receives support from at least one empirical study of social workers which suggests a relationship between level of self-awareness and practice competence (Bruck 1963).

For each of these content areas—people, problem, place, process, and personnel—there are objectives in terms of knowledge, attitudes, and skills. For instance, in learning to help senior citizens adjust to the problems of institutional living, the worker needs to have some knowledge of the biopsychosocial aspects of aging and to have interpersonal skills in relating to senior citizens. But teaching-learning also involves attitudinal changes toward the aged. It involves the dissolution of some stereotypes so that a more realistic, more optimistic attitude is developed; a change from disdain, dread and repulsion, despair, and negativism to the perception that the aged have strength and a sense of self-worth, can respond to interests, are likable, friendly, and capable of change (Cohen 1972).

Learning objectives, whatever their nature in the different content areas, should be stated as explicitly as possible and in behavioral terms that are clearly job related. "Developing a more acceptable attitude toward the offender," "understanding the drug addict," and "increasing the homefinding capacity of foster-care workers" are all educational objectives. It is not clear, however, what the supervisor hopes the supervisee will do differently as a result of such learning.

Educational Supervision versus Therapy

The task of developing self-awareness as a responsibility of educational supervision presents social work with a persistent and often-discussed dilemma. Development of self-awareness is analogous to the insight objectives of psychotherapy. How then does one discharge this responsibility while rejecting the charge that one is "caseworking the caseworker?" A distinction, then, needs to be made between educational supervision and therapy.

Resolving the apparent dilemma of being therapeutic (with a small *t*) while not engaging in Therapy, requires some adherence to guidelines. The supervisor recognizes and respects the limits and restrictions of her role. Her responsibility is to help the supervisee become a better worker, not necessarily a better person. Her legitimate concern is with the professional activities of the supervisee, but she has no sanction to intrude into the personal life of the supervisee. The concern is with changes in professional identity rather than changes in personal identity. The supervisor asks, How can I help you do your work? rather than How can I help you? Ekstein and Wallerstein (1972) note that "in supervision we aim at a change in skill, a change in the use of the professional self while in psychotherapy we aim at changes which embrace the total adaptive functioning of the individual" (p. 92).

The valid focus of attention is the supervisee's work, rather than the supervisee herself. Only as the supervisee's behavior, feelings, and attitudes create some difficulty in the performance of professional tasks, then and only then, do they become a legitimate matter for supervisory concern. The supervisor is not entitled to intervene with regard to behavior, feelings, and attitudes which, however problematic or deviant, are not clearly manifested in some job-related interaction.)

What is of exclusive concern is the supervisee's work rather than her worth. This is not to deny that professional growth does have consequences related to personal growth. The professional self is, after all, a significant sector in the total personal self configuration. But if the personal self undergoes growth and change, as is likely, this happens as an incidental, derivative by-product of the effort at professional growth.

In implementing these guidelines the supervisor keeps the discussion focused on the client's situation and experience rather than the worker's situation and experience. The discussion is work-centered not worker-centered. Further, the focus is on *what* the worker did or failed to do rather than *why* he did it. If there is any discussion of the reasons that may help explain the worker's behavior, it is centered on the current work situation rather than in any psychodynamic exploration of developmental antecedents. In indicating what should not be done, Feldman, Sponitz, and Nagelberg say:

> Supervisors, in discussing their workers' performance, put undue emphasis on discovering the inhibitions of their supervisees, looking for psychological causes. They look for the remote cause of an earlier relationship of the worker to his mother, even going so far as to think of possible frustrations in early feeding. Though any of these factors may still apply, a supervisor should examine carefully whether a worker's negative reactions are not based on the worker's present relationship with his symbolic parent, the supervisor, who should be supplying needed technical knowledge. (1953, p. 158)

Current reality as an explanation of workers' problems should always be examined first. Personal problems should be discussed through their derivative manifestations in the work assigned. A worker may

> reveal marked anxiety in trying to help a client who rejects her child. ... [The supervisor] does not explore the [worker's] early experience in his relationship with his own mother. She focuses instead on eliciting and on understanding the [worker's] feelings about *this* mother.

She directs him to consider how this woman came to feel and act as she does and she holds the worker accountable to try to understand and meet the woman's need for help. (Towle 1954, p. 123)

Although the following comments by Ekstein and Wallerstein (1972) relate to supervision of the psychiatric resident, they are pertinent to this discussion. The authors comment that

both supervision and psychotherapy are interpersonal helping processes working with the same affective components, with the essential difference between them created by the difference in purpose. (Though both are helping processes, the purpose of the helping experience is different.) Whatever practical problems the patient may bring to his psychotherapist, they are always viewed in the light of the main task: the resolution of inner conflict. Whatever personal problems the student may bring to his supervisor, they are likewise always seen in terms of the main task: leading him toward greater skill in his work with his patients. While it is true that the patient may occasionally benefit in practical matters, or perhaps even from direct practical advice, and while it is equally true that the student will frequently benefit in a personal sense, they have made these gains in the course of following the main purpose of their relationship with the helper. If the main purpose of a relationship is maintained throughout, the difference is clearly apparent between the type of relationship called psychotherapy and the one called supervision. . . . In psychotherapy the patient essentially sets his own goals, with . . . the proviso always that these goals may change as the therapeutic process itself develops and makes for change. The therapist has no vested interest in any particular degree or direction of change. In supervision, on the other hand, the clinical setting, whose representative is the supervisor, sets both its requirements and its goals in terms of standards of professional performance and clinical service currently rendered and to be attained. The institution thus furnishes the external yardstick to which both supervisor and student must measure up. (pp. 254–55, reprinted with permission of International Universities Press)

Shifting from educational supervision to psychotherapy involves an unwarranted and inappropriate shift in roles. As Stiles (1963) says, "A supervisory relationship contains an implicit contract: the worker is responsible for attempting to maximize his performance and continuing his professional development; the supervisor is responsible for helping him achieve these goals" (p. 24). The parameters of the contract, as noted, are the worker's "performance" and "professional development." Concern with personal development is an unwarranted and unanticipated extension of the explicit contract. Having consented to an administrative-educational process, the worker cannot legitimately have a psychotherapy process imposed on him. "Therapizing" the relationship suggests that the supervisor is entering areas of the worker's life concerning which he has no organizational sanction or authority.

Unlike the client in psychotherapy, the supervisee is not free to terminate his relationship with the supervisor. Thus, attempted transformation of educational supervision into psychotherapy is even more likely to be resented by the captive worker. Supervisees understandably resent any invitation to engage in a psychic strip-tease: "I had gotten into this conversation with my supervisor where he managed to dig into a whole lot of personal stuff and I bite pretty quick; if someone encourages me, out it comes. And I walked out of the office really angry with myself for having done it" (Amacher 1971, p. 225).

The attempt to convert educational supervision into psychotherapy is antitherapeutic. The worker who views himself as capable and adequate resents the implied invitation to assume the role of a client. It tends to erode supervisee self-confidence. The supervisee, as an agency employee, should be perceived quite differently from a client. We have every right to perceive the worker as essentially healty and capable and ask that he meet certain expectations.

If the supervisee becomes a client of the supervisor in a shift from educational supervision to psychotherapy, the focus of supervisory attention must shift from the agency client to the worker. The needs of the supervisee as client then take precedence over the needs of the agency client. This is a subversion of the primary responsibility and obligation of the agency toward its client.

To accept the supervisee for psychotherapy requires a modification of work standards. The criteria for a decision regarding enforcement of agency standards become the therapeutic needs of the supervisee-client rather than the needs of agency clients. This too is contrary to the primary obligation of the agency. Exercise of administrative sanctions required in maintaining adequate standards may be antitherapeutic for the supervisee-client. The supervisor cannot at the same time be a psychotherapist to the supervisee and guardian of agency standards.

To summarize, confusion results from the fact that educational supervision toward developing job-related self-awareness and psychotherapy are similar in some essential respects. Both encourage self-examination in the context of a meaningful relationship, both are directed toward personal growth and change, both provoke anxiety. The psychodynamics of both processes and the techniques employed are the same. The distinction lies primarily in purpose, scope, expectations, and sanctions employed.

The available data suggest that most supervisors and supervisees understand, and accept, the limited definition of the supervisor's responsibility as outlined here. Most of the 853 respondents to a recent questionnarie made a clear distinction between professional development and personal development. The *professional* development of the supervisee was selected by both supervisors and supervisees as one major objective of supervision. Conversely, both groups selected "ensuring the more complete development of the supervisee as a mature *person*" as among the three least important objectives. Satisfaction "in helping the supervisee grow and develop in *professional* competence" was the main satisfaction in supervision for the largest percentage of supervisors (88 percent). Less than 1 percent of them, however, checked "helping supervisees with their *personal* problems" as a source of satisfaction. Similarly, the statement of dissatisfaction in supervision least frequently checked by supervisees was "My supervisor tends to become too involved in my personal problems," indicating that transformation of supervision into psychotherapy was not currently a problem for most of the respondents (Kadushin 1974).

Supervisors responding to admonitions that they have no

right to "casework the caseworker" adhere to the dichotomy of professional versus personal development even more rigorously than do supervisees. If anything, supervisees indicate a greater willingness to accept the therapeutic intrusion of the supervisor than supervisors appear willing to offer it. In response to the incomplete sentence, "If personal problems came up in my work with clients I would prefer that my supervisor . . . ," 48 percent of the supervisees said that they wanted the supervisor to "identify the problems and help me resolve them" whereas only 30 percent of the supervisors prefer this response. Conversely, 44 percent of the supervisors would "identify the problem and help supervisees get outside help" but only 11 percent of the supervisees preferred this response. Supervisors, more often than supervisees, saw the legitimate source of help for job-related personal problems as lying outside the supervisory relationship (Kadushin 1974).

Establishing guidelines for what is appropriate in a supervisory conference is easier than applying them. The following excerpt is a supervisor's introspective review of the difficulty in making a decision in such a situation. The problem lies in deciding when a worker's difficulty is purely personal and when it is task related.

Vera [the worker] brought up the fact that she was experiencing some confusion herself about the prospect of marrying her present boyfriend and that the two of them were involved in pre-marital counseling. She expressed doubt as to her ability to help someone else deal with a problem similar to one she herself was experiencing.

I was caught a little off guard and likewise experienced a certain element of confusion—a few quick thoughts ran through my mind, and I responded by doing "nothing." My quick thoughts leading to this response went something like this: avoid taking on the role of therapist; personal problems of the supervisee are not relevant here unless they interfere with job or learning performance and there is not yet sufficient evidence to this effect; the fact that Vera is both aware of and getting outside help for her problem is good; I want to convey to her that having some problems does not necessarily prevent a person from providing effective professional help; perhaps the best way to operationalize all of the above thoughts is to simply shrug off Vera's remarks and keep the discussion focused on how to help the client. Vera had no trouble picking up the fact that I preferred not to get into a discussion of her personal problems. She did not pursue the matter any further and appeared able to continue concentrating on her client's situation. With the exception of a brief comment or two, she has not brought the matter up in subsequent sessions, nor have I.

On hindsight, I am neither totally dissatisfied nor completely over- joyed with the way I handled this matter. The basic issue is if, when, and how a supervisor should get involved in dealing with the personal problems of a supervisee. In the literature I have looked at, the issue is frequently raised and always answered in essentially the same way— that is, the supervisor should be aware of and deal with the emotional aspects of learning (fears, resistances, etc.) but should not focus on the personal needs and problems of the supervisee unless these difficul- ties are such as to significantly interfere with work performance—and then the supervisor should not "treat" the supervisee but encourage him to seek outside help.

I am satisfied that my response and the rationale behind it were in accord with the literature on this issue. However, I now question one of the basic assumptions upon which this response was based, i.e., the lack of interference with work-learning performance. In starting the process of evaluating Vera's work, I have become aware of a tendency on her part to shy away from offering help to clients in the area of mar- ital conflict, although not hesitating to offer and provide it in other problem areas (housing, child-parent relationships, etc.). Also, it now occurs to me that Vera may not have been asking for any help with her personal problems (she was already involved in outside counseling), but only for help in resolving her concern about being able to help someone else with a problem she saw as similar to her own. If this was the case, I would consider her concern to represent the kind of emo- tional aspect of learning which *is* the responsibility of the supervisor to deal with. In retrospect, viewing the pattern of Vera's work perfor- mance I think the problem was more job related than I had originally thought.

The problem is a difficult one because the worker is likely to react negatively to both indifference and excessive in- terest. If the supervisor ignores the supervisee's comment about what is apparently a purely personal problem, he is likely to feel rejected. If the supervisor shows excessive interest in the problem, it can be interpreted as an unwarranted intrusion. Recognition of the worker's statement without pursuing it might be the difficult response of choice. A frank, explicit statement by the supervisor of what he is doing might help: "I appreciate that this must be a difficult problem for you but I really don't think it is appropriate for us to discuss it at length here."

The Individual Conference

structure and scheduling

The most frequent context for supervision is the individual conference. It is often supplemented and sometimes replaced by alternatives such as the group conference (see chapter 6). Nevertheless the individual conference is still the principal locus of supervision; 86 percent of supervisors and supervisees indicated, in response to a questionnaire, that this was true in their experience (Kadushin 1974).

The individual conference is essentially a dyadic interview to fulfill the administrative, educational, and supportive functions of supervision. It is, for educational purposes, an individual tutorial. Like all interviews, the individual conference requires certain formalities, structure, and differential role assignment. It should be a regularly scheduled meeting at some mutually convenient time. It should be conducted in a place that ensures privacy and protection from interruption, is physically comfortable and conducive to good, audible communication.

The effects of failure to guard against interruptions and of differences in supervisor-supervisee orientation to conferences are illustrated in the following comment by a supervisee.

We only have one hour, which is really poor because when I do see him there are constant interruptions. And I make a list before I go in there. First of all because I know I have to go boom, boom, boom. And John doesn't go boom, boom, boom. He's much slower than me in his pace of communicating, much more thorough. I would take a quick answer and go on to the next thing. . . . Today he couldn't see me at the regular time but could see me for half an hour after the staff conference. Well the conference was late and then there were interruptions. So it's gotten so that I reduce my discussions to the most specific, concrete kinds of things. (Amacher 1971, p. 71)

Although formal scheduling is desirable, there may be occasions when informal, on-the-spot conferences are necessary. Social work is full of stressful emergencies that often cannot wait for the regular conference. At the point of crisis the worker's motivation for learning is apt to be most intense. Consequently it is good to seize the teachable moment.

However, the unscheduled, off-the-cuff, "may-I-see-you-for-a-quick-minute" conference has its own disadvantages. Because it does come up suddenly, there is no time for preparation. Judgments are made without sufficient opportunity to carefully consider alternatives. Because such conferences snatch time from other scheduled activities, they are apt to be hurried and harried. The worker may feel guilty and apologetic about intruding on time the supervisor had scheduled for other activities. In contrast, the worker can comfortably use the scheduled conference time with a guilt-free sense of entitlement. A separate time, a separate place, a planned encounter symbolically affirm the importance of supervisory conferences. Persistent requests for conferences on the run tend to depreciate their significance.

An attempt to understand the individual worker's pattern of using supervision may be helpful. Some workers may deliberately, if not entirely consciously, force the supervisor into frequent informal conferences as a way of avoiding formal conferences. This pattern may express the worker's undue dependence on, or hostility toward, the supervisor. The supervisor must decide when an emergency is truly a crisis and when it is more an expression of a supervisee's rather than a client's need.

preparation

A scheduled conference begins before it actually starts, and this is one of its prime advantages. It begins in the preparation for the conference by both supervisee and supervisor. The supervisee submits some record of his work—written recording, tape recording, log forms, work schedules, reports completed, a work plan. The supervisee's formal preparation of this material requires some explicit self-review of his work.

The supervisor reviews whatever examples of the supervisee's current activity have been made available. Reviewing the material with the responsibilities of educational supervision in mind, the supervisor develops the teaching syllabus for the next conference or series of conferences. A conscious effort is made to select some cluster of information or concepts for teaching. The supervisor, in preparation for teaching, might review his own notes and the relevant literature on the material he plans to teach. Preparation for a tutorial requires the same care as does teaching a seminar in a school of social work.

Practice knowledge and competence are indispensible for effective first-line supervision generally, and for educational supervision in particular. The power of expertise, which is a principal source of the supervisor's administrative authority, requires this. The responsibilities of educational supervision further require a solid grasp of the subject matter relevant to agency practice. The supervisor as a source of identification, as an admired practitioner, and as a model of effective practice, needs to project the image and the reality of competence.

Scott (1969) found that professionally oriented workers preferred a supervisor "to know the theoretical fundamentals of their discipline—be skilled in teaching casework methods and capable of offering professionally competent assistance" (pp. 94–95). The supervisee looks to the supervisor to have available a fund of previously developed solutions to practice problems. Studies of student evaluation of teaching show that a thorough knowledge of subject matter content is a necessary, if not sufficient, requirement for good teaching.

The worker's activity, as evidenced in the material submitted, is the "textbook" for the "course." It provides the basic relevant material for teaching, and the teaching objectives selected should be tied in with the worker's on-the-job activity; therefore the supervisor not only needs to know the content to be taught, but also to be thoroughly familiar, through preparatory review, with the worker's activity.

In administrative supervision, case records, worker's reports, and other forms are reviewed for evidence of services rendered in compliance with agency procedure; in educational supervision the same records are reviewed for evidence of deficiencies in performance which require training.

In addition to the content and context of the material to be taught, the supervisor also has to review his knowledge of the learner. Given the special learning needs and unique learning patterns of this particular supervisee, how can the selected teaching objectives be best presented? What teaching techniques and approaches might work best with this supervisee? To answer these questions the supervisor should review the educational diagnosis of the supervisee and where he is now in his learning.

Preparation involves ensuring the availability of instructional materials that might be needed in conference teaching. If the use of certain agency forms is to be taught, copies should be at hand. If policies are to be discussed, the agency manual should be accessible. If references are to be cited to support teaching and to stimulate out-of-conference reading by the supervisee, the books and articles should be obtained in advance and made available.

The advance planning and preparation provide the supervisor with a focus and a structure which she holds lightly and flexibly, ready to discard or change in response to supervisee's learning needs as they are actually manifested in the conference. Selectivity in choosing what to teach is a significant aspect of preparation. To attempt to teach everything, all at once, is to guarantee failure to teach anything. The supervisor has to select some limited focus for teaching.

process

Once the conference is under way, how does the supervisor teach? We have noted that the starting point for educational supervision is the report of the worker's activity on the job, shared with the supervisor in advance or verbally during the conference. "Supervision is 'post-facto' teaching, a retrospective scrutiny of interactions and their reciprocal effects" (Fleming and Benedek 1966, p. 238). The supervisor engages the worker

in a systematic, explicit, critical analysis of the work he did and
the work he is planning to do, with an individual client, a family, a group, or a community. The endeavor is to provide the
worker "with a structured learning situation which facilitates
maximum growth through a process which frees potentialities"
(Ekstein and Wallerstein 1972, p. 10). The conference is an opportunity for guided self-observation, for systematic introspec-
tive-retrospective review of work that has been done, for thinking about the work as "recollected in tranquillity." Experience
is fragmented and seemingly chaotic. The supervisor helps the
supervisee impose some order and meaning on experience. The
supervisor helps the supervisee identify the principles that can
guide him in understanding what he needs to do.

The supervisor does this by asking questions, requesting
clarification, freeing, supporting, stimulating, affirming, directing, challenging, and supplementing the worker's thinking. The
supervisor calls attention to errors in the worker's performance,
missed opportunities, apparent misunderstandings, gaps and in-
consistencies. The supervisor introduces new ideas, shares relevant knowledge and experience, explains and illustrates similarities and differences between this and other situations,
enlarging the worker's perspective. The supervisor poses relevant alternatives for consideration. A study of tape-recorded
conferences indicated that the supervisor's questions very seldom came across with the message of,

"I am testing you to see if you know this," but more often as
"What do you think, because we have to decide this together?" or
"What do you know about this, because I want to help fill in what you
don't know so you can help the client more effectively?" That is, [su-
pervisors] seemed interested in knowing what the [worker] thought, to
put their ideas together or to help the [worker] become more knowledgeable, not to evaluate in the judgmental sense the worker's amount
of knowledge. (Nelsen 1973, p. 190)

The supervisor can offer a small lecture, engage the supervisee in a Socratic dialogue or a give-and-take discussion, offer
a demonstration, participate in a role play, listen to and analyze

with the supervisee a tape-recorded playback, and offer material for reading.

Most supervisors apparently use a mix of expository direct teaching and dialectical-hypothetical indirect teaching procedures. Expository teaching amounts to "telling"; dialectical-hypothetical teaching involves questions and comments which help the supervisee think things out for himself and attempt to find his own answers. It comes close to the guided discussion method.

The supervisor selects her approach not only so that it is congenial with the learning patterns of the supervisee but also so that it is appropriate to the content to be taught. Agency forms and procedure can be taught didactically and by providing relevant reading material. Interviewing techniques cannot be effectively taught in that manner; role playing is the more appropriate teaching approach for this kind of content.

A supervisor says, "The worker expressed his anxiety about medical terms and his limited understanding of them, and I recommended a book which contained useful information about them," illustrating an appropriate approach for the content to be taught. In a different situation, however, another supervisor says that "her supervisee faced a difficult decision whether to recommend foster care for these children or placing a homemaker in the home. I engaged in a discussion of her thinking of the advantages and disadvantages of each of the alternatives." In each of these conferences the teaching methods were appropriate for the different content that needed to be taught.

The methods employed have to be appropriate to the ultimate objective of educational supervision, which is knowledge for use. Rapoport's (1954) definition of supervision as a "disciplined tutorial process wherein principles are transformed into practice skills" calls explicit attention to this focus. The classroom teacher can be satisfied with intellectual acquisition of content by the learner. Educational supervision has to aim at emotional assimilation of the content so that behavioral changes result from teaching. The progression is from information into knowledge, knowledge into understanding, understanding into changed behavior in interaction with the client. New behavior is then tested in interaction with the client to see whether the change is effective. Feedback from the client and the supervisor permits the worker to correct his learning, modify his behavior, test it again, and examine the feedback.

To promote transfer of learning so that the same problems do not have to be rediscussed as they are encountered in different cases, the teacher directs learning toward a clarification of general principles that can be validly applied from case to case. She moves from specificity to generality, relating the case situation to the principle and the principle to the case.

Teaching techniques have, of course, different effects depending on the attitude, skill, conviction, and appropriateness with which they are used. "What do you think?" and "How do you feel about it?" can sound like tired clichés. They can also be said, however, in a spirit which suggests that the supervisor warmly welcomes a more active participation of the supervisee in the learning process. The aim is to develop an interactional pattern of mutuality. Despite the elements of mutuality in the relationship there is, or should be, an imbalance in the knowledge and skills which the participants bring to the encounter. The supervisor has to accept the responsibility for having more experience, being more knowledgeable and skillful and having available what the profession provides in practice wisdom and problem solutions. Supervisor and supervisee are not peers. As Robinson says, "to start with an assumption of equality is to deny the student her right to any learning process" (1949, p. 42). The supervisor has the ultimate responsibility for what takes place in the teaching-learning situation.

In the following passage a supervisor describes how she found her own congenial approach to educational supervision in offering leadership in the context of mutuality.

Perhaps one of the most difficult aspects of the role of supervisor, for me, was making criticisms and suggestions. As nice as my supervisory theory sounded, when I attempted to put it into practice, I had trouble.

I found myself saying to Ruth, as she reported her meetings to me, "Did you find out about . . . ?" "Did you turn this in yet?" "Well, did you think of trying this . . . ?" Ruth's reaction to all of these "did you's" was, naturally, very defensive. Her answer was, most often, something like "Well, I didn't have time" in a very cold, flat voice, or "It seemed more important to. . . ." I was sounding more like a policeman-mother than a helpful supervisor.

I began to experiment with different ways of saying the same things, or getting the same point across, without such an authoritarian ring. My first idea was to hedge a little, to not come on so strong. I began saying "Well, you know, you might be interested in trying something like this . . ." or "Maybe one thing you could do, too, is to attempt to. . . ." When I hedged and hawed in this manner, Ruth wasn't nearly as defensive, but I still wasn't getting the desired result. Now she wasn't taking me seriously. I seemed to have no authority at all now, rather than too much. Her answer very often was "Maybe I'll try it" or "I'll think about it," very lethargically. When I realized that this approach was failing also, I put my head to work, and came up with another idea. I was trying to learn from Ruth and she from me. I needed to respect her and encourage her; I needed to give her the chance to express herself in an open and nonjudgmental atmosphere.

What I was attempting to teach her was my own techniques, my way of doing things and of thinking, of handling groups, of being a social worker. Therefore, when I suggested something to Ruth, I was giving her my ideas, what I thought, what I needed to know, what I would do. Individual supervision is a very personal experience. Therefore, I felt I could say these things to Ruth in just that way. At our next meeting together I said to Ruth, "I think what I would like to know from this girl is . . . ," "I think the first thing I might try, would be to . . . ," "For me to do this. . . ."

At first I was afraid of what Ruth's reaction would be to my great emphasis on "I," but my fears were quickly dispelled. It worked beautifully. Ruth's reactions were something like "Oh ya? I didn't think of that" or "Wait a minute, why would you do that?" When I gave her my thoughts, as a person in a supervisory capacity, she was able to relate herself to me as a person in the student role.

I realize this type of approach wouldn't work well for everyone, although it did work for me in this one case. One snag, however, that came hand in hand with this new way of doing things, was that it evoked questions such as "Why would you do that?" I was pleased she wanted to know my thoughts and that she wanted to discuss it further. Nevertheless, I didn't feel comfortable just telling her my reasons, without her having to think about it. Yet I dislike it when someone tries to "play teacher" with me, and turns my questions back around on me. I didn't want to answer, "Because X, Y and Z," nor did I want to reply, "Well, why do you think?"

My solution again stemmed from the philosophy I tried to adopt; that I was there to learn from her as well as she from me. The next time she asked me my reasons why, I told her of this dilemma; that I didn't want to give her all the answers, but I didn't want to be the quiz master either; and then we struck a compromise. If she would tell me some reasons she could find for doing it that way, I might learn some new things. Then I would tell her my reasons for taking that approach, and she might learn some new things from me.

As funny as it all sounds right now, and was at that time too, it really worked well. Whenever Ruth started to ask why, she would stop herself and say "Is that because . . . ?" To which I would always reply politely, "Yes, and not only that. . . ." It became a kind of a game I suppose, but the game, and the very ritualized aspect of it provided some very necessary elements to our interviews. It helped us both to realize our roles more fully, through spelling them out so clearly in this one aspect of the supervisory relationship. It added humor to our sessions. It helped us deal with our embarrassment, by laughing a little and thereby relieving the tension. And perhaps most importantly, it brought us closer to each other; we began to like each other and to work much better together.

Several distinctly different orientations toward supervision have been identified which tend to result in different approaches to educational supervision. An existential–supervisee-centered orientation sees supervision as concerned with the development of supervisees' self-understanding, self-awareness, and emotional growth. The emphasis is on the workers' feelings. The super*visee* has major responsibility for what he wants to learn, and the focus of supervision is on the *way* the worker does his work and the nature of his relationship to the client.

A didactic–task-centered orientation sees supervision as primarily concerned with the development of the supervisees' professional skills. The emphasis is on the workers' thinking. The super*visor* has the primary responsibility for what is taught, and the focus of discussion is on the content of *what* the worker is doing, his activities with, and in behalf of, his clients.

A scale listing these two orientations as opposite poles was offered to supervisors and supervisees (Kadushin 1974). They were asked to indicate the point on the scale which denoted the orientation that they thought worked most effectively for them.

The tendency for both supervisors and supervisees was to check the midpoint, indicating that the most desirable orientation was a rather even mixture of the two approaches. Despite the general overall agreement, however, supervisors leaned toward the didactic–task-oriented–professional growth approach somewhat more decidedly than did supervisees.

Hamachek (1971) studied the effects of different approaches to supervision, and his results

suggest the importance of *both* affective and cognitive component parts of the supervisory process. An individual who functions at high levels on affective dimensions such as empathy, respect, genuineness and concreteness may be a good counselor, but without high cognitive skills he may have trouble "teaching" or "supervising" a counselor-in-training. In other words, a supervisor cannot just respond to or focus on feelings, but he should also be able to discuss and analyze these feelings. (p. 121)

Goin and Kline (1974) videotaped those supervisors of psychiatric residents who were consistently evaluated as most competent by students. They then analyzed the videotapes of these and other supervisors in an effort to determine the distinctive behaviors manifested by such supervisors in individual conferences. "Good supervisors were shown to be those who made supervision a didactic experience with the focus of attention on the patients" (p. 213). This research finding supports the value of more didactically oriented educational supervision. Other studies of learning in supervision tend to indicate that even in teaching such interpersonal skills as empathy, a didactically oriented approach is effective (Payne, Winter, and Bell 1972).

The desirable balance between didactic and existential orientations may be different for the different levels of intervention (case, group, or community) and for different kinds of approaches at a given level. For instance Matarazzo (1971) found, in her review of teaching and learning of psychotherapeutic skills, that

the behavior-modification student-therapist requires primarily didactic training, and a much smaller emphasis is placed upon the experiential or relationship aspects, than is given to other forms of psychotherapy. The behavior therapist's task is one of observation, analysis, development of a program, and implementation of this program. The behavioral and attitudinal aspects of the program apparently are presumed to be sufficiently explicit that they depend less for their efficacy upon more general behavior characteristics of the particular behavioral engineer who administers them. (p. 919)

This observation is supported, to some extent, by transcripts of supervision sessions of behavioral modification therapists (Wolpe 1972a,b,c; 1973a,b). The following passage describes the teaching method of a behavior modification–oriented supervisor in educational supervision.

A supervisee who was working in a mental hospital with a group of psychotic, borderline psychotic and chronic alcoholic patients, had difficulty in summarizing the discussion of the treatment sessions. There were realistic barriers which interfered with the behavior of summarizing. The meetings were not always highly organized; the discussions at times were rambling; and many statements were part of the psychotic delusionary system of some of the patients. Nevertheless, both [supervisee] and [supervisor] agreed that summary was essential as part of the treatment process in order to focus the patients on those considerations, processes, and suggestions occurring during the meeting which might have been useful to them. Ideally, it was agreed that eventually the patients should summarize the material, since this was also a means of involving them and ascertaining the degree of involvement in their own treatment. Thus, the ultimate goal in this sequence was the evaluation by the patients of the therapeutic discussion. The steps in the graduated sequence which the supervisee would have to perform were as follows:
1. Describing to the instructor a summary of the discussion.
2. Summarizing one or two points of discussion to the patients.
3. Summarizing all the major points of the discussion to the patients.
4. Involvement of one of the patients in summarizing one of the points in discussion.
5. Involvement of several patients, each of whom would add a number of points for summary.
6. Involvement of a majority of the patients in the total summary of the group discussion.

The first step was already within the skill repertoire of the worker.

Following the establishment of the plan, he readily summarized to the supervisor the major points of the meeting. After this the supervisor, with the agreement of the worker, assigned him the responsibility for summarizing two points of the meeting to the patients. The same procedures were used until the worker was able to summarize most of the major points made in the meeting. Then, the supervisor assisted the supervisee to plan how he would involve one person from the patients themselves in the summarizing. After four weeks the worker was able to involve a majority of patients in the process of summarizing. It should be pointed out that after the second step, the worker was highly encouraged to take the next steps, and each subsequent success resulted in increased willingness to experiment. Success in an area where an individual has previously met with failure is a powerful reinforcer. (Rose 1970, pp. 13–14)

It should be noted that incidental learning goes on side-by-side with intentional teaching. Much is caught that is not explicitly taught. Consequently the supervisor has to be careful that her interpersonal behavior is congruent with her teaching about such interpersonal behavior. The supervisor who behaves non-acceptingly toward workers is not likely to teach the concept of acceptance successfully. In this instance the supervisor does not exemplify in her own behavior the attitudinal approach she is professing to teach.

The supervisor who says "I am telling you that what you are supposed to do is to let the client make his own decision about what he wants to do," is not teaching what he intended to teach, namely self-determination.

The following quotation shows a supervisor's awareness of incidental learning:

The client was intent on purchasing rather than renting a house and was asking for the agency's help in this regard. The worker was anxious to be of some help but was convinced that the client's decision to purchase was unwise and probably unrealistic. She asked for my advice about how to help the client to change her mind and give up the idea of purchasing. On the basis of what we knew about this client and her circumstances, I completely agreed with the worker's conclusion [that purchase was unwise and unrealistic] as well as her rationale for it. However, I saw in this situation a good opportunity to focus on the understanding and application of basic social work concepts, particularly that of client self-determination.

One way in which I attempted to teach this concept was by example—in response to the worker's request for advice about getting the client to change her mind, I refrained from telling her what to do or not do in this particular situation, allowing her the freedom to formulate and carry out her own intervention. Instead I brought up and attempted to focus our discussion of the situation in terms of the concept of client self-determination and a couple of other concepts I thought were relevant (i.e., empathy, starting where the client is). At the end of our discussion I simply indicated that next time we could discuss whatever it is the worker decides to do, and the results. I had in mind analyzing the extent to which the worker's activity represented an application of the concepts we had discussed, thus reinforcing learning through repetition and praise, if deserved.

The supervisor teaches and the supervisee learns through feedback. It would be impossible to learn to play golf if we never saw where the ball went after we hit it. We need to know how we are doing, what we are doing right, what needs to be changed. Feedback reinforces learning that "works" and helps correct faulty learning. We learn from our mistakes only if we can find out what they are and have the opportunity of analyzing them.

Whereas supervisors tend to hesitate about being critical of a supervisee's work, supervisees welcome appropriate and constructive criticism. One survey found that among the main sources of supervisee dissatisfaction was that supervisors "were not sufficiently critical so that the worker did not know what he was doing wrong or what needed changing" (Kadushin 1974). Workers seem both to anticipate and to welcome instruction, direction, and structure from the supervisor. They do, apparently, look to her to learn what they need to know in order to do their job effectively. Supervisees deserve and appreciate explicit, definite feedback. Goldhammer (1969), discussing supervision of schoolteachers, makes this point:

Perhaps the most rapid and efficient way to alienate one's supervisees is by hedging and by pussyfooting. Teacher: So you think I was really sarcastic with them? Supervisor: Uh, no, I didn't really say that. You are generally sympathetic and friendly with the youngsters, but some of your remarks today, were, uh, less kindly than I've known them to be in the past. Teacher: Some of my behavior today was unkindly? Supervisor: Well, uh, no, not really, but, uh. . . . (p. 344)

To engage in the following kind of dialogue is not very helpful: "You're doing fine! Keep it up." "Keep what up?" "Just what you're doing" (Ekstein and Wallerstein 1972, p. 145).

We can expect the workers, as reasonably healthy people, to be able to take valid criticism without falling apart. It is, therefore, not necessary to balance every criticism with a compliment. Not only does this often put the supervisor in a false position, it is also demeaning to the worker. One supervisee said, "I knew something bad was coming up because she started to give me all that sweet-talking praise." A supervisor expresses her own response to the dilemma:

Should I always temper a criticism with a compliment? Should I make up compliments, or pick out small, good points, if I can't find enough to go around? Should I just offer each compliment as it occurs to me? I'm sure it sounds silly now, but at the time, it was really a problem. The solution I arrived at was simply to play it by ear. I couldn't bring myself to make up phoney compliments, or pick out pretty points to compliment her on, or to temper each criticism with a compliment. My main focus here was to be open, honest and realistic. If something could have been done better, I felt it was important to let Carol know. If something was done well, this was also important information.

The supervisor needs to be constructively critical. This involves offering an explanation in support of the criticism, making the criticism specific, offering clear alternatives that the supervisee might consider, and making concrete recommendations for changes in his work (Miller and Oetting 1966). It is not necessarily wrong to say that a worker's performance is bad. It is only wrong if the reasons for the judgment are vague, or invalid, or cannot be documented, or if they are presented in a glib, dogmatic, authoritative manner.

If simple, helpful solutions to the professional problems the supervisee faces are available from practice wisdom, theory, the literature, or the research of social work, they should be shared forthrightly with the worker. If she can learn them in this way, it is the simplest, most direct way of effective teaching. If the worker fails to learn in response to such direct, didactic instruction, nothing much is lost and another, more indirect, approach can then be used./

Some supervisees find the Socratic approach an offensive manipulation in which they are led to develop the answer the supervisor wants them to develop. They feel it would be more efficient, and less demeaning, if the supervisor told them directly what he thought they needed to know. A supervisee writes,

> First he asks me why I think I did it? Then he asks me what I hoped to accomplish by doing it? Then he asks me what if I hadn't done it, what do I think would have happened? Then he asks me what else do I think I could have done? Then he asks me how the client might have responded if I did this? Hell, it took a half hour. In two minutes he could have told me what was wrong with what I did and what it might have been best for me to do.

Other supervisees, however, learn nothing from being told but find exhilaration in working out their own answers in response to this kind of Socratic dialogue. Once again we come to the wisdom and necessity of individualizing teaching procedures.

Feedback is important for the supervisor as well as the supervisee. Monitoring verbal and nonverbal responses, specifically requesting reaction where only limited or ambiguous reactions are communicated, the supervisor needs to be constantly alert to whether teaching is resulting in learning. What has been well taught is not necessarily well learned.

There is only one study available that attempts a systematic and detailed examination of what actually goes on in individual conferences. Nelson (1973, 1974) studied tapes of 68 supervisory conferences conducted in a variety of casework agencies. Although these conferences were between students in a school of social work and their field-instructors (supervisors), the findings are applicable to supervisory conferences generally. In response to the question, What do participants really talk about in supervisory conferences? Nelsen finds that

by the fourth taped conference, the following discussion pattern was fairly common. First, field instructor and student would together go case by case through the student's submitted written material, with field instructor asking questions for clarification or student volunteering extra details, with interrelated discussion of dynamics and handling, with occasional brief exposition by the field instructor of relevant theoretical or skills information which the student had apparently not known, and with eventual agreement on what was going on with the client and what to do next. Second, there might be brief discussions of cases on which there had been new developments but not dictation, e.g., a broken appointment requiring further action from the student. Third, there might be some, usually brief, discussions of learning content such as whether student was recording properly, or agency-field content such as monthly statistics or the need to find a resource for a client. (1973, p. 189)

Both field instructors and students usually participated actively [in the discussion]. The field instructors freely gave didactic material although not often lengthy exposition. (1974, p. 149)

Supervisors also engaged in supportive activity (to be discussed in chapter 4) and gave directives "requiring particular behavior" by the supervisee, i.e., "fill in social service cards in each case"; "to find a nursing home call the homes, find out whether they have a bed, if not find out when they will, find out the cost." Directives tended to be associated with agency administrative procedures and concrete services. The context in which the directives were given indicated a sort of summing up of mutual discussion rather than the issuing of an order. The reciprocal interaction between supervisor and supervisee is suggested by the fact that supervisors gave more directives to supervisees who more often requested direction than to those who did not.

termination
A supervisory conference, like an interview, is hard work. Consequently, after an hour or an hour and a half, it is likely to

be progressively less productive. The end of the conference should be planned at the beginning so that the agenda selected for the conference can be completed within the allotted period of time.

Toward the end of the scheduled time, the supervisor should be looking for a convenient point of termination. It should be at a point where closure has been obtained on a unit of work. The emotional level of the interaction should not be intense. The worker should have been given some prior opportunity to ask those questions and discuss those issues that were of most concern to her. To say to the supervisee, "We have two minutes left for the conference. Was there something you wanted to bring up?" is very frustrating.

Termination involves a summarization of the conference, a recapitulation of points covered and content taught. A supervisor says, "The sessions seemed more worthwhile when I reiterated at the end what we had talked about because it made it seem like we covered a lot. The ending seemed much more together and planned out when I summarized. We both saw these conclusions as a pronouncement of the end of the session. We consequently then proceeded to relax."

Since the conference terminates before it actually ends in the minds of the participants, it might be good to finish with some explicit questions for the worker to think about, some specific reading suggestions relevant to what has been discussed and in line with his interests. The questions might serve as a transition to the next conference. Thinking about the questions raised, both the supervisor and supervisee would be preparing for their next meeting.

Case Illustrations

The following vignettes illustrate the supervisor implementing the responsibilities of educational supervision in individual conferences. They have been submitted by supervisees as examples of good supervision.

The case involved my counseling a husband and wife. The wife was to come to hospital for tubal ligation and wanted an operation. She stated her husband wanted her to have the operation, but was being uncooperative in helping her arrange day care for the 3 children. She also complained bitterly about desperate financial conditions and how her husband would not follow through on his responsibilities. She stated that her husband would be willing to talk to me but would not be able to come to my office at the hospital. A home visit was arranged. After visiting the home, conditions that wife had commented upon seemed verified; the husband was civil, but not very communicative. We discussed the reason for wife's impending hospitalization, home conditions, his ability to budget. We left with agreement that they would come to my office next week. After the interview I felt I had gone to the home and unconsciously sided with the wife. I had moved too quickly in establishing a relationship with the husband and almost ended up telling him how to be more responsible. My supervisor discussed the case with me and 1) gave me positive support regarding my concern for the family and my attempted outreach; 2) supported and verified the fact that perhaps I had been "too pushy"; 3) suggested reasons why I might have acted this way (since this was not my usual style); 4) suggested how I might salvage the relationship with the family on next visit. We did a role play to help me feel more comfortable.

Supervisor noticed that the supervisee appeared to be in a state of frustrated agitation. Supervisor learned that the supervisee was immobilized because she had to be at an important meeting in the office within an hour and she had a client who needed her to do "something right now" and she had already spent over an hour talking with the client and making calls trying to find the client a place to live. The client, a 16-year-old unmarried girl with her baby, had come to the agency asking for help in finding a new place to live as her mother had kicked her and the baby out of the house the night before. The supervisor did not stand on ceremony but took initiative to help supervisee immediately. She asked the supervisee to her office to discuss the situation so that perhaps together they could figure out a solution. She assured supervisee that time is still relative, most emergencies not always what they seemed and the supervisee did have access to supervisor which could help spread the responsibility. Supervisor focussed in on the problems of the "dependent child mother" who is living with her own mother. She assessed supervisee's knowledge of family as a unit and enabled supervisee to see, and talk about, over-identification which usually occurs without sufficient facts about a problem. This enabled the supervisee to call client's mother which resulted in solution to immediate problem and demonstrated to supervisee that she did not have to face problems alone.

The problem was more clearly defined after the worker called the mother of the client only to learn that "she had not put her daughter out, but had lost her temper and her daughter had grabbed the baby and left. It had been late, they were both tired and they had quarreled over the baby's diapers!" The mother was sick with worry and came to agency. When the mother and daughter were tearfully reconciled, the worker was invited to come to their home on the next day to talk about some "real things."

During one of our conferences, I was discussing a "social study" I had completed on a client seeking individual counseling. I was relating my impressions of the client, using diagnostic labels and social work "jargon" rather freely. My supervisor listened carefully, but without commenting. When I had concluded, she smiled warmly and queried, "What's this woman like?" I was somewhat taken back, but began to describe her, again using diagnostic terminology. My supervisor interrupted me, saying, "Well you've already said that and I agree with you completely. But what is she like?"

I feel the interaction my supervisor engaged me in was extremely important, as it forced me to take a serious look at the pitfalls of using diagnostic labels too freely. I realized more clearly than before that labels should serve mainly as a helpful means of classifying behaviors and character disorders—that even though you may attach the "right" label, this does not automatically mean you understand the client. My supervisor asked me to describe a typical interaction between the client and her primary family as I would envision it having happened in her childhood. After struggling with this, she then asked me to again relate my diagnostic impressions, this time without using labels and jargon. I was successfully able to accomplish this, and feel that the steps my supervisor took were important in that they forced me to individualize my client. As a result, I was able to relate in a more personal and individual manner with my client in treatment, thus providing a more effective service.

The following is a more detailed analysis of part of an individual conference with Jim F., a worker in a state child-welfare district office.

Jim began by saying that he wanted to talk about Frank. He brought out that it was important to preserve Frank's placement—he did not think the problem would be solved by replacing him and I agreed. He thought he had made some impression on the boy, and that Frank realized he wanted to help him. I said this was good, and suggested that worker was really on the spot with foster mother ready to put Frank out if his behavior did not change. He agreed to this and said he had made it clear to Frank that he must get a job and stay away from the old crowd, since they are undesirable. I said from his recording I could see he had tried very hard with Frank—did he think it had worked?

The worker here selects the content for the teaching agenda ("he wanted to talk about Frank"). This is in accordance with the principle that learning takes place when the supervisee actively participates in the learning process. It also ensures a higher level of motivation to learn, since the worker, given the opportunity, will select for discussion that content which presents a problem for him.

The supervisor helps to clarify and define the nature of the problem situation that confronts the supervisee. The problem is not Frank's replacement but how to preserve his current placement for him.

The supervisor rewards by explicitly commending ("I said this was good"), in accordance with the principle that we learn best when we receive rewards for learning.

The supervisor communicates empathic understanding and acceptance of the worker's situation ("he was really on the spot"). This probably will be regarded as emotionally supportive by the worker, and helps to establish a good atmosphere for learning. Recognition that the supervisor is empathic and accepting makes the supervisee more receptive to content. The supervisor, however, might be concerned with teaching in saying that the worker is "on the spot." The supervisor is redefining this matter as a problem for him in his responsibility as the social worker assigned to the case. The supervisor is not concerned with Frank's behavior. That is Jim's responsibility. The supervisor is, however, concerned with Jim's behavior and case planning. The worker, rather than the client, is the immediate responsibility of the supervisor.

After Jim has shared with the supervisor what he has done on the case, the supervisor confronts Jim with a challenging question, "Did he think it had worked?" Because the question is challenging and apt to induce defensiveness, it is preceded by an introduction that makes it emotionally easier to accept: "I said . . . I could see he had tried very hard with Frank." The question, "Did he think it had worked?" solicits an objective, self-critical analysis. In inviting reflection, the supervisor is increasing the worker's involvement, intensifying his level of participation in learning.

Didactically stating that the approach was mistaken or, more gently, that it left something to be desired, might have engendered a need for Jim to defend his behavior, since this might be perceived as an attack. People learn less effectively when psychic energy is devoted to self-defense. Encouraging self-examination may result in the worker's explicit recognition of some of the shortcomings of his approach. He may then be more ready to consider alternatives.

It might be noted, too, that the supervisor has actually read the record and is using his knowledge derived from it in this conference. This in itself is encouraging to the supervisee because it indicates that the supervisor is serious about these encounters, is interested in preparing for the supervisory sessions, is keeping to their mutual agreement. Since the justification for recording lies partly in its utility in supervision, use of the recording in the supervisory session rewards the worker for having done the work. It further helps develop a positive supervisor-supervisee relationship. Emotional interaction between the two is more apt to be positive if the supervisor shows respect for the supervisee by respecting his product—the recording.

As yet the supervisor has not taught much, at least not explicitly, although he has taught something about good human relations. He has taught too, by implication, that it is helpful to define a problem clearly and to partialize it if possible. He has encouraged an attitude toward one's work—a reflective self-critical approach—which is a necessary prerequisite for the development of self-awareness. Principally, however, the supervisor is not so much concerned with teaching at this point as he is with developing an atmosphere which is conducive to learning.

Jim shook his head, indicating he was very doubtful. Then burst out with "Frank makes me mad, he's just lazy like Mrs. D says. He doesn't ever try to get work." He went on to tell how at Frank's age he had been earning his own spending money for several years by doing odd jobs that he found himself. I agreed that it would be hard for him to understand why Frank could not do this too—could he see any difference in Frank's situation and his own. He thought for a moment and then pointed out that he had his family and Frank was in a foster home. I wondered what difference that would make? He could not see that it would make any, after all Frank was only two when he went to a foster home and does not even remember his own family—it was probably the best thing that could have happened because his mother did not take care of him.

Here the atmosphere of psychological safety established by the supervisor permits the supervisee to express his negative feelings about the client. It frees the supervisee to express disagreement with some of the things for which social work supposedly stands. In effect he says the client is lazy, he's no good; if he's in trouble, it's his own fault; he makes me mad; each man is the architect of his own fate, and if Frank just tried harder he would be able to resolve his problems.

The supervisor is understanding enough to accept this outburst, and, rather than express disappointment or chagrin that a social worker should react to his client in a manner which suggests rejection, expressed empathy with the supervisee's difficulty in undertanding Frank. Responding in this way the supervisor is teaching, by exemplification, the concept of acceptance—that judging the client and his behavior in moral terms may be satisfying, but it is not very helpful; that in problem-solving it is more helpful to try to understand than to judge. She then asks a question which shifts the focus from an evaluation of Frank's behavior to an attempt to understand the behavior: what helps to explain Frank's actions, what prompts him to act differently from the supervisee.

The supervisee, whose thinking has been channeled by the

question, comes up with a descriptive statement of difference. The supervisor further questions him because this, as yet, does not explain why people should behave differently when confronted with similar situations. A less perceptive supervisor might be satisfied with the answer and develop a short lecture on the implications of differences in developmental history. This supervisor prefers to elicit the supervisee's perceptions of the implications that differences in developmental history have for behavior. This, once again, maximizes supervisee participation in learning. Implicit in the supervisor's questions are some behavioral concepts, e.g., the past is structured in the present, behavior is purposive, all generalizations need to be individualized, feelings are facts and determine behavior. These ideas, however, are not taught explicitly.

The worker continues to voice doubts about the point the supervisor is making; he questions whether this difference in background explains the difference in behavior between himself and Frank.

I suggested we think back to when all this happened. I asked how he thought Frank felt when he had to leave his parents and go to a strange place, or did it seem that he was too young for it to make any difference. Worker looked dubious and remarked that after all, a kid of two could hardly talk. We discussed this for a while, and he was thoughtful at my suggestion that it might even be harder for a little child like Frank who could feel, but was too young to understand what was happening, than for an older child. I said here we were talking about what had happened to Frank and about his feelings when he was two years old, perhaps this did not seem to have much connection with the present. He said, thoughtfully, that he could see it might, adding that Frank never hears from his family and that must be "rough on the kid"; I said he was telling me that out of Frank's life experiences and his own they would bring something different in terms of feeling to the present. With an expression of surprise, Jim commented that he felt sorry, not angry at Frank anymore, how come? Did he think it was because we were trying to understand Frank? He decided this was it, and wondered why he had not thought about all that before.

The supervisor does not directly counter the worker's doubts about her implied "explanation." She invites the worker to examine his thinking further, but this time by attempting to empathize with Frank (how did he think Frank felt? etc.). She goes on to suggest a line of thought which the supervisee grasps ("or did it seem that [Frank] was too young for it to make any difference"). Such an approach can be helpful if the supervisor senses that this is the nature of the worker's thinking but that he is either not ready or not clear enough to articulate it. The supervisor, in making it explicit, exposes it so that it can be discussed. Unless the message from a worker is clear, however, there is danger that this kind of interpretation will project onto the worker the supervisor's own conception of the situation, which the supervisee then employs for his own ends.

In any event, the supervisor is trying to make a teaching point: that a two-year-old can "know" and his "knowing" does affect later behavior—an idea with which the supervisee disagrees. At this juncture the supervisor, if she thinks the point important enough to warrant concern with its acceptance, should be prepared with didactic research material to reinforce it. What studies, if any, support the contention that a child of two can remember and that such memories affect later behavior? What clinical material supports the contention? The student has a right to know and the supervisor has an obligation to make this information available. Otherwise, the supervisor is exploiting the authority of her position to solicit acceptance of what may well be a presumption with little supporting evidence.

The past is of concern, however, not for itself but only as it affects the present. The supervisor shifts the discussion back to this area of greater importance. She does so by a question that suggests another principle in learning—that we learn best when the material being presented is meaningfully related to problems that concern us. The supervisor is trying to relate the questions she raised about Frank's past to the problems that the worker faces in dealing with Frank. The supervisee makes this connection and makes a deduction in line with what the supervisor is attempting to teach about the effects of the past.

The supervisor then summarizes and makes explicit the meaning of the interaction ("I said he was telling me" etc.). In summarizing, the supervisor uses another principle in learning—namely, we learn best and retain best if we are clear about what we have learned, if we can put it into words and look at it.

What needs to be taught is not only a change in thinking, not only the injection of new ideas for the worker's consideration (some of which may affect his thinking, some of which may not), but a change in feeling as well. The supervisor's approaching, which focuses on understanding rather than judging, leads to a change in feeling. The worker begins to feel sorry for Frank, rather than angry at him. This is an advance toward greater helpfulness but still not as helpful as an understanding of Frank, which the supervisor is aiming to teach. The approach toward developing understanding is only partly in the questions the supervisor raises ("could he see any difference between Frank's situation and his own"; "I wondered what difference that would make"; "I asked how he thought Frank felt"). It is also in the supervisor's approach to the worker. She is not judging the supervisee and his responses but rather attempting to understand why he answers in the way he does. She presents a pattern for identification which the worker might emulate in thinking about Frank.

Jim then reminded me of the foster mother's complaints and of how he had tried to handle this with Frank by telling him he should find a job and give up his "bad" associates. I said he seemed to be questioning this himself, did he think people always did what they were told to do. In the Army they did. This was always true? What about the men who went A.W.O.L.? He pointed out that they took the consequences and I agreed that we all have to do that. He reminisced about the difference in officers, how some were not liked and had a lot of trouble because the men would not obey them. In other words, I said, it made a difference how the men felt about their superiors. Of course, if they trusted them it was O.K. I said I was sure this was true, and suggested we get back to Frank. "You mean with Frank it's different, I'm not still in the Army." I thought it must be hard getting away from giving orders or carrying them out. "Yes, I see what you mean, I don't think mine are going to work with Frank."

Earlier in the conference the worker has allied himself with the foster mother against Frank ("he's just lazy like Mrs. D. says").

Here the supervisee is separating himself from the foster mother and this change follows from his change of feeling about Frank.

The supervisor uses comparison and contrast to teach a sensitivity to the unique, individualized aspects of this situation. She helps Jim factor out the essential differences between this and an apparently comparable situation, his army experience. The supervisor employs a context which is meaningful for the supervisee and which also follows the principle of moving from the familiar to the unfamiliar. The supervisor keeps to a relevant focus, however, by relating this situation to the problem which is of concern to them, how best to help Frank. To the good teacher, nothing introduced by the worker is irrelevant. It is the responsibility of the supervisor to take what has been presented and relate it to the tasks of the supervisory conference.

I asked Jim how, then, he thought he could help Frank, and he replied ruefully that he was not sure—it had seemed simple before, he would just tell him what he should do. Now he realizes Mrs. D. has been doing this right along and it hasn't worked. I asked if he thought he could help the foster mother understand Frank better. He thought he could try and added that he guessed she felt annoyed at Frank like he did. "How do you think Frank feels?" He said he had just been thinking about that and thought he might well be feeling all alone, like nobody cared, and that must be awful. I agreed and said, "I can see you do care what happens to Frank and I think if you got that over to him, maybe in time Frank can learn to trust you."

Having helped Jim come to the conclusion that the approach he had been using with Frank was not likely to work and having helped him learn why it was not likely to work, the supervisor returns to the basic question that is the focus of the conference—how to help Frank. Now the question can be discussed with greater clarity and with greater motivation on the part of Jim to consider new approaches. The preceding discussion has made possible a teachable moment. The supervisor optimizes the supervisee's involvement by asking how he now thinks he can be helpful to Frank.

The supervisor recognizes and accepts the supervisee's de-

pendence on her for suggesting possible new approaches at this
point. In response to this need she suggests an approach ("I
asked if he thought he could help the foster mother understand
Frank better").

Jim is not only achieving a greater understanding of Frank
but, in applying a general approach focused on understanding
rather than judging, he is achieving greater empathy with the
foster mother as well ("he guessed she felt annoyed at Frank
like he did"). The supervisor teaches here, as she did somewhat
earlier ("it made a difference how the men felt about their supervisors"), the importance of feelings in relationship—the fact
that people behave toward one another in terms of how they
feel about one another ("You do care what happens to Frank
and . . . maybe in time Frank can learn to trust you"). The
supervisor goes on to teach that the worker is part of this complex interaction; that his feelings toward the client are a determinant of the interaction in the relationship (feeling frustrated,
he might feel angry toward Frank); that the worker's feelings
which intrude in the relationship, once identified, can be controlled.

Jim said he too could see how it would take time whereas he had
thought he could do it all in one interview. I said it was hard to realize
that change comes slowly in people. I thought he had made a good
beginning and realized that he had noticed Frank seemed more cheerful and spoke more easily at the end of the interview. He hoped so but
felt he needed to do a lot more thinking before he saw Frank again.

He guessed it wasn't the way he thought, that you can learn all
about casework in ten easy lessons. I laughed and said it was good that
he was realizing this, but I knew it was hard too when he wanted so
much to know all the answers. When we didn't, we could feel frustrated, and perhaps that was some of the reason he had felt angry at
Frank. Jim was very thoughtful and said this helped him to understand
something that had happened in another interview and we went
on to discuss that.

Utilizing the experience Jim has just gone through, the supervisor teaches about expectations for change. Inferentially the
supervisor reassures and supports Jim by indicating that she

does not expect him to change Frank overnight—nor should Jim expect this for himself. The supervisor supports and excuses his frustration at not being able to learn all about casework in a few lessons.

The supervisor's general approach is consistent with that communicated throughout the conference. Her accepting, understanding, supportive attitude, her readiness to praise the worker where commendation is warranted, her willingness to grant the worker autonomy and to move at his pace have created a nonthreatening climate favorable to learning.

The approach is not so permissive, however, as to be totally without anxiety. There is clear indication that although the supervisor accepts Jim's current professional deficiencies, she does expect him to learn to do better. This is the best kind of anxiety for learning—anxiety based not on fear but on the discrepancy between what the worker needs to know and perhaps wants to know and what he does, in fact, know.

This section of the conference concludes before the conference itself is ended. The next section is introduced by the supervisee once again, this time on the basis of association with related problems—a natural and desirable procedure for transition, indicating the supervisee's ability to generalize his learning.

Some readers might regard the supervisor's approach as too passive or too Socratic. She might have been more active in stimulating Jim to think about certain significant aspects of the case which were largely ignored. It might have been helpful to clarify the target of change efforts—Frank, the foster mother, or both. While suggesting that Jim help the foster mother to understand Frank better, she made no effort to develop how this might be accomplished. There was little exploration of how the foster mother felt and the basis for her reaction in the situation. Rather than agreeing readily with Jim that replacement was undesirable, the supervisor might have helped him clarify his thinking about the advantages and disadvantages of replacement in this particular situation. While indicating the importance of developing Frank's sense of trust in Jim, the supervisor offers little in the way of specifics as to how this might be accomplished. The worker needs help in more clearly identifying the kinds of approaches and interventions on his part that will enhance trust. Little effort was made to explain the nature of the general social situation relating to Frank's employment and job-training opportunities. The fact that some things are not covered may reflect the principle of partialization. Only so much can be included on the teaching agenda of any one conference, and the supervisor always has to be somewhat selective.

We might further note that the supervisor was aided in her efforts by an apt, willing, and capable supervisee; that the conference might have gone less smoothly if Jim had been less cooperative and more resistive. This observation illustrates that teaching and learning require the cooperative efforts of all the participants in the interaction. The best supervisor will fail with some highly resistive supervisees with limited capacity for learning, and the worst supervisor will succeed with some highly cooperative and capable supervisees.

Educational Supervision for Supervisors

While educational supervision provides opportunity for the worker to receive training in the agency, there is less frequently a similar provision for supervisory training. Moore (1970) notes that "it is ordinarily necessary to have established professional qualifications to be eligible as an administrative professional and yet there is nothing in the *formal* training of the professional to qualify him for administrative duties" (p. 208).

On the basis of their study of supervision in 31 agencies, Olmstead and Christensen (1973) conclude that "there appears to be a pressing need for supervisory training. The function of supervision is too critical to leave to trial-and-error learning. Systematic instruction in the fundamentals of supervision warrants a high place on any list of training requirements" (p. 6).

Some training in supervision is absorbed as a consequence of being a supervisee. In one study, supervisors indicated that the most important source of learning their job was the role model of supervisors with whom they had had contact as supervisees (Olyan 1972, p. 213). Being supervised not only helps a person learn how to become a social worker; it also helps in learning how to become a social work supervisor.

In a certain sense, of course, all of the supervisor's social work education and practice have been preparation for doing the work of supervision. The knowledge, skills, and attitudes developed as a social worker are effectively employed here. However, to teach practice requires some special skills over and above those needed to do casework.

Responses from 470 M.S.W. supervisors regarding their formal training for supervision indicated that 86 percent did have some special training. About 47 percent of the supervisors had completed a "course in supervision given by a school of social work." Some had "completed a short institute or workshop given by a school of social work" or "a short in-service institute or workshop given by the agency." Others had attended a "special one- or two-day meeting on supervision at a national or regional social work conference" (Kadushin 1973). These responses indicate that most supervisors with an M.S.W. have made an effort to obtain formal training in supervision. However, the bulk of such training was obtained outside the agency.

Such formal training opportunities, either inside or outside the agency, are the principal sources of supervisory education. There is less opportunity for training through a personalized, tutorial encounter such as is available to the supervisee in educational supervision.

The supervisors of first-line supervisors are generally agency administrators. Their experience with the problem of practice is often remote. In some instances they are not professionally trained social workers but have come to agency administration via a general experience in organizational administration. Only in large public welfare organizations is it likely that the first-line supervisor will herself be supervised by a professionally trained social worker who is knowledgeable about the problems of practice and competent to help the first-line supervisor with the demands of educational supervision.

In offering supervision to the first-line supervisor, the supervisor of supervisors needs to be aware of some recurrent responses to the demands of educational supervision. Supervisors may exploit educational supervision to meet their own needs without being fully aware of doing this. The situation provides the opportunity for developing protégés, for making workers over into the supervisor's own professional image. The supervisor becomes, in such instances, more an object of direct imitation than an object of identification. The worker's success is the supervisor's success; the worker's failures are perceived as the supervisor's failures. The supervisee is less an independent entity than an extension of the supervisor.

The supervisor who, in response to the triadic situation of client-worker-supervisor, is still more a worker than a supervisor will focus too heavily on the client. Such a supervisor is still primarily interested in practice, albeit vicariously through the supervisee. He has not yet made the psychological transition from worker to supervisor. The consequence for educational supervision is that the supervisor denies the supervisee his freedom to learn. Giving exclusive priority to client needs, the supervisor is so fearful of mistakes by the supervisee that he tends to be overdirective and overcontrolling. The supervisor acts more like a guard than a guide.

A supervisor may be hesitant in sharing his knowledge and expertise with the supervisee out of anxiety about competition from a sibling. If the supervisor derives gratification from the supervisee's dependency, he will perennially tend to perceive her as "not yet ready" for next steps in education. In both these situations the supervisor tends to teach the content of educational supervision grudgingly, in small doses, at an inappropriately slow tempo. Evidence of workers' growing independence and competence is viewed with anxiety rather than pleasure. An imperious "need to be needed" on the part of the supervisor will further conflict with the responsibility to grant the supervisee as much autonomy as she can responsibly handle.

Overidentification with the worker may make the supervisor overly protective, shielding the worker from possible mistakes, anxious that the worker may not be able to accept normal failures: "She was afraid to take the risks necessary for learning and I was afraid to let her."

A supervisor who is anxious about his own relationship with the administrator may overcontrol the worker to prevent embarrassment at worker errors for which the supervisor is held responsible. Conversely, supervisors may act out their own rebellious impulses toward the agency through their supervisees, from the safety of their middle-management position.

The supervisor who has considerable therapeutic skills but limited pedagogic skills, or feels more comfortable with the role of caseworker rather than teacher, may convert educational supervision into psychotherapy. There is greater gratification in casting the supervisee in the role of client rather than that of learner. Questions brought into the supervisory conference by the supervisee tend to become personalized and interpreted as problems of personal pathology with which the supervisee might need help.

A supervisor may be sufficiently uncertain about her knowledge that she cannot permit the student freedom to experiment and to learn. A supervisor writes:

Because of my discomfort with the supervisory relationship, I found it easier to simply introduce final decisions matter-of-factly, rather than risk challenge of my own choice of alternatives in a give and take process. I was perfectly happy with this "dictator" method but feared an open exercise of authority which might be called for in joint democratic decision-making if the worker didn't accept my reasons as valid and challenged my choices.

Such a supervisor may tend to be defensive and find it difficult to acknowledge ignorance.

Educational supervision provides the opportunity for a narcissistic display of knowledge and skills. Whether or not this is educationally helpful to the supervisee becomes a secondary consideration. The supervisor who made the following comment caught himself indulging in such behavior.

> In discussing the client with the worker during that session, I made another mistake: that of "lecturing" the worker on the psychological, social, cultural and economic factors affecting clients' behavioral patterns without any reference to the particular situation at hand. And when I did talk about the client, I started to discourse on the effects of emotional and cultural deprivation on the lives of children, and the psychoanalytical implications of Henry's father having run away from the home. . . . I finally caught myself in the middle of the oedipal complex bit. "B.S.!" I said to myself and changed the subject immediately, hoping that the worker had not realized the pompousness of it all, and if she did that she would forgive me for it. I then realized how easy it is to get carried away when one has a captive audience. The "teaching" aspect of supervision is an art not easily mastered. I must remember to do more teaching and less preaching.

Some equalitarian-oriented supervisors may, on the other hand, be afraid of showing what they know. Revealing that they are actually more knowledgeable than the supervisee destroys a pretense of equality in the relationship. Teaching freely requires the ready acceptance by the supervisor that she does, in fact, know more than the supervisee and is entitled to teach it.

Some supervisors, vicariously reliving their own difficult experience in supervision, may want to give the supervisee as hard a time as they had—"Why should he have it so easy when it was so hard for me?" The supervisee becomes a target of displaced hostility over whom the supervisor has sanctioned control. Other supervisors may hesitate to be appropriately critical, fearing hostility or rejection by the worker.

Every supervisor has her own likes and dislikes regarding supervisee learning patterns. If she is not aware of such predilections, there is less probability that she can control differences in her response to different supervisees. Some supervisors like rapid, avid learners who absorb teaching quickly and voraciously; some like the slow, plodding learners who are less challenging and for whom considerable repetition of content is required. Some supervisors like the supervisee who presses the supervisor-supervisee educational relationship in the direction of peer consultation and colleagueship; others find gratification in the supervisee who accepts a parent-child relationship. Some like the exuberant, extroverted learner; some like the shy, introverted learner. Some are more comfortable with learners who do best in the individual-tutorial situation; some are more comfortable with group-oriented learners.

These are some of the considerations which a supervisor of supervisors needs to be aware of in making an educational diagnosis of supervisors.

Summary

Educational supervision is concerned with helping the worker learn what he needs to know in order to do his job effectively. Educational and administrative supervision have the same objectives, and educational supervision supplements administrative supervision by furthering the internalization of administrative controls, developing a professional orientation and a sense of loyalty among colleagues.

The following conditions make for an effective learning situation in the context of a positive relationship. We learn best if:

1. We are highly motivated to learn.
2. We can devote most of our energies to learning.
3. Learning is attended by positive satisfactions.
4. We are actively involved in the learning process.
5. The content to be learned is meaningfully presented.
6. The uniqueness of the learner is considered.

The supervisor has the responsibility of teaching the worker content regarding people, problems, process, and place and developing the self-awareness of personnel with regard to aspects of functioning that are clearly job related.

The regularly scheduled individual conference is the main locus of educational supervision. The teaching content is the supervisee's performance, and the teaching approach is based on an educational diagnosis of the supervisee. Preplanning and preparation are necessary, and during the conference the supervisor engages the supervisee in a systematic, critical analysis of the work he did and is planning to do.

chapter four

Supportive
Supervision

This chapter is concerned with the third major component of supervision—support. Supervisees and supervisors face a variety of job-related stresses. Unless some resource is available to help them deal with these stresses, their work may be seriously impaired, to the detriment of agency effectiveness. The supervisor is responsible for helping the supervisees adjust to job-related stress. Higher administrators are usually responsible for support to first-line supervisors. The ultimate objective of this component of supervision is the same as the objectives of administrative and educational supervision—to enable the workers, and the agency through the workers, to offer the client the most effective and efficient service.

If one were to categorize the research findings on characteristics associated with effective supervision and leadership, two kinds of factors turn up repeatedly. One cluster of factors relates to getting the job done, seeing that the people who do the job are provided with the facilities, services, information, and skills they need to do the job. These are the task-centered, instrumental considerations of supervision. The second cluster of factors is associated with seeing that the people who do the job are comfortable, satisfied, happy in their work, and have a sense of psychological well-being. These are people-centered, expressive considerations of supervision. Expressive tasks meet the needs of system maintenance. They are the equivalents of oiling the parts and cooling the works of a mechanical system to reduce abrasion and the possibility of overheating. Such expressive system-maintenance functions permit the achievement of instrumental goals.

Blake and Mouton (1961) employ these two variables in the development of their managerial grid—concern for production (the instrumental consideration) and concern for people (the expressive consideration). The best managerial style, both psychologically satisfying and economically productive, is an optimum combination of the two concerns. The Ohio State Leadership Studies (Stodgill and Coons 1957) identified "initiating structure" and "consideration" as the two basic dimensions of leadership. A leader who rates high on initiating structure is task oriented, organizes the work to be done, and clearly defines work objectives, group member roles and expectations. This is a concern with the instrumental aspects of the job. The leader who rates high on consideration communicates trust, warmth, friendliness and support—a concern with expressive considerations. The Ohio studies found that the most effective leaders were those who rated high on both dimensions. The Michigan Studies on Management (Likert 1967) came to the same general conclusions. The supervisor who communicates both support and high performance-goal expectations is likely to have the most effective work group.

Fiedler's (1967) research on leadership suggested that the optimum mix of these two major dimensions was largely a function of the situation. Some jobs and some settings require a greater component of instrumental, task-oriented, production-centered concern; other situations require a greater emphasis on the expressive, worker-oriented, human-relations aspects. The mix also depends on idiosyncratic needs and characteristics of the supervisees, some requiring more structure and direction, others requiring a more decidedly expressive orientation.

In studies of job satisfaction and dissatisfaction, these two aspects of supervision are, once again, clearly distinguishable. Herzberg, Mausner, and Snyderman (1959) found that worker dissatisfaction might be related to either "technical supervision" or "interpersonal supervision." Dissatisfaction with technical supervision resulted from the fact that the supervisors lacked competence in the technical skills they were assigned to supervise, the instrumental component of supervision. Dissatisfaction with interpersonal supervision resulted from failures in the human-relations responsibilities of the supervisor, the expressive component of supervision.

If these considerations operate even in the organizations that depend most strongly on machines as the means of production, they are substantially more important for social work organizations, in which the medium of service offered is the person of the worker herself. Machines do not have to feel a conviction in the work they are doing in order to do it well; they never suffer from depression, guilt, a sense of inadequacy. They are not jealous or envious of the achievements of other machines and do not feel competitive. They do not need to be inspired in order to work at an optimum level. But these kinds of feelings— and more—determine the effectiveness of the social agency worker. Consequently the social work supervisor must be concerned with the feeling reactions of supervisees to their job and their job situation. Where the technology is lodged mainly in human resources, the protection and development of human capacities will be a dominant supervisory concern.

In terms of the categorization of the major components of supervision as used in this book, both administrative and educational supervision are primarily, although not exclusively, directed toward instrumental considerations. The supportive component of supervision is primarily concerned with expressive considerations.

Administrative supervision provides the organizational structure and access to agency resources that facilitate the workers' job; educational supervision provides the knowledge and skills required for it; supportive supervision provides the psychological and interpersonal supplies that enable the worker to mobilize the emotional energy needed for effective job performance. Administrative supervision is concerned with organizational barriers to effective services; educational supervision is concerned with ignorance barriers to effective service; supportive supervision is concerned with emotional barriers to effective service.

If administrative supervision provides supervisory authority with the power of position, reward, and coercion, and educational supervision provides the power of expertise, supportive supervision provides supervisory authority with referent power. The worker complies with agency policies and procedures so that he can obtain the ego support the supervisor can make available.

The different components of supervision provide the workers with distinct but complementary models of the social worker for emulation. Administrative supervision provides a model of an efficient worker; educational supervision provides a model of a competent worker; supportive supervision provides a model of a compassionate, understanding worker.

Definition and Use

In chapter 3 we were concerned in part with some of the therapeutic aspects of educational supervision. Our concern, however, was with particular kinds of therapeutic consequences of a good supervisory relationship. These pertained to the learning objectives of developing greater self-awareness and self-understanding with reference to job-related behavior. In effect we were focusing on the insight-clarification outcomes of educational supervision.

Supportive supervision is concerned with another kind of therapeutic responsibility of supervision, related to different kinds of needs and directed toward different kinds of outcomes. The two therapeutic objectives, insight and support, while differentiated here for clarity, are often interrelated. As Towle (1954) notes, the supervisee often "gains insight as anxieties are lowered and defenses relax" in response to support (p. 145).

Supportive supervision is defined as those interventions that reinforce ego defenses and strengthen the capacity of the ego to deal with job stresses and tensions. These include such procedures as reassurance, encouragement and recognition of achievement, realistically based expressions of confidence, approval and commendation, catharsis-ventilation, desensitization and universalization, and attentive listening which communicates interest and concern. In implementing the responsibilities of supportive supervision, the supervisor attempts to help the workers feel more at ease with themselves in their work. As Bloom and Herman (1958) state, "one of the major functions of the supervisor is to provide certain emotional supports for the worker. She must encourage, strengthen, stimulate and even comfort and pacify him" (p. 403). The supervisor seeks to allay anxiety, reduce guilt, increase certainty and conviction, relieve dissatisfaction, fortify flagging faith, affirm and reinforce the worker's assets, replenish depleted self-esteem, nourish and enhance ego capacity for adaptation, alleviate psychological pain, restore emotional equilibrium, comfort and bolster and refresh. Supportive supervision is concerned with tension management on the job.

If social workers are to do their job effectively, they need to feel good about themselves and about the job they are doing. The reality is, however, that they often, for a variety of reasons to be explicated below, feel discouraged, disaffected, powerless, frustrated, devalued, inadequate, confused, anxious, guilty. Workers feel apathetic, alienated, and burdened with a sense of futility. A worker expresses disillusionment:

The supervisee is a male caseworker in a public welfare setting. He had had graduate training and this is his first job. He has been with the agency for nine months. While a number of clients have marital and parent-child problems, he feels that because of the size of his case load he cannot offer the service he would like. He feels discouraged and says that "the things I am doing, any intelligent clerk could do, they are hardly professional."

A supervisee expresses dismay:

I don't really know what the things are that are making me draw back. I think it's not really wanting to get involved in the world of Mrs. Garcia because it's such a horrible world. She has seven children and no husband and lives in a project and now she's very sick. You know that's not the nicest world and I'm not sure I want to be there. (Amacher 1971, p. 164)

Another worker expresses discouragement:

First, the girl ran away from home, fine. She took an overdose, fine. Then her mother's boyfriend is living in the house; her father's an alcoholic; her boyfriend just gave her VD and then she just found out she is pregnant. Bang, bang, bang, right down the line. (Amacher 1971, p. 159)

Inevitably it is more difficult to do an effective job when oppressed by such feelings. If these feelings are frequent in an agency, the low level of morale results in high turnover, repeated absenteeism and tardiness, loafing and inattention to work, noncompliance, frequent grievance reports, and interpersonal friction. Not a happy way to run an effective agency. Furthermore, only as the workers feel confident can they communicate confidence and hope to the client. A feeling of hope is an important variable in determining the success of worker-client interaction.

Thus far the general responsibilities of supportive supervision have been stated in a negative sense. A similarly restricted definition of physical health would be the absence of disease. We might broaden the definition of physical health so that it suggests a complete sense of physical well-being rather than merely the absence of disease. In the same way we might define psychological well-being, the goal of supportive supervision, as a state of complete emotional health, the maximum a person is capable of achieving.

In this sense the supervisor, in implementing the responsibilities of supportive supervision, not only relieves, restores, comforts, and replenishes, but more positively, inspires, animates, and exhilarates. The supervisor "motivates toward excellence," helping the worker develop those feelings and attitudes which are conducive to their best efforts, rather than "merely protecting against incompetence." Such supervision makes the difference between joyless submission and eager participation, between playing notes and making music. A supervisee writes,

I am not sure what the supervisor did or how she did it, but the spirit she inspired in the group was unmistakable. Somehow we felt hopeful, light, cheerful and optimistic. We felt confident that we could accomplish much that was good and worthwhile. It's a good feeling and it's hard to sustain but while it lasts it's a wonderful high, a really good trip.

The need for such a function has long been recognized in social work supervision. One of the earliest studies of worker turnover, in 1927–28, noted "unhappiness in work," a question of worker morale, as the second largest category of reasons for leaving the job. It included such reasons as "dissatisfaction with social work," "depressing work," "clients hopeless," and "caseload too heavy" (Pretzer 1929, p. 168). These problems would have been the concerns of supportive supervision at that time.

Supportive functions currently are seen as an important responsibility of supervision. A recent study of supervision in 31 social welfare and rehabilitation agencies, based on questionnaires to 1600 employees and detailed interviews with a sample of direct service workers, showed "support" to be one of the key functions of supervision. It was defined as "provision of emotional support to subordinates and enhancement of subordinates' feelings of importance and self-worth." "Overall, personnel report that supervisors provide a great amount of support. . . . In fact, in comparison with scores on other scales, providing support is what supervisors do best" (Olmstead and Christensen 1973, p. 189). An earlier study found that "support and encouragement" and "appreciation of efforts" ranked second and third in a 12-item listing of helpful aspects of supervision. (Cruser 1958, p. 20).

Nelsen (1973, 1974) studied tape recordings of a series of 68 supervision conferences. She found that 69 percent of the taped units "contained three or more supportive comments" (1973, p. 336), indicating the high frequency of such kinds of interventions. Relating the level of supervisor support to strain in the supervisor-supervisee relationship, Nelsen concluded that "the use of support was one of the most important skills for the [supervisor] to master if relationship strain was to be avoided" (1973, p. 340). She notes that the "technique of . . . offering support was used both more extensively and more flexibly than might have been expected" (1974, p. 153).

Sources of Job-Related Tension for the Supervisee

In implementing the responsibilities of supportive supervision, the supervisor needs to be aware of the specific, recurrent sources of tension encountered by supervisees.

administrative supervision as a source of tension
The previously discussed components of supervision are in themselves sources of tension for the worker. As discussed in chapters 2 and 5, administrative pressures toward compliance with agency policies and procedures and the requirement for work assessment and evaluation are sources of tension for the worker. Workers face the stress related to the conflict between the bureaucratic and service orientations. At the same time, good administrative supervision is, in and of itself, supportive in that it offers supervisees a well-defined structure in which to operate, a clear definition of realistic and appropriate objectives, and a chance to participate in agency decision-making, and it keeps them informed through full and free communications.

educational supervision as a source of tension
Similarly, educational supervision is a source of both tension and support. Education implies change, and the target of change efforts is the worker. Change involves, of necessity, a temporary disequilibrium, an "unfreezing" of the old equilibrium. Educational efforts, then, inevitably induce some anxiety.

New situations are encountered for which the supervisee does not have a readily available solution. Ideas that were thought correct are explicitly examined and questioned; some are found to be incompatible with new ideas to which the supervisee is introduced. The transition period is characterized by anxiety and a temporary loss of confidence. The old procedures are being rejected, but the new procedures are not yet fully accepted. Besides, the supervisee is ambivalent about taking the next step. He is "not sure that he is willing to change what it took him so long to learn" (Rothman 1973).

All learning presents the learner with a need to adjust to these emotional concomitants, but their intensity varies, depending on the nature of the subject matter. Where the subject matter is largely external and unrelated to the personal self (for example, in mathematics or chemistry), the demands of the learning situation do not pose a significant emotional problem. Where the subject matter intimately affects the perception of self and the nature of the learner's interpersonal relationships, the effects are likely to present greater difficulties. The subject matter of social work is likely to develop the kinds of intra-personal reverberations which make the changes resulting from learning more problematic. What Lazerson (1972) says about psychiatry is also true for social work: "It is important to emphasize that the very nature of what is to be learned . . . adds greatly to the stress already inherent in the learning situation and adds its own special challenge to the learning alliance" (p. 89).

Social work content is emotionally charged and ego-involved. It is content which reflects the way a person views himself and the world around him. In learning about human behavior, we are learning about ourselves, about our defences, our motives, our unflattering impulses. In dispassionately examining the sources of our most cherished attitudes and illusions, we are throwing open to question the way in which we order our lives. Whereas the usual educational situation asks that the student critically examine and hence possibly change his ideas, social work supervision is often directed toward a change in behavior and perhaps personality.

The threat of change is greater for the adult student because learning requires dissolution of long-standing patterns of thinking and believing. It also requires disloyalty to previous identification models. The ideas and behavior that might need changing represent, in a measure, the introjection of previously encountered significant others—parents, teachers, highly valued peers—and the acceptance of other models implies some rejection of these people. The act of infidelity creates anxiety.

/ Much of social work education is concerned with secondary socialization. As a consequence of primary socialization, strong attitudes have developed toward minority groups, welfare recipients, divorce, discrimination, racism, sexual deviance, crime, juvenile delinquence, violent confrontation, the class struggle, etc. The learner has become accustomed to particular patterns of behavior in relating to other people. Socialization in educational supervision requires changing those attitudes and behavioral patterns that are dysfunctional for competent job performance.

The supervisory tutorial is a threat to the student's independence. Readiness to learn involves giving up some measure of autonomy in accepting direction from others, in submitting to the authority of the supervisor-teacher. Supervisees also face a threat to their sense of adequacy. The learning situation demands an admission of ignorance, however limited. In admitting ignorance, supervisees expose their vulnerability. They risk the possibility of criticism, of shame, and perhaps of rejection because of an admitted inadequacy.

Supervisees have the choice of being anxious because they do not know how to do their work or being anxious about confessing ignorance and obtaining help. The recognition and acceptance of ignorance is a necessary prerequisite to learning. Towle (1954) presents the most detailed and perceptive analysis of the problem of tension associated with educational supervision.

While educational supervision produces these kinds of anxieties, it also contributes to reducing tensions. The knowledge and skills, the problem solutions, which educational supervision makes available give the worker a feeling of confidence and a sense of assurance in job performance. Until the worker learns what he needs to know, he is "realistically helpless, confused and fearful out of the lack of know-what, know-how and know-why" (Towle 1954, p. 33). The supervisor, in meeting workers' "realistic dependency fully and truly" (Towle 1954, p. 149), is being supportive. In learning what he needs to know, the worker can adapt more successfully to the demands of the work situation. This, in itself, is gratifying and supportively ego-enhancing.

the supervisor-supervisee relationship as a source of tension

The relationship between supervisor and supervisee is another main source of both tension and support. Mayer and Rosenblatt (1973b), who obtained some 233 protocols of stress situations encountered by social work practitioners, state that "the worker's anxieties appeared to be basically a function of the two main relationships in which he was involved, his relations with his supervisor and those with his clients" (p. 3). Furthermore, the two sources of anxiety are interrelated. "If the worker felt secure with his supervisor this was apt to make him less anxious with clients. On the other hand, if he felt insecure with his supervisor this was apt to make him more anxious with clients" (p. 3).

In her treatment of social workers, Babcock (a psychiatrist) maintained that they felt "less inadequate with clients than with the supervisor to whom they fear to reveal their inadequacies. . . . These patient-workers in discussing their work experience accept intellectually that they need the supervisor, yet . . . they often admit to unreasonable anxiety" (1951, p. 418).

Why should the relationship be a source of tension? The supervisory relationship is an intense, intimate, personalized situation that has considerable emotional charge. As is true for any highly cathected, meaningful interpersonal relationship, it becomes infused with transference elements, with ambivalence and resistance, with residuals of earlier developmental conflicts.

The supervisor-supervisee relationship evokes the parent-child relationship and, as such, may reactivate anxiety associated with this earlier relationship. If the supervisor is a potential parent surrogate, fellow supervisees are potential siblings competing for the affectional responses of the parent. The situation therefore also threatens to reactivate residual difficulties in the sibling-sibling relationship. It is a particularly fertile context for the development of transference.

A rich literature tends to support the contention that the supervisory relationship does, in fact, mobilize these kinds of tensions (Ekstein and Wallerstein 1972; Fleming and Benedek 1966; Schuster, Sandt, and Thaler 1972). The worker often reenacts his problem with the client as a problem in supervision. This has been termed a parallel process by Arlow (1963) and Fleming and Benedek (1966) and a reflection process by Searles (1955); see also Marohn (1969) and Mattinson (1975).

Doerhrman (1972) studied this reciprocal interaction by analyzing eight sets of concurrent supervisor-supervisee-client relationships over a period of 20 weeks. She studied two supervisors and four supervisees offering service to eight clients. Both the supervisors and the supervisees were interviewed each week with regard to what had happened in supervisory sessions. She was struck by the intensity of the supervisees' reactions to their supervisors. Rather ordinary action on the supervisor's part seemed, at times, to have a profound effect not only upon the therapist's feelings about himself as a therapist but also upon the way he conducted his therapy.

Following a disagreement with her supervisor, a worker said: "Just how much the supervision gets into mother images was really brought home to me. It was very clear that the degree of upset was not reasonable. . . . All it was was that my supervisor was angry with me. Well you should be able to tolerate people being angry with you. I was thrown into a massive depression. . . . I know I over-reacted" (Doehrman 1972, p. 116).

The major findings of the study were that there is a "meshing of transference and resistance patterns of the therapist and supervisor and that the therapist acts out with his patients the

effects of the conflicts engendered in him by his supervisor. . . .
It is therefore concluded the supervisors should be extremely
sensitive to unknown and intense effects that they will have
upon their supervisees, as well as effects their supervisees may
have on them, and not assume that their relationship to the
[supervisee] is a simple didactic one" (Doehrman 1972, pp.
205–6). "The results indicate that tension in the supervisory
relationship is inevitable" (p. 211). (One might parenthetically
note that it would be unfortunate if we permitted the current
disenchantment with psychoanalytically oriented psychotherapy as a treatment procedure to obscure the very rich contribution that psychoanalytic psychology can make, as an explanatory system, toward understanding complex human
interaction.)

Supervisees face a problem in determining what content is
"on-stage," or admissible for discussion in conferences, and
what content is "off-stage." Material which they have confiden-
tially shared with the supervisor in social situations on the assumption that it was "off-stage" is sometimes used in interpreting on-the-job difficulties. This is regarded as an unwarranted
use of personal information. Because of the ambiguity regarding
what information can legitimately be used by the supervisor in
conferences, supervisees are under some tension in selecting
content to communicate to the supervisor.

Tension also is generated around the interpretation of content. There may be a conflict between the supervisor's and the
supervisee's definition of the situation. The worker seeks to
"negotiate" the validity of his definition with the supervisor.
Here he is at a decided disadvantage. Since the "correctness" of
either interpretation often cannot be objectively determined,
where there is a conflict the supervisor's interpretation of the
situation is apt to prevail. As Scott (1969) points out,

The use of methods by which a caseworker's motives are scrutinized
and questioned raises problems because such tactics are subject to
abuse: from worth as a method of helping the worker to attain insight,
such procedures can degenerate into devices for the manipulation of
the worker. The danger inherent in the possibility that at any moment

the worker can be reduced from a participant in the discussion to its subject may act to curb the working out of honest differences of opinion between worker and supervisor. The worker who disagrees with his superior may be met with the response that he is "unable to accept supervision," or that he is exhibiting "resistance," or "immaturity." At worst, the supervisor becomes omnipotent: a worker is not even entitled to his own opinion in an honest disagreement with his supervisor because the latter can devalue his arguments by questioning his motives. (p. 109)

There may be further tension which results from unwarranted attempts to make the worker into a client. A supervisee discusses her relationship with her supervisor:

Feeling that "honesty" was the hallmark of the good caseworker, I included in my process recordings all of the doubts, fears and anxieties that I experienced in my interviews. At first the supervisor was delighted with my openness. However, in time she began to question what lay behind all my uncomfortable feelings. At one point, we were spending more time in discussing me than in discussing my patients. We explored my pathology in all its gory details. I would come out of the supervisory conference shaking with self-doubt and feeling vulnerable and picked apart. (Mayer and Rosenblatt 1975, p. 186)

Some conflict between worker and supervisor results inevitably from differences in perspective. The worker faces the client directly. The client is in a position to punish the worker with hostility, contempt, rejection, and apathy or reward the worker by change in behavior, by praise and appreciation. The worker is concerned with client needs for these reasons as well as in response to a desire to be helpful. The supervisor is not exposed to client reaction but is directly exposed to administrative reaction, from which the worker is buffered. The supervisor's concern is to see that agency administration is pleased with his work. Given their different positions in the agency hierarchy, the worker and supervisor have different perceptions of their world. The worker tends to see the case, the supervisor to see the caseload.

The supervisor, having already resolved many of the problems faced by supervisees, may underestimate the disturbance

table 1.

Sources of Supervisee Dissatisfaction in Supervision

	Percentage of supervisees checking item as a strong source of dissatisfaction ($N = 384$)
1. My supervisor is hesitant about confronting agency administration with the needs of his (her) supervisees.	35
2. My supervisor is not sufficiently critical about my work, so that I don't know what I am doing wrong and what needs changing.	26
3. My supervisor does not provide much real help in dealing with problems I face with my clients.	25
4. My supervisor tends to be capricious and arbitrary in the use of his (her) authority.	23
5. My supervisor does not provide enough regularly scheduled, uninterrupted conference time.	21
6. My supervisor is too controlling and dominant, so that he (she) restricts my autonomy and initiative as a professional.	20
7. My supervisor shows little real appreciation of the work I am doing.	15
8. My supervisor tends to encourage unnecessary dependency.	14
9. My supervisor is hesitant about making decisions and/or taking responsibility for decisions, so that the total burden of case decisions rests with me.	12
10. Other (miscellaneous).	22

Source: Kadushin (1973).

such problems create for them. It is easy to minimize the difficulty of these problems and to take them for granted. The supervisor may develop the unwarranted expectation that the supervisee should be as efficient as she is in dealing with these problems. The supervisor, in empathizing with the supervisee, needs to recall her own first encounter with an abused child, a client with terminal cancer, a slum tenement reeking with booze, feces, and exposed garbage, her first efforts of placing a child.

The worker often becomes explicitly aware of many of the

different kinds of tensions encountered in doing the work in discussions with the supervisor. Supervision might be perceived, by the worker, as the source of such tensions. The worker then finds "some relief in being able to blame some of his problems on the supervisor who tends to become, at this point, more or less the 'villain' " (De la Torre 1974, p. 303). Supervisee dissatisfactions with supervision point to additional sources of stress relating to the supervisor. Table 1 ranks some of them as obtained from supervisees in a questionnaire study.

If the relationship with the supervisor is a source of stress for the supervisee, for the various reasons noted above, it also is a principal source of emotional support. In contact with an understanding, accepting, interested supervisor who communicates trust, confidence, and psychological safety, the supervisee can afford to risk himself in learning and change, openly share his doubts. ventilate dissatisfactions, and obtain the emotional supplies he needs. Table 2 ranks supervisee satisfactions in supervision. It further confirms the support the worker derives from the supervisor.

the client as a source of tension
˜ Relationships with clients are an additional source of stress for the worker. Workers deal with people who are living under considerable stress. They encounter the clients at a time of crisis, when their emotional reactions are overt and strong. It is very enervating to deal with a great deal of raw emotion—anxiety, anger, depression, grief—and with the constant exposure to highly charged emotional situations while under the necessity of controlling one's own emotional responses. "The worker, face to face with the client in the interview, is exposed continually to an onslaught of unrepressed primitive feelings. The avalanche of feeling with which the . . . social worker is confronted is an unusual stress situation peculiar to the task of extending psychological help. It is, in a sense, an occupational hazard" (Feldman, Sponitz, and Nagelberg 1953, p. 153).

Workers encounter "clients" who have neither asked for nor want agency service and who are hostile and resistive to

table 2.

Sources of Supervisee Satisfaction in Supervision

	Percentage of supervisees checking item as a strong source of satisfaction $(N = 384)$
1. Through supervision I share responsibility with, and obtain support from, somebody in administrative authority for difficult case decisions.	44
2. My supervisor helps me in dealing with problems in my work with clients.	40
3. My supervisor helps me in my development as a professional social worker.	34
4. My supervisor provides the administrative access to agency resources I need to help my clients.	27
5. My supervisor provides stimulation in thinking about social work theory and practice.	27
6. My supervisor provides me with the critical feedback I need in order to know how I am doing as a social worker.	24
7. My supervisor provides me with the emotional support I need to do my job more effectively.	21
8. My supervisor provides me with some sense of agency appreciation of my work.	19
9. My supervisor helps me feel a sense of belongingness in the agency.	12
10. My supervisor helps me to grow toward greater maturity as a person.	9
11. Other (miscellaneous).	8

Source: Kadushin (1973).

their efforts to help. Despite such hostility and the workers' own very human reaction of antipathy to some clients, professional practice principles require that they act acceptingly. In the following excerpt a worker describes her feelings before an interview with a hostile client. The worker was scheduled to visit a mother whose children had been removed and who wanted them back.

I was very frightened of the upcoming visit. I have a difficult time dealing with hostility and I expected Mrs. P. to be quite hostile. . . . My anxiety mounted steadily the morning of the visit. I lingered at the office as long as I could, wanting to remain in the presence of other workers. Finally I left to drive to Mrs. P's house. I arrived at her neighborhood only too soon. I trudged up the steep hill with dragging feet, wishing with all my strength that I was going in the other direction. . . . I remember hoping that Mrs. P. would have forgotten the appointment and wouldn't be at home. But there she was, opening the door for me. I felt somehow like a condemned man at his own execution. (Mayer and Rosenblatt 1973a, p. 8)

There is stress associated with physical dangers encountered on the job. A worker providing homemaker service writes that when she came to see the children,

their uncle, whom I had met before, was standing at some distance from us on the other side of the room. He had an open switchblade in his hand which he kept flicking with his thumb. . . . All of a sudden he threw the knife at me across the room and it landed at my feet. I was panicked, but I did not move or scream or utter a sound. . . . I had a split second to figure out what to do: either run or stay and try to bluff him. The man giggled and asked if I was scared. In a voice as controlled as possible, I answered, "Yes, of course, I was scared." . . . I explained to him that I was there to try to help the children. He kept grinning and said, "It's O.K., don't worry, it's O.K." . . . He then picked up the knife, closed it slowly, put it in his pocket and moved into the other room. . . . I stayed a short while longer, and when I left I was shaking all over. (Mayer and Rosenblatt 1974, p. 58)

Clients are currently less willing to accept the worker's definition of their role in the relationship and less ready to recognize the legitimacy of organizational procedures. Previously, socialization to the role of client in a bureaucracy involved ready acceptance of organizational constraints on the worker's ability to accede to requests. This is less true today. While the worker's freedom of action is limited, the client tends to act as though the worker were a free agent, capable of meeting client demands if he were only willing to do so (Bar-Yosef and Schild 1966). Client pressure on the worker is intensified as a result of the recent development of client advocacy organizations such as the Welfare Rights Organization.

The recipient of a worker's service is a fellow human being.

The worker's decisions often have considerable implications for the client's living situation. A child is placed for adoption, a parolee can be released from prison because a job has been found, funds are obtained for a day-care center. This is an awesome responsibility, and awareness of the possible consequences of such decisions is a source of occupational stress. Often the worker has to make these crucial decisions in the face of unnerving uncertainty, ambiguity, and limited information and with a recognition that full understanding of the prodigious complexities of unpredictable human situations is beyond the wisest person's true comprehension.

Many situations encountered by child welfare workers have all the essential elements of Greek tragedies. They involve conflicting but legitimate and justifiable interests and needs. There may be a conflict between the rights and privileges of a foster parent and the rights and privileges of a natural parent. The conflict may be between the right of grown children to live autonomously and the rights of aged parents for protection and support.

There are also problems of deciding between competing needs of different clients. Devoting a considerable amount of time to one client means neglect to another. As one worker put it,

The conflict that I felt was not only between the regulations and the clients but between client and client. If you want to help clients get schooling or job training or discuss personal problems with people who may be very eager to talk to you about them, you do so with the knowledge that you are not using this time to help get basic material things to people who just as desperately need them. (Miller and Podell 1970, p. 24)

Some stress results from the workers' uncertainty about the outcome of their intervention. Certain changes are obvious—a neglected child is placed in a comfortable foster home where he is well cared for. However, many changes which social workers attempt to bring about are not so visible. Changes in parental attitudes toward children, in adjustment of a child to a foster home, in an adoptive parent's sense of security in his role, may not be overtly manifested. There may be dissatisfaction for workers in the lack of observable changes which reward their conscientiousness and competence.

the nature and context of the task as a source of tension

Stress can result from the nature of social work tasks and the conditions under which the work is done. We noted earlier that the task in which the worker is engaged interpenetrates with his own life. Encountering separation experiences, the worker is made anxious as he remembers his own separation fears at the hospitalization or death of a parent, the threat of divorce, and so on.

The work setting often produces stress. Wasserman (1970) describes a typical public child-welfare agency:

The new professional social worker's home base is usually a district office. His desk is one of many on an open floor. There is little or no privacy. He is surrounded by other workers, welfare assistants, clerks, and supervisors, all crowded together with one desk adjoining another. Telephones are constantly ringing, and there is a steady hum of conversation, typewriting, and people moving from place to place. The office is not an environment in which a worker can think clearly and calmly about the complex and painful situations he faces and the fateful decisions he must sometimes make. There is no quiet place where one can go to think for a few moments or consult with colleagues. Interviewing clients, which occasionally takes place at the agency, is carried out in a small, open cubicle. There is no privacy. In sum, the setting is not one usually conceived of as "professional"; in fact, the environmental image is more industrial than professional. (p. 95)

Workers in many large public agencies and in agencies that are newly established on the basis of innovative social-policy changes, face the stress of adapting to constantly changing directives.

Frequent interruptions of routine income maintenance and service activities further overburden caseworkers. The perpetual changes in welfare law keep administrators and caseworkers off balance, requiring them to constantly learn and relearn. When asked how often rules are changed, a Detroit caseworker answered, "Every time you put your pencil down. As soon as you make a change, a change has been made on what you just changed." An Atlanta caseworker agreed: "We get so many manual transmittals with so many changes that it's impossible to stay on top of everything." Changes are so frequent that agencies cannot keep manuals up to date. (Galm 1972, p. 30)

Other stresses result from the fact that the workers' responsibilities exceed their power and resources. Society supports social work agencies because they are part of the necessary apparatus for social control. They mitigate the effects of situations that might lead to social conflict, and alleviate the most extreme effects of social dysfunction. The limited support given to agencies allows them to perform this secondary function. The support necessary to carry out their primary functions—to provide adequate measures for prevention and rehabilitation—society is not yet willing to grant. The workers therefore have to implement a policy that reflects society's ambivalence toward the groups whom they are asked to help. Very often what they are asked to do is in conflict with society's willingness to provide the resources which will enable them to do it.

Furthermore, neither the worker nor the profession has the power to change those significant social pathologies—discrimination, unemployment, housing shortages, etc.—which directly limit what the worker can do. These crucial externalities, beyond the workers' power to remedy or change, affect their practice and determine the outcome of their efforts.

The results of the workers' best efforts to help the client in the face of overwhelming odds, under conditions which are beyond their control, lead to a sense of impotence, frustration, and failure. A clear sense of achievement is hard to come by. In addition, "the pain the staff experiences in their awareness of client sufferings is heightened by resentment that their efforts are depreciated and that they are blamed for inadequacies over which they have no control" (Arndt 1973, p. 50).

One study of M.S.W. recruits' reactions to a public child-welfare agency during their first years of employment found them "disheartened and overburdened by the large numbers of biological parents, foster parents and children with whom they had to work and overwhelmed by the large number of emergencies they had to face on an almost daily basis. . . . The worker is often overwhelmed by the cumulative impact, perhaps the cumulative terror, of a large number of cases—by the human suffering, deprivation, disorder, ignorance, hostility and casualty he must face as part of his every-day work situation. . . . The two principal feelings expressed by the twelve new professional social workers during the two-year period were frustration and fatigue" (Wasserman 1970, p. 90).

A worker writes about her reaction to trying to help in the face of overwhelming odds:

I'm tired of hearing about rats and roaches, and politely ignoring the latter as they crawl over walls and floors. I'm tired of broken boilers, toilets, and refrigerators, plumbers who never come, junkies in the halls and junkies who break into apartments and steal clocks, irons, sheets, children's clothes, food—anything they can lay their trembling hands on. I'm tired of hearing about asthma, high blood pressure, anemia, arthritis, toothaches, headaches, and "nerves." . . . I don't want to hear the same things: "He just left . . . not enough for . . . I don't know where he . . . like to work but . . . think he's you know, slow . . . not sending up heat . . . some mornings it's so bad . . . went to the clinic but they . . . do you give money for . . . need . . . teacher sent him home because he . . . only got to the eighth. . . ." Poverty jams into a mold which permits few variations. (Walton 1967)

More recently, to the stress of working against many odds has been added the stress of the accusation of betrayal. Hurvitz (1973) echoes the charge of the growing number of "radical therapists" when he says that "psycho-therapy creates powerful support for the established order—it challenges, labels, manipulates, rejects or co-opts those who attempt to change the society" (p. 237; see also Agel 1971)

Currently, the worker also carries some burden of stress that stems from the general public disillusionment and disenchantment with social services. The worker is identified with an enterprise that has less enthusiastic support than it had a decade ago. "When the profession has dubious status, the worker must not only prove his worth as a professional person but his profession's worth as a profession" (Towle 1954, p. 16).

Because the client's welfare is not necessarily equivalent to the agency's welfare, professional and bureaucratic orientations provide competing claims upon loyalty. Billingsley (1964a), who has studied this conflict in child welfare agencies, finds that

in spite of the social worker's intellectual and emotional commitment to meeting the needs of his client it is apparent that these needs must be met within the framework of structured approaches imposed by the agency and the profession, even over the worker's own estimation of the needs of the client. This is consistent with findings in studies of other professions. (p. 403)

The conflict between the two orientations leads to a strain between the agency demand that a given number of units of work be performed and the desire of the professional to do the best possible job. Billingsley identifies this as the conflict between quantitative output and qualitative performance.

A study of the work situation of public welfare workers in New York City performing public assistance and child welfare functions indicated that there was, indeed, a sharp conflict between the client-helping functions and the need to meet bureaucratic demands. As one caseworker noted, "most workers feel that they are caught between the clients and the department rules" (Miller and Podell 1970, p. 23).

There is stress in working in the context of ambiguous objectives. Society often gives the agencies a poorly defined charge. The community sometimes does not make clear what response it expects from agencies in the face of social problems. Workers ultimately have the task of making decisions in the face of poorly defined or even conflicting objectives. Should the A.F.D.C. mother be encouraged to work or stay home with her children? Should prisons serve the purpose of punishment or rehabilitation? Should the community share with the parents the burden of care for the severely retarded child? Should homosexuals be accepted as foster parents? In these situations, and others, workers frequently face the stress of making decisions and taking action about moral and ethical questions on which both they and the community are still undecided.

Some of the occupational stress to which workers are subject stems from uncertainty about what they should be doing and how they should be doing it. Techniques and approaches for helping the client are not so well established as to provide clear-cut guidelines for the workers' behavior. For many situations there is no validated professional consensus on the most effective approach. In addition to incomplete or imperfect mastery of available knowledge, workers have to accept the limitations of professional knowledge itself.

In the mid-1970s, concern about job security emerged as an additional source of anxiety for social workers. Although concern about this problem is general, bachelor-degree social workers are feeling it more keenly.

Workers in some special settings face particular stresses. All organizations interact, of course, with the environment in which they are embedded. However, not all professions are required to interact on intimate terms with other professionals. The social worker in a host setting (the medical social worker in a hospital, the school social worker in a public school, the psychiatric social worker in a mental institution) are placed in this position. They have to justify and define their decisions to a critical audience of other professionals. They have to learn a pattern of deference in interacting with higher-status professionals. Research indicates that such "boundary positions" are apt to produce tension (Kahn 1964).

The supervisor, in offering supportive supervision, needs to be aware of these multiple job stresses which impinge on the worker as a consequence of his relationship to the supervisor, the client, and the work context.

Implementing Supportive Supervision

Supportive supervision is often implemented not as a separate, explicitly identifiable activity, but rather as part of the work of educational and administrational supervision. Assigning work, reviewing work, or training for the work can be done in a manner that is supportive. The functions of educational and administrative supervision can be performed in a way that communicates respect for, interest in, and acceptance of the supervisee. As we discussed earlier, the consequences of good administrative supervision and good educational supervision can be supportive in the structure and the skills they offer the supervisees.

Beiser (1966) notes that it is very difficult to separate the precisely educational from the purely supportive components of supervision. In discussing her own supervisory practice with child-psychiatry residents, she says that "although I gave a great deal of didactic information both as to theory and specific skills, sometimes this was to alleviate anxiety, sometimes to encourage identification or to demonstrate a model of flexibility. When I tell of my own errors I use them not only to illustrate a particular point but to encourage a less experienced therapist or to interfere with hopes of omnipotence through identification with me" (p. 138).

Certain activities are, however, more explicitly supportive in their intent. The supervisor can supportively help to reduce stress impinging on the worker or remove the worker temporarily from a stressful situation. These procedures are analogous to environmental modification procedures in working with the client. The supervisor can arrange for a temporary reduction in caseload, or a temporary shift to less problematic clients. The supervisor might arrange for a temporary increase in clerical help available to the worker or provide a more private, less noisy office. If interpersonal stress between supervisor and supervisee has reached a level that is beyond any likelihood of remedial change, the supervisor might arrange a transfer to another supervisor.

Conferences, institutes, and workshops not only provide learning and stimulating personal contacts but also enable the worker to get away from the office and the caseload. They are, in effect, supportive "rest and recreation" devices enabling the worker to recharge emotional batteries. The supervisor also acts preventively to protect supervisees from stress by protesting against unreasonable demands by administration. These procedures make the stress encountered by the worker easier to cope with.

Such environmental modification may be particularly necessary for group workers and community organizers.

From time to time the supervisor may need to encourage the worker to reduce his contacts with the group in order to maintain his own family interests and responsibilities. The worker cannot lead a normal family life if he is out of the house four or more evenings a week, sleeps late in the mornings, and is generally unavailable to his family during critical evening hours and weekends. Personal maladjustments may result in the worker's own family from his hectic pattern of professional or agency life. A supervisor will want to encourage the worker periodically to dilute his exposure to the street experience, and reinvest himself in the normal routines of family life. (Spergel 1966, p. 260)

The supervisor provides support by communicating that he is available and approachable. Even if the worker chooses not to discuss some problems with the supervisor, there is still comfort in knowing that he is available for such help. The supportive supervisor practices an "open door policy"; this suggests some limits, as contrasted with a "no door policy," but also considerable flexibility. The supervisor is not only physically and administratively available, he is also psychologically available. Recognizing that there are, inevitably, social distance factors that act as psychological barriers, to free communication between supervisor and supervisee, the supervisor attempts to mitigate these.

When a supervisor communicates her confidence in the worker, she is supportively reassuring to the worker.

R came in at one o'clock and seemed worried. She [said] . . . she was worried about her relatives' group. She didn't feel helpful, involved, connected, etc. She said loudly, "I just don't know what to do; I am at the end of my rope." (In previous conferences, I found myself either becoming overwhelmed by her despair and making psychological interpretations, prematurely reassuring her, or directly solving her concerns. I was determined to help her begin to assume greater responsibility for various practice binds.) I said, gently but firmly, "In our last few conferences, we haven't looked at your records; you have a lot of material; let's look at your concerns more specifically. Why don't you begin reading the record?" She hesitated, stating that parts were left out and the recording wasn't really accurate about what happened; she forgets to record important things. I said firmly, but gently again, that she had recorded a lot of material—we should look at what was in there before we learned about what wasn't, and again asked her to begin reading. She paused, looked at me, and I encouraged her to begin. She shook her head in agreement and began to read clearly. She read the contract at the beginning of the group and said that she wondered, is it OK? I asked her what she thought. She responded that her efforts were very specific, but she did talk too much. She thought some more and continued that she did get what she wanted and the people seemed to dig into their concerns right at the beginning. I added that I thought that her being very specific about many of their concerns certainly helped them make a beginning. (Gitterman 1972, p. 36, reprinted with permission of Jossey-Bass)

The supervisor can be supportive by frankly sharing some of his own difficulties with the supervisee. This confirms the fact that examined failure is acceptable and that the supervisee need not feel so guilty and inadequate.

Gretchen then commented that it was so hard to know when she should say something to someone and when she should keep quiet. I asked her what she meant. She said, . . . "if the girls want to talk about sex, I let them talk about sex even if I know that maybe I am going further than they want to go." I agreed that this was a rough struggle, one that I was going through too. I elaborated by saying that many times I was torn when Gretchen asked me something as to whether or not to tell her or to let her do the work. This struggle, I said, I could feel with her since it was a struggle that I had too. Gretchen looked at me and said, 'Do you really?' I said that I did. She looked very comfortable and at ease with this. (I cannot describe the look but at that moment I felt that there was a strong feeling of closeness between Gretchen and me.) (Gladstone 1967, p. 9)

The worker may be upset about a problem he is facing with the client. Discussing it with a supervisor who is calm about the situation is supportive. Some of the supervisor's calmness is contagiously communicated to the worker. A supportive orientation encourages expression of feelings, which is in itself supportive. Nelsen (1973) found that supervisees "volunteered feelings after they had been encouraged *and* supported in expressing feelings on a conference by conference basis" (p. 209, emphasis in original).

It is presumed that anxiety is reduced by externalization, by open expression of anxious feelings. Consequently, encouragement of ventilation, of catharsis, tends to be supportive. The supervisor who suspects that the supervisee feels anxious about his next visit to a family, his next group meeting, or his next community-action planning conference, might supportively ask, "How do you feel about this meeting?" Or she might hazard an inference coupled with an invitation: "You seem somewhat upset about this upcoming meeting. Would you like to talk about it?"

Considerable stress is encountered in exercising control and communicating acceptance in response to a client's hostility and rejection. To react with anger, defensiveness, or withdrawal (eminently human and socially acceptable reactions) would be regarded as a violation of professional norms. Such a response would then evoke guilt and a feeling of professional failure. Even the thought of such reactions creates discomfort. "The client aroused some negative feelings in me—like anger, impatience and frustration. And I became angry at myself for having these feelings" (Mayer and Rosenblatt 1973a, p. 8).

While holding to the norms of professional conduct, the supervisor can supportively sanction such feelings. Paraphrasing Freud, the supervisor might say that the professional superego is like a good hotelkeeper who doesn't care what goes on in the privacy of the individual rooms as long as it doesn't disturb other guests. All thinking and feeling is acceptable as long as it is not manifested in unacceptable behavior. A worker says,

I think that one of the important functions of supportive supervision is to help the worker deal with negative feelings about the client. Social work attitudes tend to reinforce general societal constraints about thinking negative thoughts about other people. So this is quite a job for supervision. In my case I was asked to physically describe a client. I proceeded along the line of height, weight, etc. when my supervisor asked me if the person was attractive. I was really caught off guard and felt hesitant about expressing my thoughts that, no, the person wasn't attractive at all. With the supervisor's support I have become more at ease with expressing negative thoughts and feelings and have come to accept these as part of any relationship.

The supervisor supports workers in carrying out tasks they have to do but that cause anxiety. Workers are often initially reluctant to reverse the usual pattern of amenities and ask intimate details about the life of a relative stranger, the client. Such behavior is seen as an unwarranted intrusion on client privacy, a manifestation of unacceptable "aggressive voyeurism." The supervisor supports the workers by reassuring them about their entitlement to such information if they are to do the job of helping the client.

Reinforcement, or confirmation, of the workers' decisions is supportive because it assures them that the supervisor shares the responsibility for what they are doing or planning to do. It is reassuring for workers to know that their decisions are in line with more expert opinion.

Mayer and Rosenblatt (1973a,b) found, in their study of stress among social workers, that new workers had an unrealistically high expectation of what social work could accomplish. When this overly optimistic picture met with inevitable failure, the workers tended to blame themselves. The supervisor can offer the exculpation of a practiced professional who reduces guilt by excusing failure. The supervisor helps the worker move from an unrealistic sense of idealistic omnipotence to an acceptance of a realistic limitation of themselves, social work technology, and the clients. The shift is supportive and results in less anxiety and guilt. The supervisor legitimizes limits of expectations. The supervisor depersonalizes responsibility for some failures and relieves the worker of the burden of unearned guilt.

One significant aspect of supportive supervision is concerned with what Stelling and Bucher (1973) have identified as "vocabularies of realism." "Acquiring a language for coping with failure and human fallibility can be seen as part of the process of acquiring a professional orientation and frame of reference towards the work of the profession" (p. 673). The need for vocabularies of realism is greater in those professions where risk of failure is high and the consequences of failure are significant. "A profession which rests on a body of knowledge characterized by uncertainties and gaps runs a relatively high risk of error and failure" (p. 673). These factors are operative in social work. As a consequence, collective responses to recurrent probabilities of failure have tended to develop, and the supervisor passes these on in supportive supervision. Stelling and Bucher, studying these procedures in medicine and psychiatry, identify basic exculpatory themes that are similar to those employed in social work. One theme is "doing-one's-best"; a second is "recognition-of-limitations." In the following example we see the doing-one's-best theme communicated supportively by a supervisor to a psychiatric resident.

Another very important time came when one of my supervisors said to me, in dealing with this very manipulative patient, "Look, you know, she may commit suicide, we may lose her—we could try, but there is a very good chance that she will kill herself sooner or later, no matter what you do," and I think once I had accepted that idea that patients do kill themselves and that . . . there are some things I can do to prevent this, but there are also some things that I can't, I think I had kind of an "aha" experience. (Stelling and Bucher 1973, p. 667)

The second theme supportively communicated in supervision is a recognition of limitations, expressed by the following psychiatric resident:

One thing one learns in this residency program is not to have therapeutic ambitions in anywhere near the quantities that you have when you first come here. Patients thwart that right, left and center, and you learn that it is therapeutically unhelpful to have a large therapeutic ambition for patients. . . . I can now say that there are large numbers of people who suffer symptomatically, but who are untreatable. . . . I had many sorts of rescue fantasies about patients when I came into the residency, and it's taken me a long time to shift focus and learn that I didn't have to rescue everybody, that, one, it wasn't necessary, and two, it wasn't possible. (Stelling and Bucher 1973, p. 669)

The supervisor reduces tension by helping the worker resolve the problem of conflicting role obligations. If the worker is torn between finishing a report or helping a client facing an emergency, the supervisory can sanction delaying the report so that the worker can devote full attention to client needs. Where two performance objectives conflict, for instance detailed intensive interviews with clients at intake and the need to expeditiously complete intake interviews so as to process more applicants, the supervisor can reduce anxiety by officially assigning clear priority to one of the objectives./

The supervisor provides the support of perspective. The view that both the client and the relationship are fragile often inhibits workers from doing what may be helpful. The supervisor can validly reassure the worker that both the client and the relationship can survive a mistaken intervention, a poor interview, or a temporary lapse in professional conduct. Unlike the experienced worker, the new worker "does not have a backlog of successful cases to which he can refer in reverie when things don't go well with the client who is sitting across from him. When things go awry in relationship to a particular client nothing can shore up a therapist's defenses faster than his recall of the many successful cases he has terminated" (Mueller and Kell 1972, p. 104). Borrowing the perspective of the more experienced supervisor can be supportive.

A beginning worker might express doubts about his ability to be helpful to the client. The supervisor can supportively universalize by sharing the fact that most new workers feel this way, that she has been able to assist others to be helpful, that she has confidence in the worker's ability to learn, and that she would be available to discuss with the worker the problems he meets in trying to be helpful. This single intervention contains a number of different kinds of statements, all of which have a supportive intent.

Supervisors provide support for workers in helping them formulate a clearer conception of agency policies, their own work goals, and their role within the agency. Unless supervisees have a reasonably clear idea of what they are supposed to be doing, why they are doing it, toward what objectives, they are likely to be burdened with unnerving doubt and confusion. Uncertainty is generally related to increased tension. A worker whose supervisor clearly communicates performance objectives, performance standards, and performance expectations, feels a sense of support in such clarity. Unfortunately, a sizable minority of social workers reported a lack of clarity with regard to goals and policies of the agency (Olmsted and Christensen 1973, table 81, p. 218). The following supervisee writes of the nonsupportive effects of lack of clarity regarding objectives:

I was given the task of being an indirect leader in a new setting. I continually reported back to the supervisor what I was doing and what problems existed. The supervisor briefly commented that what I am doing is good. When I asked direct questions such as what goal does the agency have as a priority now, or what are new developments from conferences, the supervisor answered that there are no goals, no new developments, you do your own thing. I feel that a task like the above is extremely difficult and threatening, demanding support and a certain amount of direction from the supervisor, which serves the purpose of giving the supervisee a sense of direction and support in the work setting itself. The supervisor's lack of direction made my task more difficult.

The supervisor, in discharging the responsibilities of supportive supervision, attempts to provide workers with the opportunity to experience success and achievement in performance of professional tasks and provides increasing opportunities for independent functioning. Herzberg, Mausner, and Snyderman (1959) found that feelings of achievement and responsibility were two of the most potent sources of job satisfaction. Both help people feel good about the job they are doing.

The supervisor supports by praising and commending good performance and communicates agency appreciation for the workers' efforts. Compliments from the supervisor are particularly gratifying and ego-enhancing because they come from someone who is identified as capable of making valid evaluations. In sharing their victories with an appreciative supervisor, workers know that they are talking to someone who understands the difficulty of the task they have successfully achieved. Such phrases as "good," "nice job," "well thought out," or "really helpful to the client" were typical examples of supervisors responses which were coded as supportive in one study. In one instance the worker came up with a "rather insightful idea" to which the supervisor responded, "using a tone of special warmth and respect, 'you know, that's true'" (Nelsen 1973, p. 129).

Partial praise should be offered where warranted: "It was good you realized something was going on here, but I am not sure this was the best way to respond to it. Let's talk about how to handle clients' anxiety." The worker is commended for knowing that something needed to be done, even though what she did was not especially helpful. One supervisor writes, in detailing her supportive intervention,

On the days I didn't find a lot of glory to give her, I gave her encouragement and pointed out that at least she was aware of what she did wrong and how it could have been improved. When she had a miserable meeting with the girls and was angry with herself, I tried to interject some realistic reassurance. When she had a good meeting, I tried to help her feel justified in her high spirits. I'm sure that getting along together as people had a great deal to do with it as well.

Unwarranted praise, however, is antisupportive. It may reflect the supervisor's rather than the supervisee's anxieties, which then tend to decrease the supervisee's self-confidence. "He seems much too worried about me, like I am about to fall apart or something"; "I get the feeling that he is afraid to criticize me, afraid that I can't take it"; "I don't think I am so fragile, but he is so supportive about not hurting my feelings that I begin to wonder if he thinks I am fragile"; "I appreciate the

gentleness of her approach to me but it suggests a kind of con-
descension that I tend to resent."

As was true for educational supervision, the act and its intent may be at variance with the effect. Just as teaching is not
learning, supportive activity on the part of the supervisor may
not be perceived as supportive by the supervisee. The supervisor must be sensitive to any feedback that gives information
as to the actual effect of her behavior. Reassurance may not reassure; catharsis may lead to an increase in anxiety.

The following are two examples of situations that were
regarded by workers as good examples of supportive supervision:

One conference dealt with the relationship of the supervisee in working with a group of severely mentally handicapped children. The
worker mentioned the fact that such children "make me physically ill,"
"they are repulsive to me." I pointed out how I could understand her
feelings and how I myself had at one time shared somewhat the same
feelings. I went on to talk about my growth in this as a result of experiences I had had in working in a school for retarded children, the
warmth of relationships that had developed.

I do not know if she has changed her bias, but I know that she did
a good deal of thinking about it, and told me how I had helped her
manage her feelings so that she could work more effectively in that
program. What helped the supervisee was some understanding and
sympathy toward her feelings coupled with warmth and empathy and a
positive stand on what this type of work could entail, how it could be
meaningful, etc.

A worker in a surgical ward of an acute-care hospital expressed to her
supervisor her resistance to visiting a patient, long known to her, who
was in terminal stage of cancer. Supervisor helped worker to express
her fear, and then to look at why she was afraid. Worker finally concluded that she was afraid patient might die while she [worker] was
visiting her. Further exploration revealed that the worker had many
warm, close and positive feelings about the patient and the worker was
afraid she would break down and cry. The supervisor's response to this
was, in effect, "so what!" Discussion followed regarding the reality of
such fears and emotions, the need for the worker to remain an individual whose real feelings are not to be confused with concepts of "pro-

fessionality," and that expression of honest feelings can only serve to strengthen relationships between people. Subsequently, the worker reported freedom to share feelings with the dying patient. The supervisor had effectively provided support to the worker, had accepted her fears and emotions, enabled her to express them, and freed her to overcome fears.

A limited number of studies are available which demonstrate the positive effects of supportive supervision. One study experimentally tested the effects of supportive and nonsupportive orientations to supervision (Blane 1968). Counseling students who experienced supportive supervision showed a significant difference in empathic understanding after such supervision as compared with scores before supervision. Students who experienced nonsupportive supervision did not show this change.

Another study testing the differential consequences of the two approaches showed that nonsupportive supervision tends to shift the worker's focus of concern away from the client and toward himself (Davidson and Emmer 1966). Blau (1960) found that reductions in the level of workers' anxiety as a result of supportive supervision were related to a less rigid use of agency procedures and encouraged better service to clients.

In general the supervisor, in implementing the responsibilities of supportive supervision, engages in the same kinds of intervention that characterize supportive psychotherapy. The supervisor acts to prevent stress, reduce stress, or temporarily remove the worker from stress. The supervisor praises the workers' efforts where warranted, reassures and encourages, communicates confidence, depersonalizes and universalizes the workers' problems, affirms workers' strengths, shares responsibility with workers, for difficult decisions and/or lends his sanctions to the workers' decisions, listens attentively and sympathetically, providing an opportunity for cathartic release. All of this takes place in the context of a positive relationship characterized by respect, emphatic understanding, acceptance, sympathetic interest in and concern for the worker as a person. The fact that such interventions are employed in the context of a meaningful positive relationship increases the saliency of the supervisor's communications. Praise, reassurance, encouragement, any supportive comment expressed by the supervisor, have greater significance for, and effect on, the supervisee because they come from somebody whose responses he values highly.

The aim of supportive supervision is to reduce anxiety, allay guilt, increase self-esteem, enhance the workers' capacity for adaptation to the demands of the work situation, and free psychic energy for more adequate job performance. By increasing the supervisees' feeling of emotional well-being, the supervisor increases their emotional fitness to offer more effective service.

It needs to be recognized, however, that even the best supervisory relationship is not potent enough to resolve some dissatisfactions and job-related conflicts which derive from the nature of the work itself and the conditions under which it frequently has to be performed. Some potential dissatisfactions are inherent in agency structure, the social work task, the state of available professional technology, the position of the social work profession in modern society.

It would be asking far more of supervision than it is capable of achieving if a good supervisory relationship is expected to eliminate work dissatisfaction, worker disenchantment, and worker turnover. This is part of the vocabulary of realism for supervisors.

Additional Sources of Support for Supervisees

the client

The supervisor is not the only source of support for supervisees in dealing with stresses encountered on the job. Clients can be a source of support as well as stress. In their responses to workers, and to the service offered by workers, they confirm the workers' competence and sense of self-worth. Appreciative comments regarding the workers' efforts are supportive. Client movement and change provide workers with a gratifying feeling of achievement.

the peer group

The informal agency structure provides the worker with an additional source of support. Some interpersonal relationships in the organization are required by agency structure—the supervisor has no choice but to establish a relationship with the supervisee, and vice versa. Informal relationships are voluntarily selected; they are the primary, close relationships one establishes in the organization in response to personal interests and preferences without reference to any formal work requirements.

The agency is, after all, a small social system composed of a network of human relationships that follow idiosyncratic desires rather than the organizational chart. The formal structure reflects the needs of the organization. The informal structure reflects the needs of the individuals.

Resorting to the informal structure, workers turn to others with whom they feel comfortable to talk about their dissatisfactions, discouragements, doubts about the job, to express feelings of anxiety about inadequate performance and feelings of guilt about mistakes made. The peer group on the job, the work clique, is very often the primary resource to which workers turn to talk about such concerns. These are people who most likely have experienced similar problems. They are knowledgeable about the job situation and can discuss these matters with some sophistication. The worker who feels the need to talk about these feelings and the peer group to whom he turns share experiences and a common frame of reference, increasing the likelihood of empathic understanding. In addition, they have no administrative power to evaluate the worker. Consequently the worker may feel freer in sharing his doubts and dissatisfactions with fellow workers than with his supervisor. The peer group has the additional advantage of being not only psychologically accessible, since social distance between peer and peer is minimal, but also physically available. You do not have to make an "appointment" with co-workers.

Co-workers provide mutual support, assistance, and protection. They use each other as models for identification and teach each other much that is important about the job. "A social worker may use the [peer] group as a sounding board for a particularly difficult case problem or ways to get around a trying regulation may be devised" (Peabody 1964, p. 72). Parallel to the formal system of administrative, educational, and supportive supervision there exist the administrative, teaching, and supportive functions as performed by the peer group. The person holding the position of supervisor is formally invested with the title but should recognize that the supervisee has, in fact, other "supervisors" without title or official position.

The idea that the peer group and the supervisor are alternative sources for meeting similar needs is supported by Marcus's (1961) research. He found that those workers who were supervised by unpopular supervisors interacted more with each other and sought each other out more often. Blau and Scott (1962) have detailed the supportive activities of the peer group:

Discussions among colleagues served to relieve the tensions engendered by conflicts with clients. Informal observation over a period of several months and interviews with the staff revealed that there were three topics of conversation prevalent among staff officials during working hours. The most frequent topic involved complaints about clients. An interviewer would, in effect, say to a colleague, "Look what this client did to me!" These discussions served as an escape valve for releasing aggressive feelings against clients in a harmless form. But this could not have been their sole function, for they often occurred after an official had penalized a client, perhaps by sending a notification that might disqualify him from further unemployment benefits. In these cases, the practice did not serve to relieve pent-up aggression, which had already been expressed directly by penalizing the client, but to obtain social support for one's decisions and thereby mitigate feelings of guilt. The sympathetic listener, who laughed at the client's stupidity or expressed indignation at his impertinence, implicitly justified the speaker's punitive or inconsiderate action by condemning the client's behavior, and this social approval relieved impending feelings of guilt.

A second type of discussion took the form of joking about clients. Ridicule is a form of agression, but it also relieves guilt. The laughter elicited by a story about a client constituted social evidence that his behavior was ludicrous or incongruous, thus placing the blame for the client's troubles on his own shoulders and relieving the official from having failed to mitigate these difficulties; it conveyed the message, "Nobody could have helped such an impossible person!" Joking about clients not only relieved tensions created by work situations but also strengthened group cohesiveness by uniting its members in laughing together. . . . Finally, some interviewers did not joke or complain about clients but often told colleagues about outstanding clients they had encountered. This third topic of conversation was characteristic of the interviewers who were most considerate in their treatment of clients. Their sympathetic attitudes toward clients constituted overconformity with the service ideals in violation of group norms, according to which concern with helping clients must be tempered by willingness to "put them in their place" when necessary. By selecting for their conversations with colleagues accounts of exceptional clients who clearly deserved special consideration, interviewers with overly favorable attitudes toward clients sought to escape the onus of being defined as deviant by soliciting social approval of their treatment of clients. In these cases, the listeners were invited to agree, the extremely considerate treatment was surely justified. Thus, [workers] felt compelled to seek the social approval of colleagues for both inconsiderate and overly considerate treatment of clients, because the former violated their service philosophy and the latter their unofficial norms. These discussions about clients furnished social support and reduced tensions. (pp. 84–85)

Peer-group gripe sessions are effective cathartic devices permitting discharge of tension and providing release and relief.

supervisees' adaptations

Supportive supervision is further supplemented by the workers' own adjustive capacities. Presthus (1962) has categorized three kinds of adjustment that workers make in response to organizational and work pressures. One group of workers accept and commit themselves to organizational demands and conform, in a dedicated manner, to organization policy, procedures, and objectives. This mode of adjustment is characteristic of workers defined as "upward mobiles," who are able to compete in the bureaucratic framework and who expect to be rewarded. Another group of workers, termed "indifferents," accommodate to organizational and work pressures by withdrawal. They distance themselves from their work, invest little of their real selves in the job, and seek their primary satisfaction in other areas. The job is a way of making a living. They neither seek nor expect promotion. A third group, the "ambivalents," want the rewards that conforming to agency demands might provide but feel uncomfortable about, or openly resistive to, conforming to those demands. This last group is apt to be devoted to principle and to be the most critical, alienated, and disaffected.

Merton (1957) describes a somewhat different set of accommodations to the demands of the job. He identifies the "conformist" who accepts both the objectives and the procedures of the agency, the "ritualist" who compulsively accepts procedures as ends in themselves and who has no concern for objectives, the "innovator" who accepts objectives but rejects agency procedures, the "rebel" who rejects both objectives and procedures, and the "indifferent" who does what is asked of him without commitment to or rejection of either objectives or procedures.

In discussing supervisees' reactions to the supervisory situation, the social work literature tends to give recognition almost exclusively to the workers who are, in Presthus's terms, upward mobiles. These are the workers who are committed to the agency's goals and who identify with such goals. Because they have the educational and personal qualifications that permit them to compete successfully in the organization, they receive satisfactions and rewards from conforming to expectations. Dedicated to the goals of the organization, they feel little conflict between what they are asked to do and what they prefer to do. Such an orientation might characterize a sizable number of the staff in small, highly professionalized private agencies; it is likely to characterize a smaller percentage of supervisees in large public welfare agencies. Some of the supervisees in the latter agencies are more likely to be among the indifferents. They accommodate to organizational demands by doing what they need to do, without enthusiasm or conviction. Tension between their personal preference and agency policy is resolved by keeping their thoughts to themselves and implementing the role they are asked to perform without investing anything of their real self in the performance. Lacking either the personal or the educational qualifications for upward career mobility, they withdraw from the struggle and look to their off-the-job life for principal satisfactions.

More frequently now than in the past, agency supervisors encounter a "new breed of social workers" (Walz 1971) who might be classified as ambivalents. Identifying themselves as professional social workers, committed to the goals of the agency, having the qualifications for upward mobility, they feel a strong conflict between their definition of acceptable social work and agency goals and procedures. They want the rewards of upward mobility which can be gained by adherence to agency directions but are reluctant to pay the price of organizational loyalty and discipline which, for them, means violation of their own standards and beliefs. They see themselves as too principled to play the game employed by indifferents, "think one thing, do another."

Supervisees respond to the stress of supervision by actively "psyching out" the supervisor. Their purpose is to determine the kinds of behavior that will obtain acceptance and those that will elicit disapproval. Supervisees then manage a presentation of self that will net maximum approval and minimum disapproval. What Goldhammer (1969) says of teachers in supervision can be applied equally well to social workers. They have learned, in adapting to stress in the supervisory relationship, "how to second guess the supervisor, how to anticipate what will please him, how to stage appropriate performances for him to observe and how to jolly him up for their own protection" (p. 64).

Humor helps reduce worker tension by making the impermissible, permissible. The friendly sarcastic remark permits an excusable expression of hostility towards clients and supervisors. It suggests that the worker does not really mean what he is saying and expects to be excused. If the supervisor reacts punitively, it is an indication that he cannot take a joke. "The supervisor said she was stumped, she really did not know what to suggest. A smile slowly spread over the worker's face as she said in a gentle voice, 'My, that really surprises me—I thought you were all-knowing, all-loving and all-forgiving.' "

Supervisees have developed a series of well-established, identifiable games that are, in effect, defensive adjustments to the threats and anxieties which the supervisory situation poses for them. In the description that follows, these games are grouped in terms of similar tactics. It may be important to note that some supervisees almost never play games. However, even the least anxious supervisees resort to such adjustive games occasionally. Supervisors also play games for similar reasons. These are discussed following the description of supervisees' games.

Supervisees' Games *

manipulating demand levels

One series of games is designed to manipulate the level of demands made on the supervisee. One such game might be titled "Two against the Agency" or "Seducing for Subversion." The game is generally played by intelligent, intuitively gifted supervisees who are impatient with routine agency procedures. Forms, reports, punctuality, and recording excite their contempt. The more sophisticated supervisee introduces the game by noting the conflict between the bureaucratic and professional orientation to the work of the agency. The bureaucratic orientation is one that is centered on what is needed to ensure efficient operation of the agency; the professional orientation is focused on meeting the needs of the client. The supervisee

---

* Much of the material in this section originally appeared in my article entitled "Games People Play in Supervision," *Social Work* 13 (1968): 23–32. It is quoted with permission of the National Association of Social Workers.

points out that meeting client needs is more important, that time spent in recording, filling out forms, and writing reports is robbed from direct work with the client, and further that when he comes to work and goes home is not important as long as no client suffers as a consequence. Would it not therefore be possible to permit him, a highly intuitive and gifted worker, to schedule and allocate his time to maximum client advantage and should not the supervisor be less concerned about his filling out forms, doing recording, completing reports, and so on?

It takes two to play games. The supervisor is induced to play this game because he identifies with the supervisee's concern for meeting client needs; he himself has frequently resented bureaucratic demands and so is, initially, sympathetic to the supervisee's complaints; and he is hesitant to assert his authority in demanding firmly that these requirements be met. If the supervisor chooses to play the game, he has enlisted in an alliance with the supervisee to subvert agency administrative procedures.

Another game designed to control the level of demands made on the supervisee might be called "Be Nice to Me because I am Nice to You." The principal ploy is flattery. "You're the best supervisor I ever had," "you're so perceptive that after I've talked to you I almost know what the client will say next," "you're so consistently helpful," "I look forward in the future to being as good a social worker as you are," and so on. It is a game of emotional blackmail in which, having been paid in this kind of coin, the supervisor finds himself unable to hold the worker firmly to legitimate demands.

The supervisor finds it difficult to resist engaging in the game because it is gratifying to be regarded as an omniscient source of wisdom; there is satisfaction in being perceived as helpful and in being selected as a pattern for identification and emulation. An invitation to play a game that tends to enhance a positive self-concept and feed one's narcissistic needs is likely to be accepted.

In general, the supervisor is vulnerable to an invitation to play this game. The supervisor needs the supervisee as much as the supervisee needs her. One of the principal sources of gratification for a worker is contact with the client. The supervisor is denied this source of gratification, at least directly. For the supervisor the analogous satisfaction is helping the supervisee to grow and change. But this means that she has to look to the supervisee to validate her effectiveness. Objective criteria of such effectiveness are, at best, obscure and equivocal. To have the supervisee say openly and directly, "I have learned a lot from you," "You have been helpful," is the kind of reassurance needed and often subtly solicited by the supervisor. The perceptive supervisee understands and exploits the supervisor's needs in initiating this game.

redefining the relationship

A second series of games is designed to lessen the demands made on the supervisee by redefining the supervisory relationship. These games depend on ambiguity in the definition of the supervisory relationship; it is open to a variety of interpretations and resembles, in some crucial respects, analogous relationships.

One kind of redefinition suggests a shift from the relationship of teacher and learner in an administrative hierarchy to worker and client in the context of therapy. The game might be called "Protect the Sick and the Infirm" or "Treat Me, Don't Beat Me." The supervisee would rather expose himself than his work, and so he asks the supervisor for help in solving his personal problems. The sophisticated player relates these problems to difficulties on the job. If the translation to worker and client is made, the nature of demands shifts as well. The kinds of demands one can legitimately impose on a client are clearly less onerous than those imposed on a worker. The supervisee has achieved a payoff in a softening of demands, and since so much time is spent discussing his personal problems there is less time left for discussing his work.

The supervisor is induced to play because the game appeals to the social worker in him (since he was a social worker before he became a supervisor and is still interested in helping those who have personal problems); it appeals to the voyeur in him (many supervisors are fascinated by the opportunity to share in the intimate life of others); it is flattering to be selected as a therapist; and he is not clearly certain that such a redefinition of the situation is impermissible. All the discussions about the equivocal boundaries between supervision and therapy feed into this uncertainty.

Another game of redefinition might be called "Evaluation Is Not for Friends." Here the supervisory relationship is redefined as a social relationship. The supervisee makes an effort to take coffee breaks with the supervisor, invite her to lunch, walk to and from the bus or the parking lot with her, and discuss common interests during conferences. The social component tends to vitiate the professional component in the relationship. It requires increased determination and resolution on the part of any supervisor to hold the "friend" to the required level of performance.

A more contemporary redefinition of the supervisor-supervisee relationship is less obvious than the two kinds just discussed, which have long been standard. The game of "Maximum Feasible Participation" involves a shift in roles from supervisor and supervisee to peer and peer. The supervisee suggests that the relationship will be most effective if it is established on the basis of democratic participation. Since he knows best what he needs and wants to learn, he should be granted equal responsibility for determining the agendas of conferences. So far so good. However, in the hands of a determined supervisee, joint control of agenda can easily become total supervisee control. Expectations may be lowered and threatening content areas avoided.

The supervisor finds himself in a predicament in trying to decline the game. There is truth in the contention that people learn best in a context that encourages democratic participation in the learning process. Furthermore, the current trend in working with social agency clients is to encourage maximum feasible participation, with as yet ambiguously defined limits. To decline the game is to suggest that one is old-fashioned, undemocratic, and against the rights of those on lower levels in the administrative hierarchy—not an enviable picture to project of oneself. The supervisor is forced to play but needs to be constantly alert in order to maintain some semblance of administrative authority and prevent all the shots being called by the supervisee-peer.

reducing power disparity

A third series of games is designed to reduce anxiety by reducing the power disparity between supervisor and worker. One source of the supervisor's power is, of course, his position in the administrative hierarchy vis-à-vis the supervisee. Another source of power lies in his expertise and superior skill. This second source of power disparity is vulnerable in this series of games. If the supervisee can establish the fact that the supervisor is not so smart after all, some of the power differential is lessened and with it some of the need to feel anxious.

One such game, frequently played, might be called "If You Knew Dostoyevsky like I Know Dostoyevsky." During the course of a conference, the supervisee alludes casually to the fact that the client's behavior reminds him of Raskolnikov's in *Crime and Punishment,* which is, after all, somewhat different in etiology from the pathology that plagued Prince Myshkin in *The Idiot.* An effective ploy, used to score additional points, involves asking the supervisor rhetorically, "You remember, don't you?" It is equally clear to both supervisee and supervisor that the latter does not remember—if, indeed, he ever knew. At this point the supervisee proceeds to instruct the supervisor. The roles of teacher and learner are reversed; power disparity and supervisee anxiety are simultaneously reduced.

The supervisor acquiesces to the game because refusal requires a confession of ignorance on his part. The supervisee who plays the game well cooperates in a conspiracy with the supervisor not to expose his ignorance openly. The discussion proceeds under the protection of the mutually accepted fiction that both know what they are talking about.

The content for the essential gambit in this game changes

with each generation of supervisees. My impression is that currently the allusion is likely to be to the work of the conditioning therapists—Eysenck, Wolpe, and Lazarus—rather than to literary figures. The effect on the supervisor, however, is the same: a feeling of depression and general malaise at having been found ignorant when his position requires that he know more than the supervisee. And it has the same payoff in reducing supervisee anxiety.

Another game in this genre exploits situational advantages to reduce power disparity and permit the supervisee the feeling that he, rather than the supervisor, is in control. This game is "So What Do *You* Know about It?" The supervisee with a long record of experience in public welfare refers to "those of us on the front lines who have struggled with the multiproblem client," exciting humility in the supervisor who has to try hard to remember when he last saw a live client. A married supervisee with children will allude to her marital experience and what it "really is like to be a mother" in discussing family therapy with an unmarried female supervisor. The older supervisee will talk about "life" from the vantage point of a veteran to the supervisor fresh out of graduate school. The younger supervisee will hint at his greater understanding of the adolescent client since he has, after all, smoked some marijuana and has seriously considered LSD. The supervisor, trying to tune in, finds his older psyche is not with it. The supervisor younger than the older supervisee, older than the younger supervisee, never having raised a child or met a payroll, finds himself being instructed by those he is charged with instructing; roles are reversed and the payoff to the supervisee lies in the fact that the supervisor becomes a less threatening figure.

Another, more recently developed, procedure for "putting the supervisor down" is through the judicious use in the conference of strong four-letter words. This is "Telling It like It Is," and the supervisor who responds with discomfort and loss of composure has forfeited some amount of control to the supervisee who has exposed a measure of the supervisor's bourgeois nature and residual Puritanism.

Putting the supervisor down may revolve around a question of social work goals rather than content. The social action–oriented supervisee is concerned with fundamental changes in social relationships. She knows that obtaining a slight increase in the budget for one client, finding a job for another client, or helping a neglectful mother relate more positively to her child are of little use since they leave the basic pathology of society unchanged. She is impatient with the case-oriented supervisor who is interested in helping a specific family live a little less troubled, a little less unhappily in a fundamentally disordered society. The game is "All or Nothing at All." It is designed to make the supervisor feel he has sold out, been co-opted by the Establishment, lost or abandoned his broader vision of the "good" society, has become endlessly concerned with symptoms rather than with causes. It is effective because the supervisor recognizes that there is an element of truth in the accusation for all who occupy positions of responsibility in the Establishment.

controlling the situation

The games mentioned have, as part of their effect, a shift of control of the situation from supervisor to supervisee. Another series of games is designed to place control of the supervisory situation more explicitly and directly in the hands of the supervisee. Control of the situation by the supervisor is potentially threatening since he can then take the initiative of introducing for discussion those weaknesses and inadequacies in the supervisee's work that need fullest review. If the supervisee can control the conference, much that is unflattering to discuss may be adroitly avoided.

One game designed to control the discussion's content is called "I Have a Little List." The supervisee comes in with a series of questions about his work that he would very much like to discuss. The better player formulates the questions so they relate to problems in which the supervisor has greatest professional interest and about which he has done considerable reading. The supervisee is under no obligation to listen to the answers to his questions. When question 1 has been asked, the supervisor is off on a short lecture, during which time the supervisee is free to plan mentally the next weekend or review the last weekend, taking care merely to listen for signs that the supervisor is running down. When this happens, the supervisee introduces question 2 with an appropriate transitional comment, and the cycle is repeated. As the supervisee increases the supervisor's level of participation he is, by the same token, decreasing his own level of participation, since only one person can be talking at once. Thus the supervisee controls both the content and the direction of conference interaction. The supervisor is induced to play this game because there is narcissistic gratification in displaying one's knowledge and in meeting the supervisee's dependency needs, and because, in accordance with good social work practice, the supervisee's questions should be accepted, respected, and, if possible, answered.

Control of the initiative is also seized by the supervisee in the game of "Heading Them Off at the Pass." Here the supervisee knows that her poor work is likely to be analyzed critically. She therefore opens the conference by freely admitting her mistakes—she knows it was an inadequate interview, she knows that she should have, by now, learned to do better. There is no failing on the supervisor's agenda for discussion to which she does not freely confess in advance, flagellating herself to excess. The supervisor, faced with this overwhelming self-derogation, has little option but to reassure the supervisee sympathetically. The tactic not only makes it difficult for a supervisor to conduct an extended discussion of mistakes in the work but also elicits praise for whatever limited strengths the supervisee has manifested. The supervisor, once again, acts out of concern with troubled people, out of his predisposition to comfort the discomforted, out of pleasure in acting the good, forgiving parent.

Another variation is "Pleading Fragility." The supervisee communicates "that he is extremely brittle, is easily hurt or may even go over the brink if pushed too hard. This communication effectively prevents the supervisor from exploring any painful or threatening issues with the supervisee" (Bauman 1972, p. 253).

Control can also be exerted through fluttering dependency, a case of strength through weakness. It is the game of "Little Old Me" or "Casework à Trois." The supervisee, in his ignorance and incompetence, looks to the knowledgeable, competent supervisor for a detailed prescription of how to proceed: "What would *you* do next?" "Then what would *you* say?" The supervisee unloads responsibility for the case onto the supervisor and the supervisor shares the caseload with the worker. The supervisor plays the game because, in fact, she does share responsibility for case management with the supervisee and has responsibility for seeing that the client is not harmed. Further, the supervisor often wants the gratification of carrying a caseload, however vicariously, so that she is somewhat predisposed to take the case out of the supervisee's hands. There are, in addition, the pleasures derived from acting the capable parent to the dependent child and from the domination of others.

A variant of this game in the hands of a more hostile supervisee is "I Did like You Told Me." Here the supervisee maneuvers the supervisor into offering specific prescriptions on case management and then applies them in spiteful obedience and undisguised mimicry. The supervisee acts as though the supervisor were responsible for the case, he himself merely being the executor of supervisory directives. Invariably and inevitably, whatever has been suggested by the supervisor fails to accomplish what it was supposed to accomplish. "I Did like You Told Me" is designed to make even a strong supervisor defensive.

"It's All So Confusing" attempts to reduce the authority of the supervisor by appeals to other authorities—a former supervisor, another supervisor in the same agency, or a faculty member at a local school of social work with whom the supervisee just happened to discuss the case. The supervisee casually indicates that in similar situations his former supervisor tended to take a certain approach, which is at variance with the approach the current supervisor regards as desirable. And "it's all so confusing" when different "authorities" suggest such different approaches to the same situation. The supervisor is faced with defending his approach against some unnamed, unknown competitor. This is difficult, especially because few situations in social work permit an unequivocal answer in which the supervisor can have complete confidence. Since the supervisor was somewhat shaky in his approach in the first place, he feels vulnerable to alternative suggestions from other "authorities," and his sense of authority in relation to the supervisee is eroded.

A supervisee can control the degree of threat in the supervisory situation by distancing techniques. The game is "What You Don't Know Won't Hurt Me." The supervisor knows the work of the supervisee only indirectly, through what is available in the recording and shared verbally in the conference. The supervisee can elect to share in a manner that is thin, inconsequential, without depth of affect. He can share selectively and can distort (consciously or unconsciously) in order to present a more favorable picture of his work. The supervisee can be passive and reticent or overwhelm the supervisor with endless trivia. In whatever manner it is done, the supervisee increases distance between the work he actually does and the supervisor who is responsible for critically analyzing it with him. This not only reduces the threat to him of possible criticism of his work but also, as Fleming and Benedek (1966) point out, prevents the supervisor from intruding into the privacy of his relationship with the client.

Supervisors' Games

It would be doing both supervisor and supervisee an injustice to neglect a description of games initiated by supervisors. Supervisors play games for the same reasons that supervisees play. The games are methods of adjusting to stresses encountered in performing their role. Supervisors play games out of felt threats to their position in the hierarchy, uncertainty about their authority, reluctance to use their authority, a desire to be liked, a need for the supervisees' approval—and out of some hostility to supervisees that is inevitable in such a complex, close relationship.

One of the classic supervisory games can be called "I Wonder Why You Really Said That." This is the game of redefining honest disagreement so that it appears to be psychological resistance. Honest disagreement requires that the supervisor defend her point of view and be sufficiently acquainted with the literature to present the research evidence in support of her contention. If honest disagreement is redefined as resistance, the burden is shifted to the supervisee. He has to examine the needs and motives that prompt him to question what the supervisor has said. The supervisor is thus relieved of the burden of validating what she has said, and the onus for defense now rests with the supervisee.

Another classic supervisory game is "One Good Question Deserves Another." A supervisor writes:

I learned that another part of a supervisor's skills, as far as the workers are concerned, is to know all the answers. I was able to get out of this very easily. I discovered that when a worker asks a question, the best thing to do is to immediately ask for what she thinks. While the worker is figuring out the answer to her own question (this is known as growth and development), the supervisor quickly tries to figure it out also. She may arrive at the answer the same time as the worker, but the worker somehow assumes that she knew it all along. This is very comfortable for the supervisor. In the event that neither the worker nor the supervisor succeeds in coming up with a useful thought on the question the worker has raised, the supervisor can look wise and suggest that they think about it and discuss it further next time. This gives the supervisor plenty of time to look up the subject and leaves the worker with the feeling that the supervisor is giving great weight to her question. In the event that the supervisor does not want to go to all the trouble, she can just tell the worker that she does not know the answer (this is known as helping the worker accept the limitations of the supervision) and tell her to look it up herself. (H.C.D. 1949, p. 162)

Some games are designed to validate the supervisor's authority on the basis of ascription. Subtly appealing to experience or credentials, the supervisor solicits endorsement of authority and seeks to deflect any challenge to such authority. Playing "Parents Know Best," the supervisor asserts her unquestioned authority on the basis of her M.S.W. or years on the job (Hawthorne 1975).

Some supervisor's games are concerned with protection from the burden of supervision. The supervisor can avoid the inconvenience of individual conferences by finding justifiable reasons to postpone or cancel conferences or significantly shorten those which are unavoidable. The game might be termed "I Can Hardly Catch My Breath." The supervisor indicates that because he has suddenly received an administrative request for a special report or some special statistics, he is very sorry but the scheduled conference will have to be postponed (Hawthorne 1975).

A judicious arrangement of the supervisory conference agenda may provide protection from the need to confess inability to help. The more difficult questions are relegated to the last ten minutes of the conference. Then, regretfully noting that "I wish we had more time to discuss this," the supervisor gives these questions a cursory and hurried review, leaving no time for possibly embarrassing questions.

Appealing to the limits of the supervision power protects the supervisors from some difficult decisions. In playing "I Would if I Could but I Can't," the supervisor indicates that she would be willing to go along with some request that the supervisee is making except for the fact that the administration will not permit it.

The worker has considerable administrative discretion in how liberally or rigidly she might interpret agency policy in contact with the client. The supervisor has similar maneuverability in applying administrative requirements in supervision. The supervisor creates an obligation by leniency in enforcing agency procedures. "After All I Did for You" is a supervisor's game which seeks to cash in on such obligations. It calls for explicit attention to the obligations which the supervisee has incurred and asks that restitution be made. "After all I did for you" can be communicated almost as effectively nonverbally as verbally. The pained expression, the sigh of resignation at impending disappointment bring the supervisee up short.

The supervisor is selective in her demands for adherence to agency rules and procedures or modulates the vigorousness with which she requires such adherence. The extent to which the supervisor feels free to do this depends on the security she feels in her own relationship with administrators to whom she is responsible and the number of "reciprocity credits" that she has earned with them.

The obverse of reciprocity credits is of course "obligation deficits." Supervisees seek to obligate the supervisor for extra work they have done in meeting the request for a report on short notice, in agreeing to cover an uncovered client, and so on. Being "obligated" to the workers, the supervisor has to reciprocate by softening, for a time at least, her demands on the workers in order to maintain their loyalty.

Countering Games

Although such defensive games help the supervisee cope with anxiety-provoking stress, they may be dysfunctional and subvert the purposes of the supervisory encounter. Consequently the supervisor may be required to break up the games.

The simplest and most direct way of dealing with games introduced by the supervisee is to refuse to play. Yet a key difficulty in this approach has been implied by discussion of the gains for the supervisor in playing along. The supervisee can successfully enlist the supervisor in a game only if the supervisor wants to play for her own reasons. Collusion is not forced but is freely granted. Refusing to play requires that the supervisor be ready and able to forfeit self-advantages. For instance, in declining to go along with the supervisee's request that he be permitted to ignore agency administrative requirements in playing "Two against the Agency," the supervisor has to be comfortable in exercising her administrative authority, willing to risk and deal with supervisee hostility and rejection, willing to accept the accusation that she is bureaucratically, rather than professionally, oriented. In declining other games the supervisor denies herself the sweet fruits of flattery, the joys of omniscience, the pleasures of acting as therapist, and the gratification of being well liked. She incurs the penalties of an open admission of ignorance and uncertainty and the loss of infallibility. Declining to play the games demands a supervisor who is aware of and comfortable in what she is doing and who accepts herself in all her "glorious strengths and human weaknesses." The less vulnerable the supervisor, the more impervious she is to gamesmanship—not an easy prescription to fill.

A second response lies in open confrontation. Goffman (1959) points out that in the usual social encounter each person accepts the line put out by the other person. There is a process of mutual face-saving in which what is said is accepted at its face value and "each participant is allowed to carry the role he has chosen for himself," unchallenged (p. 11). This is done out of self-protection since, in not challenging another, one is also ensuring that the other will not, in turn, challenge one's own fiction. Confrontation implies a refusal to accept the game being proposed; instead, the supervisor seeks to expose and make explicit what the supervisee is doing. The supervisory situation, like the therapeutic situation, deliberately rejects the usual rules of social interaction in attempting to help the supervisee.

Confrontation needs to be used, of course, with due regard for the supervisee's ability to handle the embarrassment and self-threat it involves. The supervisor needs to be aware of the defensive significance of the game to the supervisee. Naming the interactions that have been described as "games" does not imply that they are frivolous and without consequence. Unmasking games risks much that is of serious personal significance for the supervisee. Interpretation and confrontation here, as always, require compassionate caution, a sense of timing, and an understanding of dosage.

Another approach is to share honestly with the supervisee one's awareness of what he is attempting to do in adjusting to work-related stress but to focus the discussion neither on the dynamics of his behavior nor on one's reaction to it, but on the disadvantages for him in playing games. These games have decided drawbacks for the supervisee. They deny him the possibility of effectively fulfilling one of the essential purposes of supervision—helping him to grow professionally. The games frustrate the achievement of this outcome. In playing games the supervisee loses by winning.

Job-Related Tension for the Supervisor

The supervisee is not alone in encountering job-related tensions that call for adjustive responses and supportive help. The supervisor also struggles with problems that create tension for him in becoming, and being, a supervisor. Promotion to supervisor involves a drastic change for the worker. The newly appointed supervisor "is essentially entering a new occupation, not simply a new position. This occupation will have its own set of job specifications . . . precedents . . . expectations. In the performance of his duties he finds himself in a new set of role relations with his former peers, with his new administrative colleagues and with his new superiors" (Moore 1970, p. 213).

Becoming a supervisor may involve moving to a new agency and all that this implies in the way of adjustment. But even if the worker stays in the same agency after becoming a supervisor, the shift requires some of the adjustments involved in accepting a new job. As one beginning supervisor said, "Rather than being at the top of the ladder as a caseworker, I was starting all over at the bottom again in my new trade—supervision" (H.C.D. 1949, p. 161). The shift has been compared with that of a person who has often ridden as a passenger in a car and who now has the responsibility for driving the car, watching traffic, getting the group safely to its destination.

In becoming a supervisor the direct service worker gives up a role with which he has become familiar and in which he is comfortable. He is asked to make a transition to a new and unfamiliar role which requires implementation of functions that he has not as yet learned. He may have some anxiety about his ability to meet the demands of the new job.

Some of the stress related to becoming a supervisor was detailed in a study of the reaction of 40 supervisors to the experience of transition (Woodcock 1967). Becoming a supervisor was regarded as a career crisis, "the first and most striking finding being the degree of alarm that the prospect of supervision proved to arouse" (p. 68). Since few supervisors had had formal training in supervision prior to the appointment, they felt considerable anxiety about whether they could do the job. This fear related particularly to the demand of educational supervision. Did they know enough to teach others to do the work? New supervisors reported "increased reading, thinking, consulting, attending lectures, seminars, meetings, anything which would illuminate the road ahead. . . . One supervisor said, 'I bought a pile of social work books, only one of which I read.' Another 'made notes on the principles of casework and determined to exemplify all these in all cases' " (p. 69). They had doubts about the adequacy of their qualifications and consequently about their entitlement to the position. In making the transition, it takes time before one begins to think like a supervisor. This involves an acknowledgment and acceptance of the difference between worker and supervisor in level of skill and authority.

Becoming a supervisor forces one to explicitly examine one's practice in order to conceptualize it for teaching. "Supervising forced me to put my ideas, knowledge and experience together. I was placed in the position of having to communicate or try to communicate what I knew."

In moving into supervision, the worker assumes the stress of greater responsibilities. She has responsibility to the supervisees for administration, education, and support, and ultimate responsibility for service to the client. She assumes greater responsibility for policy formulation in the agency and community-agency relationships. Whereas previously the worker was responsible only for her own work, she now has the larger responsibility for the work of a number of others. Instead of being responsible for a caseload, the supervisor is now responsible for a number of caseloads.

In becoming a supervisor, the worker gives up the satisfaction of direct practice and contact with clients. She has to learn to offer service through others. One supervisor said, "As a caseworker I was very 'social work' oriented. I enjoyed working with clients and helping them if possible. As a supervisor I no longer feel the stimulation I did as a worker" (Miller and Podell 1970, p. 36). Some supervisors ask for a small direct-practice caseload as a way of meeting the need for these satisfactions.

The shift from diagnosis of clients' social problems to diagnosis of supervisees' educational problems, from helping in the personal development of the client to helping in the professional development of the worker, involves a shift from therapeutic techniques previously acquired to pedagogic techniques that need to be learned. Accepting the title of supervisor involves a shift in self-perception from a treatment person to an administrator-teacher.

Some stress derives from the defensiveness that a supervisor might feel in comparing administrative work with direct service work. According higher status to direct service activity as the only work worth doing in an agency. the supervisor may be somewhat apologetic about a desk job without client contact (Berliner 1971).

As discussed earlier, some of the administrative requirements of the supervisor's job run counter to the ethos of social work. The need to exercise authority, the need to judge the worker, the need to deindividualize the client in formulating and implementing policy require some adjustments in attitude. The beginning supervisor also has to make other adjustments in perspective. He moves from a process orientation as worker to a more focused concern with product as a supervisor. He has to become more organizationally oriented.

The movement from worker to supervisor is accompanied by a stronger identification with the agency, increased support, loyalty, and commitment to the organization and its policies. Agency policy and actions now seem more justifiable, acceptable, morally correct and fair. The new supervisor's attitudes become more like those supervisors whose ranks he is joining and different from the attitudes of direct-service workers from whom he is disengaging.

Lieberman (1956) tested the hypothesis that a person's attitudes will be influenced by the role he occupies in a social system. "Johnny is a changed boy since he was made a monitor in school"; "She is a different woman since she got married"; "You would never recognize him since he became foreman" (p. 385). He studied the attitudes of men in industrial concerns before and after they became supervisors. He found that, since the supervisory role entails being a representative of management, workers who were made supervisors did tend to become more favorable to management.

The change from worker to supervisor involves a change in reference group affiliation, which leads to changes in attitudes and therefore behavior. The change in functions performed also requires changes in behavior. Attitudes are revised so that they are consistent with changed behavior required by changed functions. One supervisor expressed her change in orientation as follows:

My orientation definitely changed as I moved from the role of supervisee to the role of supervisor. In the first place, I took agency policy much more seriously. I also felt a marked increase in responsibilities and in the importance of realizing the full responsibilities of this position. I also saw problems in a wider scope and found it easier to analyze them when the details and the client were not as close to me.

As he moves from worker to supervisor, the new supervisor becomes more sensitive to the effects on policy, agency survival, and agency image of actions taken with, or in behalf of, individual clients. He adopts an administrative perspective with regard to service decisions (Piven and Pappenfort 1960). This change in orientation may be stressful for some supervisors who perceive it as evidence of "going over to the enemy" or "joining the Establishment."

Some problems arise from the fact that the supervisor, in a position immediately adjacent to the caseworker, has the same professional background and experience as the supervisee. Identified and empathic with the problems and orientation of the direct service worker, the supervisor nevertheless represents management. "This creates both a role conflict and a personal dilemma for the supervisor. Professional norms stressing autonomous integrity for practitioners still make a claim on him which he considers legitimate but so does the organization's need for control" (Abrahamson 1967, p. 83).

The supervisor is apt to be pulled between conflicting expectations from above and below. Placed at the boundary between the direct service worker and agency administration, the supervisor is simultaneously a member of both the working unit and the organizational unit. As is true for all who operate in boundary areas, the supervisor is in a difficult position. He has only marginal membership in each unit and is faced with pressure from both as he attempts to act as a buffer and mediator between them. Sometimes the directives from administration and the demands from the workers are contradictory. In responding to one group, he risks incurring the hostility of the other group and compromising his power to influence.

Becoming a supervisor requires changes in the worker's relationships with others in the agency. The supervisor is no longer a member of the peer group of direct service workers. She has become one of "them." Not only is the new supervisor deprived of what may have been a satisfying source of pleasure and support, but she is further penalized by feelings of rivalry and jealousy from former colleagues. There may be "a certain feeling of distance that I had arrived and they hadn't" or "that I was doing better than them" (Woodcock 1967, p. 69). A new supervisor says,

One's colleagues like to see a person get ahead all right—but not too far ahead, and not too fast. If fortune seems to be smiling too often and too broadly on one person, his friends begin to sharpen their knives to even up the score a bit. I was philosophical about this, as by this time I realized that an occasional knife in the ribs goes with supervision just as June bugs go with June and must be accepted as stoically. I marked my promotion by buying a bigger brief case, enrolling in an advanced seminar in supervision, and having a drink with a few sympathetic friends—also supervisors. (H.C.D. 1949, p. 162)

Social distance is increased between the worker-turned-supervisor and his former peers. There is more formality, less spontaneity in their interaction, a greater guardedness and hesitancy in communication. The talk slows down and alters as he sits down to drink coffee with them.

Charles Lamb noted this change in his essay "The Superannuated Man":

To dissipate this awkward feeling, I have been fain to go among them once or twice since; to visit my old desk fellows—my co-brethren of the quill—that I had left below in the state militant. Not all the kindness with which they received me could quite restore to me that pleasant familiarity which I had heretofore enjoyed among them. We cracked some of our old jokes, but methought they went off but faintly.

Former peers wonder about the new supervisor. Will he act with favoritism toward best friends; will he pay off grudges against old enemies; will he grow into the job or just swell? "He must neither commit the sin of officiousness nor the folly of fraternity."

The ghosts of one's predecessors can be a source of tension. The new supervisor wonders if she can be as good as the former supervisor; if, in changing some of the patterns of work established by the former supervisor, she will insult the old loyalties of the supervisees and incur their hostility.

Having lost her old peer group, the new supervisor has to obtain acceptance in a new peer group, that of the other supervisors. Maintenance of some marginality, some social distance, from both groups to which the supervisor is hierarchically related, the supervisees who are his subordinates and the administrators who are his superiors, is functionally useful. Blau and Scott (1962) found that "detachment from subordinates was associated with high productivity and independence from superiors with greater solidarity in the work group and [that] both kinds of social distance, although the two were hardly related to one another, were associated with commanding the loyalty of subordinates" (p. 238).

Supervisors, like supervisees, face heavy work pressures. Wasserman (1971) questions whether "the supervisor, responsible for five workers with a total of 175–200 cases or more, can make reasoned and balanced judgements about any problematic human situations, particularly when he must base his judgements on what the workers say about clients" (p. 91). A recent study of supervisors' work load in a public welfare agency concluded that "casework supervisors did not have time to supervise" (Galm 1972, p. 34). Faced with such pressures, supervisors feel anxious about the kind of job they can do. A supervisor writes:

My greatest dissatisfaction came with the realization that supervision takes an incredibly large amount of time. I now understand why I have received so little of it in my former placements. To do the job correctly, one needs to devote great time and energy to supervising each [worker]. It resembles teaching anything. To maximize effectiveness, the teacher must prepare several hours for each hour spent actually instructing. I would have liked to have been able to analyze each recording of the worker, for instance, in depth, prior to our discussion of it, but instead I found myself listening to it for the first time in conference and responding spontaneously.

Supervisors are aware of, and feel concerned about, the limits of the help they can give supervisees. A supervisor says: "A big part of my anxiousness is that I won't know the answers for them and that I won't satisfy them with the answers that I have to give. I think even our profession doesn't know that much and that's a hard thing. They walk out feeling they didn't get what they wanted" (Amacher 1971, p. 262). Workers can stand the uncertainty of doubt better than the supervisor can because they feel that if they do not know the answers they need, the supervisor can make them available. The worker has the sanctioned luxury of acceptable dependence on the supervisor. The supervisor is granted the dubious prerogative of independence. She becomes the question-answerer rather than the question-asker. Furthermore, she has little opportunity to turn to others in the hierarchy who might be able to answer her own questions. The worker's status gives absolution from some mistakes; supervisor's status reduces the grant of immunity. In meeting the needs of the worker, the supervisor requires a confidence in her convictions and in decision-making that is hard to come by. The pressure to act with certainty, when inwardly one feels very uncertain, is stressful.

There is also stress which results from the lack of clear definition in many agencies of the supervisor's tasks, responsibilities, and authority; and stress as a consequence of current attacks on the legitimacy of the position of supervisor. The discussion in the literature, which suggests that supervision is an archaic, unnecessary drag on the profession, tends to erode the confidence of supervisors that they are engaged in a meaningful and appreciated task.

Supervisors worry that they may be growing away from the job they have to supervise. In some measure the supervisor's image of practice is not as it is but as it once was; practice in the supervisee's experience is as it is today. Such anxiety is exacerbated by the rapidity of change. "Given the rapid changes in knowledge and state of the arts, the administrative professional is in danger of losing 'professional authentication'" (Moore 1970, p. 211). Changes involve new orientations and new techniques. Supervisors may often lack mastery of some of the new techniques and knowledge about some of the new programs. Hanlan (1972) cites an example of this:

The merger of a number of small independent, sectarian agencies in Philadelphia under one administrative organization is one illustration of how the change in functions has broad ramifications throughout all levels of the organization. In this particular case, the tension was particularly noticeable at the level of the first-line supervisor. The situation became critical when supervisors who formerly performed casework teaching functions were now required to train their staff and themselves in a wide range of community-organizing functions. (p. 43)

The supervisor has to deal with the stress of competitiveness between supervisees while diplomatically maintaining a cooperative spirit in the group. "Several workers with the same supervisor are like a big family, each demanding the . . . attention of a busy mother who has her own housework to do. The supervisor has to learn to give each what he needs without seeming to give anyone more than the others" (H.C.D. 1949, p. 163). Here, too, the supervisor walks a tightrope.

The limits of the supervisor's responsibility are less definite than the worker's. Consequently, some beginning supervisors find themselves working harder than ever before. "I soon found that I was doing about twice as much work as I had done formerly. When I brought this to my executive's attention she was very nice about it. She patiently explained that this was one of the privileges of my new position" (H.C.D. 1949, p. 161).

In addition to the indefiniteness of limits, which acts as a stress toward more work, there is also a very real expansion of responsibilities. There is a greater legitimacy to claims on the supervisor's time for involvement in professional activities, there is increased responsibility as a representative of the agency to the community. It is not as easy now to claim that extra-agency, but professionally related, matters are "off limits."

If the principal sources of stress for the supervisee are the client and the supervisor, the principal sources of stress for the supervisor are the worker and the administration. I noted earlier that the supervisor is dependent on the worker to some extent. In terms of instrumental needs the supervisor gets compliance, communication, and information from the worker; in response to expressive needs, the supervisor gets appreciation, respect, and loyalty from the worker. Failure or refusal of the worker to meet the instrumental and expressive needs of the supervisor creates a stress for the supervisor. The worker can be uncooperative, resistive, make the work of the supervisor more difficult, threaten the supervisor's good conception of herself and her competence. The supervisor is identified with her supervisees in the agency and in the community, and any complaints about their work reflects negatively on her.

Certain situations present special problems for the supervisor. In some instances the official hierarchical relationship is contrary to the usual pattern of social arrangements. The younger person is generally expected to defer to older people; people with less experience on the job are expected to defer to those with more experience. Despite recent changes, there is still some persistence of the attitude that there is something strange about a man being hierarchically subordinate to a woman. Consequently, when the supervisor is younger than the supervisee, has less experience on the job or is a female supervising a male, the situation presents additional problems. The supervisor in such instances may feel less secure, more defensive, less certain of her entitlement to the position. (Positional authority is called into question because it runs counter to social expectations.)

If there is a substantial age difference between supervisor and supervisee, there is a problem of generational gap, of "cultural lag" between the older, experienced supervisors and the younger, recently trained supervisees. However, the young supervisor with the young supervisee faces other kinds of problems. A young supervisor with limited practice experience writes:

I feel that my age and amount of experience in social work are both my greatest strength and my greatest weaknesses. They are strengths because it has only been a few months since I was in the same position as my supervisee, with strong feelings of inadequacy and nervousness. They are weaknesses because I don't feel that I know enough about social work yet to supervise and teach someone else.

Where supervisor and supervisee are of different races, some of the problems of race relations in society at large are apt to intrude in the relationship. The more frequent pattern is of a white supervisor and a black supervisee:

The black worker felt that I was not meeting her needs, probably because of our racial differences. The worker was angry and I felt threatened (maybe I am a racist). We spent a great deal of time discussing these feelings. We got a lot of talk going but no real change in attitude. Finally I said, "Look, we've talked about it long enough. Let's get on to the business of the agency. If a specific example comes up that seems related to our differences in race we can then discuss it." The situation improved after this. It seemed to me in retrospect that the worker was suffering from insecurity about how she was doing the job. I got hooked onto looking at racism (with some valid concern) when actually the worker needed more help to feel she could do the job.

A black worker brought up her concern about racism within the agency. I asked her to go over all such situations she knew of. I took them to administrative staff who were only partially receptive to change. I told the worker of these activities and asked her to begin thinking about how she could operate with certain givens and continue to work to change a few things. This approach certainly helped develop a good relationship between worker and supervisor. We got a few changes made in the agency and I helped the worker look towards how she wanted to use herself in future agencies.

I think the approach I used was helpful because it brought out a sore subject and got some openness between worker and supervisor; it helped the worker learn how to present problems and to explore where the limitations were. The areas of progress were brought about by presenting some alternatives. This took it away from a gripe session only, toward looking at ways to deal with the problem.

Where a black person supervises a white person, positional authority is again in contradiction to the usual social arrangement pattern. Few whites have experienced a situation of subordination to a black person. A black woman supervising a white woman writes about the learning advantages of such an arrangement: "This was an opportunity for the worker to get information on black life styles, feelings, etc., that she may otherwise not have had a chance to learn. It also gave me a chance to teach some therapeutic techniques to use in dealing with black clients that aren't usually printed in the literature." Royster, a black social worker, notes that "the black supervisor must decide whether or not to assign white workers to black clients, given the prevailing belief in much of the community that black workers are more effective with black clients and given the knowledge of racism within each white person" (1972, p. 81).

Royster feels that the black supervisor may have even more difficulty with black workers. The black supervisor, representing management in agencies that often have racist policies, may be in conflict with those black workers who are more whole-heartedly oriented to the views of the black community (p. 80). There is very limited research on race problems in supervision, and the few studies that are available have been conducted in simulated experimental situations (Mayhand and Grusky 1972; Richards and Jaffee 1972).

The dissatisfactions expressed by supervisors suggest some of the kinds of stresses they encounter in their role. These are listed in table 3.

Coping with Stress—Supervisors' Adaptations

In general, supervisors have fewer supportive resources available to help them cope with work-related stresses than do supervisees. Griping as a form of cathartic release is not as readily available to the supervisor.

Caseworkers could freely complain about agency policies and even, on occasion, defy them, but such options were hardly open to supervisors. Supervisors did critically discuss some aspects of agency functioning in supervisory staff meetings, and such discussions sometimes resulted in policy changes, but many regulations were outside their control, having been set by legislative bodies and the lay board. Regardless of their own feelings, supervisors were expected to enforce all current agency policies. These circumstances created problems for all supervisors, although professionally oriented supervisors were placed in a particularly difficult position. It was their task to help workers to accommodate to the agency's program—to reconcile bureaucratic requirements with professional principles. (Scott 1969, p. 133, reprinted with permission of Macmillan Publishing Co.)

There appear to be fewer provisions made for the formal induction of supervisors into their new role and fewer formal, regularized channels provided to assure support for new supervisors during the transitional period. Perhaps the assumption is that if the person is experienced enough to be selected for the position, he or she should be able to operate independently without the need for such support. A supervisor wryly expresses some resentment about this:

table 3.

Supervisor Dissatisfaction in Supervision

	Percentage of supervisors checking item as strong source of dissatisfaction (N = 469)
1. Dissatisfaction with administrative "housekeeping"—red tape, details in caseload audits, time sheets, statistical reports, etc.	71
2. Dissatisfaction because other heavy responsibilities of the job not related to work with supervisees prevent me from giving as much time as I would like to supervisees.	53
3. Loss of the direct worker-client contact and relationship.	46
4. Dissatisfaction related to need to get workers' adherence to agency policy and procedure with which I disagree.	41
5. Dissatisfaction with having to work with supervisees who are resistive or hostile or dependent or slow learners, etc.	39
6. Dissatisfaction from being tied to the desk and to the office.	27
7. Anxiety at the responsibility of making decisions for which there is no clear-cut agency policy or procedure.	27
8. Dissatisfaction associated with the conflict between administrative evaluative aspects of the relationship with supervisees and the educational aspects.	26
9. Anxiety from not feeling certain that I know enough to be an adequate supervisor.	22
10. The need to exercise administrative authority in relation to supervisee performance and to evaluate the work of the supervisee.	21
11. Dissatisfaction at the socially and professionally isolated position of the supervisor in my agency.	21
12. Dissatisfaction with the physical aspects of my job—office, equipment, parking, etc.	18
13. Dissatisfaction at finding myself becoming part of the Establishment.	15
14. Anxiety from being responsible for somebody else's work and being looked to for leadership.	12
15. Anxiety at having to supervise workers who are older and/or more experienced than myself.	2
16. Other (miscellaneous).	2

Source: Kadushin (1973).

My first supervisee was a rather dependent person, who, as we expressed it professionally in her evaluation, "worked best with considerable reassurance and support." In practical terms, this meant that I propped her up while she propped the clients up, and in the end the whole weight fell on me. This left me in need of "considerable reassurance and support" too, but no one thought of that. I was the supervisor and I was paid to have shoulders that were broad. I soon became accustomed to this, however, and eventually I was able to prop several workers up—something like the bottom man in a human acrobatic act—and hardly feel it at all. (H.C.D. 1949, p. 162)

The supervisory peer group is less often a resource for emotional support than is the direct-worker peer group. There are not as many supervisors, so there are fewer possibilities for choice of those with whom one might feel comfortable and congenial. Supervisors do not meet and interact with each other as regularly as do direct service workers. Competition for promotion becomes keener as one moves up the administrative ladder because there are progressively fewer positions available. Consequently there is less tendency for the supervisors to act as a group and a greater tendency to act as individuals in seeking administrative favor.

A study of supervisors in a public welfare agency notes that "all supervisors felt that they needed someone with whom they could discuss problems that faced them and in most instances the immediate supervisor assumed the support role" (Colorado State Department of Public Welfare 1967, p. 10). The supervisee is an additional source of support in offering positive feedback. If the supervisee learns well and performs competently, this achievement is also a source of reward and support for the supervisor. A supervisor writes: "My supervisee's feedback and interest were satisfying. I was also very happy when she made new discoveries on her own and shared them with me." In making the transition from worker to supervisor, people are often helped by the realization that many of their social work skills are adaptable and applicable to the demands of the new role. Furthermore, looking back at their earlier experience as supervisees permits them to empathize with and understand their own supervisees.

Supervisors, in adjusting, make deliberate efforts to buffer themselves from supervisees. Too much social contact, too little distance, exposes the supervisor to constant pressure from the demands and needs, explicit or implicit, of the supervisees. But since the supervisor needs the cooperation of the supervisees, and a positive relationship with them, too great a social distance is undesirable. In a somewhat formalized, controlled contact the supervisor seeks an optimum balance between too great a familiarity, which risks constant pressure, and too little, which encourages supervisee resistance and alienation.

Some supervisors may adjust to the stresses of the position by becoming indifferent and doing the minimum to satisfy the requirements. Such a supervisor rewards supervisees who handle their assignments without bothering him, who do not bring any problems, who do not have any complaints themselves and do not generate any complaints from clients or other agencies, who do not allow emergencies to develop and, when they do develop, handle them by themselves. The supervisor's actions are motivated not by a concern with helping the supervisees develop autonomy but rather by a desire to be trouble free. He settles for the absence of negatives in the performance of his supervisees rather than the presence of positives. He is not concerned with noncompliance as long as the supervisees take the risk and are not too blatant about it so that it comes to his explicit attention.

There are numerous compensating gratifications that offset, and make acceptable, the increased stresses occasioned by the appointment to supervisor. Table 4 ranks satisfactions in supervision as described by supervisors. The listing points to the kinds of social and emotional returns from their jobs which sustain supervisors in dealing with job-related tensions.

Comparative Enactment of the Principal Components of Supervision

These are the three principal components of social work supervision—administrative supervision, educational supervision, and supportive supervision. The three components effectively

table 4.

Supervisor Satisfaction in Supervision

	Percentage of supervisors checking item as strong source of satisfaction (N = 469)
1. Satisfaction in helping the supervisee grow and develop in professional competence.	88
2. Satisfaction in ensuring more efficient and effective service to more clients through my supervisory activity.	75
3. Satisfaction in sharing my social work knowledge and skills with supervisees.	63
4. Satisfaction in the greater opportunity and leverage to affect changes in agency policy and procedures.	45
5. Satisfaction in the stimulation provided by curious, idealistic and enthusiastic supervisees.	44
6. Satisfaction in helping the supervisee grow and develop as a person.	37
7. Satisfaction in a more diversified job.	31
8. Satisfaction in having others look to me for leadership, advice, direction.	24
9. Satisfaction in being able to provide emotional support to supervisees when needed.	23
10. Satisfaction in increased salary that goes with job.	23
11. Satisfaction in contacts with professionally qualified and interesting fellow supervisors.	18
12. Satisfaction in the status and authority the position gives me.	9
13. Satisfaction in being free from contact with difficult clients and a heavy caseload.	5
14. Satisfaction in helping supervisees with their personal problems.	1
15. Satisfaction with the physical aspects of the supervisor's job—better office, parking, privileges, etc.	1
16. Other (miscellaneous).	2

Source: Kadushin (1973).

cover both the instrumental and expressive responsibilities of supervision—ensuring that the work is done, by people who know how to do it and who feel good about themselves and their job while doing it.

Supervisors tend to view the administrative component of

supervision as less important than other components. "Ensuring that the client gets full entitlement to service" and "ensuring the professional development of the supervisee" are ranked as the two most important functions of supervision. "Ensuring compliance with agency policy and procedure" and "ensuring accountability for the use of public funds" are ranked among the least important functions of supervision (Kadushin 1974).

In general the evidence available seems to show that the responsibilities of supportive supervision are more effectively implemented than the responsibilities of either administrative or educational supervision. A study of the reactions of 211 beginning social workers (caseworkers, group workers, and community organizers) to their job indicated that a major source of dissatisfaction was the technical competence of the supervisors. At the same time, the workers were very much satisfied with the interpersonal relationships they enjoyed with their supervisors. Expressive needs were satisfied, instrumental needs were not (Miller 1970).

A study of the differences between the social work students' ideal picture of supervision and actual supervision encountered shows the greatest discrepancy with regard to the "cognitive-structuring behaviors" of their supervisors. These included such instrumental problem-solving aspects of supervision as the following: "As I need them, he suggests specific intervention techniques"; "He helps me to apply theoretical concepts in the analysis of my practice"; "He assists me in systematically structuring my own thinking in the problem areas where I am not clear" (Rose, Lowenstein, and Fellin 1969).

Similarly, Kadushin (1974) asked supervisors to describe their conception of an ideal supervisor by reacting to a series of 39 statements about different kinds of supervisory behavior. Supervisees were given the same statements and asked to describe their current supervisor. The 39 statements offered were designed to cluster into six different dimensions. (1) supervisor interest in supervisee ("ready and willing to meet the supervisee and shows real interest in discussing the supervisee's work"); (2) empathic understanding of the supervisee ("when the supervisee is discouraged or anxious, supervisor seems to recognize this"); (3) acceptance of supervisee ("creates the kind of emotional atmosphere so that supervisees feel free to discuss their mistakes and failures as well as their successes"); (4) willingness to grant autonomy ("can permit the supervisee to make his own mistakes"); (5) openness ("is ready to acknowledge occasional inability to help supervisee"); (6) competence ("has a detailed accurate grasp of agency policies and procedures"). Discrepancies between the ideal picture of supervision and the actual picture of supervision were frequently greater with regard to the technical competence–instrumental components rather than with the expressive–relationship skill components.

The nationwide study of social agency supervision by Olmstead and Christensen (1973) shows that supervisors were ranked lowest on "work facilitation" scales involving such activities as "showing personnel how to improve performance and providing help in solving job-related problems" (p. 195). Supervisors were ranked considerably higher, however, on scales concerned with supportive activities in supervision.

The apparently greater success in implementing the supportive responsibilities of supervision may merely reflect the fact that, in implementing this function, the supervisor is closer to the job for which she was trained and which she knows best. Supportive supervision is more like the professional social work direct-service function than is either administrative or educational supervision.

Summary

Supportive supervision is concerned with helping the supervisee deal with job-related stress and developing attitudes and feelings conducive to maximum job performance. Whereas administrative and educational supervision are concerned with instrumental needs, supportive supervision is concerned with expressive needs.

The main sources of job-related stress for the supervisee are the performance and compliance demands of administrative supervision, the learning demands of educational supervision, the clients, the nature and context of social work tasks, and the relationship with the supervisor.

In implementing the objectives of supportive supervision the supervisor seeks to prevent the development of potentially stressful situations, removes the worker from stress, reduces stress impinging on the worker and helps her adjust to stress. The supervisor is available and approachable, communicates confidence in the worker, provides perspective, excuses failure when appropriate, sanctions and shares responsibility for different decisions, provides opportunity for catharsis, helps the worker clarify goals and roles, provides opportunity for independent functioning and for probable success in tasks achievement.

The client, the peer group and the worker's own adjustive capacities are additional sources of support for the supervisee.

Supervisors are also subjected to a variety of job-related stresses. The transition to supervisor is a difficult change involving a reorientation of relationships with colleagues, alterations in self-perception and in attitudes toward agency goals.

Both supervisors and supervisees engage in a variety of games which are designed to help in dealing with job-related tensions.

chapter five

Evaluation

Evaluation in supervision is defined as the objective appraisal of the worker's total functioning on the job over a specified period of time (Schmidt and Perry 1940). It is a process of applying systematic procedures to determine with reliability and validity the extent to which the worker is achieving the requirements of his position in the agency. An evaluation should be a judgment based on clearly specified, realistic, and achievable criteria reflecting agency standards. It is job related and time limited. It is concerned with both the "quality of performance and the quantity of accomplishment." Evaluation is an administrative procedure that should, and can, contribute to professional growth. It is therefore a component of both administrative and educational supervision.

Evaluations are as ubiquitous and necessary as they are inevitable. There is no way of not communicating an evaluation message. Refraining from evaluating is, in itself, an evaluation. An anxious worker to whom no evaluation is communicated may read the message as "I am so bad he can't even tell me about it"; the cocksure, conceited worker may read the same message as "my work is so exemplary that there is nothing to discuss."

Every time the supervisor nods in agreement, says "yes," "okay," "you're right about that" in response to something the supervisee has said, an evaluation is being made. Every time a pained expression crosses the supervisor's face, every time he gestures impatiently, every time he says gently, "come now, I am not so sure about that," or more forthrightly, "I disagree with you about that," an evaluation has been made.

We cannot abstain from informal assessment, and workers are aware of this. Each supervisor has some idea of how she ranks a particular worker as compared with others in terms of a level of performance she regards as adequate. Evaluations require us to formalize such assessments, to make them explicit, to communicate them to the workers, and to defend them if necessary.

The formal evaluation conference differs from the on-going assessments which are, or should be, part of each supervisory conference. In the individual conferences the focus of concern is the current case situation. The formal evaluation conference is concerned with an overview of the entire caseload. It is a period of stock-taking and review. As Pettes (1967) says, it is "a chance to see how the whole orchard is growing rather than concentrating on individual trees" (p. 114). Given the uncluttered opportunity to take a more general view of the worker's activity, the worker and supervisor make a conscious effort to discuss general patterns of performance.

Values of Evaluation

Evaluation has value to the client, the agency, the supervisor and, most importantly, to the supervisee.

value to the worker

Evaluation relieves supervisees' anxiety since it helps them know where they stand. The only thing more anxiety provoking than evaluation is no evaluation. Supervisees are then in doubt about how adequately they are meeting agency expectations and how they compare with other workers of similar education and experience.

A period set aside for formal evaluation gives supervisees a perspective on change and achievement. Assuming that a worker has improved during the period of time covered by the evaluation, the process tends to encourage him and to enhance a sense of accomplishment. For the worker the evaluation is an opportunity to obtain explicit approval of his work from somebody who is thought to have the information, ability, and experience to make such a judgment. It provides the worker with a presumably objective, authoritative perspective on his abilities and deficiencies. Recapitulating the real progress in professional development made by the worker while acknowledging the existence of deficiencies, the supervisor helps the supervisee to view his work more realistically and optimistically. This mitigates the counterproductive tendency, particularly on the part of young, conscientious workers, to deprecate their achievements.

Evaluations help motivate, direct, and integrate learning. The supervisee is stimulated to learn and change in order to achieve a good evaluation. A systematic review of what one has learned helps to consolidate it. Having identified explicitly what he has learned to do, the supervisee can recognize the learned behavior and more easily repeat it.

Evaluations help direct learning. The standards by which he is evaluated help to clarify for the supervisee the specific kinds of activities on which he has to focus. Selection of a task for inclusion in an evaluation-assessment instrument increases the visibility and significance of that task. The workers are likely to expend more energy in learning such tasks and pay more attention to the performance of such tasks.

Evaluation helps make learning conscious, because it requires an explicit assessment of performance. It points to how much the worker has learned, how far he has come. At the same time it helps to clearly identify the nature of performance weakness and what needs to be learned more adequately. It makes possible further goal-directed teaching. An evaluation is concerned with an assessment in the present of work during the immediate past period, for the purpose of determining future teaching and learning activity.

Evaluations help set the pattern for self-evaluation by the supervisee. Before standards of service can be internalized for self-regulation, they need to be clearly identified for the worker. Having become acquainted with performance standards and criteria as a result of evaluation conferences, the supervisee is in a better position to critique his own work. Evaluation "increases self-awareness to further self-improvement."

Every worker has the responsibility for self-evaluation and self-regulation. The worker's continuous, critical assessment of his own performance is the best guarantee of effective and efficient service. But to do this analysis requires not only the will to engage in critical self-evaluation but a knowledge of the standards and criteria that distinguish good practice from poor practice, learned as a consequence of evaluation conferences.

value to the agency

Discharging the responsibility toward public accountability by evaluating the extent to which the agency is achieving its goals and objectives starts with an evaluation of the degree to which the individual worker's performance is meeting agency standards. Just as the agency is accountable to the community, so the individual worker is accountable to the agency.

Periodic, systematic evaluation of worker performance may point to needed changes in agency administration. Careful review may show that the workers are not failing the agency but that instead the agency is failing them. Evaluation then leads to communication from supervisors to administrators regarding administrative procedures that are adversely affecting worker performance.

A review of a series of evaluations of a number of different workers can help in planning in-service training programs and staff-development procedures. Such analysis may disclose consistent weak spots in staff performance to which agency administration needs to give attention. Evaluation helps define for the staff generally, and for the individual worker in particular, those aspects of professional performance that require further special attention and effort, and it points to the kinds of learning experiences that need to be provided. Evaluation further helps the agency to identify special skills manifested by individual staff members who might then be assigned special tasks.

If promotions, dismissals, reassignments, and merit pay increases are necessary and acceptable responsibilities of administrative supervision, then we must accept as legitimate and necessary the procedures that permit such decisions to be made on a reasonable and defensible basis. Evaluation also helps validate agency policy regarding worker selection. Through evaluation the agency can determine if its selection requirements do, in fact, tend to result in the recruitment of personnel capable of doing an effective job.

value to the client

Social work, like other professions, claims the freedom to operate without control by outsiders. One justification frequently advanced to support the demand for autonomy is that professionals will regulate each other to prevent abuse and ensure efficient practice. The professional-association code of ethics exemplifies such self-regulation by members of a profession. But the sanctions available in the professional codes of ethics are rarely applied, and then only for the most egregious violations. The community, in granting a profession freedom from outside regulation, control, and interference, has a right to expect some more immediate, more routinely applied measures of control. The principal benefit of evaluation for the client is that as a consequence he is more likely to be assured of effective service and protected from continuation of inadequate service.

Having noted the values of evaluation, we may now ask, Who might best be delegated the task of making evaluations? The logical response is that the person in the agency who is most directly and intimately acquainted with the details of the worker's day-to-day activity would be in the best position to make a reasoned and defensible assessment of performance, i.e., the worker's immediate supervisor. Consequently it is not surprising that when any organization requires a formal, periodic evaluation of worker performance, almost invariably the immediate supervisor is given this responsibility.

Dislike of Evaluations

Despite the value and necessity of evaluations, they trouble most supervisors and tend to be avoided, if not actively resisted. There are a number of reasons which explain supervisors' dislike of evaluations./

Evaluation is among the supervisory procedures that most explicitly call attention to the difference in status between supervisor and supervisee. As such, it tends to increase the social distance between them. It is difficult to maintain the fiction that supervisor and supervisee are colleagues in a peer relationship when the supervisor has the responsibility and authority to evaluate the work of the supervisee. The possible reward-punishment consequences of evaluation clearly express the power of the supervisor, which on other occasions may be muted and obscured. Some supervisors feel uncomfortable with the authority inherent in their position. In many other kinds of supervisor-supervisee interactions their authority need not be explicitly employed and so can be conveniently ignored; in evaluation it is openly exercised.

Any evaluation of the worker is in effect an indirect evaluation of the supervisor. If the worker is performing inadequately, the evaluation might reveal that the supervisor has not taught the worker what he needs to know, has not given the worker the help he had the right to expect. A supervisor reports:

> I felt a pressure to give her a good evaluation, and I wonder now if my desire to do this was because I felt it was therapeutic for her. It was also a kind of reward for myself for being a good therapist in helping Ms G. become a better worker. Both of these reasons are inappropriate but it was a kind of validation that I was a good supervisor.

Evaluation can evoke strong negative feelings. Supervisors may be anxious that evaluation will precipitate a hostile reaction from the supervisee; there is guilt at the possible consequences of a negative evaluation, consequences that have considerable significance for the job status and professional career of the worker. A supervisor says:

If I told Mr. R what I really think—that he's a lousy worker—he'd blow his top and I'd have psychic debris all over the office. Besides, he would challenge me on every word, and I am not so sure I could cross the *t* and dot the *i* on my judgments. So who needs all that grief? I kind of tone the evaluation down.

There is a reluctance to be appropriately critical because the criticism might be discouraging to the worker. The supervisor may hesitate to inflict pain and discomfort or may fear that the supervisee will like her less as a result. The supervisor's task is to be uniformly helpful, not invariably popular, to be consistently useful and responsible rather than consistently loved. Aware of this ambivalence, a supervisor notes:

I was flattered by his evident liking and respect for me. It gave me pleasure. I was not so ready to risk this by arousing his hostility if I pressed him about some of the things he was doing poorly, which needed improvement. If I did what I thought I had to do I would be giving up, or at least risking, some of the satisfactions for me in the relationship.

To be comfortable with the threats implied in evaluating, the supervisor must accept the legitimacy of the evaluation process and feel entitled to make an evaluation. The supervisor has to feel confident that she is capable of making a valid judgment, that she has enough accurate information on which to base a valid judgment, and that the standards on which the judgment is based are clearly defined and defensible. However, many supervisors question the legitimacy of evaluation and lack a sense of entitlement. They do not think they should or can judge the work of another. Further, they are oppressed by conflicting, ambiguous evidence of performance and by imprecise, vague standards available for judging performance. Consequently they neither feel qualified to make such a judgment nor confident that they can make a true evaluation. Such doubts may make supervisors hesitant about being critical—not being without sin, they are reluctant to cast the first stone. As one supervisor said,

I know the agency wants us to recommend dismissal for workers who don't meet minimum requirements. But I am not so sure what these requirements are or how to measure them and how much emphasis to place on achievement versus individual progress. It's hard for me to be confident recommending dismissal for even my poorest supervisees so I give them a passing evaluation.

A positive evaluation is an endorsement, a certification of proficiency. Hence it involves a considerable responsibility to the general community, to the specific community of clients, to the agency, and to professional peers. Being invested with, and having to carry out, such a responsibility is apt to be somewhat unnerving.

The requirement for evaluation seems to contradict the ethos of social work. The professional value orientation puts great emphasis on being nonjudgmental. Evaluations, of necessity, involve a judgment of performance. The admonition to be responsibly critical, frank, and direct in rigorous evaluation clashes with the professionally inculcated disposition to be accepting and compassionate, supportive and reassuring. The felt conflict causes discomfort.

Most supervisors are aware of the possible loss of staff as a result of a negative evaluation. This realization suggests an additional motive for resisting evaluations. A study of worker attrition in the New York City Department of Public Welfare showed that "workers with one or more positive evaluations were about half as likely to leave the Department within nine months of their appointments as those with none; workers with a plural number of negative evaluations showed a significantly greater tendency to leave the Department than those with one or none" (Podell 1967, p. 22).

Every time a supervisee with some experience is fired or quits in response to a negative evaluation, a new, inexperienced worker has to be hired in his place. During the period of transition, extra burdens are placed on the supervisor. The uncovered caseload has to be temporarily assigned. Prospective candidates for the position have to be interviewed and a selection made. Once a person has been hired, the supervisor again faces the tasks of worker introduction and orientation. The supervisor can avoid all this additional work by placating the supervisee with a laudatory, if not entirely accurate, evaluation.

(Evaluations generally tend to be avoided, but negative evaluations tend to be avoided most of all) Yet such evasion only compounds the supervisor's problem. Refraining from critical evaluation does the worker an injustice and promises future difficulty. Performance failures that are ignored do not disappear. The worker continues to practice his mistakes and becomes more proficient in making them. With time the errors become more serious and, having been ignored, are more difficult to deal with. The easy avoidance of critical evaluation today comes back to haunt the supervisor tomorrow.

Hesitancy to deal openly with deficiencies in performance becomes in itself an incentive to continued concealments. The supervisor is aware that if she raises the problem for discussion after some delay, the worker can justifiably accuse her of early dishonesty and deception.

Failure to be appropriately critical substitutes a problem of group morale for a problem of individual morale. The worker who is appraised too leniently may be happier, but his fellow workers will be less happy. Peers are perceptive in their evaluation of each other's competence. If a worker whom they know to be inefficient and ineffective is given a raise along with better workers because the supervisor has not been appropriately critical, they feel resentful and cynical. They become suspicious about the validity of the supervisor's evaluation of their own work. They are robbed of some of the motivation to improve their own performance, since the system appears to reward good and bad work equally.

It may reassure supervisors to note that most social work supervisees recognize and accept the fact that the agency, as their employer, has a right to evaluate the work they are doing. They face this challenge along with millions of other employed workers. In fact, one study found that supervisees expressed strong dissatisfaction with the fact that supervisors were not sufficiently and specifically critical of their work. Anxious to do a better job, supervisees looked to their supervisor for help in identifying deficiencies in their work which needed correcting. They were disappointed when they failed to receive such critical analysis (Kadushin 1974). When supervisees raise objections to evaluation, the reason is not the legitimacy of agency entitlement to evaluate their work but rather the fact that evaluations are often inequitable, arbitrary, and unhelpful.

Desirable Evaluation Procedures

Despite the clearly identifiable reasons which feed supervisory antipathy toward evaluation, it is both necessary and inevitable. What approaches are most likely to contribute to a productive evaluation?

1. Evaluation should be a continuous process rather than an occasional event. The formal evaluation conference may be a summation of the small evaluations that take place as part of each conference. Regularly devoting some part of each conference to evaluation, however brief, helps desensitize the worker's anxiety regarding it. This practice also helps prepare her for what is likely to be shared at the formal conference so that it does not come as an unexpected, disconcerting surprise. As one worker complained, "The supervisor never mentioned my overidentification with Jane [a girl on probation] until the evaluation conference. If I had been aware of it sooner I certainly could have made some effort to control overidentification in my contacts." The formal, periodic evaluation is a summary-recapitulation of familiar, previously encountered assessments rather than an unexpected, unanticipated critique for which the worker is unprepared.

2. The supervisor should discuss the evaluation procedure in advance with the supervisee. Supervisees may be less anxious if they know in advance when evaluations are to be scheduled, what information and standards are to be used as a basis for evaluation, what they might be expected to contribute to the evaluation, with whom the evaluation will be shared, what use will be made of the evaluation. But, of even greater importance,

supervisees will be in a better position to prepare for the evaluation over a period of time and to participate more productively in the process. This approach implies that the evaluation outline should be shared with workers in advance and that they be given the opportunity of asking questions about the outline for clarification.

3. The evaluation should be communicated in the context of a positive relationship. The positive relationship acts as an anodyne to the pain of criticism (however warranted) and makes the worker more receptive to, and accepting of, the criticism as a basis for constructive change. If the supervisor and supervisee dislike each other, the supervisee is predisposed to reject the criticism as invalid and unfair.

All criticism of performance should be offered out of a sincere desire to help, not out of pleasure and satisfaction in criticizing. The supervisor needs to be sensitive to the worker's reaction, to manifestations of anxiety and resistance. These feelings can then be discussed openly, and appropriate reassurance and support can be offered.

A formal evaluation generates anxiety because it is a threat to narcissism and self-esteem. There is a fear of failure and rejection. It raises such questions as, Will I be able to measure up to expectations? Will I be able to maintain the good opinion of me held by people I like and respect? How do I compare with my peers? What effect will this have on my professional future? Evaluations become part of our official records. There is much at stake. A good supervisory relationship helps support the worker through this anxiety-inducing procedure.

4. The evaluation procedure should be a mutual, shared process. The supervisor should attempt to maximize the worker's participation in, and contribution to, the evaluation. The worker could be asked to write a self-evaluation or to write a critique of the supervisor's evaluation. The worker's reaction to the evaluation should be solicited. Mutuality implies not only encouraging the worker's participation but also active use of those contributions that are valid and applicable in the final evaluation write-up. Evaluation is done "with" the worker, not

"to" the work. Mutual participation in the evaluation process increases the probability of a more valid evaluation and of its acceptance and use by the supervisee.

Participation lessens anxiety. Having been invited to participate, the worker retrieves a measure of control of the proceedings. Sharing in control and being able in some measure to determine content, direction, and emphasis in the evaluation conference, the supervisee tends to feel less anxiously helpless. Participation also tends to reduce the discomforting imbalance in power between supervisor and supervisee. Power is manifested in the ability to control. In encouraging the supervisee's active participation in the evaluation process, the supervisor is sharing his control.

5. Evaluations should be made with some recognition and consideration of reality factors that might be determinants of the worker's performance. The supervisor needs to assess whether or not the worker's caseload was atypically heavy or included more than the usual number of specially difficult cases. Was this a period when the turnover in personnel was greater than normal, when things at the agency were unusually hectic? Allowances need to be made for situational aspects of the job—lack of office space, lack of secretarial help, the unavailability of essential support services, periods of low agency morale which adversely affect workers' performance. The worker who has a routine caseload of minimum complexity, imposing few unusual decision-making responsibilities, is in a different position from the worker with a caseload of clients who frequently present unique and complex problems.

6. The principal, if not the exclusive, focus of evaluation should be the work performance of the supervisee rather than any evaluation of the worker as a person. The only social role of concern to evaluation is that of the supervisee as an employee of a social agency and, specifically, as the person assigned to do a particular job in this agency. None of the other aspects of the worker's life are legitimate areas for review. This concept is stressed by the Family Service Association of America in defining evaluation as "an accurate appraisal of the performance of

the incumbent [of the position] in relation to specific duties assigned" (1957, p. 53).

7. The evaluation should review both strengths and weaknesses, growth and stagnation, and should be fair and balanced. Isolated, atypical examples of the worker's performance should not be used to make a general case for failure. Rather, recurrent patterns of behavior in job performance are the legitimate bases for evaluation statements. Nor should the supervisor's personal standards be substituted for agency standards as a basis for evaluation.

Fair evaluation focuses on behavior because "behavior provides structure and articulation for objectives and judgments that might otherwise be vague and excessively open to interpretation" (Goldhammer 1969, p. 326). The total configuration of the worker's performance needs to be considered. Recent incidents may overinfluence the evaluation because of their very recency, and dramatic incidents because of their vividness. Furthermore, if behavior patterns are cited as factors in the evaluation, there should be some reason to believe that the worker's behavior had some significant positive or adverse effect on the client.

Admittedly, fairness is difficult to achieve. It has been said that what makes life so complicated in supervision is that the supervisee can almost always find some technical defense for his actions while his supervisor can almost always find some basis on which to criticize them (Goldhammer 1969, p. 172).

8. A good evaluation is not like a final game score but rather a review of how the game was played. It should be more than a listing of good and bad performance, being instead an analysis of why certain behaviors and procedures are desirable and effective and why other behaviors and procedures are not. As one worker said in complaining of her evaluation conference, "The supervisor said my work was satisfactory but what was satisfactory about it or why it was satisfactory she didn't say, so I don't know."

9. The evaluation should suggest tentativeness rather than finality and should focus on modifiable aspects of the worker's

performance; this is the way the worker performs at this particular time; the expectation is that she will develop and improve. The good worker can become a better worker, and the poor worker a good worker. The spirit of the evaluation should communicate the idea that "success is not final; failure is not fatal." The evaluation is, after all, not an unchangeable verdict but an incentive for change.

10. Evaluations should be formulated with some consistency. Both intra- and inter-supervisor consistency is desirable. The supervisor needs to apply the same standards in the same way to all of her supervisees who have approximately the same education and experience. Likewise, different supervisors responsible for different units of workers with similar backgrounds need to act similarly in evaluating their respective supervisees. It is difficult to think of any other factor so corrosive of morale as differences in evaluation procedures applied to a homogeneous group of supervisees.

11. It is desirable for the supervisor to indicate a willingness to accept evaluation of his own performance from the supervisee. If the process of evaluation is helpful in the development of the supervisee, it can likewise contribute to the supervisor's professional development.

The supervisee will be more accepting of evaluation, and less likely to see it as a manifestation of capricious authority, if she has the opportunity, in turn, to evaluate the supervisor. Certainly, as a recipient of supervision, as the consumer of the product, she is in a position to assess the supervisor's performance. Teaching faculty currently are more and more frequently open to student evaluation; it is difficult to defend supervisor immunity from supervisee evaluation. Two-way evaluations exemplify agency orientation toward evaluation. Evaluation of the worker's performance should be only one manifestation of the overall evaluation of personnel at all levels as part of a periodic review of the agency's total program.

12. Involvement of staff in establishing evaluation criteria is likely to ensure the selection of more relevant criteria, to intensify commitment to the evaluation process, and to clarify ex-

pectations with regard to evaluation. Workers who have helped develop standards to which they will ultimately be held accountable will feel a greater obligation and responsibility to see that the evaluation process achieves its objectives. Research indicates that ability to have significant input in determining evaluation criteria and procedures is clearly related to satisfaction with evaluation (Dornbusch and Scott 1975, pp. 186–87).

Evaluation Conference—Process

scheduling the conference

The worker should be informed at least a week in advance about the specific date and time of the evaluation conference. In some agencies, evaluations are scheduled at regular intervals—every half-year or every year. In other agencies, evaluations are tied to transition points in the supervisee's professional career, for example, at the end of the probationary period, when the worker's assignment is changed, when there is a change of supervisors, when the worker is leaving the agency, when a merit increase is due.

supervisor's conference preparation

The supervisor prepares by reading a sampling of the worker's recording, reports, special project write-ups, by reviewing the statistical material, time sheets, and supervisor's notes or logs covering the period of performance to be evaluated, as well as by reviewing previous evaluations.

In a more general fashion the supervisor's preparation should be a continuous process. Utilizing all sources of information, the supervisor should make notes of ongoing activity that illustrates the worker's typical performance. She should be constantly alert for critical incidents that relate performance to agency standards. A thorough knowledge of the details of the worker's performance is one of the most effective antidotes to supervisory anxiety about making evaluations. Criticism can be shared with less anxiety if there is a feeling of certainty that it is warranted and if the criticism can be adequately documented.

The supervisor further prepares by introspectively examining his attitudes toward, and feelings about, the supervisee which might contaminate an objective appraisal of performance. The supervisor needs to be aware of such feelings as hostility toward the supervisee which might make him punitive in evaluation, a desire to control which might make him manipulative, or a tendency to identify with and defend the supervisee which might make him overprotective. The supervisor has an investment in the professional progress of his supervisees; eager for their success, which is the supervisor's success once removed, he may be reluctant to perceive the workers' failings.

The supervisor should also prepare for the conference by reviewing some of the classic and persistent pitfalls in evaluating, in order to avoid them. These include the "error of central tendency"—the tendency, when in doubt, to rate specific aspects of the worker's performance as "fair" or "average"; the "halo effect"—the tendency to make a global judgment about the worker's performance and then to perceive all aspects of the worker's performance as consistent with that general judgment; the "contrast error"—the tendency to evaluate using oneself as a standard, the very conscientious supervisor seeing most workers as less conscientious, the highly organized supervisor tending to see others as less well organized; "leniency bias"— a reluctance to evaluate negatively and critically.

The halo effect is a major hazard to objective evaluations. The relevant research shows that "those individuals who behave in such a way as to satisfy the personal needs of the supervisor will generally be rated higher; those subordinates who interfere with the satisfaction of the personal needs of the supervisor will generally be rated lower. The specific ratings by supervisors are likely to be determined by the more global, conscious or unconscious, reaction to subordinates" (Kallejian, Brown, and Wechsler 1954, p. 168). A good evaluation may reflect the ability to please the supervisor rather than objectively superior performance in contact with the client.

Green (1972) notes that research on supervisory evaluations tends to indicate that an evaluation "begins with a field instruc-

tor's assessment of a student's *overall* performance which then
determines whether he or she will not find any specific qualities which are being sought" (p. 53). This is the halo effect in
operation.

Similarly, leniency bias is a considerable problem for social
workers. Educational Testing Service has the contract for administering and scoring the reference vouchers and tests used
for certification to The Academy of Certified Social Workers
(A.C.S.W.). The Service's review of the judgments of supervisors and peers on the reference voucher rating forms indicates
"a strong 'leniency effect' in the ratings which is evidenced by
uniformly high average ratings, low variabilities and a total reluctance by the rater to employ the low or unfavorable categories" (Educational Testing Service 1973, p. 3).

worker's conference preparation

The worker should also prepare for the conference by reviewing the agency evaluation outline or evaluation rating form
which has been shared with her. She might follow the outline
in thinking about and making notes for a self-evaluation. In addition, she might be asked to consider the way her performance
six months or a year ago compares with her performance now,
what she thinks she has accomplished during the period to be
covered by the evaluation, where she thinks she needs more
help, and the kinds of professional experiences she missed and
would like to have.

Despite the desirability of familiarizing the supervisee with
the criteria of evaluation, a large percentage of supervisees responding to a national study reported that they were not given a
formal statement which informed them of these criteria. Only
about one in four supervisees was asked to formulate her own
evaluation statement in preparation for the evaluation conference. Less than half indicated that they were given a written
evaluation that was supplemented by an oral discussion. Almost
half of the supervisees (46 percent) reported that no formal, individual evaluation conference was scheduled with them.

When such conferences were scheduled, they usually occurred at one-year intervals (Kadushin 1974).

evaluation conference interaction

If both supervisor and supervisee thoughtfully prepare for the evaluation, there may be much agreement to begin with. The following are an excerpt from a self-evaluation review by a supervisee and an excerpt, related to the same problem, from her supervisor's preliminary evaluation note.

Supervisee self-evaluation:
With both Jane [an unmarried mother] and the Allens [a foster family] I continued to demonstrate what appears to me to be excess zeal. Jane was more capable of handling her problems than I gave her credit for and did not need as much help as I was ready and anxious to offer her. She was capable of applying for A.F.D.C. without my intervention. The Allens too had enough skill and practice as parents to do an adequate job of making Paul [the foster child] comfortable with the transition to their home without all my hovering over them. In these, and in several other instances, I tend to be the all-loving, over-protective, anxious mother figure.

Supervisor's preliminary evaluation:
Miss M [the supervisee] frequently manifests a need to be helpful, to encourage the dependency of clients, to solicit client approbation and appreciation by doing for them what they can, perhaps, do as well for themselves. The general attitude of concerned helpfulness which Miss M manifests is a desirable attitude for which the worker should be commended. However, Miss M's current indiscriminate, helpful behavior needs to be exercised with more self-control and self-discipline. Miss M needs to learn to offer her help more discriminatingly in situations where it is appropriately required. In such situations and under such circumstance her help is likely to be more truly helpful. Perhaps we can, in future supervisory conferences, center on the criteria which will enable Miss M to distinguish when a client is truly objectively dependent on her for her intervention and when the client can do for himself.

The mutual awareness of the same general problem may be a tribute to the supervisor's continuous efforts at assessment during the regularly scheduled on-going supervisory conferences. Sharp differences in how the supervisee and supervisor assess the performance would suggest some difficulty in the relationship, some failure in communication.

At the beginning of the evaluation interview, it may be useful to deal explicitly with worker anxiety, to review the procedure, and to briefly recapitulate what will be covered. If made at all, these comments should be very brief; the worker is primarily concerned about the evaluation itself. Another tactic in opening the evaluation conference is suggested by a supervisor who said, "I asked the supervisee to check her case load with me for the period to be sure nothing had been omitted. I find this is a good comfortable way for both supervisor and supervisee to get into the evaluation conference, and it sets the tone for the supervisee as an active participant."

Since the supervisee is probably anxious to hear what the supervisor has to say, this is one conference in which the supervisor should take the initiative. The supervisor should open the main body of the conference-interview by presenting clearly, simply, and unambiguously a general evaluation of the worker's performance as she sees it. Evaluation provides explicit formal feedback. Its effectiveness is intensified if it is specific, if it can be communicated so that it is appropriate to the needs of the worker, if it is clear and accurate.

The supervisor, in his anxiety, can be so careful that he drains the assessment of all meaning and significance. Euphemisms and qualifications are often added to elaborate circumlocution so as to soften the message to the point where it fails to be communicated.

I said that, on occasion, I had some feeling that in particularly difficult situations, with overly demanding clients, when she herself was hurried and harassed, her behavior tended to reflect aspects of an attitude which suggested some elements of disrespect—even though I recognized that generally this might not be typical of her approach. I wondered if she herself thought this was the case—did she think there was some truth in this or perhaps not.

The formal evaluation is the opportune time for plain, direct statements adequately supported by specific citations from job performance. Workers may feel puzzled by ambiguous evaluation statements. "I guess I am doing all right because she didn't say I wasn't." "She talked a lot about my mature approach to people but I don't know exactly what she meant."

The main body of the conference is a discussion of the worker's performance in terms of criteria in an evaluation outline such as those described in a later section of this chapter. The conference concludes, as does any good interview, with a summary of the principal points covered. The implications of the conclusions for immediate future conferences are explicated and outlined. There is a clear statement of "where we go from here." Attention is paid to the supervisee's emotional responses to the evaluation at the end of the conference, and an effort is made to resolve, or at least mitigate, the most disturbed feelings.

Having explicitly identified some aspect of the worker's performance needing improvement, the supervisor and supervisee might give some consideration, in terminating the conference, to a plan of action for change. Both participants should agree on a specific period of time during which the objective for change will be accomplished. Some evaluation forms even have an entry labeled "Development Plan: List specific plans for improvements, objectives to be achieved, schedules for development to be undertaken."

The evaluation conference is not finished when the participants leave the room. Both supervisor and supervisee continue to mull it over. Hopefully, this reflection on what was discussed will lead the supervisor to a better understanding and appreciation of the supervisee's work, and the supervisee to a better awareness of his strengths and weaknesses as a social worker.

But even when the conference has finished, the evaluation process continues. Each evaluation is directed toward the ultimate achievement of the termination of evaluations, when the worker is truly self-directed and capable of valid self-evaluation. At that point in his professional development, an objective, critical outside review of his work can still be helpful, but the agency has sufficient confidence in the worker so that formal evaluations are no longer administratively required. It is then that evaluation is terminated.

Communication and Use of Evaluations

The supervisee is not in a position to accept or reject the evaluation, as would be true if the relationship were consultative. The agency cannot grant the supervisee this option if it is to responsibly meet its obligation to the community and the clients. Assuming the evaluation is valid, the supervisee is given the option of modifying his behavior so that it meets the standards of performance required by the agency.

The supervisor, in preparing an evaluation, needs to have confidence that recommendations for administrative action, which follow from the evaluation, will be supported by the administration. The relationship with the supervisee can be undermined if the supervisor's recommendations are rejected by administration. However, the ultimate responsibility for implementing the consequences of the evaluation rests with administration. This practice protects the supervisee from possible arbitrary evaluations and accompanying negative recommendations. Thus, if the supervisor needs the confidence that administration will generally accept his evaluatory recommendations, he also needs to be aware that good administration will make a considered rather than an automatic decision to support such recommendations.

Once the evaluation has been formulated, it should be written out and the worker should have an opportunity to read it and to keep a copy. N.A.S.W. Standards for Social Work Personnel Practices, as revised in 1971, require a written statement by the agency "of standards of performance" as the basis for evaluation. Furthermore, "the evaluation shall be in writing . . . and the employee shall be given the opportunity to read it, to sign it (signifying he had read it) and to file a statement covering any points with which he disagrees. A copy of the evaluation shall be furnished the employee." The statement notes that "the authority of the evaluator must be recognized on both sides and final authority belongs to him" (National Association of Social Workers 1971, p. 19).

Administrative procedures should be available for appealing an evaluation which the supervisee thinks is unfair. In writing an evaluation, the supervisor can be more deliberate and precise. She can review it carefully and reconsider it at leisure for possible changes in content, emphasis, and balance. None of this is possible in the heat and stress of an oral evaluation, when a word uttered is beyond recall or change. Because they are a matter of record, written reports have the advantage of being available for use by those who might supervise this worker in the future.

Several arguments can be made in support of having the worker read the evaluation. Oral evaluation is open to misinterpretation and is the source of considerable fantasy about what the supervisor actually said. A written evaluation is definite and available for rereading and rechecking. While still open to some misinterpretation, it is not as readily distorted as an oral evaluation. It is easy for the worker to fail to hear what he does not want to hear or to supress what he has heard but is reluctant to remember. It is possible, but more difficult, to engage in such defensive maneuvers with a written document. The evaluation conference is often a stressful experience during which the supervisee finds it difficult to absorb what is being said. The opportunity to read the material improves the chances for distortion-free communication.

Being permitted to read the evaluation reduces any anxiety the worker may feel about whether the evaluation that is shared verbally is the same as the written evaluation actually filed with administration. The privately written evaluation is often more critical than the evaluation verbally communicated, and supervisees are aware of this. The fact that the evaluation will be read acts as a constraint on the supervisor. It is likely to intensify the care with which the statement is prepared and increases the probability that the evaluation will be more objective and accurate.

The context provided for reading the evaluation is important. The worker should have the opportunity to read the evaluation in the presence of the supervisor. If he has questions or objections regarding content, or desires clarification of ambiguously phrased material, this can be handled immediately. If the evaluation is negative, the presence of the supervisor provides an immediate target for hostility or an immediately available source of reassurance and support.

If objections are raised which the supervisor accepts as valid, the evaluation statement is ammended accordingly. If objections are raised which are not agreed to by the supervisor, the supervisee should have the right to ask that a statement of her reservations be included in her file in her own name. Evaluation forms often include provision for supervisor signature, supervisee signature, and signature of agency administrator. Alongside the supervisee's signature the forms might include a proviso such as the following: "The contents of this evaluation have been shared with me. My signature does not necessarily mean agreement."

Some supervisors claim, with a certain amount of justification, that a careful safeguarding of the supervisee's right to read the evaluation will result in less useful and perhaps less valid evaluations. Torn between doing justice to agency administration and agency clients and protecting themselves from enervating argumentation, supervisors may choose to write bland, noncommittal, generally favorable evaluations, saying little to give offense but, at the same time, saying little that is significant. Hunches, intuitions, sharp guesses which supervisors feel are true but which they cannot actually substantiate by citing the specific supporting evidence, will tend to be excluded.

Some supervisors also feel that such procedures suggest that the supervisor is not trustworthy, that supervisory evaluations are likely to be unfair, unjust, and untruthful. They reject and resent such implications. These supervisors assert that where the supervisory relationship is positive, the professional

self-discipline of the supervisor is a sufficient guarantee that the
evaluation will be fair and honest—without the requirement
that the supervisee have a right to check it.

After their final formulation, evaluations are employed in
making a variety of significant administrative decisions. They
are used as a basis for retention or separation, salary increases,
promotion, caseload assignment, work or supervisory reassignments, reclassification, and as a source of basic information for
letters of reference. The two most frequent administrative uses
of evaluations are as a basis for retention and separation and for
salary increases (Kadushin 1974).

In summary, both supervisor and supervisee should prepare for the conference by reviewing their notes and tentatively
formulating an evaluation. After they have discussed their respective perceptions of the worker's performance in the evaluation conference, the supervisor writes a formal evaluation statement. This is given to the worker for reaction and comment.

Evaluation Outlines and Rating Forms

Many of the suggestions to make the evaluation process more
positive and productive depend for their effective implementation on the availability of an evaluation guide or outline. An
evaluation outline ensures more precise definition and specification of the criteria for evaluation; it suggests the explicit kinds
of information that need to be obtained for evaluation; it assures
a greater likelihood that uniform standards will be followed by
different supervisors and by the same supervisor with different
supervisees; it tends to depersonalize the evaluation for the
supervisee since the outline is an all-agency guide, and reduces
a supervisor's guilt and anxiety as she employs agency-spon-
sored standards and is protected from her own subjectivity; it
increases the certainty of covering the same points in succes-
sive evaluations; it simplifies sharing with the supervisee, in
advance, the areas of performance to be covered by an evaluation.

The availability of an evaluation outline related specifically to the job responsibilities of a classified group of workers in a particular agency ensures that the process of assessment will be directed to the worker's performance on the job, a job for which the duties have been clearly defined. The evaluation outline further serves as a convenient interview guide for evaluation conference discussion.

Evaluation outlines in any social work agency reflect basic social work skills, methods, and general objectives—the enhancement, support, or restoration of psychosocial functioning. Hence, it is to be expected that evaluation outlines have some general similarities. However, since each agency has a particular responsibility, a particular problem area of concern, operates in a particular community, with staff of some particular composition, each agency has to adapt and modify a generally applicable outline to make it optimally appropriate to its own situation. One agency may be concerned with use of community resources, another with the development of those resources; workers in one agency may be involved in considerable collaborative effort with other professional workers; in another agency they may have minimal working contact with other professionals. These factors would alter the kinds of competencies that need to be evaluated.

Any evaluation, of necessity, starts with a statement of objectives and a description of the job the worker is being asked to perform. It is axiomatic that we cannot tell how well we are doing unless we know what we are trying to do. The process of evaluation involves the explication of worker tasks; the clear, concise, and meaningful definition of criteria by which we can measure the extent to which the tasks have been achieved; and the actual measurement of worker performance in terms of the criteria which reflect the task objectives. A criterion is a standard against which a comparison can be made.

One of the difficult problems faced by the social work profession, and shared with other human-service professions, is establishing standards of productivity in the absence of a standard product. The ultimate aim of social work intervention is the more effective psychosocial functioning of the client—individual, family, group, or community. The most immediate criterion, then, in evaluating the productivity of the worker is the number of clients who have been helped, as a consequence of the worker's activity, to achieve more effective psychosocial functioning over a given period of time. Any review of the literature concerned with evaluating the outcome of social work service will testify to the problems of definition, measurement, and data procurement which would be encountered in applying such a criterion in evaluating the worker's performance. In recognition of the difficulties of evaluating worker performance in terms of outcome, the content of evaluation in virtually all agencies has been generally concerned with second-order criteria, which are easier to apply. The use of such criteria is based on the supposition that if the worker possesses relevant knowledge, displays professionally approved behavior, manifests the proper attitudes, and follows professionally prescribed procedures, clients will be helped. Consequently, the evaluation is focused on relevant knowledge, approved behavior, proper attitudes, and prescribed procedures rather than on the frequency, consistency, and quality of client change, as such, attributable to worker intervention.

Evaluation on the basis of process and procedure rather than outcome is defensible because so many factors that determine outcome are beyond the control of the worker. One might often legitimately claim that "the operation was a success although the patient died."

With the recent use of behavior modification approaches and the specification of identifiable, measurable objectives to be achieved through the worker's intervention, evaluation on the bases of outcome variables has become more frequent. The worker's performance is evaluated in terms of the degree to which specific, measurable objectives have been achieved.

An overview of the principal content areas usually included in reasonably comprehensive evaluation outlines follows.

I. Ability to establish and maintain meaningful, effective appropriately professional relationships with client system.

A. Attitudes as manifested in appropriate worker behavior toward client: interest and desire to be helpful; respect; empathic understanding; nonjudgmental acceptance; nonstereotyped individualization; assent to client self-determination; warmth and concern.

B. Objective, disciplined use of self in relationship in behalf of client: empathy and sympathy without overidentification.

C. Adherence to professionally accepted values in client contact: confidentiality.

II. Social work process—knowledge and skills.

A. Social study (data-gathering) skills: discriminating ability to discern psycho-social-cultural factors of significance to service situation that needs to be explored; ability to gather relevant information from client, collaterals, records, tests; observation and exploration of relevant items of social study are accurate and appropriately detailed.

B. Diagnosis (data assessment) skills: demonstrates understanding of interrelationship of intrapsychic, interpersonal, and environmental factors; effectively applies knowledge of human behavior and social systems so as to derive meanings from social study data; shows appreciation and understanding of client's perceptual, cognitive, and emotional frame of reference; capable of formulating a descriptive, dynamic diagnostic or data-assessment statement.

C. Treatment (intervention) skills: capacity to plan and implement a program of remedial action based on understanding (diagnosis), derived from the facts (social study); ability to use, as appropriate to the client's situation, specific treatment interventions, e.g., environmental modification, psychological support, clarification, insight, advocacy, brokerage, social action; interventions are appropriately timed and relevant.

D. Interviewing skills: ability to establish, with client, clear interview purpose; ability to maintain interview focus in order to achieve interview purpose; maintains a good balance between flexibly and responsibly following client lead and offering appropriate direction and control; ability to tactfully and nonthreateningly help client communicate feelings as well as facts.

E. Recording skills: recording demonstrates capacity for organization and communication of worker's thinking and feelings; recording is discriminating, selective, accurate, succinct.

III. Orientation to agency administration—objectives, policies, procedures.

Knowledge of, commitment to, and identification with agency objectives, policies, and procedures; ability to work within limits of agency policies and procedures; imaginative use of agency policies and procedures in helping client; takes responsibility for working toward orderly change in policies and procedures which require improvement.

IV. Relationship to, and use of, supervision.

    A. Administrative aspects: prepares adequately for conference, is prompt and regular in attending scheduled conferences, provides supervisor with necessary, appropriate material for conference.

    B. Interpersonal aspects: freedom in seeking and using supervisor's help without undue dependency; acceptance of supervision and instruction without subservience; positive orientation to supervisory authority; active and appropriate participation in supervisory conferences; ability to recognize when consultation is needed and how it might appropriately be used.

V. Staff and community relationships.

Contributes to harmonious and effective relationship with agency staff at all levels; develops positive relationship with, and makes appropriate use of, colleagues from allied disciplines; constructively represents the agency to other professionals and to the general community; has good knowledge of relevant community resources.

VI. Management of work requirements and work load.

Covers work load with regularity and adequacy; shows ability to plan and organize work schedule within time allotted; shows capacity to set selective, valid priorities and to schedule work accordingly; is prompt in submitting recording, statistical reports, time sheets, service reports, etc.

VII. Professionally related attributes and attitudes.

Realistic critical assessment of own limitations without undue anxiety; adequate level of self-awareness and capacity for self-evaluation; flexible and cooperative on the job; enthusiasm for, and conviction in, the work he is doing.

Generally behaves on the job in accordance with the values and ethics of the profession; shows identification with the profession; takes responsibility for continued professional development by reading, informal discussion, participation in relevant, available training programs.

Evaluation outlines like the preceding one result in a narrative statement of performance. There is a growing dissatisfaction with detailed narrative statements and increasing use of standardized check forms as guides to evaluation. The use of such a form imposes less of a burden on the supervisor, it results in a more precise product for comparative evaluation of one worker with another or the same worker with himself at different points in time, and it encourages greater standardization in evaluation. It is an expeditious way of summarizing evaluative statements.

From experimental study, Schubert (1960) concludes that "application of a schedule to student process records has been found an effective and relatively economical means of making objective evaluations of performance and discriminating between several levels of performance" (p. 298).

On the facing page is a humorous, but clear, example of an objective format for performance evaluation.

The following examples illustrate different kinds of formats used in social work evaluation forms. The material comes from evaluation forms obtained from a number of schools of social work and a wide variety of agencies. The items have been modified and edited to suit our present purpose. I have included only a limited number of items in each form but have varied the content so that, in aggregate, the items employed illustrate the kinds of content areas included in a comprehensive evaluation outline.

The following example illustrates the use of a step scale. Each step in the scale identifies the level of performance which relates to a particular area of performance.

What are the worker's attitudes toward clients as shown in supervisory and/or group conferences?
1. Acceptance without sentimentality, without overidentification, without denial of unlikable qualities in client.
2. Acceptance tinged with overidentification, but not so much so as to impede learning.
3. Acceptance varies in different cases; predominantly positive attitude toward clients.
4. Some negative attitudes toward clients, but these are not so excessive as to impede learning.
5. Strong overidentification impedes learning.

Performance factor	Performance level				
	Far exceeds job requirements	Exceeds job requirements	Meets job requirements	Needs some improvement	Does not meet minimal requirements
Quality of response	Leaps tall buildings with a single bound 1.__	Must take running start to leap over buildings 2.__	Can only leap over short building or medium with no spires 3.__	Crashes into building when attempting to jump over 4.__	Cannot recognize buildings much less jump over them 5.__
Tempo of performance	Is faster than a speeding bullet 1.__	Is as fast as a speeding bullet 2.__	Not quite as fast as a speeding bullet 3.__	Would you believe a slow bullet? 4.__	Wounds self with bullet when attempting to shoot gun 5.__
Communications skill	Talks with God 1.__	Talks with the agents 2.__	Talks to himself 3.__	Argues with himself 4.__	Loses the argument 5.__

6. Hostile, withholding attitudes impede learning.
7. Neutral and guarded attitudes.

To what extent does the worker perceive his own part in the worker-client relationship?
1. Sees that his own feelings affect work with the client, and tries to handle his own feelings for the client's benefit.
2. Acknowledges feelings but does nothing about them.
3. Protests or denies feelings.
4. Guarded in acknowledging feelings; maintains a bland surface, so there is nothing to take hold of in teaching.

What is the quality of the worker's diagnostic perception as revealed in verbal and written evidence?
1. Very high quality both in recording and in verbal material. Expresses diagnostic thinking freely. Sees the total problem and implications. Sees the meaning of behavior both in the client's life situation and in the worker-client interaction. Explores supervisory suggestions rationally. Weighs evidence.
2. High quality, but less consistently or pervasively so than in 1.
3. Mixed quality: variations in different cases, or sees major problem but not its implications.
4. Mixed quality: does fairly well verbally but does not organize ideas on paper very well.
5. Limited quality: diagnostic thinking is in general rather thin or something distorted, but enough is going on that there is something to take hold of in teaching.
6. Poor quality: distortions in thinking do not yield to discussion, or observation is so superficial that clues are not available for supervisory discussion.

What attitudes does the worker characteristically show in the conference with the supervisor?
1. Thoughtful, spontaneous, generally postive.
2. Somewhat scattered, spontaneous, positive.
3. Challenging and somewhat hostile; but hostility not so great as to impede learning.
4. Guarded; apparently some fearfulness of the supervisor's intent; bland.
5. Passively hostile; negative attitude that impedes learning.
6. Actively hostile; negative attitude that impedes learning.
7. Other

What is the level of the worker's attempts to engage client participation?
1. Very high: imaginative, individualized, relevant, with full recogni-

tion of obvious factors and some recognition of the less obvious. Flexibly related to case situation. Well-timed.

2. High: individualized and relevant, with recognition of obvious factors; fairly flexibly related to case situation; fairly well-timed.
3. Moderate: incomplete or inadequate or superficial, but not predominantly irrelevant, inappropriate, inflexible, or poorly timed. May be somewhat inconsistent.
4. Low: predominantly somewhat irrelevant or inappropriate, and/or mildly distorted or rigid; not very well-timed.
5. Very low: predominantly irrelevant or inappropriate, and/or grossly distorted or rigid; poorly timed.

Table 5 shows a five-step scale with a further gradation of two different points within each step.

The evaluation instrument might be a check form with evaluation items stated, giving the supervisor four or five possible choices of responses. The performance response levels might be stated in several ways.

1 = clearly above expected level	1 = excellent	1 = outstanding
2 = above expected level	2 = above average	2 = very good
3 = at expected level	3 = average	3 = good
4 = below expected level	4 = below average	4 = poor
5 = clearly below expected level	5 = poor	5 = unsatisfactory

A zero is often provided to be checked when the supervisor does not have sufficient information or when the item is not relevant to the worker's job assignment. Any one of these three scales might be employed with the following evaluation-item listing.

Evaluation items	Performance level
a. Is aware of own feelings in relationship and controls them so as not to impede help to client.	1 2 3 4 5 0
b. Establishes a relationship characterized by rapport, ease, psychological safety.	1 2 3 4 5 0
c. Able to communicate acceptance of wide variety of different kinds of behavior while not condoning unacceptable behavior.	1 2 3 4 5 0

(list continued on p. 306)

table 5. A step scale.

For each factor to be rated select the behavior description along the 10-point scale which *most nearly describes* the worker. Decide which of the two numbers above the behavior description represents the more accurate, most consistent description of the worker and circle this number. Rate each factor without reference to any other. If you have had no opportunity to observe the worker in the relevant activity, circle 0. (National Association of Social Workers n.d.)

	0	1 2	3 4	5 6	7 8	9 10
1. Ability to develop and maintain working relationships with clients.	No opportunity to observe.	Difficulty in forming relationships even in relatively uncomplicated situations.	Able to form productive relationships but this may be inconsistent and the range may be limited.	Generally forms productive relationships; but has some difficulty in unfamiliar situations.	Consistently forms productive relationships in familiar situations and often in unfamiliar and challenging situations.	Unusual and consistent ability to form relationships with wide range of persons in complex situations.
	0	1 2	3 4	5 6	7 8	9 10
2. Ability to take professional action on behalf of clients.	No opportunity to observe.	Usually expresses little concern for the rights of clients.	Recognizes the rights of clients but generally does not stand up for the client.	Sensitive in general to the rights of clients and takes a stand for the client in usual situations.	Greater than usual sensitivity to rights of clients and leadership in advocating for those rights.	Has in-depth awareness of the rights of clients in complex situations and consistently takes a stand for clients.

	0	1 2	3 4	5 6	7 8	9 10
3. Diligence and dependability in performing assigned work.	No opportunity to observe.	Frequently does not work hard or long enough or has "forgotten" to carry out assignments.	Some supervisory prodding necessary to get work done.	Works fairly steadily at assigned tasks.	Can be depended on to stick to a job until it is finished.	Puts every possible effort into his work.
4. Commitment to continuing professional development.	No opportunity to observe.	No apparent interest in professional development. Not self-critical, apathetic about increasing skill and knowledge, very limited view of professional responsibility. Does not respond to stimulus. Not committed to continuing professional development.	Inconsistently responds to outside stimulus to increase knowledge and skill, rarely takes initiative. Commitment somewhat questionable.	Usually responds to outside stimulus but does not initiate many efforts toward increasing knowledge and skill. Interest somewhat restricted but there is some positive evidence of commitment.	Definite evidence of commitment to continuing professional development, though this may be spasmodic or limited to particular areas. Some initiative in self-evaluation. Demonstrates some sense of professional responsibility beyond immediate tasks.	Consistently seeks to extend knowledge and improve skill, evaluates own practice, formulates ideas and shares them, clear sense of professional responsibility beyond the immediate job, systematically prepares self for new responsibilities.

Evaluation items (continued)	*Performance level*

d. Able to obtain clear and accurate picture of problem situation with which client wants help.   1   2   3   4   5   0

e. Able to organize and synthesize social study data in understanding client in his situation.   1   2   3   4   5   0

f. Confirms, refines, modifies diagnostic formulation as appropriate.   1   2   3   4   5   0

g. Able to mobilize community resource in client's behalf.   1   2   3   4   5   0

h. Able to accept limited treatment goals without feeling immobilizing frustration.   1   2   3   4   5   0

i. Facilitates client communication in interview.   1   2   3   4   5   0

j. Understands and responds to nonverbal as well as verbal communication in interview.   1   2   3   4   5   0

k. Recording reflects nature of worker-client interaction and worker's diagnostic thinking.   1   2   3   4   5   0

l. Is constructively and appropriately critical of agency policies and procedures which impede service.   1   2   3   4   5   0

m. Able to contribute constructive disagreement in supervisory conference.   1   2   3   4   5   0

n. Takes responsibility for establishing own learning needs in supervision.   1   2   3   4   5   0

The following three items illustrate the use of a seven-point scale anchored by descriptive statements at the high and low ends, clearly defining the behavior being evaluated.

1. Relationship with client (individual or group): *Level of rapport, warmth, acceptance*

    HIGH   Has regard, respect, and concern for person regardless of behavior which worker may reject; established warm, nonthreatening, nonpunishing, easy, relaxed, psychologically safe atmosphere; compassionate, gentle, sympathetic; client given freedom to be himself, to express himself freely, in all his unlovely as well as lovely aspects; client feels at east and is encouraged to communicate since he trusts worker and has confidence in him.

    __ 1. Extremely good.

    __ 2. Very much better than average.

    __ 3. Somewhat better than average.

    __ 4. Average.

___5. Somewhat poorer than average.
___6. Very much poorer than average.
___7. Extremely poor.
___8. Not enough information available to make confident judgment.

LOW   Moralistic and judgmental; cold, distant, aloof, derogatory, disapproving, critical; establishes an atmosphere which is psychologically threatening and potentially punitive; client not permitted freedom to be himself; client feels uneasy, unrelaxed, hesitant to communicate since he mistrusts worker and has little confidence in him.

2. *Diagnostic skills* (individual or group)
   HIGH   Recognizes, identifies, demonstrates understanding of and appropriate use of psychosocial, individual and group dynamics; tends to individualize diagnosis using pertinent social-study material; capable of conceptualizing and verbalizing psychodynamics of client situation and psychodynamics of the worker-client (individual or group) interaction; uses theoretical constructs regarding individuals and groups to make relevant, valid inferences from appropriate case data; technical language precisely and/or appropriately used.

   ___1. Extremely good.
   ___2. Very much better than average.
   ___3. Somewhat better than average.
   ___4. Average.
   ___5. Somewhat poorer than average.
   ___6. Very much poorer than average.
   ___7. Extremely poor.
   ___8. Not enough information available to make confident judgment.

   LOW   Misses most significant psychosocial, dynamic cues; understanding of client's situation and dynamics of worker-client interaction superficial and/or distorted; tends to stereotype client and apply theoretical constructs inappropriately; technical language imprecise and/or inappropriately used.

3. *Management of work load*
   HIGH   Management of work load is smooth, efficient, inconspicuous, requiring little or no prodding or checking; worker output and efficiency high; meets deadlines, fulfills assignments.

          __1. Extremely good.
          __2. Very much better than average.
          __3. Somewhat better than average.
          __4. Average.
          __5. Somewhat poorer than average.
          __6. Very much poorer than average.
          __7. Extremely poor.
          __8. Not enough information available to make confident judgment.

LOW   Management is poor, seems unable to manage work load without considerable reminding, prodding, checking; work output and efficiency low; frequently fails to meet deadlines or fulfill assignments.

More precise distinctions can be made on a scale such as the following. The supervisor is requested to check the scale at the point which appropriately reflects level of performance.

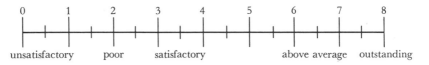

The scale is repeated for each of the items such as the following:

a. Recognizes and disciplines own biases, prejudices, negative reactions to client.
b. Accepts limitations in clients' capacity and motivation and works with clients at their own tempo.
c. Uses good judgment in determining what information needs to be obtained in a particular situation.
d. Makes relevant inferences from social study data through appropriate application of social work theory.
e. Able to use the relationship as a medium for help.
f. Achieves good balance in treatment between stimulating the client to act on his own behalf and, when necessary, acting in behalf of the client.
g. Can identify and utilize appropriate strategies of intervention relevant to client system need.
h. Understands client's latent as well as manifest communication in interview.
i. Effectively handles pauses, silence, transitions in interview.

j. Recording is well organized and reflects essentials of case situation.

k. Understands his position in agency structure and the appropriate channels for intra-agency communication.

l. Shows little need to defend himself against learning in supervision.

m. Shows evidence of use of supervisory learning in subsequent client contacts.

n. Able to function as a productive, contributing member of a team of colleagues.

With recognition of the difficulty of making precise distinctions in levels of performance, some evaluation forms provide only for very broad categorizations, i.e., acceptable, needs improvement, unacceptable.

An evaluation form can include negative as well as positive and neutral statements. The following examples are taken from such a form.

Instructions: Below are listed some statements which relate to evaluation of worker task performance. Using your knowledge of the worker's activity, please mark each statement according to how strongly you agree or disagree that this is characteristic of the work. Mark the statement +3, +2, +1 or −1, −2, −3 to represent the following:

+3 I strongly agree	−1 I disagree slightly
+2 I agree	−2 I disagree
+1 I agree slightly	−3 I strongly disagree

__a. Demonstrates an interest in client's problems.

__b. Tends to be cool and aloof in contact with clients.

__c. Tends to respond punitively to the hostile, resistive client.

__d. Shows empathic understanding of most client behavior.

__e. Participates actively and willingly in supervisory sessions.

__f. Accepts and acts on constructive criticism.

__g. Lacks sensitivity to dynamics of self in supervisory relationships.

The content of the evaluation outline and the content items included in the above illustrative standardized forms are designed to be generic and applicable with some adaptation to all social work methodologies. In addition to the core generic items illustrated, it may be helpful to list some performance items that are more specific to group work and community organization.

Group work:
1. Skill in the use of group process to effect individual change.
2. Skill in helping individuals establish positive, productive group relationships.
3. Skill in the use of program activities to effect group change.
4. Skill in participating effectively in group interaction.
5. Knowledge of, and ability to use, a variety of group roles in effecting group movements.
6. Skill in discriminating and appropriate use of program media.
7. Skill in effecting change in intragroup interaction.
8. Skill in relating to group members as individuals.
9. Knowledge of various types of groups and their differentiated structure and function.
10. Skill in group leadership.

Community organization:
1. Skill in assisting community group to articulate needs and problems.
2. Skill in helping community residents develop organizational capacity necessary for effective social action.
3. Skill in establishing positive and productive relationships with leadership people at a variety of levels.
4. Skill in employing a range of educational and/or promotional techniques to enhance community understanding and support of social welfare programs.
5. Knowledge and understanding of community dynamics and power structure.
6. Skill in bringing together disparate citizen groups, professional groups, and social agencies in a working relationship addressed to the solution of community problems.
7. Skill in translating expressed community concerns into a feasible course of remedial action.
8. Skill in increasing motivation and participation of community residents in problem-solving activities in their own behalf.
9. Skill in negotiating with citizens' groups and community agencies.
10. Skill in effecting change in intergroup relationships.

In applying rating scales, supervisors make use of the knowledge which comes from experience with the performance of different workers. A lack of such experience makes it difficult to use some rating scales, as one supervisor notes:

> It was difficult to evaluate using ratings such as above average, average, below average. Having no substantial supervisory experience other than this year's, it was difficult to determine what average behavior would be. This must be a dilemma faced by other beginning supervisors, who have little other than their own behavior by which to compare.

Even the most detailed rating form may fail to include a performance item that is of particular significance in the case of an individual supervisee. Furthermore, a valid evaluation is a complex configuration of many discrete items. The standardized form tends to fractionate performance since it is generally a listing of separate items. It is clear that something more is required, which involves putting the items together in some general, inclusive statement that relates the different items to each other. Using the same itemized information, one can get quite different evaluations depending on how one interpretively puts the items together. Failure to understand the interrelationship of discrete performance items is illustrated by the efficiency expert who evaluated the work of members of a symphony orchestra. He noted that for

> considerable periods the oboe players had nothing to do. The number should be reduced and their work spread out more evenly over the whole of the concert, thus eliminating peaks of activity. It is noted that all twelve first violins were playing identical notes; this seems unnecessary duplication. There is too much repetition of some musical passages. No useful purpose is served by repeating on horns and woodwinds a passage which has been already adequately handled by the strings.

In an evaluation, as in an orchestra, the whole is greater than the sum of individual parts.

In view of the need for a summary statement that integrates the itemized listing, most standardized forms leave space for this at the end. The instruction to the supervisor might ask her to "consider and assess the staff member's total performance as a social worker during the period covered by the evaluation, taking into account those factors covered by the form and any others you might believe to be important." More succinctly, the form might end by asking for the supervisor's general overall impression of the worker. All items in the outline or on the standardized scale appear to have equal value, but some are more mechanical, more peripheral, and require less skill than others. The overall summation is an opportunity to give differential weighting to the more significant aspects of the worker's performance which require more skill and competence.

The rating forms generally provide for face-sheet information which includes the name of the worker, classification of the worker, education, the name of the supervisor, the identifying department or unit, the date of the evaluation, the reason for it, the period it covers.

Once a standardized rating scale has been formulated, it might be helpful to schedule meetings of supervisors alone, supervisees alone, and of the two groups together in order to discuss the use of the form. Such training in the use of the scale will ensure more uniform and efficient use of the instrument.

The evaluation outline or rating form is uniformly applicable to all the workers in the same job classification, that is, those positions having similar duties and responsibilities and requiring similar levels of knowledge and skill. Because the workers have the same classification, they have the same status in the agency and receive similar pay.

The standard for a job activity is defined as the quality of performance and the quantity of accomplishment which the agency feels it is legitimate to ask from all the workers assigned this job activity who have similar levels of education and experience. Evaluations for the same job classification differ in terms of experience on the job. The evaluation outline for the Caseworker I employee with five years of service is necessarily somewhat different from that for the newly hired Caseworker I. The performance items are similar in many instances. The difference lies in the greater consistency, adequacy, appropriateness, and autonomy of performance by the experienced worker. It calls for a performance executed with greater self-assurance as applied to a caseload of greater complexity. For example, the evaluation outline in table 6 makes distinctions in expectations varying with experience.

Sources of Information for Evaluation

In addition to knowing what to look for, which is spelled out in the criteria of the evaluation outlines, we have to know where to look in sampling worker performance. The supervisor needs to be able to obtain sufficient valid and reliable information representing the typical performance of the worker if she is to apply the criteria in making an assessment. The possible sources of information available to the supervisor regarding the worker's performance might include:

1. Supervisee's written records.
2. Supervisee's verbal reports of activity.
3. Tape recordings of supervisee-client (individual, group, or community) contacts.
4. Video tapes of supervisee-client contacts.
5. Observation of supervisee's performance via one-way screen.
6. Observation of supervisee in joint interviews.
7. Observation of supervisee's activity in group supervisory meetings.
8. Observation of supervisee's activity in staff meetings and/or joint professional conferences.
9. Client evaluations of supervisee's performance.
10. Supervisee's correspondence, reports, statistical forms, weekly schedule, daily action logs, monthly performance records, etc.

A study of the actual sources of information utilized by supervisors in formulating evaluations indicates high dependence on a very limited group of sources, principally the supervisee's written record material and the supervisee's verbal reports of activity. Less frequently utilized, but of some importance, are correspondence, reports, and statistical forms, and worker activity in staff meetings and group supervisory meetings. Audio and video tape recordings, direct observation

table 6.

Distinctions in expectations, based on experience.

Performance criteria	1st year	Experience level	
		3rd year	5th year
Understanding of the relationship of this agency to other agencies	beginning understanding	good understanding	full grasp
Commitment to agency program	awareness and a feeling of responsibility	growing facility	full commitment
Anxiety level	still a good deal of unfocused anxiety	no pervasive anxiety except in particular cases—expect some regression	anxiety minimal; worker should handle it herself except in serious cases
Degree of enthusiasm for work	high degree	still some unbridled enthusiasm	seasoned with compromise
Capacity to take criticism and deal with it constructively	accept with some objectivity; needs help in dealing with it	take and use with a minimum of help	take and use without defensiveness
Capacity for effective functioning as team member	growing awareness of need to fit self in; still needs much help	accomplished fact	accomplished fact plus helping others to do it
Use of supervision	willingness to expose but still quite dependent; produces material but not too clear on what needs to be learned	takes initiative; use of time for specific needs; knows what he wants	consultation

of the worker, and client evaluations are almost never utilized (Kadushin 1974).

The use of audio and video tapes and one-way-screen observation is discussed in detail in chapter 8, which is concerned with innovations in supervision. I might note here, however, that other human-service professions use such devices in supervision much more frequently, and there is beginning acceptance of their use in social work as well. There is likewise growing acceptance of clients' reactions as a source of information regarding workers' performance. Client reaction has frequently been a productive source of information in program-evaluation research. Clients can provide equally valid information regarding their reaction to contacts with individual workers.

Controversial Questions

There is some controversy about whether evaluation should be concerned with assessing the worker against objective, uniform standards or against the worker's own development. A profession accountable to the community and concerned with effective service to the client cannot, it seems to me, accept as legitimate an orientation toward evaluation which employs the worker's own development as the standard. Some minimal external requirements need to be met. Even if the worker is ten times more proficient today than yesterday, if he still does not meet minimum standards of acceptability we do the clients an injustice in retaining the worker on the job. We are concerned about individual development, but as measured against some general, established standard.

Earlier I mentioned the controversy around separating administrative and educational supervision. The proponents for separation suggest that the administrative responsibility of evaluation be given to the supervisee's peers. Studies have shown that when peers are provided with the necessary information about a worker's performance their assessment of performance correlates very highly with evaluations of the same work made by the supervisor (Friesen and Dunning 1973). Under usual conditions, however, workers do not know enough about the work activity of their peers to make a reasoned judgment. Social work generally involves face-to-face activity between worker and client in privacy rather than any public performance open to observation by others. Studies of doctors in a clinic performing under analogous conditions indicated that they did not have enough knowledge of their peers' activity to judge their performance validly and reliably (Freidson and Rhea 1965).

Evaluation by peers would require sharing with each other all of the recordings, case reports, and statistical forms ordinarily used as a basis for evaluation. Even if such materials were shared with peers openly and willingly, the peers would be still denied the rich information that supervisors obtain from the conference-to-conference discussion of work activity. The limited availability of basic information needed for valid evaluation, and the time expenditure such a procedure would impose, make peer evaluation for educational purposes open to criticism. Peer evaluation as a basis for administrative decision would be open to even more serious question. Where peers are in competition for scarce resources (a merit raise, a promotion, a more desirable caseload), the burden of trying to be fair, honest, and objective in evaluating one's competitors is very great.

The same problems regarding adequate knowledge of the worker's total performance would militate against assigning the responsibility for ongoing educational supervision to one person in the agency and responsibility for evaluation to another. Other aspects of this controversy are discussed in chapter 8.

There is a question about the reliability and validity of supervisors' judgments in evaluation. The supervisor is faced with a very difficult, albeit inescapable, task in evaluating. Unable to observe worker performance directly, denied access to a clearly defined finished product, employing imprecise criteria applied to activities which are difficult to measure, the supervisor is asked to formulate an evaluation that accurately reflects the reality of the worker's performance.

There is general agreement that standards for evaluation in social work have been vague, "pragmatic, observational and intuitive rather than precise, standardized and scientific" (Kagan 1963, p. 18). But they have not been totally unsophisticated, casual, and without merit. No recent research has tested the reliability with which different supervisors will evaluate the same sample of performance. However, we do have available an experiment conducted in 1955 under the sponsorship of the Council on Social Work Education (Lutz 1956). Records of four casework interviews were sent to casework faculty of schools of social work throughout the country for independent assessments. Records of four group-work meetings were sent to group-work faculty. Faculty members were asked to evaluate the performance of the caseworker or group worker as reflected in the record on a seven-point scale from "definitely inadequate" to "definitely superior." A total of 143 responses were received. In three of the four casework records the consistency in judgments made was at a level of statistical significance ($p = .01$). This indicates that there was considerable consensus regarding judgments. However, there were some supervisors who rated the same record "definitely inadequate" while others rated it "definitely superior." Consistency in rating all of the group-work records was statistically significant, and there was less variability in the ratings. There is therefore reason to believe that supervisors can achieve close agreement about the level of performance of a particular worker, based on some generally accepted criteria.

The general difficulties in evaluation are compounded currently by rapid changes in social work responsibilities, procedures, and acceptable methodological approaches. For example, the psychoanalytically oriented supervisor has great difficulty in evaluating the work of the behaviorally oriented supervisee. Accepting that "different" does not necessarily imply "better" or "worse," the supervisor is not in a position to evaluate work based on a much different basic orientation to the clients.

Recognizing and accepting the necessity for evaluation and the difficulties that reduce the likelihood of achieving a wholly satisfactory, reliable, and valid evaluation, what can one say to supervisors faced with this responsibility? The task and concomitant authority are inherent in the position. To accept the position of supervisor involves acceptance of the task. In accepting the task one must also, unavoidably, accept the burden of guilt and anxiety associated with it. But this is a truth to which the supervisor is no stranger. The social worker offering service to the client accepts the burden of guilt and anxiety associated with implementing decisions that are frequently made on the basis of tenuous evidence and hazardous inference. Every decision of consequence to which one is a responsible party excites a keen and discomforting awareness of personal fallibility.

One might further say to supervisors that they should recognize and accept their humanity, that *all* evaluations have, inevitably, elements of subjectivity, that all are, in a measure, in error. But the supervisor, in immediate contact with the day-to-day work of the supervisee, is best informed about the work and best able to evaluate it. The measure of probable error in the supervisor's evaluation is less than the supervisee would be subjected to if evaluated by anyone else. And the systematic, conscientious effort at assessments by the supervisor, despite subjectivity and error, is "far kinder (and more accurate) than the commonly employed gossip by which professional judgments are circulated in the absence of a structure" (Ekstein and Wallerstein 1972, p. 291).

It must be recognized and accepted that, however fallible it may be, the best instrument currently available to make complex judgments, such as performance evaluations, is the trained, perceptive, informed mind of the supervisor. More precise instruments are desirable but not yet devised. Currently, "the making of such assessments is as much an art to be cultivated as it is a science to be applied" (Green 1972, p. 54). Neither the community, the agency, the clients, nor the supervisee can legitimately ask for infallibility in evaluation. What they can ask for and expect is a "reasonable approximation to an estimate" (Reynolds 1942, p. 280). This, most supervisors are capable of offering, while striving for infallibility.

Summary

An objective appraisal of the worker's total functioning on the job over a given period of time, in terms of clearly defined criteria reflecting agency standards, has value for the supervisee, supervisor, agency, and client. It is a responsibility of administrative supervision.

Supervisors dislike evaluating because they are reluctant to accentuate status differences, feel dubious about their entitlement and ability to evaluate, perceive evaluation as an indirect assessment of supervision, regard it as contradictory to the ethos of social work, and fear the strong negative affect which might be evoked.

Evaluation should be a continuous process that encourages active supervisee participation and input. It is based on defensible work-related criteria that are openly shared with the supervisee. It takes situational factors into consideration, is tentative and concerned with both strengths and weaknesses. It is enacted in the context of a positive relationship, and the supervisor is ready to accept an evaluation of his own performance.

Both supervisor and supervisee prepare for the evaluation conference by reviewing the work done during the evaluation period. The conference is concerned with a mutual sharing of the outcomes of the reviews, using the evaluation outline as the basis for discussion. The final evaluation is written and given to the worker.

A variety of performance evaluation outlines were presented. The worker's written and verbal reports of her work are the principal data used in assessing performance. Evaluations are most frequently used in making personnel decisions.

chapter six

The Group Conference in Supervision

Although the individual conference is the most frequent context for supervision, it is not the only one. In a few agencies the group conference is the principal form of supervision. In many more agencies the group conference is used in addition to, and in supplementation of, the individual conference.

A 1973 questionnaire study of some 1500 supervisors and supervisees showed that the group conference was the principal context for supervision for about 15 percent of the respondents. For about 60 percent of the respondents the individual conference was the main context for supervision, supplemented by group conferences held once or twice a month. For about 25 percent of the respondents the individual conference was the sole context for supervision (Kadushin 1973). Group supervision was much more frequently a supplement to individual supervision than was individual supervision a supplement to group supervision.

Definition

Group supervision is distinguishable from other procedures which employ a group setting to achieve agency administrative purpose. Staff meetings, in-service training sessions, agency institutes, seminars, and workshops all use the group setting as the context for conducting agency business and for the purpose of educating staff. However, the term "group supervision" is here defined as the use of a group setting to implement the responsibilities of supervision. In group supervision the supervisor, given educational and administrative responsibility for the activities of a specific number of workers, meets with them as a group to discharge these responsibilities. In group supervision the agency mandate to the supervisor is implemented in the group and through the group.

The supervisory conference group is a formed group. It is a structured group with a task and an agenda. Membership in the group is defined as a consequence of being a supervisee of a particular group leader–supervisor. These groups are organized under agency administrative auspices. They are formed with the expectation that certain objectives will be achieved; they have a designated place in the formal structure of the agency and have a designated leader in the unit supervisor.

This definition of group supervision solves some of the decisional problems regarding group formation. How large the group should be and whether it should be heterogeneous or homogeneous in composition are questions answered by the definition. The size of the group is determined by the number of supervisees for whom the supervisor has administrative responsibility, generally four or five. The supervisees assigned to any one supervisor probably have some similarity in education and training, but even more probably are concerned with similar problems and similar service. As a result, the group is likely to be homogeneous with regard to significant factors that determine group interests and concerns.

The fact that members of the group share concern about the same social problems and the same group of services suggests that they have high interaction potential. Sharing significant concerns, they have much to talk about, and much of what they have to talk about is mutually understandable. Since they are all social workers in the same agency, they share a common frame of reference. These factors make for considerable mutual predictability, enhancing group members' trust and confidence in each other.

The primary ultimate objective of group supervision is the same as the ultimate objective of all supervision: more effective and efficient service to agency clients. Unlike group therapy or sensitivity training groups, group supervision is not directed toward the personal development of the supervisee, personal problem-solving, or satisfaction derived from group activities and interaction.

An agency introducing group supervision as a substitute for, or a supplement to, individual supervision needs to prepare its workers for the change. This modification of supervision should be introduced only with the concurrence of staff, with whom the reasons for the change have been discussed. The specifics of how group supervision will operate should be clearly interpreted following the acceptance of the desirability of the change. There are distinct advantages and disadvantages to group supervision that can be made explicit.

Advantages of Group Supervision

One clear advantage of group supervision is economy of administrative time and effort. Administrative communications regarding standardized policies and procedures can be communicated once to all the supervisees in a unit. Matters that are of common concern can be most economically communicated to individuals as members of a group. Kaslow (1972) has confirmed the fact that there are financial savings to an agency that moves from individual supervision to group supervision, since the latter involves less expenditure of supervisory personnel's time.

Group conferences make possible the efficient utilization of a wider variety of teaching-learning experiences. A presentation by a specialist can be scheduled, a film can be shown, a tape recording can be played, a role-playing session can be organized, a panel presentation can be arranged. Such learning experiences are designed primarily for the group context.

Group supervision provides the opportunity for supervisees to share their experiences with similar problems encountered on the job and possible solutions which each has formulated in response. "All of us are smarter than any one of us." However similar the assignments, the aggregate of all the caseloads (which is the total pool for discussion in the group) provides a greater variety of experiences than is available in any one worker's caseload. Consequently the sources for learning are richer and more varied than in the individual conference. Different members of the group can further provide a greater variety of points of view for learning. "The right explanation of behavior (one's own!) yields to the possibility of multi-dimensional understanding. The one right treatment approach (one's own!) bears reexamination" (Judd, Kohn, and Shulman 1962, p. 102).

The sharing of relevant experiences in the group supervisory conference is illustrated in the following excerpt. This conference of psychiatric social workers in a mental hospital setting is concerned with "factors affecting casework movements with psychiatric patients." One supervisee, Mr. N, reported that his client

had regressed since his admission to the hospital. The patient's wife had noticed this further withdrawal and had discussed with Mr. N her concern about this observation. Mr. N pointed out that he felt he had been able to help the patient's wife understand that regressions during psychotic episodes occurred frequently.

Addressing the group, the supervisor pointed out that Mr. N had helped the relative to anticipate what so commonly happens during the course of mental illness and its treatment: that there were frequent vacillations in reality anchorage and in observable responses to treatment. The supervisor wondered if the others hadn't observed examples of these swings in their case assignments.

Miss Delmar said she had a patient who had recently been taken off of ECT and had regressed immediately afterward. Mr. Drake explained that he had a case like Miss D's and also one like Mr. N's. So far, most of Miss Gleeson's patients had been responding very well to treatment; however, when discharge plans had been mobilized with one of her cases, the patient had regressed, showing worse symptoms than had been shown on admission to hospital. The reversal had been sudden.

The group expressed its opinion that temporary regression at the time of discharge or termination is a common reaction among clients. (Abrahamson 1959, pp. 89–90)

Members of the group also act as a source of emotional support. Group members console, sympathize with, and praise each other during the course of group meetings. The group not only provides the opportunity for lateral teaching—peer to peer—but provides opportunities of mutual aid of various kinds. This opportunity for a supervisee to share her knowledge and to give emotional support to peers is a gratifying, morale-building experience that reinforces a feeling of belonging to the group.

In the following passage, Cohen (1972) notes the mutually reinforcing aspects of interaction in group supervision—for better and for worse. The setting is a geriatric center and the supervisor is reporting.

Vividly I can remember the day that the first client in the unit caseload had died. The [worker] rushed into my office, tears streaming down her face, sobbing "Mrs. H died and I wasn't there and I didn't know anything about it." Intuitively the three other [workers] in the unit came out of their offices and the four of them sat with me for the next hour as we talked about their own feelings about dying and death. Real comfort was derived for each of them, and for me too, as in a very poignant manner we lent support to each other.

The reverse side of the coin of mutual support can be one [worker's] negativism or pessimism feeding into others. During a [group] meeting one [worker] began with "If this is what it's like to grow old who wants it. It's terrible." Whereupon each [worker] began to share the depressed, upset, gloomy feelings that had been accumulating. (p. 175)

The opportunity for the sharing of common problems encountered on the job is, in itself, a therapeutically reassuring contribution to individual morale. In the interchange made possible through group supervision, a worker often becomes aware that his problems are not unique, that his failures and difficulties are not the result of his own particular ineptitude, that all the other workers seem to be equally disturbed by some clients and equally frustrated by some situations. The group context permits a living experience with the supportive technique of universalization. The worker is given a keen appreciation of the fact that these are "our problems" rather than "my problems."

It decreases the tendency to personalize problems and increases the likelihood of objectifying them.

For some workers the group situation is the most comfortable learning environment. For some, the one-to-one tutorial conference is too intense a relationship. They need a more diffuse relationship with the supervisor to feel sufficiently comfortable to devote all their energies to learning; they need the give and take of the group interaction. It is easier for some workers to accept criticism, suggestions, and advice from peers than from parental surrogates such as the supervisor. For some supervisees, then, the group context has the advantage of meeting their idiosyncratic educational needs.

The group context provides the safety in numbers which individual supervisees may need in order to challenge the supervisor. In the highly personalized, isolated context of the individual conference, the supervisee may be afraid to articulate his questions and objections to what the supervisor is saying. "In the individual conference . . . there are only two opinions available and in case of disagreement the supervisor's opinion will usually prevail" (Pointer and Fishman 1968, p. 19). Given the support of potential allies, the supervisee may find the courage to present his differing opinions in the protected setting of the group conference.

Workers find it difficult to assess their comparative competence because they perform their tasks in private and discuss their performance in the privacy of the individual supervisory conference. Group supervision gives workers an opportunity to "see" the work of others and provides them with a basis for comparison. A worker can develop a clear sense of how he is doing as compared with other workers of comparable education and experience. Not only does the worker get a different perspective on his colleagues and their work through group supervision, he also gets a less threatening perspective of the supervisor. "The supervisor seems less the personalized judge, jury and evaluator as he is seen functioning in relation to the cases of others" (Judd, Kohn, and Shulman 1962, p. 102).

Through group conferences the individual supervisee develops a sense of belonging to a unit in the agency, a sense of group and professional identity, of group cohesion. It is true that supervisees working in close proximity in a common enterprise develop some sense of solidarity through informal interaction. Group life is inevitable in any agency and is fostered by coffee breaks, lunching together, and working together on the job. The group supervisory conference supplements and reinforces what happens naturally and ensures that feelings of affiliation and commitment will, in fact, develop. Furthermore, formal group interaction in supervisory sessions feeds back to intensify and improve informal staff interaction outside these sessions.

The group conference provides the supervisor with the opportunity of observing the supervisee in a different kind of relationship. Individual conferences permit the supervisor to understand how a supervisee reacts in dyadic relationship; the group conference shows the supervisee in action in a group. It provides the supervisor with an additional perspective of how the supervisee functions. As a consequence the supervisor may be in a better position to supervise the worker more effectively in the individual conference. This result is illustrated in the following vignette:

Mrs. D is a kindly middle-aged worker who does a fine job with her clients but tends to overprotect the underdogs to the extent of denying them room for growth. Mr. L, her supervisor, has been unsuccessful in handling this with Mrs. D in individual supervision. In group supervision Mrs. D assumes the same role, becomes protector of Miss T, the soft-spoken new worker. With direct observation of this interaction, Mr. L is able to assess with Mrs. D how needful Miss T is of this protection, how Miss T might be allowed to try coping with criticism on her own at future meetings, perhaps even considering how needful Mrs. D is of this role. (S. Moore 1970, p. 19)

Group supervision permits an advantageous specialization of function. Any ongoing system, individual conference or group supervisory conference, requires the implementation of both expressive and intrumental roles. Some things need to be done to see that the system is kept operating harmoniously, some things need to be done to see that the system successfully completes its assigned task. In the individual conference the supervisor has to perform both roles, to see that the work gets done while maintaining a harmonious relationship between supervisor and supervisee. The instrumental demands may at times be antithetical to expressive needs. To insist that expectations be met, to confront in order to get the work done, conflicts with the need to comfort and reassure. The supervisor has to be simultaneously both the "good" and the "bad" parent.

Group supervision permits the separation of these sometimes conflicting role responsibilities. While the supervisor is communicating support to some member of the group, the group may communicate expectations. While the supervisor is acting to confront, members of the group may act to reassure. Because the group situation allows delegation of different functions to different people, the task of the supervisor is in some ways simplified. He can let the group carry the instrumental tasks, confronting, demanding, raising uncomfortable questions, while he devotes his attention to supportive interventions. At other times the supervisor can do the needling, counting on the group to be supportive.

It may be easier for the supervisor to achieve modification of a supervisee's behavior through the medium of the group conference than in an individual conference. If members of the peer group indicate, in the group discussions, an acceptance of the supervisor's point of view, the individual supervisee may be less resistive to change. Learning from peers with whom one feels identified can be easier than learning from a supervisor. Learning from peers is free of the feelings of dependency and authority that complicate learning from the supervisor. Taking advantage of these benefits of the group conference, the supervisor consciously uses them to influence workers toward desirable changes in their behavior.

Blau and Scott (1962) studied workers in a public welfare agency and found that the attitude of the group was a significant determinant of individual worker behavior (p. 101). Despite differences in commitment to the desirability of service to the client, those workers who were assigned to a group where a pro-client attitude was dominant were more likely to offer service than workers in an anti-service-oriented group.

As Moore (1971) notes, "Norms formulated in the group through peer interaction are more readily internalized by workers than are the standards handed down from the supervisor as an authority figure. Workers are more apt to incorporate peer-formulated standards into improved work performance (p. 5)." This process is illustrated in the following extract:

> Shortly after the group supervisory meeting opened, Mr. L, a case-worker, complained that the meetings were dealing with material that was "too elementary," and they should move on to getting more "advanced" help with their cases. The supervisor, Mr. W, had anticipated this complaint and was prepared to answer; but he kept silent a moment and his patience was soon rewarded when Mr. M and Miss C came to his defense, itemizing instances where the so-called elementary material helped them with clients. Further, they suggested that some of the problems workers were having (the shoe seemed to fit Mr. L) were because they ignored elementary techniques and wanted to be self-styled psychiatrists. The force of the remarks at this point was greatly enhanced by having come from workers rather than the supervisor. (Moore 1971, p. 5)

Just as the group conference permits the supervisor to observe the supervisee in a somewhat different set of relationships, it permits the supervisee to observe the supervisor under different conditions. This setting provides the supervisee with the opportunity for using the supervisor as a model in learning group-interaction skills. Through the individual conference the worker learns something about dyadic interaction; through group supervision the worker learns something about group interaction. With the growing acceptance of multimethod responsibilities for all workers, and the increasing use of group approaches by caseworkers, there is a clear advantage to learning about group interaction through group supervision.

Group supervision provides a gradual step toward independence from supervision. The movement is from dependence on the supervisor, to a lesser measure of dependence on peers, to autonomous self-dependence. Group supervision offers an effective medium for power sharing and power equalization between supervisors and supervisees. Consequently it can serve as a half-way house in the movement toward independent functioning (Weinberg 1960).

I have emphasized that the agency, and particularly the supervisory personnel, should move in the direction of actively encouraging the development of greater independence in functioning by all workers. For the worker who comes to the job with professional qualifications, such as a master's degree in social work, the move should be toward rapid and nearly total relinquishment of supervisory controls. For the worker who comes without any prior knowledge of social work, the tempo is less rapid and the relinquishment less total. The direction is the same for all workers, toward a decline in the amount and extent of supervision, although the rapidity with which the change is accomplished varies.

Group supervision requires active participation of the worker in lateral teaching of peers, by peers. Such sharing among colleagues emphasizes a greater measure of practice in dependence than is true for individual supervision. Not only does the supervisor share with supervisees responsibility for teaching in the group conference, the power of the supervisor is also shared. The supervisees have a greater measure of control and a greater responsibility for the initiative in the group conference. Even responsibility for evaluation is shared. What is evaluation in the individual conference becomes feedback from peers in the group conference. Hence, if at the beginning there is much individual supervision and only a limited amount of group supervision, the movement toward independent, responsible practice should see a change in this balance. Gradually there should be less individual supervision and a greater measure of group supervision. In line with this idea, some agencies have used group supervision in explicit recognition of its potential as a vehicle for fostering independence and autonomy from supervision. Judd, Kohn, and Shulman (1962) have reported on their agency's use of group supervision "in helping the worker achieve greater independence and thereby accelerate his professional development" (p. 96).

Disadvantages of Group Supervision

The great advantage of the individual conference is that teaching and learning can be explicitly individualized to meet the needs of a particular supervisee. The group conference has to be directed toward the general, common needs of all the supervisees and the special, particular needs of none. As a consequence, the interest in group activity may be highly variable for the individual supervisee. At one moment the group may be concerned with something of vital interest to a particular worker; a half-hour later the matter under discussion may be boring or repetitious and of no concern. The principal disadvantage of the group conference is that it cannot easily provide specific application of learning to the worker's own caseload.

If the supervisee can learn more easily in a group conference through identification with peers, unencumbered by feelings of dependency and hostility toward the authority of the supervisor, the group presents its own impediments to learning. The group situation stimulates sibling rivalry and peer competition. Each supervisee may be concerned that another will say the smart thing first, will get more of the attention, approval, and affection of the supervisor. Each may be anxious about how well he compares with others in the group.

This problem was noted by Apaka, Hirsch, and Kleidman (1967) in describing the introduction of group supervision in a hospital social-work department. "There was hostility and competitiveness among workers that previously had been concealed effectively. It became clear that the group process was potent in underscoring and bringing out all the previously underscored or unacknowledged subtleties of staff interrelationships" (p. 58).

It is more difficult to incorporate a new appointee into a supervisory group than to provide the same appointee with individual supervision. A group with any continuity develops a

group identity, a pattern of interpersonal relationships, an allocation of roles, cliques and subgroups, a set of shared under-
standings. The newcomer, a stranger to all of this, threatens the
established equilibrium and is apt to be resented. Group supervision thus imposes a particular problem for new appointees.

The individual conference forces the supervisee to come
up with his own answers, his own decisions regarding the problem he faces. The group context permits the supervisee to abdicate such responsibility and to accept group solutions and
decisions. He is forced to participate and respond in the individual conference; he can hide in the safety of numbers provided by the group.

If a group offers a larger pool of possible sources of insight
and support, it also offers more sources of critical feedback. It is
easier to expose your feelings to one supervisor in the privacy
of an individual conference than to present somewhat inadequate work publicly to a group of four or five peers. If a worker
is seeking and can accept critical feedback, the number of
participants is an advantage of group supervision; if she is hesitant and anxious about critical feedback, it can be a disadvantage. There is a similar risk for the supervisor. The threat to
self-esteem and narcissism from saying something stupid in
front of a group is greater than the risk of a similar failure in the
individual conference. Supervisory ineptitude is exposed simultaneously to many rather than to one.

Operating with confidence as a group leader requires more
self-assurance than does successfully conducting an individual
conference. The group context is more complex and demanding. The complexity of interaction increases geometrically as
the number in the group increases arithmetically. Four times as
many people makes a 16-fold increase in possibilities for interaction. In any group there are simultaneous interactions between (1) individual group members, (2) individual group
members and the supervisor, (3) the group as a whole and individual members, (4) the group as a whole and the supervisor, (5)
a subgroup and individual members of subgroups and the supervisor. There is therefore a greater diversity of informational

cues and pressures to which the supervisor has to adjust and accommodate as compared with the less complex, more manageable, individual supervisory conference.

The safety of numbers which allows the supervisee to raise critical questions and comments also presents a danger that the peer group may organize against the supervisor in the group conference. The supervisor may feel more comfortable in the individual conference, where there is a greater likelihood that she can control the interaction. There is a greater threat to such control in the group situation. Consequently some supervisors might be uneasy about employing group supervision.

In group supervision the supervisor risks loss of control of the meeting. Stimulating, encouraging, and supporting more active participation by the group and granting a larger measure of responsibility for interaction to the group are acts of control by the supervisor. She consciously decides to encourage such activity because she feels that it is desirable. But the group may decide to do some things the supervisor does not feel are desirable. Having encouraged maximum participation and fuller responsibility for action on the part of the group, the supervisor may find that the group has taken the play out of her hands. In the individual conference, when something comparable to this occurs the supervisor can reassert control. In the group situation, she is outnumbered. Faced with the solidarity of a group in opposition to her, the supervisor may find it difficult to regain control of the situation. Because of the risk in sharing control of the supervisory conference with the group, the need for personal security on the part of the supervisor is greater.

Accepting the responsibility for group supervision requires additional learning and a reorientation of focus for many casework supervisors. They have to learn about, or at least refresh their knowledge of, group interaction, group dynamics, and the psychology of individual behavior in the group context. They have to move from an accustomed focus on the individual as the center of interest to perceiving the group entity as the center of concern. If a supervisor cannot successfully reorient her focus, she may find herself engaged in an individual supervisory conference in the presence of others. Her tendency might be to respond to a collection of individuals rather than to the group.

Competent leadership in the individual conference requires a knowledge and understanding of social work, the educational process, and individual behavior. Competent leadership of the group requires all of these plus a knowledge and understanding of group dynamics and group process. (The fact that group supervision does require special competence for its effective implementation is a disadvantage that limits its use.)

The more cohesive a group is, the more the individual member feels identified with the group, the greater are the felt pressures to conform to group thinking and group attitudes. This cohesion is both a strength and a weakness of group supervision. It operates as an advantage in influencing individual supervisees to accept agency procedures and professionally desirable approaches in interaction with clients. On the other hand, it tends to stifle individuality and creativity. Considerable strength and conviction are needed to express ideas and attitudes that run counter to those held by the group. Sometimes these atypical ideas may be valid and helpful to the group in more effectively implementing its tasks. The supervisor, as group leader, needs to act so as to preserve the advantages of group cohesion but mitigate its disadvantages. In achieving this aim, the supervisor supports the expression of atypical attitudes and ideas, is sensitive to a supervisee's ambivalence about expressing them, and establishes as a norm for group interaction the accepting encouragement of such contributions to group discussion.

Research on the Value of Group Supervision

The question of relevant advantages and disadvantages of group supervision has been the subject of some empirical research. The University of Michigan School of Social Work conducted an experiment in which a sample of students assigned to group supervision in fieldwork was compared with a sample of students assigned to individual supervision (Sales and Navarre

1970). Comparisons were made in terms of student satisfaction with mode of supervision, content of supervisory conferences, time expended in supervision, the general level and quality of participation in conferences, and evaluation of practice skills as the outcome of training.

In general the experiment indicated that "students performed equally well under each mode of supervision when supervisors' ratings of student practice skills were compared." However, "field instructors using individual supervision spent substantially more time per student in supervisory activities than those who employed group supervision." Since both "modes of supervision result in equivalent overall student performance" and since the difference in time expended "unequivocally favors group supervision," "the time factor may become pivotal to a choice" (Sales and Navarre 1970, pp. 39–41).

In addition to the greater efficiency in time expended in group supervision, the study further confirms some of the other hypothesized advantages of the approach. "Students in group supervision felt greater freedom to communicate dissatisfaction with field instruction to their supervisors and greater freedom to differ with them about professional ideas"; "students in group supervision most liked the varying ideas, experiences, and cases made possible by this mode of supervision" (p. 40). On the other hand, confirming the individualizing advantage of individual supervision, "students in individual supervision most liked the specific help, the help in specific problem areas provided by this method" (p. 40).

An experiment that tested the two supervisory procedures in training counselors arrived at similar conclusions. The group of trainees were randomly assigned to individual supervision and group supervision. The data regarding training outcomes

suggest that the individual method is not significantly different from the group method in producing some desirable outcomes. It is reasonable, therefore, to use group supervision at least as an adjunct to individual supervision until further research suggests that a different method is obviously superior. Additional considerations, such as cost and time, may be important enough to take what appears to be a small risk that individual supervision is significantly superior to the group method. (Lanning 1971, p. 405)

Because both individual and group supervision provide special advantages and disadvantages, because both are more or less appropriate in response to different conditions and different needs, it is desirable to employ them as planned, complementary procedures. Frequently the agenda for group conferences derives from recurrent problems discussed in individual conferences; frequently the group discussions are subsequently applied in individual conferences to individual supervisee case situations. The flow is circular, from individual conferences to group conferences to individual conferences. Since the same supervisor is generally responsible for both the individual and group conferences, the two different procedures can have unity and continuity. The supervisor has the responsibility of determining how each approach can best be used to further the learning needs of individual supervisees.

The decision as to what should be taught on an individual basis and what should be taught through the group must be based diagnostically on the educational needs of the learner. For example the staff member whose own personal deprivation in early childhood makes it difficult for him to accept placement of children away from their own homes will require considerable help and support in understanding how his own emotional experience influences the way he works with clients. For such a worker, learning would have to have an internal focus where, on a case-by-case basis, he could be helped to change his attitudes toward inadequate parents. The same staff member, however, could also profit from group consideration of this problem. He may discover, for example, that [other staff members] feel this way about such parents and that disapproving attitudes can stem from what is conceived to be a violation of our social values as well as from judgments growing out of individual developmental experiences. In a group the individual may get a different perspective which enables him to grapple more successfully with his own attitudes. This, in turn, may help him to feel less guilt as he works on the problem more introspectively in individual supervision. (Blackey 1957, pp. 62–63)

Group Supervision—Process

Many considerations to which we might call attention regarding the process of group supervision are not particular or unique to the group supervisory situation. They are generally true for any circumstance in which a group is used as the vehicle for achieving the desired objective. Consequently, social workers familiar with the different uses of groups in providing agency service already know much that is applicable to the use of the group in supervision. This is true not only for group-service social workers but for caseworkers who have employed group approaches in adoption, foster care, protective service, public assistance, corrections, and family therapy, and for community organizers who operate in a group context. Awareness of the procedures that are most productive, the recurrent problems in group interaction that are likely to be encountered, is applicable, with some adaptation, to the group supervisory situation. The objective in this section is to review some of these considerations, translating the generally applicable material to the special context of group supervision.

group setting

Physical arrangement is a determinant of group interaction and needs to be given careful attention by the supervisor in preparing for a group supervisory conference. A circle of chairs in a room of moderate dimensions for the size of the group is perhaps the most desirable arrangement. Too large a room makes the group feel insignificant and lost; too small a room may produce a cramped, uncomfortable feeling and may require too great a closeness and intimacy between members. A circular arrangement permits everybody to look at and talk to everybody else. Being able to look at, as well as listen to, everyone else permits easier perception of nonverbal communication messages. A circle maximizes the chances that each person in the group will have access to direct communication with everyone else. A circle, furthermore, has no identifiable status position, no front-of-group position. The supervisor can melt into the group by taking his place unobtrusively anywhere in the circle. While the circle does not entirely neutralize the supervisor's dominant status in the group, it helps somewhat to mute it. Freedom from competing noises and from disruptive interruptions are other components of desirable physical arrangement.

A schedule specifying the hour and day for meetings should be clearly established and adhered to with some regularity. It helps give the group continuity and becomes a necessary part of group structure. It shows respect for the workers' time and permits them to schedule other appointments in advance with assurance that there will not be a conflict. In general it might be good to avoid scheduling group supervisory meetings early in the afternoon. The lethargy that follows lunch tends to dampen group interaction.

purpose
The group meeting, like the individual conference, needs to have a clearly defined purpose. Formed by the agency to achieve agency purposes, the group is not entirely free to determine its own purposes. Group and individual supervision have the same ultimate objectives, and group conferences are required to have purposive outcomes that further these objectives. A considerable amount of expensive agency-personnel time is invested in each group supervisory conference. A meeting of eight people for an hour and a half costs more than a day's pay for one worker. The supervisor consequently has some responsibility to attempt to direct the group interaction so that purposes congruent with the general objectives of supervision are selected and so that such purposes are more or less achieved.

Group members are also personally investing their own limited time and energy. If the group meeting serves no productive, useful purpose, they have every right to feel disappointed and resentful. In a study of social work students' reactions to group supervision, a major dissatisfaction was "time wasted in tedious, irrelevant discussions" (Sales and Navarre 1970, p. 40).

leadership and planning

In group supervision, group interaction is employed as a "method used toward a specified end and group supervisory discussions are bounded discussions," bounded by the objectives of supervision (Perlman 1950, p. 335). Consequently the supervisor in the group conference is a leader in the explicit sense of having "the authority and the obligation to guide and to direct and often to require. . . . He must take responsibility both for stimulating discussion and for controlling it; both for releasing the (supervisees) energies and for insistently directing them to the task for which they have been freed. He is responsible not only to promote movement but literally to 'steer the course' so that direction is not lost. He must not only keep the [group] going but help it to arrive" (ibid.).

However equalitarian his approach, the supervisor cannot entirely shed the mantle of group leadership. His status in the agency hierarchy and his position inevitably give him a special status in the social system of the group. This status is reinforced by his education and experience, which give him some special knowledge and skill that he is responsible for using, and is expected to use, in behalf of the group.

Discussion, in and of itself, is not a particularly efficient procedure for learning, problem-solving, or decision-making. Discussion "has been known to confuse and confound rather than to systematize and clarify thinking. As Towle (1954) said, discussion which is not focused through the direction of a leader and organized and reorganized through intermittent summarization can become a flight into purposeless activity— activity which, in not attaining its aims, often breaks down into noisy fragments or sinks into silence. . . . For just as the client's unburdening will not necessarily reeducate or heal, just as the caseworker must direct him to talk to a purpose and help him focus and relate his production toward activity in the solution of his problem" (p. 359), so the supervisor as group leader must take some responsibility for purpose and focus of group discussion.

Although leadership of the group is primarily the responsibility of the supervisor, it is not her responsibility alone. The group itself has considerable responsibility for the many decisions that relate to group purpose and functioning. The supervisor is here, as in the individual interview, only first among equals. Furthermore, it is clear that rigid, insistent adherence to an approach that emphasizes supervisory control is self-defeating and counterproductive. Supervisees can be required by the agency to attend group meetings, but there is no way to compel their participation. While physically present, supervisees can absent themselves psychologically and emotionally and hence defeat the purposes of group supervision. The purpose of the meeting and the nature of group interaction have to meet, in some measure, not only the needs of the agency but also the needs of the supervisees themselves.

The amount of leadership exercised by the supervisor should be the minimum necessary to assure that the group can do its job. As in the individual conference, the supervisor, as group leader, faces the dilemma of leading without imposing, directing without controlling, suggesting without dictating. Over a period of time in the history of the group, the supervisor should be progressively less active, and an increasing proportion of the initiative, responsibility, control, direction, and activity should pass over to the group itself.

If the supervisor is invested with the responsibility for defining and implementing, however tentatively, however gently, the aim and objectives of the group, adequate preparation for group meetings is mandatory. The supervisor has to have a clear idea of what she will propose for group consideration, however experimentally. She must decide the points that need to be raised for discussion, the content that needs to be communicated and taught. The supervisor needs to think out the answers to some of the more difficult questions that can be anticipated. She needs to clarify for herself which points will encounter greatest resistance and which may require repeated emphasis. In effect, she needs to imagine the general scenario of the meeting as it might, in actuality, unfold.

Some plan—flexible, subject to change and if necessary to

abandonment—is desirable. Having an outline of how the group meeting is likely to go is, in itself, reassuring. However, a plan is advantageous only if used as a guide. If it becomes a crutch, the supervisor will resist deviating from it even when that appears necessary to follow the legitimate interests of the group, since she is psychologically dependent on it. The supervisor's preparation also involves bringing in the supporting books, pamphlets, articles, forms, and directives that are pertinent to the content of the meeting.

The general purpose of group supervision may be clear, but since it is often stated in a very global way the supervisor has to help translate it into specific, clearly identifiable objectives for each particular meeting. "Learning to offer more effective and efficient service" does not answer the question of what the group will actually do when it meets next Tuesday morning from 9:00 to 10:30. The supervisor, whose experience and perspective give her a clear idea of what supervisees need to know, to do, and to be, should be in a position to derive from the general purpose the topics for a series of meetings. However, while it would be helpful for the supervisor, as group leader, to propose specific topics for group meetings, it would be best if these were advanced tentatively as suggestions for consideration rather than as requirements for acceptance. The group itself may have suggestions for relevant and significant topics that have greater priority and interest for the members. However, achieving a shared purpose is not easy. Often the purpose that interests one subgroup is of little or no interest to others in the group. The objectives on which the supervisor is administratively required to focus may be accepted with reluctance or covert resistance.

A clearly stated purpose that has group understanding and acceptance is one of the best guarantees against overcontrol and overdirection of group activities by the supervisor. The group rather than the supervisor gives direction and meaning to group interaction, determines the relevance of contributions, and structures group activity. Knowing what to do and being motivated to do it permit the group to exercise self-direction.

Consideration needs to be given not only to the plan for a particular meeting but also to the way this meeting relates to the meeting that precedes and follows it. To what extent, and in what ways does this specific meeting fit into some overall plan for group supervision?

Planning should include consideration of the most advantageous format for the kind of content with which the meeting is concerned. Sometimes a case presentation might be best, sometimes a movie, a role-playing session, or a panel presentation. Different kinds of presentation procedures involve different levels of participation, involvement, and necessary preparation from different members of the group.

content and method

The content of group supervisory meetings includes matters of general concern to social workers in any agency—recording, interviewing, referral procedures, psychological tests, caseload management, worker-client interaction, use of consultation, and so on. Often it is specific to the clientele served by a particular agency—understanding the delinquent, the adoptive child, the patient with a terminal illness, the unmarried mother. Sometimes it is concerned with procedures, forms, and reports that are particular to a given agency, with communications to workers from administration, or with problems identified by workers which they are anxious to communicate to administration. It may also be concerned with the particular community in which the agency operates—community composition, community problems, agency resources in the community, and the nature of the relationship between this agency and other agencies.

Group supervision may, by deliberate choice, become individual supervision in a group setting. The group of supervisees might decide to conduct sessions in which the work of a particular member of the group is singled out for discussion. Rather than discussing matters that are of general concern, each meeting is devoted to the particular concerns of some individual member through case presentations.

On occasion, general agency situations determine agenda items. If the agency is concerned with formulating a budget, this might be the opportune time to discuss budgeting matters as they relate to the unit's operations; if a state case-audit is scheduled, it makes reviews of some related content relevant; if evaluations for unit members are scheduled for the immediate future, the evaluation form and associated questions might be discussed. Agenda items for group meetings are frequently, and most desirably, derived from interests and problems recurrently identified in individual supervisory conferences as common to a number of different workers.

Traditionally, clinical case material is the most frequently used stimulus for group supervisory discussions. Such material vicariously replicates actual situations with which group members are grappling, making it vivid and interesting, and motivating group involvement. For most productive use, case material needs to be carefully selected and prepared. Its very richness permits all sorts of digressions that have little real yield. Consequently, selection of case material should be in line with clearly defined objectives of the group meeting. In preparing the material for distribution, the supervisor may profitably condense and paraphrase so as to sharpen the focus for teaching. Often a section of dramatic interaction may be excerpted from a longer case record for group discussion purposes.

Although case material by definition is concerned with some individual instance, the focus of the discussion cannot remain tied to the individual case situation if learning is to be generalizable and transferable. At some point the group (and if not the group, the supervisor) needs to determine what the particular case situation offers for learning about such situations in general.

When a group member presents his own material for discussion, there are additional problems. The supervisor may work with the supervisee toward selecting a case for presentation that is likely to have greatest value for both the supervisee and the group. The supervisee may need help in preparing the case for group presentation; he may also need the supervisor's support in coping with the anxiety that case presentation arouses and help in clarifying what group reactions he is likely to encounter. Because this is a case situation in which the agency has ongoing contact, the presentation may run the risk of group supervision of the worker which parallels the individual supervisory conference in deciding on specific planning for the case. The more appropriate use of the case situation in the group context would, again, be a general focus that permits group members to apply learning from this case to situations in their own caseloads.

Role playing is a procedure often used in group conferences. It can be improvised readily and offers a dramatic episode for discussion. The outlines of the proposed role play have to be clearly presented to the group—what is the nature of the problem to be acted out, and who are the participants? Situations for role playing could include an application interview at a department of public welfare, a welfare rights advocate's meeting with an agency director, a rejection interview with an adoptive applicant, an interview with an unmarried mother struggling to decide whether to surrender a child, a first interview with a parolee after his return to the community, an interview with a daughter concerned about institutionalization for her aged mother. Beyond the definition of the situation and identification of participants, the approach of the worker can also be defined. The worker can be asked to play the role in Rogerian terms or behavioral terms, punitively or acceptingly.

Willingness to participate in role playing requires a considerable sense of security in the group. Particularly in early meetings, obtaining volunteers may be difficult. It is easier if initially the supervisor volunteers to play the worker—the more difficult role. Her playing the worker may inhibit spontaneous critical comment but this depends partially on the freedom to criticize which the supervisor communicates to the group. Using the role-playing names of the participants helps to depersonalize the discussion afterward. It is not "Mr. P" (the actual name of the supervisor whose work the group is discussing) but rather "Mr. Smith," the name the supervisor used in the role play.

The group can move into role playing through the use of brief playlets. In the midst of some discussion, the supervisor can suggest that, for the moment, she play the client they have been talking about. "As the client, I have just said to the worker, 'I got so mad and discouraged that I sometimes feel like I just want to get away and never see the kids again.' How would you, as a worker, respond to that? Let's play it for a minute." Frequent use of such role-playlets provides a good group introduction to role playing.

Role-play participation enables the workers to understand more clearly, through vicarious identification, how an assistance applicant, an unmarried mother, an adoptive parent, or a parolee feels about his situation. However, like a thematic apperception test, role playing permits and encourages self-revelation. Without realizing it, we tend to act ourselves and expose to the group some parts of ourselves that were previously hidden. Consequently, role playing makes participants vulnerable. The supervisor has to be sensitive to the need to protect participants from destructive criticism. There is also a possibility that a role-playing session which generates strong feelings may become a group therapy session.

Films and audio and video tapes are appropriately used as the basis for group discussions. Adequate preparation is invariably necessary. Showing a film without previewing it can often be disappointing and time wasting. The description in the film catalogue may be only remotely related to the film itself. Familiarity with the equipment and with the room used for showing is also necessary. Countless groups have been frustrated because an extension cord was not long enough to meet an outlet, because there were no blinds to darken the room, because nobody could thread the film correctly and it kept fluttering or the sound track was garbled.

Checking the equipment and the material to be used is equally important for audio and video tapes. Audio tapes are often difficult to understand, and the strain of listening to unclear, disembodied voices can leave the group without energy for discussion. (If possible, written transcripts of the tapes should be made available to the group. They not only permit people to follow what is said but make subsequent discussion easier as people refer to the transcript in making a point.)

learning in the group conference

Just as the supervisor has inducted supervisees into the social system of the individual conference and has interpreted the respective, differentiated responsibilities of supervisor and supervisee in that system, she similarly inducts supervisees into their role as members of the group supervisory conference. The nature of reciprocal group-membership role expectations and obligations should be clearly outlined. Supervisees are given to understand that they have some responsibility for preparing for the meetings, for reading any relevant material that is distributed in advance. They have responsibility for contributing to group interaction and keeping such contributions pertinent to the discussion; they have responsibility for listening to others with respect and attention and should refrain from making interventions that will create unproductive conflict and tension, and should help in dealing with such conflicts and tensions as do arise. They need to indicate respect for other members of the group, to display a willingness to accept them as resources for learning and demonstrate some commitment to help achieve group goals.

Most of the principles of learning that are applicable to the individual conference are equally applicable to the group conference. As in the individual conference, the supervisor is responsible for establishing a context that facilitates learning.

The supervisor, as group leader, engages in many of the same kinds of behavior he manifests in individual conferences—asking questions, soliciting and supporting the expression of ideas, attitudes, and feelings, requesting amplification of supervisees' points of view, restating and clarifying supervisees' ideas and feelings, summarizing, recapitulating, enabling, expediting, facilitating, focusing and redirecting, resolving conflicts, making suggestions and offering information and advice, supporting and reassuring, while also challenging and communicating agency expectations. The supervisor, as group leader, raises the provocative suggestion, acts as devil's advocate, calls attention to what has been missed, stimulates productive conflict to enhance instruction, acts as a traffic cop to the interaction. She acts as catalyst, mentor, arbiter, and resource person.

The supervisor orchestrates the activities of the individuals who make up the group. She maximizes individual contributions, coordinates and synthesizes them, weaves them together into a pattern. "The discussion leader must be able to focus discussion so that, for all its diversity, it maintains an essential wholeness, a basic unity. . . . Periodically the discussion leader 'pulls together' related points of the discussion. If discussion is visualized as the spokes of a wheel radiating from the hub, the leader may be said to 'rim the wheel' " (Perlman 1950, p. 336).

Groups, like individuals, resist the often difficult, unpleasant, uncomfortable tasks that need to be worked on if productive purposes are to be achieved. Groups manifest ambivalence and resistance by irrelevant digressions, unproductive silences, fruitless argumentation, and side conversations among subgroups. The supervisor has the responsibility of holding the group to its purpose, of stimulating and rewarding the kind of group interaction that will optimally help the group achieve its purpose.

At the same time the supervisor delays disclosure of her own views in order to prevent premature closure of discussion. Ultimately, of course, she is obligated to share them with the group, clearly and explicitly. But if, as in the individual conference, she indicated early in the discussion what she thought, this would act as a constraint on free exchange and would relieve supervisees of the stimulus and responsibility in finding their own answers. If challenged with "well what do *you* think?" the supervisor can legitimately say, "I'll be glad to share that with you later but at this point I think you all have some thoughts about this that we can profitably share with one another."

The pattern of informal group interaction which takes place in the agency outside the group meetings is brought into the group supervision meetings. Some people like each other, some dislike each other, some are indifferent to each other. Workers play out these feelings in the way they relate to each other during the total work time. The supervisor needs to be aware of these patterns of relationship and how they might influence subgroup formation and reactions to what a particular individual says in the group. A knowledge of individual needs and the pattern of informal interaction outside the group helps the supervisor identify the nature of "hidden agendas" that help explain otherwise inexplicable in-group behavior. The supervisor knows a great deal about the individuals who make up the group and actively uses this knowledge in evaluating and understanding group interaction.

Each supervisee brings to the group meeting his own needs and anxieties which eventually find expression in the way he behaves in the group. The supervisor has the problem of responding to individual behavior in a way that furthers the purposes of the group and at the same time meets the individual's needs. Often the best that can be achieved is some compromise between individual need and group need. Reconciliation of conflicting group and individual needs is sometimes impossible, and the supervisor, giving priority to group needs, may have to ignore or actually deny the satisfaction of individual need. The persistent disrupter who seeks to use the group for satisfaction of insatiable attention-getting needs may have to be suppressed; the time allotted to monopolizers of group discussion may have to be firmly limited; the cynical demolisher of group morale may have to be resolutely moderated; the consistently passive supervisee may need to be prodded out of his lethargy. To keep all the group interested and motivated the supervisor must, without guilt, limit his concern for any one person in the group. Needs of the group, as a group, have priority.

The supervisor's responsibility denies him flexibility of accepting any contribution as subjectively correct for the person advancing it. If our claim to being a profession has substance, it means that we have established some procedures, practice principles, and approaches that are objectively more correct, more desirable, more efficacious than others. It is these responses that the supervisor is helping the group to learn and accept. Consequently some contributions from the group need to be challenged and rejected by the supervisor. Since the hurt of rejection in the presence of a group is sharper than in the individual conference, the supervisor has to be even more sensitive and compassionate here.

The group-supervision equivalent of "reject the sin but not the sinner" is to "reject the comment but not the commentator." The supervisor does this subtly and understandingly: "I see you have given this considerable thought but if we did it this way what negative consequences could result?" "It's easy to get confused about this. The point you are making is based on somewhat outmoded information. Actually the average assistance payment for a family of four is currently. . . ." "I know that what you say is a point of view held by many people, but studies relating to this show that. . . ." Sometimes the supervisor can accept part of the comment and by reinterpretation or change of emphasis convert it into an acceptable contribution. "It may be, as you say, that the social system rather than the client needs changing, but how can we help Mrs. F, for whom something has to be done this afternoon?"

It would be best, of course, if the group itself takes the responsibility for correcting, rejecting, or amending erroneous information and approaches that might do a disservice to the client. But the group is not always aware of what needs correcting, and the supervisor cannot abdicate her responsibility for this. Since members of the group are frequently on the same level in terms of education and experience, the nature of the error is not as readily evident to them. In addition, they identify as peers with other group members, and they are understandably reluctant to confront them. Reluctance to criticize also derives from hesitancy about creating friction in the group. Refraining from necessary criticism in order to maintain group harmony is one of the weaknesses of group supervision. Maintenance of a good group relationship may take precedence over the desirability of engaging in some difficult activities necessary for the optimum achievement of the group's objective. Expressive needs prevent fulfillment of instrumental tasks. Furthermore, because the supervisor has administrative responsibility for the work of every individual member of the group, there is hesitancy about intruding on her responsibility. Group members may feel limited responsibility to critique the work of a peer since this responsibility is formally invested in the individual supervisor-supervisee relationship.

For a number of different reasons, then, willingness to be openly critical develops slowly in most groups. In reporting on her own experience as a group supervisor, Smith notes that "for the first dozen sessions we were very supportive and encouraging towards the other participants, and few challenging or critical comments were made during the early reticent stage. Since then, workers have become more clear, direct and specific with their observations and thoughts" (Smith 1972, p. 15).

When necessary expressive functions—group maintenance functions—are not performed by members of the group, the supervisor performs them. She mediates between conflicting subgroups; she prevents, or tempers, scapegoating; she offers help and support to group members who are fearful or reticent about participating; she tries to influence the monopolizer to accept a more quiescent role. Good discussion leadership does not necessarily imply that everyone participates equally, only that everyone has the opportunity for equal participation.

The supervisor attempts to protect individual members from the hostile reaction of the group and protects the group from its own self-destructive, divisive tendencies. While protecting the weak from the assaults of the strong, the supervisor has to act in a noncondemning manner, redirecting or redefining the hostile intervention so that only the comment is rejected.

Task and group-maintenance problems are interrelated. The group that is effective in accomplishing its tasks is likely to have better morale and a greater sense of cohesion. A group that seems to accomplish little, that never gets anywhere, is more likely to encounter expressions of dissatisfaction and divisiveness. The supervisor who effectively aids the group in accomplishing acceptable objectives is also, at the same time, helping to develop more positive patterns of interaction among group members.

In ending the group supervisory meeting, the supervisor summarizes the main points covered in the meeting, relates them, if possible, to conclusions of previous meetings, and ties them in with the topic of the next meeting. Material for the next meeting is distributed, and the group is reminded of specific responsibilities previously contracted for by individual members for the next meeting. If such continuity has not been previously established, the leader needs to reserve a block of time before the end of the meeting for a firm decision on what the group will be doing the next time it meets.

Whereas the frequency of participation on the part of the supervisor decreases (as it should) as the group continues to meet, the nature of her interventions remains rather constant. Most often the supervisor's interventions are concerned with direct teaching, e.g., giving technical information about agency procedures; explaining agency policy; explaining social work theory, or questioning to stimulate further discussion, get clarification of thinking, elicit negative and positive feeling reactions, get further information from the group. In addition, interventions offer support to the group or to some individual member, clarify the nature and direction of group discussion, provide active leadership to the group (i.e., initiating and terminating group activity) and summarizing. See table 7.

Illustration of Group Supervision

The following long extract is from the supervisor's report of a group supervisory meeting of a protective-service unit in a county public welfare agency. It illustrates some aspects of the process of group supervision. The group consists of the seven workers who are assigned to the unit. Five of them have a mas-

table 7.

Activity of the Supervisor in 25 Consecutive Weekly Fieldwork
Group-Supervisory Sessions

	Supervisor responses during:			
Activity	Weekly sessions no. 1–8	Weekly sessions no. 9–17	Weekly sessions no. 18–25	Total responses
Direct Teaching	21	26	12	59
Support	16	7	9	32
Helping to express negative feelings	2	0	0	2
Active leadership	24	7	8	39
Clarification and Mediation	10	6	7	23
Questioning	23	16	10	49
Total	96	62	46	204

Source: Adapted from Lawrence E. Cooper, Raymond C. Every, Alice L. Garvey, and Margaret E. Morris, "A Study of Group Supervision in a Field Work Placement," Master of Social Work group research project, Graduate School of Social Work, University of Washington, 1957, as reprinted by Abrahamson (1959, p. 56).

ter's degree in social work. All have at least one year of experience in the unit. The group meetings, scheduled for one and a half hours every two weeks, supplement individual conferences held once a week. The supervisor is administratively responsible for scheduling and conducting the meetings. The meetings are held in the agency conference room around a large, boat-shaped table. The first 30 to 40 minutes of this meeting were devoted to some general announcements followed by a discussion of techniques in helping abusive parents to make changes in their behavior.

George had been, as usual, a rather inactive participant. I observed that he had taken some notes, had nodded his head in apparent agreement with others at different times and had leaned forward at other times in apparent interest in what was being said. However, he himself had contributed little to the discussion. At this point, however, his non-verbal activity seemed to increase in intensity. He crossed and uncrossed his legs, leaned forward and back in his chair, and rubbed the back of his neck. I interpreted this to suggest that he might respond to a direct invitation to participate so I chanced it and, taking advantage of a slight pause in the discussion, I said, "George, I wonder if you would care to share your reactions to what has been said?" I tried to make the invitation tentative and general so that he would not feel an obligation to respond to any particular point made in the discussion but could feel free to respond to anything that had been said. I attempted to make the tone of my invitation light rather than peremptory so as to suggest that it would be all right if he declined my invitation to participate. I tried to catch his eye as I said this, pausing a little after calling his name. He, however, kept looking at his notebook.

There was a moment of silence which increased the pressure on George to respond. Having initiated the invitation out of a conviction that George, like any other member of the group, had an obligation to contribute his fair share to the discussion, I wasn't going to rescue George too early by breaking the silence without waiting a while. He shifted in his chair but continued to look down. He said, "Well," and then paused. Then, looking at the wall, avoiding eye contact with any member of the group, he started up again, saying, "I guess the whole discussion kind of pisses me off. Here we are trying to figure out how to be nice and understanding and accepting of these lousy parents who crack skulls and belt a defenseless infant around. I say to hell with them. They had their chance to care for the kid adequately and they didn't. Out of protection to the kids we ought to petition the courts for termination [of parental rights] and place them. And then take legal action against the parents for abuse. That's the only way to discourage this sort of behavior and this is the way to protect other children from this sort of thing."

The more he talked, the more vehement he became. When he finished there was a kind of dead silence. I recognized that he had articulated a strongly felt, but often suppressed, attitude that was generally characterized as "unprofessional," a component of the protective social worker's ambivalence that was rarely openly expressed—at least in officially sponsored meetings (it is frequently said by one worker to another in informal contacts in the washroom, coffee breaks, etc.). Consequently, after a short pause, but not giving anybody else a real chance to respond, I said, "Well, there is something to what you say. It's understandable that social workers concerned with child abuse might get to feel this way. What do others in the group feel about this?"

I was deliberate in taking the initiative because I wanted to protect George from any direct criticism from others, which would be easy to do, because he was expressing an "unfashionable" opinion. Secondly, some members of the group might be threatened by what George had said because it was a feeling that they themselves were struggling to control and be prompted to attack him in an effort to protect their own equilibrium. Thirdly, I wanted to give official sanction to George's comments—not as a correct point of view but one which was acceptable for open discussion. Fourthly, I suspected that many in the group had hostile feelings toward abusive parents (you would have to be either pretty callous or pretty saintly not to, after some of the things we had all seen) and might welcome a chance to discuss it now that it was brought out in the open. Consequently, I was more directive than usual in taking the initiative here but did it consciously and deliberately for the reasons cited.

In saying what I said, to focus the discussion on the point of view raised, I tried to depersonalize it and universalize the comment. Not "What do you think about what George has said?" but "Social workers might feel this way. What do you think?" Having said what I said I sat back, physically withdrawing, my intent being to give the initiative back to the group and suggest that they were once again in control and responsible for the proceedings.

It didn't work. George's comment was too threatening or too tempting. Perhaps some felt that once they started expressing hostility to the abusive parents, they might not be able to control themselves. I really don't know what was operating internally in members of the group. I do know that nobody responded to what I had said and the continuing silence was growing more oppressive. Something needed to be done and I, as the one officially in charge of the group (the leader?), had the responsibility for doing it.

After a silence which seemed eternal (but was really only about 7–10 seconds) I intervened again. I was also pressured by the fact that I was conscious that George, for all the vehemence with which he had said what he had said, was now growing more and more uncomfortable about being responsible for getting us into this impasse—so I felt an obligation to protect him again. My intervention this time was designed to deliberately sanction negative feelings toward abusive parents and consequently to make acceptable the open expression of such feelings in the group.

Very briefly I told the group about a call I had made in response to a report about a baby crying continuously, apparently uncared for. The apartment was in a rundown rooming house, and the baby, in a crib, had apparently not been fed for some time. It was covered with sores and the diaper had not been changed for days. Feces and urine had dribbled down the child's legs and covered the bottom of the crib. In addition, the child's face was bruised as a result of a beating. The mother was lying on a bed in a drugged or drunken stupor. As I stood there taking in the situation I kept saying to myself openly but in a low voice, "You shit. You lousy bastard"—because that's the way I felt at the moment.

Having finished, I sat back again. I shared this with the group in giving further sanction to expression of negative feelings. Assuming that some in the group identified with me, openly sharing my own reactions might prompt a response.

I had, during the 7–10 second silence, briefly considered, and then rejected, an alternative intervention. I knew from our individual conference meetings that Sandra had strong negative feelings about abusive parents. I was tempted to use this knowledge and call on Sandra to share her feelings with the group. However, I felt that would be a breach of confidentiality which Sandra might resent. It might also make the others anxious about my use of any information they had confided in the individual conference.

An uneasy silence followed what I said and then Paul (bless him) said that as he thought about it this reminded him of his reaction with the "R" family. (Paul, 27, who did a 2-year stint with the Peace Corps in Guatamala, is the indigenous leader of the group.) Paul's comment started a general discussion which lasted for about 35 minutes during which I said nothing. The initiative and control remained with the group throughout. All I did was nod and "mmm-mmm" on occasion and in general indicated I was an active, interested, accepting listener.

Paul's comment, focused on his hostile feelings toward some parents, was followed by similar expressions of feeling by Ann, Cathy, Bill, and George again. As each one took the ball in turn, there was less hesitancy and stronger feelings expressed. The sense of group contagion was almost palpable. There was, particularly at first, a good deal of embarrassment, tension-relieving laughter—the kind one hears in middle-aged, middle-class groups when sex is discussed. Neither Lillian nor Ruth said anything, but they listened avidly and reacted, nonverbally, with approval to what was said. They really enjoyed hearing the group tear into abusive parents. It was clear (at least to me) that the effect was cathartic (and needed) by the group—and was not as likely to have happened in the individual conference where each member of the group reacted in isolation.

After a time, however, this expression of such previously suppressed feelings kind of ran its course. Once again, Paul initiated a change in direction of the group discussion. He said something to the effect that that's all well and good but how does that help the kids. Perhaps it was satisfying to feel punitive toward the parents, but we all knew that in most instances the courts would not terminate parental rights even if we petitioned for it and furthermore, in most instances, we would be abusing the child if we opted for removal and placement. He used the "R" case, once again, to discuss the fact that even though, sure, he felt hostile toward the parents, his job was to do what was best for the kid and even here he felt that preserving the home for the kid by helping the parents change was the best thing he could do to protect the child.

This changed the direction of the discussion. It returned to the earlier focus—how does one help the abusive parent to change, but with a difference. There was a conviction that this was a necessary and correct approach in helping the child and that, while hostility toward the parents was an understandable and acceptable reaction, it got us nowhere. We needed to control our feelings because if we all responded punitively toward the parents, this would get in our way in trying to establish a therapeutic relationship with them. If we were going to keep the child in the home by changing the parents, we would kill our chances by communicating hostility toward them.

Once again the discussion with regard to this question was pretty general and for the most part I stayed out of it completely. Members of the group used their own caseload (as did Paul with the "R" case) and their own experience to illustrate the futility of hostility toward parents if your aim was to help the child.

The meeting went about 10 minutes beyond scheduled time. At the official end-time the discussion was still pretty active so I let it run for a while. When it began to slow down and get somewhat repetitious I intervened to sum up and recapitulate. I rapidly reviewed the course the meeting had taken from general discussion on approaches in helping abusive parents to change, to a cathartic expression of hostility, to a discussion of the pragmatic need to control negative feelings if we were going to do our job effectively.

I was conscious of the need to do this rapidly (3–5 min.), because once the scheduled time is past some people stop listening and get restive ("overtime" is an imposition), others get anxious because they may have interviews scheduled. But I was also conscious of the need for closure and for a transition to the next meeting. Consequently I kept the group a moment longer and said that, while we had established a pragmatic reason for self-discipline of feelings, perhaps we could discuss what makes abusive parents act this way. Perhaps we could come to the desirability of self-discipline of hostile feelings through understanding. I threw in the old "to understand is to forgive," first in French (pandering a bit to my narcissism—a venial sin). I proposed that we think about this as the focus for our next group meeting, and if the group thought that this would be helpful to discuss, to let me know before next Tuesday (meetings are on Thursday afternoon).

The supervisor has acted consciously and deliberately to help the group move productively toward the achievement of some significant learning related to their work. Each intervention he makes is the result of a disciplined assessment of the needs of the group at that moment. The exercise of direction is not restrictive but tends to enhance group participation. The supervisor tries to limit his interventions to those necessary to expedite the work of the group, giving direction and control back to the group as soon as possible.

He shows a sensitivity to verbal and nonverbal reactions of individual members of the group as well as perceptiveness to the general climate of the group as a whole.

At every point the supervisor is faced with a series of possibilities. For instance, when the group was silent the supervisor might have chosen to focus on group dynamics or steer the discussion in a direction which developed greater group awareness of group-dynamics interaction: "I wonder what prompts the silence; perhaps it might be productive to discuss how each of us is feeling now." This would have encouraged a transition away from the question of dealing with abusive parents and it would have led to teaching regarding group process. (By focusing group attention, by his interventions on one or another aspect of the situation, the supervisor can narrow, widen, or change the focus of discussion.)

Summary

Group supervision is the use of the group setting to implement the administrative, educational, and supportive functions of supervision. It is most frequently used in supplementation of, rather than in substitution for, individual supervision.

Among the advantages of the use of the group setting for supervision are: it ensures economical use of administrative time and effort; it ensures efficient utilization of a wider variety of teaching-learning experiences; it provides a forum for discussion of problems and experiences common to group members which not only aids in the formulation of possible solutions but also provides a wider variety of experiences to each worker; it provides emotional support; it provides an opportunity for the supervisees to share their own knowledge and give support to others; it aids in the maintenance of morale; it provides a comfortable learning environment, one that is potentially less threatening than the individual supervisory conference; it provides an opportunity for the supervisees to confront the supervisor with some degree of safety; it provides each worker with an opportunity to compare his work with that of the other supervisees; it gives the supervisees a chance to feel more involved with and a part of the agency as a whole; it provides the supervisor with the chance to see the supervisees in a different light; it allows the sharing of supervisory functions between the supervisor and the group; it facilitates modification of the supervisees' behavior through giving them a chance to learn from peers; it allows the supervisees to see the supervisor in a different light; and it permits the development of greater supervisee autonomy.

Among the disadvantages of the use of the group setting for supervision are: group-learning needs take precedence over individual learning needs; it fosters peer competition; the supervisee can abdicate responsibility for developing his own work-problem solutions; it threatens the loss of supervisor's group control; group pressures to conform may stifle individual creativity; it demands considerable group-work skills from supervisors.

The basic principles of group process and dynamics and the general principles of learning are applicable to group supervision. The supervisor as group leader shares with the group the responsibility for stimulating and focusing group interaction.

chapter seven

Supervision of
Paraprofessionals

Family service and child welfare agencies have always employed a small number of "case aides" or "social work assistants." The literature of the 1960s reports a series of experiments in the use of aides in a variety of social work contexts (Birnbaum and Jones 1967; Family Service Association of America 1969; Ferrar and Hemmy 1963; Jones 1966; Mayer and Matsushima 1969). But for the most part these workers formed a very limited proportion of workers in the social welfare field, and their utilization was always regarded as a temporary expedient. Widespread employment of paraprofessionals, clear identification of such workers as a designated component of agency staff, and their acceptance on the basis of their special contributions rather than expediency have their beginnings about 1963.

A number of different pressures converged to heighten concern with employment of paraprofessionals during the 1960s. The civil rights movement resulted in efforts to provide more and better jobs for minority groups. The "rediscovery" of poverty was followed by mobilization of efforts to reduce the number of families living in deprived circumstances. This too led to a search for new possibilities of employment. The civil rights movement and the War on Poverty reinforced each other, since a disproportionately high percentage of minority-group members are living in poverty. Growing concern with the increase in public assistance rates led to more active efforts to find employment opportunities for recipients and potential recipients in ghetto areas. There was a growing dissatisfaction on the part of clients, and those needing service but reluctant to apply, with the social welfare service-delivery system. It was felt that white, middle-class social workers did not, or could not, understand the lower-class, minority-group client, that they were not sufficiently identified with or committed to the needs of the client group. Pressure was developed to employ residents from the local community to help reduce the social distance between agency and community and make the agency more aware of, and responsive to, client-community needs. This attitude was reinforced by the trend toward participatory democracy and community control of local institutions, which led to proposals for inclusion of local residents on the agency staff.

There was, during the latter part of the 1960s, an equalitarian denigration of "professionalism" and the "credential society." Questions were raised about whether or not the diplomas and degrees needed for access to many positions really reflected functional requirements for competent performance on the job. This debate led to a greater emphasis on performance rather than certification of training as the standard for determining job allocation.

These pressures from the client community were augmented by others from the professional community. These were principally pressures of staff shortages and the need for more personnel. Associated with them was the professionals' dissatisfaction with time and energy devoted to routine tasks which, they felt, could be adequately performed by staff with little or no training. Staff shortages were particularly acute in some special areas. Social workers were reluctant to take jobs in agencies offering service to the most deprived segments of the population, and staff turnover was highest there.

Each group had a different investment in the various determinants that triggered what came to be called the New Careers movement. Professional social workers were more concerned about personnel shortages and the possibility that employment of paraprofessionals promised for conserving the social workers' time and energy for the more professional aspects of their job.

The paraprofessionals were more interested in jobs, in access to the community opportunity structure, in the possibilities of a career not dependent on formal credentials, and in local control of local institutions. Social reformers were interested in the New Careers movement as a lever for restructuring traditional agencies and changing service-delivery approaches.

One of the earliest responses to these different pressures was a large-scale experiment in delinquency control, Mobilization for Youth, in New York City. This organization employed a significant number of paraprofessionals in 1963. With the publication of *New Careers for the Poor* (1965) by Arthur Pearl and Frank Riessman, the movement was given a name, an identity, and a program.

Pressure to employ New Career workers was not distributed equally over all sectors of the labor force. The pressure was most intense on those human services where employment possibilities for such workers could most likely be generated— health, education, and welfare. The human-services sector of the economy was destined to grow very rapidly during the 1960s, accounting for a large percentage of new jobs created. In line with these considerations, the legislative mandate for creation of New Careers employment was directed mainly toward human-service agencies and institutions.

With the adoption of the Scheuer amendment to the Economic Opportunity Act in 1966, the Federal government required that efforts be made to employ members of economically deprived groups as paraprofessionals in human-service jobs. This provision was later incorporated in amendments to the Social Security Act, which required the training and employment of welfare recipients as service aides in public assistance, child welfare, and health programs. The 1967 amendments required implementation of these provisions by 1969. The Allied Health Professions, Personnel Training Act of 1966, the Vocational Rehabilitation Act amendments of 1968, the Juvenile Delinquency Prevention and Control Act of 1968 and the Drug Abuse Act of 1969 incorporated the New Careers concept in one form or another. The National Institute of Mental Health established a New Careers Training Branch to provide support for New Careers training programs. The Department of Health, Education, and Welfare established an Office of New Careers.

A sizable number of paraprofessionals found employment in newly organized, multiservice neighborhood centers and in community-action programs. With the reduction in funds available for the support of such organizations at the beginning of the 1970s, the number of such New Careers jobs was reduced. By 1970, in a growing climate of dissatisfaction and disenchantment with innovative social programs on the part of Congress, some of the steam went out of the New Careers program. The Scheuer amendment New Careers Program was replaced by a Public Service Career Program which offered less support to New Careers.

By 1972 it was clear that some of the original high expectations of the New Careers movement were proving to be illusionary (Riessman 1972). Instead of earlier optimistic predictions of more than 100,000 New Careers jobs in the human services, the reality seems to be more modest. Part of the difficulty for analysis comes in obtaining information on actual numbers for an accurate perspective.

A detailed summary of data available indicates that in 1971 some 76,000 paraprofessionals were employed in social welfare and rehabilitation services (Rigdon 1972, p. 33). This is, of course, a substantial number but rather less than proponents of the New Careers movement had originally anticipated. However, numbers alone do not adequately reflect the significance of the New Careers movement for social work. Once the New Careers movement started, it proceeded in response to an impetus of its own. It developed institutionalized structures and procedures parallel to, but somewhat independent of, the social welfare profession. Local organizations of New Careerists were established, and a newsletter was published to give voice to the movement (*New Careers Newsletter,* now called *New Human Services Review*).

The State, County and Municipal Employees' Union has organized paraprofessionals working in schools, hospitals, and other public agencies. The American Federation of Teachers has organized educational aides, and the American Public Health Association has a special, officially recognized section of nonprofessionals in the health-care system. Such workers have begun to organize themselves in standard-setting protective associations such as the National Association of Human Services Technologists and the National Association of New Careerists.

A large-scale educational apparatus has developed in relation to the New Careers movement. There is growing recognition of a group of applicants for social service positions who have graduated from community colleges with associate degrees, preparing them for community-services technician positions. This group of workers is achieving growing visibility, a recognizable identity, and increasing self-consciousness. This is a new and recent source of manpower for social agencies.

The development of such educational programs has been rapid. By 1972 at least 8000 students at some 200 community colleges were preparing for employment in child care, mental health, and human services generally (Schindler 1972). Titles that identify the graduates of such programs include "social work assistant," "social service technician," "social service worker," and "community service worker." About 30 percent of the students in the programs are from minority groups. Preparation is most frequently generic and includes some field placement experience.

Recognition of this new level of education for the social services has been granted by the Council on Social Work Education. The Council has completed two surveys of such programs (Feldstein 1968; Schindler 1972), formulated a guide for their development, offered consultation, and by 1975 was beginning to consider seriously the need for development of standard-setting procedures. Several schools of social work have offered courses or institutes in training professionals to work with and supervise paraprofessionals. Social work practice organizations have, likewise, shown a concern with these developments:

In 1968, a joint report of the National Association of Social Workers (NASW) and the Council on Social Work Education (CSWE) endorsed the concept of new careers as an important new manpower resource, and recognized "the inclusion of personnel indigenous to the client system as part of social work manpower." The report went on to recommend that jobs be developed with tasks stemming from the needs of clients rather than from those which social workers do not want to do; that there be vertical and horizontal mobility; that education for career advancement be provided; that a team concept of service be developed; and that training be provided for professionals in how to better work with paraprofessionals. (Gartner 1971, p. 101)

In June the N.A.S.W. Division of Professional Standards issued a policy statement which defined six levels of social service manpower—two preprofessional and four professional. The statement gives official recognition to the aide and technician positions (N.A.S.W. News, June 1973, p. 9).

Preprofessional levels

1. Social Service Aide	Entry is based upon assessment of the individual's maturity, appropriate life experience, motivation, and skills required by the specific task or function.
2. Social Service Technician	Entry is based upon completion of two-year educational program in one or another of the social services, usually granting an Associate of Arts Degree.

Professional levels

1. Social Worker	Entry requires a baccalaureate degree from an approved social work program.
2. Graduate Social Worker	Entry requires graduation from an accredited Master of Social Work program.
3. Certified Social Worker	Certification by (a) the Academy of Certified Social Workers as capable of autonomous, self-directed practice, or (b) licensed by state regulation.

Professional levels

4. Social Work Fellow   Completion of a doctoral program, or substantial practice in the field of specialization following A.C.S.W. certification.

The first preprofessional classification level—social service aide—comes closest to the indigenous paraprofessional. The social service aide "works under close supervision and is required to be able to read and count" and to have "knowledge derived from accumulated life experience paralleling the consumer community."

In employing indigenous paraprofessionals, agencies have sought to achieve varied, and sometimes contradictory, objectives. Such workers have been employed: to meet the need for additional staff; to permit more efficient use of professional staff's time by relieving them of tasks that can be performed by paraprofessionals; to provide employment for low-income people; to reduce the personnel budget of the agency by covering some of the work through use of lower-paid staff; to make the agency more receptive to the client through contact with indigenous workers and to provide treatment approaches that may be more successful with low-income clientele; as a therapeutic procedure—by helping others as a paraprofessional, the client learns to deal more effectively with his problem. This is sometimes termed the "helper therapy" procedure.

Within a short recent period, we have seen the development and institutionalization of jobs, training, and legislative and organizational support for a group of workers previously encountered only rarely in social welfare agencies. They are currently firmly entrenched as part of the social welfare service-delivery system. It is difficult to determine the number of such workers employed, but it appears to be sizable. Such workers need supervision, and that responsibility rests primarily with the professionally trained workers. This is a new, substantial, and, in all likelihood, a growing charge to the profession's supervisory cadre (Teare et al. 1974).

Definition

Social agency staffs include a heterogeneous group of people, of whom only a limited percentage might be regarded as fully professionalized because they have the requisite graduate training. This chapter is devoted to supervision of a particular group of the nonprofessionals. For clarity I shall call this group of workers paraprofessionals and identify them as follows: Social welfare paraprofessionals are those workers who perform explicitly defined functions at entry-level competence. Performance of such functions does not require traditional education, and they are generally the kinds of services that have often been received by the paraprofessionals who are now called upon to deliver them.

The nature of this supervisee group needs to be made clear because much of the discussion in previous chapters was concerned with another significantly large group of social welfare supervisees who are frequently termed nonprofessionals—workers who hold a bachelor's degree but have no special educational background in social work. While not professionally trained, these workers have had advanced formal education. Paraprofessionals more often have limited formal education rather than, as is true for the B.A. group, being differently educated.

Nomenclature is a problem. The term paraprofessional may have negative connotations for some, but none of the alternative terms that have been suggested are wholly successful and without difficulty. These include such terms as "ancillary," "preprofessional," "new professional," "nonprofessional," "subprofessional," "case aide," and "social service assistant." Other professions, namely, guidance counseling and vocational rehabilitation, often use the term "support personnel" for such workers. Terms such as "co-professional" and "dawning professional" have also been used.

"Paraprofessional" is the label of choice because it is more neutral than some of the other terms and comes closest to delineating the actual position of such workers. The prefix comes from the Greek word that means "by the side of" or "alongside," but it also implies a subsidiary relationship which reflects accurately the position of the paraprofessional vis-à-vis the professional with whom she works. The term is beginning to gain general usage in professions other than social work. There are, for example, paramedical and paralegal training programs. In all of these instances the term reflects the reality that the paraprofessional works, for the most part, under the direction and guidance of professionally trained personnel.

The term is, admittedly, used loosely in the social work literature. The general term includes a heterogeneous group from paraprofessionals in day care, with limited grade-school education, to paraprofessionals in mental health centers, who may have a master's degree in some subject other than social work. Consequently, a further distinction needs to be made between the "ubiquitous" paraprofessional and the "indigenous" paraprofessional (Reiff and Riessman 1965, p. 5). Ubiquitous paraprofessionals may be recruited from the same general background as the professional staff; they are widely distributed in the population. Indigenous paraprofessionals are a more limited group who are "native to" the population to whom they will offer service.

Mental health paraprofessionals, for instance, are often second-career people. They frequently have had work experience and some college education but in a field other than mental health. Such paraprofessionals are more likely to be ubiquitous paraprofessionals. Because the clientele of mental-health agencies is heterogeneous in terms of socioeconomic background, selection of paraprofessionals for such agencies is not likely to involve matching in terms of life experience and life styles.

The indigenous paraprofessional, however, is explicitly recruited so as to match the ethnic, racial, educational, and socioeconomic background of the client group. Most frequently this means that the indigenous paraprofessional is black, has grown up and lives in the ghetto, shares the experience and life style of residents of the disadvantaged community, and often has been, or is, a public welfare recipient.

While the ubiquitous paraprofessional is often seen in terms of the help he can offer the professional with whom he works, relieving him of routine nonprofessional tasks, the indigenous paraprofessional is seen in terms of the help he can offer the client. The objective in employment of the ubiquitous paraprofessional is frequently to remove "low-level functions" from the "high-level" professional to increase his productivity. The objective in employment of the indigenous paraprofessional is more often to make available a different approach to a disadvantaged clientele through the mediation of a person who has special attributes not possessed by the professional staff. A particular life experience, rather than academic credentials, provides the basis for the indigenous worker's special expertise.

The indigenous paraprofessional is expected to serve as a bridge, a human link, between the agency and those needing its service. By virtue of her identification with the disadvantaged community, her special knowledge and understanding of the community and its residents, she is more likely to be able to develop rapport with such clients and be of special help to them. Sharing the clients' frame of reference, experience, life style, and language, the indigenous paraprofessional is thought to be in a better position to teach, influence, and act as a role model for the clients. The agency can benefit from "those socially useful skills and capacities [that] many have acquired by virtue of being poor. In this sense, what other job-creating concepts have treated as an obstacle for employment becomes a qualification for employment" (Pruger and Specht, 1968, p. 23).

The term "indigenous" has also been used to refer to those who were previously members of a group sharing a common problem—the former alcoholic, prisoner, drug addict, or mental health patient. Having personally been involved with such problems, they can identify and empathize with people currently disabled by them.

The New Careers program discussed above is most directly concerned with the indigenous paraprofessionals. Under the aegis of the New Careers program, "Persons from disadvantaged backgrounds are prepared, through on-the-job training and other methods, to assume entry-level positions in human service agencies." Entry-level jobs, sometimes called first-level positions, require "minimal skill and education [and are] open to previously uncredentialed persons." People holding such positions "assist professionals in the delivery of human services" (Pointer and Fishman 1968, pp. i–ii).

Supervision of ubiquitous paraprofessionals is an extension of the supervisor's traditional administrative and educational responsibility for volunteers and newly employed workers with advanced education but without any prior social-work education, and the material in previous chapters is applicable to this group of paraprofessionals. In some identifiable ways, however, supervising indigenous paraprofessionals presents new problems. While directing attention to the special problems in supervision posed by this group of supervisees, I wish to emphasize the fact that much of the generic content regarding social work supervision is appropriately applicable to this group as well.

A useful caveat might be entered here regarding some of the points made in this chapter: there is little empirical evidence for many of the statements made. This is true of the material on social work supervision generally, but with reference to traditional kinds of supervisees this lack is offset somewhat by the rich fund of practice wisdom made available by long years of experience with supervision. We lack any similar, substantial body of practice wisdom concerning indigenous paraprofessionals, since social work experience with them is recent and limited.

Paraprofessional Functions

Clearly delineating the functions that might be appropriately assigned to paraprofessionals is one of the most difficult problems faced by the agency that employs them. By implication, the agency must also solve the problem of clearly delineating

the tasks that the professional social worker performs, further
specifying the components of such tasks and the level of skill
required to perform the same tasks at different levels of competence. All of this is a problem which the supervisor is required
to solve. The degree of difficulty which the supervisor encounters in actually assigning tasks to paraprofessional supervisees depends on the success with which the profession, and
the agency through the profession, solves this problem. However, it would be a digression to discuss in detail the various efforts currently being made to deal with the general problem of
differential task conceptualization, other than to note that it is a
problem which requires resolution and a problem which affects
the supervision of paraprofessionals. More appropriately for our
purposes here, we will move to a description of what paraprofessionals are actually doing.

One of the professional's main rewards for accepting the
paraprofessional employee is freedom from the performance of
necessary but less professionally demanding tasks. Delegation
of such functions tends to increase the professional productivity
of the trained workers as they devote themselves more exclusively to professionally appropriate functions (however these
are defined).

Many professionally less demanding tasks have been assigned to paraprofessionals. They range from what one paraprofessional called "gopher jobs"—gopher coffee, gopher office
supplies, gopher transportation—to jobs whose responsibilities
are difficult to distinguish from those carried by professional
staff. In public assistance programs, indigenous paraprofessionals have:

1. Offered direct, concrete services—emergency baby-sitting;
   shopping for, and with, the client; transporting and escorting
   clients to hospitals, recreation centers, employment offices; helping clients to find jobs and housing, obtain surplus food, use family planning services.
2. Provided clients with information about community services and
   assisted clients with forms, eligibility verification, application
   procedures in using services; helped clients to use service

through an outreach program; acted as translators for clients using services; acted as client advocates. Paraprofessionals helped steer clients through the complexities of the welfare service system and helped clients "get around the runaround."
3. Counseled with and educated clients regarding housekeeping, child care, money management, budgeting.
4. Offered supportive services through friendly visiting, companionship, sympathetic listening.

Katan (1974) studied seven human-service organizations using indigenous workers. He concluded that "mediating tasks in relation to clients and simple routine tasks within the organization may be considered the common 'core' of the indigenous workers' activities" (p. 462). During the mid-1960s, the nationwide project ENABLE, sponsored by the Family Service Association of America, employed 200 indigenous aides in 59 programs of local family service agencies. The range of their activities is reflected in the report of one aide:

Mrs. F followed up on several referrals from one of the parent groups. She secured work appointments for eight young people—some were children of group members; other were referred by them. She also helped prepare a social summary on Mrs. J who had been referred for mental care to the state hospital. A case of child neglect was referred to her by group members, and she was able to assist the protective service of the county welfare department in making plans. She also referred two mothers from a former group to jobs as aides in a local OEO program. Five group members were referred to day camp and family camp opportunities. She secured Legal Aid service for one group member. She also provided escort service for parents to explore the possibility of financial assistance. (Birnbaum and Jones 1967, p. 628)

This quotation reflects the variety and complexity of tasks performed by nonprofessionals in a nationwide survey of some 185 mental health programs (Sobey 1970). Titles given paraprofessionals are a testimony to the diversity of their tasks—mental health aide, activity aide, family service aide, day-care aide, expeditor, rehabilitation aide.

Some of the heterogeneity in task assignment is the result

of social workers' willingness to encourage the development and use of the full potential of paraprofessionals. Some of it results from pressure by paraprofessionals who resent being saddled with inconsequential functions and who feel entitled to, and demand, meaningful roles. Some of it results from an acceptance by the agency that indigenous paraprofessionals bring some special aptitudes, resulting from their indigenousness, that make them particularly suited to perform certain tasks. According to this view, the paraprofessional is "not functionally beneath the professional, he is simply functionally different," the difference being based on "an expertise in the folk knowledge of slum life" (Hardcastle 1971, p. 57).

Administration and Supervisory Problems

The administrator who accepts paraprofessional staff must also accept the necessity of making some changes in agency organization, promotional procedures, supervisory patterns, and staff attitudes if the innovation is to succeed. These are problems of general agency administration, but the consequences of these policy decisions directly affect the supervisor–paraprofessional supervisee relationship. Any supervisory position requires clarifying directives and support from agency administration; for supervisors assigned responsibility for indigenous paraprofessionals, such back-up is essential.

A prerequisite for successful supervision is clarity regarding the paraprofessionals' assignment. There needs to be clear definition of a task to be done and general acceptance on the part of agency personnel that this particular job is the responsibility of the paraprofessional staff. Introduction of paraprofessionals requires either creation of new tasks or redefinition and reassignment of previously allocated tasks. Such job creation and reassignment can only be done by agency administration. The outcome of supervision is dependent on the readiness with which administration formulates the changes and the success it has in obtaining acceptance of them throughout the agency.

The need for clarity in job assignment and the difficulty in differential task assignment were expressed by one paraprofessional homemaker when she said, "You need to know what your job is and what is expected of you. You're not a social worker and you don't play at being a social worker—although the difference between what is and what is not being a social worker is paper thin."

Staff attitudes toward the paraprofessional supervisee are conditioned by the respect their supervisor commands within the agency. Hence it would be helpful if administration selected the agency's more respected supervisor to work with paraprofessionals. Having a powerful and respected supervisor front for them will give the paraprofessional supervisees an advantage that they need to a greater extent than other supervisees.

There is (despite the fiction that there is not) a hierarchy of status and prestige associated with the kinds of workers a supervisor supervises. The supervisor who supervises those workers with the most professional training is likely to rank higher in the agency pecking order than other supervisors. A supervisor may feel that being assigned the responsibility of supervising paraprofessionals is a threat to her status in the agency. The assignment therefore may be accepted with reluctance and resentment. If the supervisor does not come to terms with these feelings, they may be communicated to the paraprofessional supervisees. In counteracting the tendency to disparage such a supervisor, administrators might make a point of according this assignment some special tokens of respect. These might include a better office for the unit supervisor, special secretarial help, or a letter of commendation about the supervisor addressed to the staff.

Administration has to be ready to accept the burden of additional costs involved, at least initially, in training and supervising paraprofessionals. Working with paraprofessionals requires more supervisory time than is needed for other workers. The Family Service Association of America notes that "all the experience reported from member agencies in the use of social work assistants points out the *heavy investments of su-*

pervision required both during their training periods and on the job" (Family Service Association of America 1969, p. 8).

Not only does the supervisee have to be trained, the supervisor of indigenous paraprofessionals also requires some special training or retraining. Hallowitz (1969) notes that the supervisor often needs help in assuming the responsibility for supervising paraprofessionals. He suggests that provision for such help be structured from the very beginning of the experience and that group meetings of supervisors are often helpful. Here, too, the administrator has to provide the resources and sanction the use of time for retraining.

If the paraprofessional's distinctive contribution is as a bridge to the community, the linkage must flow in both directions. Administration should be receptive to paraprofessional input in effecting changes in agency policy and service-delivery patterns. If administration is not receptive, the supervisor will be faced with a problem of dealing with paraprofessional dissatisfaction at the derogation of their contribution.

Beyond defining and assigning appropriate entry-level tasks, administration must resolve a more subtle long-range problem relating to careers. The agency can have a staff policy of compartmentalization, which means that there is a clear layer of personnel with paraprofessional qualifications, who do a paraprofessional's job, another layer of B.A. workers, who do somewhat different tasks, and still another layer of fully professionally qualified M.S.W. workers, who are assigned still other responsibilities. The three groups of workers are perceived as distinctly different, and there is little movement of workers from one group to another.

A different agency policy might accept and encourage the movement of workers from one layer to another. The paraprofessional whose capabilities and experience are suitable might be helped to move up to the B.A. level of task assignment and then to the M.S.W. level. Worker competence, rather than educational credentials, would be the criteria for progressively more responsible task assignment. Given such an open system of upward mobility, the supervisor would have the responsibility for continuously offering more advanced training to the worker, constantly testing the limits of the worker's capacity. The supervisor would have the further responsibility of assigning more complex tasks as the paraprofessional supervisee was perceived as being ready for them.

Limiting the opportunities for advancement impairs motivation for training and makes educational supervision more difficult. One supervisor, in talking of her agency, said: "We are in a position to provide more training to paraprofessionals to increase their skills. We are not, however, in a position to increase their salaries or to promote them when they acquire more skills. Under these circumstances it is unreasonable to ask paraprofessionals to participate in additional training" (Gould, Smith, and Masi 1971, p. 81). A compartmentalized system, limiting the career possibilities of the paraprofessional, risks lowering paraprofessional morale and increasing feelings of frustration and dissatisfaction, leading to higher paraprofessional job turnover. The supervisor is asked to help the worker with such feelings related to the job and faces the burden of constantly training new workers at the starting line.

The supervisor has to recognize that the paraprofessional may feel dissatisfied with his position and his possibilities for advancement. At the beginning of the New Careers movement in the early 1960s, it was perhaps realistic to expect that paraprofessionals would be satisfied with the mere fact that they had been given agency jobs. By the 1970s, the expectations of the New Careers employees had gone well beyond this, and they felt entitled to meaningful roles within agency service and to the possibility of advancement beyond entry-level positions.

Except in a limited number of instances, paraprofessionals have achieved jobs and not careers. A study of paraprofessionals in 10 mental-health settings in New York City found that although "the preponderant majority of administrators, supervisors and clinicians perceive the paraprofessional's work as at least partially overlapping the work of the professionals . . . only two of the institutions had developed career ladders" (Gottesfeld, Rhee, and Parker 1970, p. 287).

A recent follow-up study of paraprofessionals in human services agencies found that such workers have been absorbed in these agencies "with far less difficulty than had originally been predicted. The early fears of many professionals and traditional civil service personnel have been dispelled or transformed into recognition of the substantial contribution paraprofessionals can make—the major failure has been the inability to provide new careerists with opportunities to advance through career ladders beyond the entry level" (Gould, Smith, and Masi 1971).

The administrative problems regarding career opportunities for paraprofessionals exemplify the fact that some of the main barriers to successful supervision of paraprofessionals are attitudinal. Difficulties are presented not only as a result of attitudes held by supervisors themselves, but also by those of other staff groups with whom the supervisors must work in representing the paraprofessionals in the agency. The paraprofessional group is a threat to professional staff and to clerical staff as well.

Clerical staff may resent the kinds of assignments that are offered to paraprofessionals. Such workers often have more educational preparation than paraprofessionals and, having worked in the agency, are very knowledgeable about agency policies, procedures, forms, and services. In agencies that have developed a career ladder for paraprofessionals, clerical staff have sometimes demanded to be included in promotional possibilities.

The paraprofessionals' demand for career opportunities also threatens the professional staff. Until very recently, existing and projected staff shortages were offered as a rationale for employment of paraprofessionals. By 1975 the gap between need and availability of personnel seemed to have evaporated. Job shortage rather than staff shortage became a matter of concern. Social work journals were, for the first time in the history of the profession, listing advertisements by professionals seeking positions. Consequently, professional social workers feel more strongly threatened by competition from the heterogeneous group of "other trained" or "partially trained" or "untrained" preprofessionals, nonprofessionals, and paraprofessionals who are claiming title to some, or all, of the social worker's functions. An administrative policy decision to permit an open career line giving paraprofessionals access to all agency positions that they are capable of filling, without regard to formal credentials, is likely to make professional staff anxious.

In one study of paraprofessional employment in a welfare agency, a supervisor expressed this anxiety in the form of a rhetorical question. "With the community voice becoming more powerful in this agency, what will happen to us professionals? When they open all opportunities to neighborhood people, where will we go?" (Gould, Smith, and Masi 1971, p. 110) Professional acceptance of such groups of workers within agency settings controlled by professionals may be more problematic in the future than it has in the immediate past. The supervisor will find it difficult to develop a climate of receptivity for her paraprofessional supervisees among professional staff.

Almost more important than the threat of job security is the blow to professional narcissism. As Rioch (1966) says, "If we have invested long years of hard work in achieving high professional status, including many courses that were dull and many examinations that were nerve wracking and we are told that some young bit of a girl with no training can do the job as well, or better than we can, it is natural that we should try to find some objections" (p. 291). This is a threat to the professional's perception of himself as a more competent, more skilled worker, differentiated from paraprofessionals by virtue of his more adequate educational preparation.

The problem is related to the difficulty of clearly and irrefutably establishing the relationship between educational preparation and the nature and level of task performance in social work. Where differences in level of job performance are clearly and observably related to differences in level of educational background, one need not emphasize differences in educational credentials. The product of the worker's performance is, in itself, testimony to his greater ability. Where job output is not so clearly related to job performance, there is a greater need to stress differences in educational background to ensure that the professional will be regarded differently. As Bandler (1973) says, "The new careerists by their existence, by their achievements, by their functioning, add a further dimension to the identity crises of the social work professional" (p. 101).

Indigenous paraprofessionals also represent a variety of ideological threats to which professionals are not insensitive. The New Career movements has challenged the legitimacy of the traditional patterns through which the professions control access to positions in their areas of concern. The movement has advocated a critical reanalysis of professionalism and credentialism, a priority entitlement to human service jobs on the basis of life experience and performance rather than on the basis of professional education, an equalitarian orientation that rejects many of the presuppositions of organizational hierarchical structure, and a decided emphasis on agency accountability to the client community in opposition to primary accountability to the general community. New Careerists, implicitly or explicitly, have challenged professionals to justify their preferential access to positions of status, their higher pay, their claim that their education prepared them for clearly superior performance.

In a more conciliatory vein, New Careerists have said repeatedly that paraprofessionals, far from being a threat to the professionals' status, enable them to dedicate their training and skills more fully to their own professional functions. Professionals are not readily convinced of this and frequently feel uneasy. Uneasiness leads to anxiety, and anxiety to defensiveness, hostility, and rejection—staff reactions that the supervisor needs to recognize in representing his paraprofessional supervisees in the agency community.

Because they are social workers, holding convictions which reflect the profession's values, staff and supervisors feel guilty about their uneasiness—which only intensifies it. They are ideologically sympathetic to the basic thrust of the New Careers movement. They agree that social justice demands access to jobs with a meaningful future for groups who had previously been excluded from full participation in American society. However, the goodies available in any organization are finite.

There is just so much power, just so much money, so many good offices, so many desirable duties. Increasing the availability of these rewards to one group increases the risk of diminishing it for another. There is a real conflict of interests.

There are still other factors in the relationship between indigenous paraprofessionals and professional staff that the supervisor needs to be aware of. A supervisor in an agency employing paraprofessionals pointed to some of them when she said:

> The paraprofessional represents the role of the community while I, as a supervisor, represent the role of the professional. Then another factor gets introduced into this issue: black/white polarization. The black represents the community to which the agency is directing its service and the supervisors, who are primarily white, represent union-protected professionals in middle management. This situation is currently aggravated by the fact that paraprofessionals are still in provisional employment status whereas the supervisors and professionals have permanent status, tenure and full protection of their rights. (Gould, Smith, and Masi 1971, pp. 110–11)

The indigenous paraprofessional is quite different in social characteristics from the usual non- or preprofessional B.A. supervisee with whom supervisors have had experience. The largest group of indigenous paraprofessionals are lower-class black mothers, in their late 20s or early 30s, with less than a high-school education who are, or have been, receiving public assistance (Gartner 1971, p. 7). Supervisors are generally white, middle class, and well educated. The differences in race and class background present a problem of social distance between supervisor and supervisee. There is a similar gap between paraprofessionals and a large proportion of other agency staff.

In supervising paraprofessionals, the supervisor faces the problem of establishing a working relationship with people who are quite different from herself—racially, socioeconomically, and in terms of life style and life experience. The supervisor may have had contact with such groups previously, but most often in the structure of the worker-client relationship. In supervision the interactional context is quite different. If the supervisor is not already familiar with the subculture of the supervisees, she should make some effort to learn about it and should reexamine her attitudes toward working with lower-class blacks. Is she predisposed to feel guilty and apologetic about her middle-class, educated, professional status? Does she tend to be permissive and solicitously ingratiating in an effort to make restitution for white oppression of minority groups, or does she react by excessive formalization of the relationship? What residuals of racism does she carry into the relationship?

Paraprofessionals present other, more subtle, kinds of threats to professional staff. Paraprofessionals' activity often involves an assault on professional mystique. "Words such as 'psychotherapy,' 'casework' or 'nursing care' have magical meanings to particular professions and make it difficult for their representatives to consider the possibility that paraprofessionals could perform such functions, this despite the fact that evidence has been accumulated that the preprofessional often can perform these functions adequately" (Hadley, True, and Kepes 1970, p. 33). Associated with this threat is the anxiety that the client group, through the paraprofessional, might find out that some aspects of the professional mystique have, in fact, little substance; that the emperor is without clothes.

The professional feels threatened by removal of the "shield" of routine tasks when nonprofessionals are given these tasks to perform. He now has to prove his worth in dealing with the more sophisticated problems for which his advanced training supposedly prepares him. One reaction to a reduction in caseload so that intensive casework can be offered is an increase in the worker's anxiety (Schwartz and Sample 1972). "As the subprofessional assumes roles within the professional structure, there is a necessity for the fully qualified professional to develop new and more advanced skills than those which are currently included in his repertoire" (Gordon 1965, p. 343). Thus one of the advantages for professional staff of employment of paraprofessionals, namely, that they can be free to be professionally creative, poses a challenge that is often perceived as a threat.

Professional secrets and client secrets present other problems. The agency is "backstage" for the professional staff. At staff meetings, at coffee breaks, in the staff lounge, in informal peer interaction, the professional staff express some of their ambivalence toward clients and their work. They regain their emotional equilibrium by expressing some of their hostility toward the client group, their doubts about agency procedures, the gaffs they have made, their cynicism about certain aspects of their work, their use of administrative discretion in behalf of favorite clients and in opposition to overly demanding clients. They need a place where they can safely engage in these tension-reducing activities, which Goffman (1959) has aptly termed "collusive intimacies and backstage relations" (p. 206). They feel free to do this in the presence of other professionals. They are uneasy, however, about revealing such "secrets" in the presence of paraprofessionals. Paraprofessionals have not committed themselves to loyalty to the professional staff in maintaining secrecy if they become party to this information. In effect, the client community represented by the paraprofessionals becomes a witness to all of the professional's secrets, including those which are unflattering and unlovely.

Professionals are reasonably certain that fellow professionals will honor the implicit pledge of reciprocal loyalty. They can count on each other for support against client opposition and criticism. The agency's control over the paraprofessional's behavior is tenuous, however, and the paraprofessional's adherence to norms of professional conduct is open to question. The felt need for circumspection denies the professional staff a safe refuge for such functionally important, backstage activities. Denied opportunities for safe release, the professional staff resents the presence of paraprofessionals who are the source of the difficulty.

The situation presents a conflict for the paraprofessional as well. Although identified with the client group, the paraprofessional nonetheless feels some loyalty to the agency. She then experiences a conflict regarding how much of this secret, backstage knowledge she can, or should, share with her neighbors in

the client community. The reverse problem is even more difficult for the paraprofessional (Levinson and Schiller 1966). Her
closeness to members of the client community frequently
makes her a party to secrets that are of concern to the agency
but that have not been disclosed by the client. The paraprofessional learns of many instances in which clients have conned
and manipulated the agency in a wide variety of imaginative
ways. What is she to do with the information? How does she
share it with the agency without risking her loyalty to the client
group; how does she withhold it form the agency without risking her loyalty to the agency?

Agency staffs are aware that these sitations are potentially
problematic. A large county department of public welfare posed
these problems as an element in recruitment procedures:

> Two situations in the applications questionnaire we used for
> screening aides were designed to bring out the applicant's attitude
> toward sharing "confidences" with social workers: 1) A client you have
> visited several times tells you she does not like her social worker be-
> cause she is cold and disinterested. What would you say or do? 2)
> When visiting a client to discuss budgeting the client tells you she is
> working half-time but has not told her social worker because she does
> not want her welfare grant discontinued. What would you say or do?
> There was less unanimity of response to these questions than to any of
> the others—demonstrating the applicants' initial conflict over the is-
> sues. (Cudabeck 1970, p. 217)

The effort to highlight, for greater visibility and recognition, the problems a supervisor of paraprofessional supervisees
might encounter, tends to overemphasize the difficulties. Many
of the projects that utilize paraprofessionals report a receptive
attitude on the part of staff and a sincere effort to work cooperatively and productively with paraprofessionals. It is difficult to
know how valid and realistic these difficulties are. The pertinent research is contradictory. For instance, Hadley, True, and
Kepes (1970) report that program administrators may grudgingly
concede that paraprofessionals might be able to do adequately
many things professionals can do, but they "hasten to add that if
given the chance of spending money on professional or prepro-

fessionals, they would hire professionals" (p. 49). Sobey (1970) found, however, that mental-health project directors would, given the chance, "clearly not utilize professional staff" in 55 percent of the cases (p. 156). Consequently the pervasiveness of the threats felt by professionals remains a matter for future study.

In the meantime, what can the supervisor do in discharging the administrative responsibility of helping her paraprofessional supervisees achieve acceptance in the agency community? Some of the objections to paraprofessionals are based on concern with maintaining agency standards and a disquiet about possible reduction in the quality of service offered clients. There is some doubt about the capacity of paraprofessionals to perform adequately, and acceptance of the paraprofessional depends, to some extent, on paraprofessional performance. Thus one of the most effective methods of ensuring staff acceptance of paraprofessionals lies in the supervisors' helping such supervisees to perform their tasks as effectively as possible. As one paraprofessional said, "When everybody found out that we really could do what we were supposed to be doing, the rest of the staff began to appreciate us and accept us."

The supervisor might also point out that paraprofessional skills are complementary to those of professionals and that the work done is most often at a different level of complexity. Neither the professional nor the paraprofessional can offer the client optimum service without the other. The work of the paraprofessional is needed to increase the effectiveness of the service the professional offers, and the paraprofessional needs the professional for the more effective performance of his role. While doing different things, both are discharging necessary and significant tasks. Reflecting this attitude one paraprofessional, discussing her relationship with a social worker, said, "I can't do her job; she can't do my job. I need her to help me do my job; she needs me to help her do her job."

The supervisor needs to watch for, and explicitly discuss with workers, their tendency to disparage the work of paraprofessionals, to restrict them to menial, unimportant tasks. Such responses may derive from defensiveness and fear of the implications of paraprofessional staff. Just as paraprofessionals need to be prepared by the supervisor in order to take their legitimate place in the agency, professional staff members have to be prepared to welcome them.

The Process of Paraprofessional Supervision

general approach

Often the paraprofessional is assigned to work in collaboration with, or ancillary to, a direct service worker. The worker then is given some responsibility for supervision of the paraprofessional. Sometimes the staff is organized into teams—two professionally trained workers, two paraprofessional assistants, and a clerical worker making up a team. The senior professional worker is designated as team leader. The most frequent supervisory situation, however, is the traditional one-to-one relationship between the paraprofessional supervisee and a supervisor. It is this last context that is the basis for the following discussion.

Supervisors of indigenous workers approach the assignment with a variety of attitudes that condition their relationship with the paraprofessionals. Hallowitz (1969) has perceptively described some of these attitudes:

The expectations of professionals in relation to indigenous workers can be described as polarized along a continuum consisting of the "doubters" on one hand and the "idealists" on the other. The doubters were those professionals who tended to have low expectations of the aides' potential for making a significant contribution to service delivery. They tended to cast nonprofessionals in the roles of dependent clients or handymen in the service of the professionals. In this context the workers often reacted by assuming roles to fit the supervisors' expectations, thus creating a vicious circle. For example, in the teacher aide program one teacher tended to treat her aide as an overgrown student instead of a classroom assistant. Fairly early in his experience the aide perceived what was expected of him, and he played the role to the hilt. The result was that the teacher received little in the way of concrete help from him and he regarded himself as a failure as a classroom assistant.

At the opposite end of the spectrum were the idealists, who had inordinately high—in some cases unlimited—expectations of aides' capacities. Virtually all regarded the aides as practitioners. This included teachers who, in effect, believed that the aides could perform instructional tasks indiscriminately, caseworkers who voiced expectations that aides could perform intensive therapy, and so on. They seemed to view the worker as a "noble savage," who, by virtue of being poor and minimally educated, could outperform the professional, while at the same time retaining his identity as a nonprofessional person with roots in the client population. One consequence of this kind of approach was that the aide was continually expected to produce beyond his capacity. When he failed, the supervisor frequently became disenchanted. As a result, neither party got what he wanted. The aide received neither realistic nor practical skills or knowledge and the supervisor did not get the "all-American indigenous worker."

A fairly sizable subgroup of idealists were those professionals whose perceptions of their role can best be described as "warriors in the War on Poverty." They were inclined to view the nonprofessionals as potential allies in a struggle to change the human service Establishment. In many instances, the aim of these professionals was to effect change in the total agency, in which service delivery was an incidental element. Concomitant with their interest in broad-scale organizational change, these professionals also operated as advocates of the aides vis-à-vis their attempts to become integrated in the system.

An intermediate point on the spectrum was a third group consisting of professionals who might be termed "pragmatic experimentalists." These were individuals who, although committed to the acceptance of the nonprofessional's potential, took the approach that, at this juncture, no one could realistically "know" what that potential was, but that it should be tested out. They were inclined more consistently to orient their behavior to meeting the learning needs of the nonprofessionals as indicated in the job definitions and to try to evaluate performance on the basis of what was done on the job rather than on what ideally could have been done. (pp. 184–85, reprinted with permission of the National Association of Social Workers)

It would be good for any supervisor assigned paraprofessional supervisees to make explicit for himself where he stands on this continuum.

Some of the behavior that results from these different attitudes is described in a study that compared the supervisors who evoked the most positive responses from paraprofessionals and those who were least positively regarded.

The most positively regarded supervisors expressed delight with [paraprofessionals] and praised their capacity to learn new tasks and to perform at a high level. The typical personality style of these supervisors was found to be open and enthusiastic—qualities paralleling those of many of the paraprofessionals themselves. These supervisors appeared to relate to paraprofessionals in much the same way as the paraprofessionals relate to the community: that is, on a highly human level, with an ability to communicate well, to understand and to empathize. (Gould, Smith, and Masi 1971, p. 90)

Summarizing her supervisor's approach, which she thought worked well for her, one paraprofessional said, "My supervisor didn't make me feel like a dumbbell, although to tell the truth I was somewhat of a dumbbell. It was the confidence she had in me which gave me the confidence in myself" (ibid.). Supervisors who were least positively perceived

indicated dissatisfaction with so many changes in the agency and in the city. They displayed discomfort and a lack of familiarity with direct interactive relationships with minority groups and members of the client community. They indicated preferences for the older mode of relationship of superior and subordinate, and appeared also to lack the experience and the skills needed for direct relationships with staff on a team basis. These supervisors evaluated the [paraprofessionals] on their staff principally in terms of their adherence to time schedules, the orderliness of their written work and the promptness of their report submissions. Most described the role of supervisors as that of a person who is held accountable by his superior for the accountability of his staff.

One supervisor complained that a [paraprofessional] who was rebuked for lateness retorted, "You're late as often as I am." The supervisor replied, "That is not your concern, it's my supervisor's." This supervisor criticized this attitude as lacking in deference and respect, and suspects it is indicative of hostility, racial hostility. The interview with the paraprofessional referred to indicated that he viewed this supervisor as negatively as the supervisor viewed him. He said, "I do my job very well, he has no complaints," and the supervisor indeed did not report any problem with work performance. On a human level, both interviews indicated that no relationship had been established and no communication took place. Disregard was mutual. (Smith, Gould, and Masi 1971, p. 91)

administrative supervision

One of the administrative responsibilities of the supervisor with regard to all new workers is to help them get "placed" in the agency. This involves not only an interpretation to other workers in the agency as to where the new worker fits in but also the others' acceptance of the new worker's place in the agency. This task is more difficult to accomplish for the paraprofessional and consequently needs more emphasis by the supervisor.

The difficulty lies in the fact that the agency often has had little familiarity and experience with paraprofessionals. There is, therefore, little prior socialization regarding the place of such workers on which the supervisor can draw in eliciting understanding. The supervisor of paraprofessionals, in trying to help her supervisees find their place in the agency community, often is faced with limited acceptance of such workers and considerable confusion as to what they are supposed to do.

Clerical staff as well as professional staff need to be introduced to the paraprofessional and given some information about her job assignment and how she fits into the agency. It would help to repeat this process with people with whom the paraprofessional is likely to come into regular contact in carrying out her assignments—key staff in the neighborhood housing project, the community hospital, the employment office. It helps to have some written material which supplements the verbal interpretation.

The paraprofessional may have a job but he does not have a role until:

1. His role is defined in terms of specific behaviors appropriate for his position.
2. Both the "paraprofessional and all significant groups with which he interacts reach a level of consensus about what is expected of him."

3. "His position has an accepted status or social location."
4. There is acceptance of the validity of his claim to the role the agency has defined for him.

The quotations are from Neleigh and co-workers (1971, p. 36). Helping the paraprofessional achieve entitlement to a role, as defined above, is the larger aspect of the supervisor's responsibility for placing the worker in the agency.

The supervisor is charged with promoting attitudes of acceptance and understanding between paraprofessionals and the rest of the staff and interpreting, for recognition and appreciation, the contribution which paraprofessionals can, and do, make to the work of the agency. A changing perception of the agency by the former client, now a paraprofessional, has to be matched by the staff's changing perception of the paraprofessional, its former client.

The supervisor may have to be more active and assertive than usual in advocating the paraprofessionals' entitlement to agency resources. The status of the fully professional staff worker permits her to confidently ask for supplies, clerical help, the use of the dictaphone and the copier machine, with clear expectation that her requests will be granted. The paraprofessional worker has less status, and her requests can be more easily ignored or refused. The supervisor may then have to lend some of her clout to the paraprofessional group in seeing that such resources are made available.

The usual supervisee is familiar with the "culture" of the social-service organization. For the paraprofessional, this is either unfamiliar territory or familiar in a distorted way. If she has known the agency as a client, her view of its operations may come from a narrow and particular perspective. The supervisor has to act as a guide to the culture of the organization for those paraprofessionals who have had no prior contact and to correct misperceptions and distortions on the part of those who have had client contact.

As a paraprofessional, the worker is asked to support and administer policies that she may have previously opposed as a client. She frequently sees herself as an advocate of the client against the agency. The supervisor must help the paraprofessional successfuly manage the dual aspects of her role—her responsibility to the agency and her responsibility "to the client group of which she may formerly have been a member" (Leon 1973, p. 42). Budner, Chazin, and Young (1973) note this attitude in reporting on indigenous workers in a multi-service center. The worker's orientation was toward

working directly with the client; . . . this tendency limited the worker's concern with administrative requirements of the agency. The perceived reality was the worker-client set; the [agency] was merely the framework in which this reality was carried out. (p. 355) . . . Because the outreach [indigenous] staff sees its role in almost missionary terms—helping with overwhelming exigent problems—they tend to consider agency-imposed responsibilities, like recording, as irrelevancies and distractions. In addition, because the staff believe that they are effective in meeting their primary obligation, record keeping and accountability inevitably become functions honored more in the breach than in the observance. (p. 358)

Illustrating this pattern, one indigenous worker says:

Keeping records is difficult for the indigenous worker—one of the hardest things he has to do. Being with people and working with them sets up a relationship that cannot be conveyed in words. Most of the time the essence of what takes place cannot be put down on paper. The indigenous worker knows that it is a great achievement to get his client's trust and that most of what is said is confidential. Why, he feels, should he share it with someone else? (Normandia 1967, p. 65)

In discharging administrative responsibilities, the supervisor may need to assist the paraprofessional in learning and accepting the role of a worker in an organization. Merely relating to the world of work, its rhythm, requirements, and structure, is something new to the paraprofessional, who often has had little or no formal work experience.

The world of work requires the readiness to be on the job at certain times, follow directions, adhere to procedures, accept evaluation, discharge responsibilities, relate to hierarchical authority. Most supervisees that the supervisor has encountered have been already shaped by the work matrix so that these fundamental considerations do not have to be explicitly taught. With paraprofessionals one cannot presume that this is the case.

New careerists are likely to have had limited work experience, particularly experience in large bureaucratic agencies. They will need extra help in learning to maintain work schedules, keep records, use written resource material, exploit agency channels of communication, and participate productively in staff meetings. Simple office procedures—answering phones, leaving messages, filing material—may need to be specifically taught. (Cudaback 1970, p. 217)

In helping paraprofessionals accept administrative rules, the supervisor does best if she can present them as functionally justifiable and useful requirements. A director of a settlement house day-care center, in talking to professionals who will be supervising paraprofessionals, emphasizes the need for functional justification of job requirements:

What I have tried to stress so far is what *you* can do to create an environment of mutuality. It is also fair that you have a right to ask for certain things in return. You have a right to expect your aide to be on time, to dress appropriately for work with children, to be where she is supposed to be and not goof off. These may be foreign ideas to a girl who has never held a job that meant anything to her before. You don't have the time for extended therapy with your aides, so I suggest the best thing you can do is just give it to them straight. *Tell* them the reason why it is important to be on time, that is, the *real* reason, which is that the *important job* that *she* has to do will be neglected if she's late. And give her a good reason for not goofing off: which is that the children need her attention. These are *real,* positive reasons, and if the girls have positive jobs to do, these reasons make sense. We started a new aide last Thursday, and one of the things we stress at the outset is to call in if you are going to be absent or late. On Monday Joann didn't show up, and on Tuesday, when she came in she offered no explanation. So I asked her. Quite innocently and truthfully, I am sure, she said, "I was sick, and I went to Receiving Hospital early in the morning before the nursery opened. I had to go early, otherwise I'd wait all day." She was, you see, concentrating on an immediate problem, and the importance of her notifying the nursery had not yet impressed itself. It's true, I had *told* her what to do, but she hadn't yet learned it from experience. After the girls are with us for a few weeks, they rarely stay away without notifying us.

I didn't scold Joann. I told her I hoped that she would remember next time, because one of the teachers was hoping to take a group of children to Belle Isle and couldn't go because Joann wasn't there to help. It was the truth, and I think Joann was sorry; not sorry that she broke a rule, but sorry that because of her the children missed a treat. There's quite a difference. (Linden 1972, pp. 12–13)

Having more limited educational background in preparation for doing the job, having had less opportunity in a structured work situation to develop habits of punctuality, routine job organization, and efficient work procedure, experiencing difficulties with or resistance to written report forms which often serve as administrative control devices, the supervisee may initially need more frequent reviews of her work. The need for greater supervisory contact with paraprofessionals is explicitly recognized by the National Association of Social Workers in its definition of the different levels of workers. The paraprofessional is expected to be less autonomous, less capable of self-directed performance.

Initially the supervisor needs to be willing to be somewhat more informal about scheduling conferences and to be more readily available at other times. Frank and Quinlan (1973), detailing their experience in training welfare clients as mental-health paraprofessionals, state that "back-up supervision and easy access to supervisors became critical for our students to win their way through to a reasonably staunch view of themselves as effective and self-assertive human beings" (p. 102). Short daily conferences rather than a single longer weekly conference may be desirable. Sometimes a simple log form, listing clients to be contacted or work to be done, is used as the basis for a structured verbal report.

The paraprofessional's familiarity with the community of clients places him in a vulnerable position from which he may need to be protected by the supervisor. Yielding to personalized pressures, made more potent by his strong identification with the client, the paraprofessional may make a commitment to the client that is difficult to implement without conflicting with agency policy. "This situation may require a continuous series of bail-out, back-up or back-down maneuvers by the agency in order to square organization policy with the various commitments which have been made" (Meyer 1969, p. 48). These paraprofessional decisions may require discussion with, and sanctioning by, the supervisor.

Although paraprofessionals may be different in terms of background and education from other members of the direct service staff, it is easy to exaggerate the implications of such difference. Consequently it is unfortunate if paraprofessionals are not routinely included in staff meetings. The generally desirable rule would seem to be that unless there is a compelling, explicitly defined reason why paraprofessionals should not be included, the supervisor should invite them to any and every staff meeting. Such a procedure symbolizes the full membership of the paraprofessionals within the agency.

The supervisor must make sure that all pertinent communications are shared with paraprofessionals. Workers in large agencies often break up into four units—clerical staff, paraprofessional aide staff, professional staff, supervisory and managerial staff. The groups are separate at coffee breaks, lunch breaks, leisure time get-togethers. The more traditional supervisee is a member of the informal communication network of professional staff. The paraprofessionals, separated from the professional staff, may miss much important information unless the supervisor is aware of this problem and makes provisions for redress.

educational supervision

Educational supervision requires individualization of the worker. There is as much heterogeneity among paraprofessionals as among professionals. However, our more limited familiarity with paraprofessionals is conducive to stereotyping. "There are many different types of non-professionals: some are earthy, some are tough, some are angry, some are surprisingly articulate, some are slick, clever, wheeler-dealers, and nearly all are greatly concerned about their new roles and their relationship to professionals" (Riessman 1967, p. 104; see also Kramer 1972).

In discharging the responsibilities of educational supervision, the supervisor has to have a conviction in the value of training. While recognizing and affirming the paraprofessionals' knowledge and understanding gained as a consequence of life experience, it is also necessary to acknowledge that education is necessary if the paraprofessional is to make the most effective use of what he knows. Educational supervision is the "guidance mechanism" that makes explicit the worker's knowledge and understanding, gives it purpose and direction, and makes it consciously available for use in job performance.

The paraprofessional's spontaneity, naturalness, intuition, and lack of inhibition are sometimes cited in derogation of training, the implication being that, given the necessary personal attributes for working with the client, training is unnecessary and may even be harmful. Cudabeck (1968) says, however, in analyzing the results of a paraprofessional demonstration project, "In my work with aides I have moved from believing that all we needed to do was free aides to use their native sensitivity and common sense to my present view of their needing some disciplined, formalized educational program and theoretical framework to augment their considerable natural abilities—and aides are the first to request this additional instruction" (p. 3).

Pearl and Riessman, founders of the New Careers movement, strongly support the need for training paraprofessionals:

Nothing could undermine the New Career concept so much as allowing untrained persons to do meaningful work with the romantic notion that their unskilled lower-class status is sufficient qualification for helping others. The non-professional without training is *not* an asset; he can in fact be a menace to the service. Not only is he unaware of his active role, he also has no idea of what he must *not* do. (1965, p. 157)

Seconding the need for educational supervision, Hallowitz (1969) comments that some myths currently prevalent should be laid to rest. Specifically, the poor do not necessarily have special knowledge, insight, or intuition not available to the more affluent; neither is the poor person, ipso facto, more sympathetic to others in the same plight, nor does his poverty give him special knowledge about effective administration, program planning, interviewing skills, community action, and the like for the urban poor. He does not necessarily understand his community or culture better than an outside professional. On the whole, the poor and disadvantaged were found to be no more free of prejudice and snobbery than any other group in society (The one clear advantage of the indigenous nonprofessional is that he understands the language, style and customs of his neighbors. (p. 168))

Paraprofessionals themselves are very anxious for educational supervision. Some 20 paraprofessionals in a public welfare agency were asked about strains on the job which lead them to seriously considering quitting. The second-ranking dissatisfaction, offered by about half of the respondents, was the fact that "they felt that they were not getting enough help from their supervisors" (Creecy 1971). Sharing a similar life experience may help the paraprofessional in achieving contact with the client, but once contact has been made, effective service needs to be offered. Reaching is different from helping, and helping requires training.

In discharging the educational function of supervision, the supervisor is not only helping to increase the effectiveness of the paraprofessional staff but also making them more acceptable to the agency. The professional staff have some assurance that paraprofessionals are being socialized to the norms of agency behavior, and that their behavior is thereby becoming more predictable.

Having some conviction about the value of training of paraprofessionals, the supervisor has to have further conviction in the paraprofessionals' capacity to benefit from training. She needs to accept some basic New Careers concepts—that people learn in a variety of ways and that formal schooling may not be the best procedure for everyone; that lack of formal credentials is not indicative of what the supervisee is capable of doing; that the paraprofessional does bring some special knowledge, some

unique qualities, and a special kind of competence which results from life-experience learning; that previous lack of experience with formal training does not impair capacity to learn; and
that such supervisees are capable of learning what they need to
be taught.

For many of the professionals, this will be their first experience in
training disadvantaged people. They will have many unspoken doubts
about the ability of the trainees to be of any help to other people and
about their own ability to teach such trainees. One of the best ways of
dealing with their anxieties and doubts is to introduce the [super-
visors] to [other] supervisors who have had experience with indigenous people. Visits to agencies using Human Service Aides, neighborhood centers, local hospitals, child care centers and residential
centers for juveniles, provide an opportunity for the supervisor to see
and talk with nonprofessionals in action. (Pointer and Fishman 1968, p.
14)

It is not likely that the paraprofessional will succeed unless
the supervisor can communicate to her some conviction in her
ability to succeed. At the same time the supervisor has to guard
against developing a mystique about the indigenous paraprofessional. Such a mystique involves a derogation of professional
skills and learning and an excessive evaluation of the paraprofessional's supposed uniqueness: "The neighborhood workers
know the community; the professionals know only book learning"; "they have a magic pipeline to the people" (Morrill 1968,
p. 409).

Romanticizing the special attributes of the paraprofessionals may lead the supervisor to expect more from them than
they are actually capable of delivering, or to make him feel less
confident and more apologetic about what he can teach them.
While not exaggerating the importance of the professionally
based knowledge he has available to share with the paraprofessional, the supervisor needs some quiet confidence in the value
of what he can teach.

Paraprofessional supervisees present special difficulties for
supervisors in developing and maintaining the relaxed, comfortable, psychologically safe, give-and-take relationship necessary

for effective educational supervision. Paraprofessionals inevitably bring with them a configuration of attitudes developed in response to the reality they have repeatedly experienced. They feel fear, suspicion, distrust; they anticipate exploitation, rejection, betrayal, and discrimination; they may be predisposed to react with anxiety, hostility, and barely concealed aggression; and they are prepared to con and manipulate. Residuals of class conflict and racial conflict are brought into the supervisory situation. In explicating the paraprofessional's attitude toward supervision, one indigenous worker says:

At the start the indigenous worker sees the professional supervisor as part of the structure that has always been telling him that he is wrong. It takes time for him to accept the concept of supervision but he responds gradually to constructive criticism—the worker feels that the purpose of supervision should be to guide him to perform better rather than to control his way of acting. He believes in action and that this is more important than filling out forms. (Normandia 1967, p. 65)

Having practiced surface acceptance of authority as a pattern of accommodation in society, paraprofessionals have to be encouraged to learn through open questioning of authority. A handbook of paraprofessional training states that one of the objectives in supervision is to "develop a sense of personal freedom and self-confidence for open communication within the trainee-supervisory relationship. This means such things as being able to discuss 'I don't like . . . ,' 'I don't see why . . . ,' 'I don't understand . . .' and 'why can't we try it that way?' It means seeing supervision as really learning to think together rather than 'the place to go to get answers.' " The emotional interaction in the teaching-learning situation involving paraprofessionals is complex:

Out of their life experiences—probably largely out of their school experiences—nonprofessionals tend to see supervision not as a learning process, but as a threat. Their suspiciousness makes it difficult for them to believe that criticism is meant to be constructive, and it is not unusual for them to react defensively and argumentatively. Sometimes this leads to their withholding information and avoiding supervisory conferences. As this was examined by the Lincoln Hospital staff, we realized that we were more comfortable with a dependent—even over-dependent—relationship that fed our narcissism and self-esteem, whereas the hostile reactions of the nonprofessionals threatened our potency and self-image and frustrated our wish to be of service. In an attempt to avoid this hostility, we too often placated the worker, a ma-neuver that he tended to see as a cop-out, or reacted to with coun-terhostility, which simply tended to escalate the conflict and create a power struggle. (Hallowitz 1969, p. 170).

Language presents a problem. The same words often have different connotations to supervisors and to paraprofessionals, so that explicit care needs to be given to word usage in educa-tional supervision.

One aide remarked, "That slum you keep talking about is my home." Another wanted to know if clients were people—not without irony. The use of such expressions as "you people" usually wakened some hostility in aides. One aide stated that she thought an indigenous per-son was someone who had some kind of health problem.

The professional proclivity for labeling social phenomena was miscon-strued. The neighborhood workers felt that the term "lower income" was being used not merely in a descriptive but in a pejorative sense. (Goldberg 1967, p. 200).

Word usage is more than a question of semantics. It expresses differences in attitudes between paraprofessionals and super-visors. Consciously examining the words he uses may help the supervisor become more aware of attitudes that are barriers to an effective relationship. In general, non-jargonal plain English is preferred to "high fashion talk."

In implementing the tasks of educational supervision, the supervisor will find similarities and differences in approaching the paraprofessional. The general principles of learning are equally appropriate and applicable with this group. The proce-dures and techniques that facilitate learning for supervisees with professional education also facilitate learning for parapro-fessionals. Although the label identifying the paraprofessional might be different, she is, as a person, very much like all other supervisees. Consequently, whatever the supervisor knows about establishing good human relationships and about teaching is clearly relevant here.

The need to adapt teaching approaches to make them suitable for adults is even more pronounced with paraprofessionals than with other supervisees. As a group, paraprofessionals tend to be older. They have had long years of experience in struggling with a very stressful reality. Their life experiences have demanded an independence and maturity that intensify their sense of adulthood as compared with those more protected, middle-class fellow supervisees with advanced degrees. They are truly adult learners.

Untrained does not necessarily imply unskilled or unknowledgeable. We credit the younger, educated supervisee with knowledge derived from his advanced education and (limited) experience and draw on this in educational supervision; we credit the older paraprofessional with the rich knowledge derived from life experience and (limited) education and draw on this in educational supervision. The balance of education and life experience is different. Both are valid sources of learning, and each can provide content to be used by the imaginative supervisor for teaching-learning. If the supervisor knows how to employ the relevant life experience of the paraprofessionals, there can be as much give-and-take in this relationship as with other kinds of supervisees. In training a group of "hard-core delinquent drop-outs" to work as research aides, the supervisor taught statistics by "pointing out to them that they already knew a lot about probability theory. They knew it was a 2 to 1 bet not to make a 10 in a crap game. But as much as they knew, I knew more and we went through a simulated crap game and I showed them how much money I would have won if we'd been playing for real because it isn't an even money bet against a 6 or an 8; it's 6 to 5 against the shooter" (Popper 1968, p. 40). The client's life experience is the text for teaching.

Another factor that distinguishes paraprofessionals from other supervisees is that they are likely to have been out of school for a longer time. They are less likely to have well-habituated, formal patterns of studying and less likely to have had recent practice in reading, note-taking, and paper-writing procedures so basic to the formal educational experience. Paraprofessionals have had less opportunity to learn how to learn.

There are several consequences of this fact for choice of teaching approaches in educational supervision. The supervisor needs to deemphasize reading as a source of learning and to depend more on didactic, repetitive, personal discussion with the paraprofessional as the preferred procedure. Paraprofessionals are not likely to read articles or books or agency manuals. Many of the words frequently used in written communication, but rarely in speech, are unfamiliar and confusing, making reading difficult.

Straightforward instruction of what needs to be communicated seems less devious and more acceptable to the paraprofessional than do Socratic question-answer procedures. The need to partialize learning is greater here. The supervisor needs to select limited objectives for each supervisory session; therefore, shorter and more frequent supervisory conferences are desirable. If the supervisor realizes that many things are likely to need repetition, she is less likely to show impatience at the third or fourth, or perhaps the fifth time around on the same regulation or the same procedure. Didactic, repetitive presentations can be made more effective if material can be diagrammed or made visual in some other way.

Material to be taught needs to be clearly structured, and precisely defined. Theory has to be translated into action terms, and the behavioral implications of principles have to be specified. On the other hand, if simplification is overdone the paraprofessional may feel he is being talked down to or patronized. Pearl and Riessman (1965) summarize the preferred teaching approach:

Many illustrations should be used, details should be carefully spelled out, assumptions should be explicitly stated. Ideas that are often taken for granted in other types of presentation should be enunciated almost compulsively and material should be repeated frequently. . . . Presentations should be well organized, few disgressions permitted and frequent summaries made available. Transitions should be clearly indicated and breaks in continuity should be held to a minimum or else explicitly designated. (p. 172)

(Pearl and Riessman also suggest heavy emphasis on role playing as a preferred teaching procedure.) It is "concrete, motoric, emotionally stimulating, and represents engagement with real live problems as against intellectual theorizing." Role-playing and job-simulation sessions are regarded as congenial to the learning predispositions of lower-class paraprofessionals (Riessman and Goldfarb 1964). These teaching procedures are problem centered, action oriented, informal, and gamelike.

(If, in general, people learn by doing, this fact needs particular emphasis in educational supervision of paraprofessionals.) Their life experience has been one of learning by doing. They become easily impatient with teaching that is not directly and observably related to job tasks. The New Careers slogan "jobs now, training to follow" has pertinence here. "Considerable anxiety develops in the nonprofessional until he gets into 'action.' . . . Consequently it is extremely important that he actually begin performing some tasks as soon as possible" (Reiff and Riessman 1965, p. 20).

The following outline for a supervisory group session illustrates educational supervision of paraprofessionals. It is directed toward newly hired paraprofessionals and is concerned with teaching effective use of the telephone. The material was developed by the Training Bureau of the California State Department of Social Welfare as part of a program of induction and training of case aides.

A. *Objective*
   To identify and discuss . . . proper telephone usage.
B. *What do you do when the telephone rings?*
   1. First impressions are lasting impressions.
   2. A prompt and courteous handling of telephone calls creates a helping environment for agency work.
   3. When a caller has to wait on the line through several rings he is apt to be annoyed. *Always answer the phone promptly.*
      a. A situation to consider:

You are working with some materials across a room when the telephone rings. The phone rings several times before you can answer. You answer the telephone and say what?
  b. A possible response for the situation:
     "Mr. Smith speaking. I'm sorry to have kept you waiting; I was not at my desk when the phone began to ring."
     Ask the group to offer alternative responses and select the one which seems the best response.
4. Use "please" and "thank you" liberally in your conversation—this helps to make a good impression.
5. Always identify yourself when answering the telephone.
C. *Talking on the telephone*
  1. Don't talk too fast or too slowly. Adjust your speed to the pace set by the person you are talking with.
  2. Be careful not to speak in a monotone. Use the many inflections of which your voice is capable.
     a. A situation to consider:
        "Mr. Smith, I'm so glad you called."
     b. It should sound better when "Mr. Smith" and "so" are emphasized (or "Mr. Smith" and "glad"). Ask the members of the group to try different voice inflections.
  3. Speak in a normal conversational tone. Don't shout or let your voice drop too low.
  4. Pronounce your words clearly.
D. *What to say and what not to say*
  1. Maintain a focus on the purpose of the telephone call.
  2. Answer the caller's questions.
  3. Volunteer any information he may need.
  4. Listen carefully to what he has to say.
  5. Maintain conciseness and politeness, but don't be so brief as to sound discourteous.
E. *Examples*
  Here are two examples of how two Case Aides handled similar telephone calls. What one do you think does the better job?
  Mrs. Smith handled it this way:

  "Mr. Jones' desk; Mrs. Smith speaking."
  "Mrs. Smith, this is Mr. Johnson."
  "How are you, Mr. Johnson? And the wife and children?"
  "All in good health—now what I was calling about was my appointment with Mr. Jones tomorrow at 2:00 P.M."
  "Oh yes, Mr. Johnson, I can see from Mr. Jones' schedule that he does have an appointment with you tomorrow. I hope the weather is better tomorrow when you come in."

"Well, what I was calling about was that I'd like to postpone my appointment until about 3:00 P.M. I have a job appointment earlier in the afternoon and I doubt if I can get to your office any earlier."

"Oh what a shame, Mr. Johnson. I'm sure Mr. Jones will be disappointed. I can have Mr. Jones telephone you later this afternoon to let you know if he can see you at 3:00. Will that be satisfactory, Mr. Johnson?"

"Yes, thank you. Goodbye."

Mrs. Brown handled it in this way:

"Mr. Jones' desk, Mrs. Brown speaking."

"This is Mr. Johnson, Mrs. Brown."

"May I help you, Mr. Johnson?"

"I'd like to postpone my appointment with Mr. Jones tomorrow from 2:00 to 3:00 P.M. I have a job appointment earlier in the afternoon and I doubt if I can get to your office earlier."

"I'm not sure whether Mr. Jones has that time open on his schedule, but I can have him telephone you later this afternoon and tell you if he can see you at 3:00 P.M. Will that be satisfactory, Mr. Johnson?"

"Yes, thank you. Goodbye."

F. *When taking calls for someone else*
  1. Find out who is calling.
     You might say:
     (1) May I tell Mr. Jones who is calling, please?
     (2) Mr. Jones would like to know who is calling.
     (3) Could you tell me who is calling, please, so that I can announce your call to Mr. Jones?
     Ask participants which response they believe is most appropriate.
  2. If you are screening telephone calls, you may want to find out what the person wants.
     You might say:
     (1) Perhaps I can help you.
     (2) May I tell Mr. Jones what you're calling about, perhaps I might be able to help.

G. *Some do's and don'ts*
  1. If you are taking a message, jot down the most important words—then complete writing the message as soon as you hang up the telephone.
  2. Don't start anyone on a wild goose chase. If you are not sure who should handle the call, *don't transfer it.* Instead, offer to call the person back and then find out who has the information he wants.

3. If you get someone who has been traveling from one extension to the next, do not transfer the call again, even if you know who would have the information. That person may not be at his desk. Instead, offer to have that person telephone them back.
4. Remember to return telephone calls, respond to messages, and follow through.

There are conflicts between the recommended procedures for training paraprofessionals and the press toward a career rather than a job. It has been recommended that training for paraprofessionals be "job-related rather than general. An adequate training program can be generated only if it is attuned to a precise job description. Training must provide the nonprofessional with a portfolio of specific skills" (Pearl and Riessman 1965, p. 157). But if, in discharging her responsibilities of educational supervision, the supervisor adheres to this prescription she is, in effect, restricting the employment maneuverability of the supervisee. Such training prepares the worker for a specific job in a specific agency. The possibilities of both lateral movement to another job in another agency and vertical movement to a more advanced job in the same agency are reduced.

Another conflict that the supervisor may experience is the conflict between what have been termed "bridges" and "ladders." The special quality which the indigenous paraprofessional brings to the agency is her identification with the client community, and her special contribution is to serve as a bridge to that community. At the same time, the paraprofessional wants the opportunity of advancing along a clearly delineated career line, a ladder, to more responsible, more prestigeful, better-paying positions in the agency. This movement requires that she become more professionalized, better trained, more closely identified with the agency. Moving in this direction, experiencing these changes, reduces the indigenous paraprofessional's identification with the community. She becomes progressively, and inevitably, more middle class, less like the client group. Climbing the ladder makes her a less effective bridge. The supervisor may have to help the paraprofessional with the felt conflict between these opposing pressures.

The problem is one of professionalizing performance while

at the same time not professionalizing the performer. Riessman's solution to the dilemma is to regard identification as less
important than commitment. As long as the paraprofessional
remains committed, he can operate as an effective bridge even
though his identification may be eroded. However, if commitment rather than identification is the primary operative consideration, it diminishes the strength of the argument for employing indigenous paraprofessionals because of their uniqueness.
Sensitive, well-trained, middle-class professionals often have a
strong commitment to the needs of the client community and
thus can operate as effective bridges. The supervisor, then, has
a problem of socializing the paraprofessional to agency and professional norms without "bleeding out" his identification with
the client group, to educate without "contaminating." It has
been suggested that one way to do this is for the supervisor to
develop and communicate a conviction in the desirability of the
indigenous worker's community orientation. "If the paraprofessional perceives that the [supervisor] both recognizes and values the strengths in the client community and his own special
contributions, he is free to remain true to himself and his community. If, however, he detects through overt and subtle cues
that the [supervisor] derogates the client community, he seeks
to disassociate himself from patterns and ties which are dysfunctional to his aspirations" (Richan 1972, p. 58).

The conflict between the desirability of training paraprofessional workers and the undesirability of "remolding them in the
professional image" is resolved, for some, by formulating the
training program so as to increase the paraprofessionals' skill in
their own special style and approach. As an alternative, Hardcastle (1971) has suggested that indigenous paraprofessionals be
placed in special units and supervised in a group of their own
peers. Such compartmentalization "would shield the nonprofessional from the dysfunctional influences of the agency and reinforce the functional influences of his peers" (p. 61).

the supportive component

The nature of the tasks often assigned to paraprofessionals
increases the risk of discouragement and job dissatisfaction and

calls attention to the third component of supervision—support and maintenance of worker morale. These tasks are often the ones that call for the least skill and are most apt to be routine and repetitive. Paraprofessionals may feel that they are not doing anything of much importance. "It's just babysitting"; "it's just being a chauffeur"; "it's like being a Seeing Eye dog, leading people to where they have to get." Sometimes, admittedly, it is just that. The supervisor can often legitimately point out, however, the broader significance of what the paraprofessionals are doing. Chauffeuring can provide the kind of emotional support that the client needs in a critical situation; accompanying an anxious older client to the local Social Security office may be just the measure of human companionship that the person needs to make it through the application experience (The supervisor has the responsibility of recognizing possible supervisee dissatisfaction with the paraprofessional task assignments and giving some thought to how the more significant aspects of such tasks might be interpreted.)

Coming to the agency without the usual qualifying educational credentials, paraprofessionals are apt to feel somewhat defensive. Having been out of the labor market for some time and having no recent, prolonged experience in proving themselves in a formal work situation, they are somewhat anxious about whether or not they can measure up to agency expectations. Being affiliated with the lower-income group and having often known the agency as supplicants, the paraprofessionals may be somewhat intimidated by the professional staff. Conversely, they may have developed contempt for, or hostility toward, the professional staff.

Paraprofessionals often find themselves assigned to a job that is poorly defined, in an agency that is ambivalent about their status and that has limited experience with paraprofessionals. "When I first came to this project," said one paraprofessional worker, "I had no idea of what I was supposed to do. I sat around and shook, scared as hell of all the self-assured people on the staff" (Rigdon 1972, p. 5). Anxious about their acceptability to the rest of the staff, their position in the agency, and

the adequacy of their performance, the paraprofessional supervisees may require more supervisory time devoted to support
and maintaining morale.

Conflicts encountered in meeting organizational demands
at the expense of client needs generate feelings in paraprofessionals of being a traitor to the group. The paraprofessional may
feel a sense of marginality to both the staff of the agency and
the client group with which she was formerly affiliated. She
may begin to feel that she holds membership in both worlds but
does not fully belong in either. These are morale problem calling for supportive supervision.

Given the lack of initial confidence on the part of many
paraprofessionals, for whom the role of paid employee may be a
new experience, the supervisor has to be more careful in task
assignment. In assigning tasks to any supervisee, the supervisor
tries to maintain the delicate balance between stimulation that
encourages learning new skills and excessive requirements that
may undermine self-confidence. In the case of the paraprofessional, whose self-confidence is initially tenuous, greater care
needs to be given in maintaining this balance.

The supervisor has to reward the good performance of the
paraprofessional with frequent praise. The paraprofessional,
who has no prior training, is even more uncertain than other
supervisees about whether her performance has been satisfactory. The active effort of the supervisor in praising good work
reassures the worker and gives her necessary feedback on how
she is doing and some basis for judging her own performance.

The supervisor may be faced with dealing with the ri-
valrous dissatisfactions of paraprofessional supervisees. Complaints may be made about salary differences, difference in assignments, about better offices for professionals, better
treatment of professionals in that the latter have "secretaries
and a variety of status symbols" (Pearl and Riessman 1965,
p. 203). While paraprofessionals may rationally recognize the
basis for differences in financial, symbolic, and psychic rewards, these still foster feelings of resentment. Requests for
changes in title reflect this feeling of rivalry with professional

staff. In one agency, "aides" requested that they be called "professional assistants" or "special work assistants" and later, after having obtained some experience, requested a further change to "family service workers" (Ayers 1973).

(Paraprofessionals may have to be supported in professionalizing their relationships with some clients, out of self-protection.) Some measure of professional distancing from clients is functional. Lacking this, paraprofessionals may find themselves exploited in baby-sitting arrangements for temporarily abandoned children, lending food or money in emergencies, and feeling personally hurt by a client's rejection. Paraprofessionals may also need support and protection from their own high expectations and consequent disappointments. The trained worker has developed some sense of the limits of what is possible. Paraprofessionals may be frustrated in their attempts to deal with situations that have little leverage for change.

Paraprofessionals are made anxious by a lack of real job security. Often they are hired for an innovative project on a demonstration basis. Frequently the jobs are in recently established, tenuously funded agencies or in new units of an established agency. Institutionalized backing may not exist for either the job title or funding for the job. The paraprofessional needs support in dealing with anxiety which comes from having a precarious foothold in the agency and on the agency budget.

Given the nature of the socioeconomic background and current living arrangements that characterize a large percentage of the paraprofessional group, the supervisor can anticipate many situational problems that require support. Having lacked access to good medical services, paraprofessionals are apt to have a high rate of absenteeism because of ill health. Many are single parents and are responsible for the care of young children; this too may increase absenteeism. Living on the limited paraprofessional salary, without financial reserves, the group is financially vulnerable and frequently faced with money problems. The agency pay period of two weeks or a month, which is convenient for middle-class employees with some financial reserves, may pose a hardship for paraprofessionals. Administrative authorization of weekly pay periods may reduce the number of personal crises that supervisees bring to supervisors for help. Furthermore, an agency that hires paraprofessionals should consider making available some situational supports to the group—child-care facilities, a low-interest loan fund, pay advance procedures.

evaluation of paraprofessionals

The usual difficulty of adequately defining task-performance criteria for purposes of evaluation is even greater because our experience with paraprofessionals is limited. There is little material available in the literature to help the supervisor in evaluating the work of paraprofessionals. The tendency is to assess performance from the traditional frame of reference of the profession. The supervisor has to make a conscious effort to assess attitudes, behavior, and work performance from the paraprofessional frame of reference. Their spontaneity, informality, and tendency toward overidentification have to be assessed on their own merits rather than in terms of traditional professional standards.

The supervisor must also decide what she thinks is the principal rationale for paraprofessional employment: is it to provide more effective agency service to the client or to provide an income and rehabilitation for the paraprofessional? If the supervisor sees rehabilitation as the raison d'être of paraprofessional employment, she will be reluctant to assess the work of the paraprofessional critically. A negative evaluation might mean the loss of a badly needed job for a worker who is not otherwise employable. If client service is the principal purpose, however, then the supervisor can move freely to deal critically with inefficient, ineffective performance that is potentially damaging to clients. The supervisor can feel more comfortable about holding the paraprofessional to realistic standards of performance.

Critical, objective evaluation is made more difficult for the supervisor as a consequence of racial and class differences between supervisor and supervisee. The supervisor may be hesitant to criticize because this might be perceived as an expression of racism—and the supervisor may not be entirely certain that she is without guilt in this respect. In some agencies the unquestioning, excessive enthusiasm for the paraprofessional's contribution, an attitude which Barr (1967) characterizes as "professional beneficent colonialism," has resulted "in a tyranny of the indigenous nonprofessional" (p. 16). It becomes difficult to be objectively critical of their work. This, combined "with the frequent application of reduced standards of work and of administratiove accountability for the indigenous workers as compared to other workers," can lead to resentments to which the supervisor will have to respond.

The supervisor may hesitate to criticize because of possible repercussions. The paraprofessional can exploit her relationship to a power base in the community to intimidate her supervisor into muting criticism and making a positive evaluation. This is not generally done openly, but the supervisor may act out of fear that the paraprofessional "can turn the neighborhood against the agency." Grosser states that agency administrators "frequently felt inhibited in reassigning or dismissing indigenous paraprofessionals because of fear of community reprisals" (1969, p. 128; see also Gartner 1971, p. 12). A special report on paraprofessionals in community-action centers noted a tendency "on the part of program directors to fire virtually no one irespective of performance" (Riessman and Popper 1968, p. 7).

What Pointer and Fishman (1968) say about evaluation of paraprofessionals in on-the-job-training evaluation is equally applicable to performance evaluation by the social work supervisor.

Many On Job Training supervisors will be tempted to tell the trainee he did well when he actually did not. This is usually done either to avoid a confrontation with potential discomfort for both the trainee and the supervisor, or because the supervisor really does not expect very much from the trainee and is willing to accept poor work from "these poor people." In such situations the trainee is not fooled! He knows how well he has done, and he is likely to reach these conclusions: that he is immune to criticism because his supervisor either pities him or is afraid of him, or that the training program is phony and everyone is just putting in time and drawing a salary. (p. 18)

The clients, the workers, the agency, and the community pay a price for a supervisor's failure to evaluate performance objectively and critically. It does not really matter whether this failure results from ignorance of valid standards, charity to the paraprofessional, intimidation, or low expectations. Readiness and willingness to accept low-level performance for any reason communicates minimal-level expectations which encourage minimal-level performance.

Group Supervision of Paraprofessionals

(Group supervision is regarded as a particularly advantageous and appropriate approach for paraprofessional workers.) It is often said that "poverty culture is a peer culture" and that the peer group is an important element in lower-class life. As a new worker, and feeling isolated, the paraprofessional may need the group to strengthen her sense of identity and obtain support of peers. The minority-group paraprofessional may feel uncomfortable in the more intimate one-to-one situation with a white supervisor and may need the comfort of the presence of ethnic allies. "The peer group can be invaluable in maintaining and supporting the aides' specific identity, in helping the aides continue to feel pride in their own special and separate abilities so that they are not reduced to finding status by being 'junior' social workers" (Cudabeck 1970, p. 219).

Reinforced by the presence of peers in the group, the paraprofessional can more adequately deal with problems of status and authority vis-à-vis the white supervisor. Since power differences are even greater here than in other supervisor-supervisee combinations and since they are often exacerbated by racial and class differences, the paraprofessionals' need for group support to equalize power is also greater.

Techniques that are thought to be most appropriate for paraprofessional education, such as peer learning, role playing, and job simulation, all require the group context and hence group supervision.

Paraprofessionals are initially reluctant to speak up in

groups and need considerable encouragement. Knowing that feelings can be manipulated, they are reluctant to talk of them. Acting cool or "gritting," maintaining silence and appearing unaffected, are accepted peer reactions that work against effective group interaction.

Group supervisory conferences, while perhaps less threatening to paraprofessionals than the individual tutorial conference, present their own hazards. A free-wheeling discussion of a problem often involves the presentation of contradictory ideas and viewpoints. The group member has the difficult task of organizing in her own mind some coherent conclusions from the contradictory presentations. This is a more difficult task for the paraprofessional, who has had less experience with this procedure than more formally educated supervisees, many of whom have sat through innumerable class discussions. In using group supervision as an educational device with paraprofessionals, the supervisor needs to make certain that the meeting ends with some clear, explicit recapitulation of the principal teaching points derived from the discussion.

Summary

There has been a great increase in the employment of paraprofessionals in social agencies recently as a result of a variety of factors—the civil rights movement and the pressure to hire minority group workers; expanding the job opportunities for welfare recipients in response to public concern with increasing welfare costs; problems encountered by middle-class, white social workers in making effective contact with lower-class nonwhite clients; the criticism of educational credentials as the ticket to job openings; the growing demands for local control of, and participation in, the activities of social agencies; and chronic agency staff shortages.

Paraprofessionals, who work alongside professionals, are defined as workers with limited education who are assigned tasks requiring entry-level skill and competence. Indigenous paraprofessionals come from the same community as the client group and share their culture and life experience.

Supervision of paraprofessionals presents some special problems and requires adaption of traditional supervisory approaches. Funds and time have to be made available for additional training of both supervisors and supervisees, tasks have to be clearly defined, and some consideration needs to be given to career advancement opportunities. The supervisor needs to have respect for what she can teach paraprofessionals and confidence in their ability to learn. Educational supervision requires a didactic, repetitive approach with an emphasis on concrete illustrations and liberal use of role playing. Supportive supervision is needed in response to the marginal position of the paraprofessionals in the agency and special life stresses encountered by them.

Supervisors are more than usually threatened in evaluating paraprofessionals because of lack of experience with this group and because of political reasons. Group supervision is particularly appropriate for this group of supervisees.

chapter eight

Problems and Innovations

At different points in the earlier chapters, I have alluded to persistent problems that confront supervisors in social work. Some relate to inadequacies in current procedures for supervision; some are more basic and relate to the desirability of, and the justification for, supervision per se. The first series of problems is primarily technological in nature; the second series deals with professional policy issues. The intent in this chapter is to pull together and make explicit the different sets of problems and to review the innovative methods and procedures that have been proposed to deal with them.

Observation of Performance

The supervisor faces a technological problem related to access to the supervisee's performance. If the supervisor is to be administratively accountable for the worker's performance and if she is to help the worker learn to perform his work more effectively, the supervisor needs to have clear knowledge of what the worker is doing. However, the supervisor most often does not have access to direct observation of the worker's performance. This is particularly true in casework. The caseworker-client contact is a private performance, deliberately screened from public viewing. Concealment of what takes place in the physically isolated encounter is reinforced and justified by dictates of "good" practice and professional ethics. Protecting the

privacy of the encounter guarantees the client his right to confidentiality and guards against the disturbances to the worker-
client relationship which, it is thought, would result from intrusion of an observer. What Freud said of analysis is applied to
the social work interview: "The dialogue which constitutes the
analysis will permit of no audience; the process cannot be demonstrated."

Although most of the interview is private, some aspects
may be open to supervisory observation if the performance
takes place on agency grounds: meeting the client in the waiting room, accompanying her to the door on termination. The
worker who contacts a client in the field is shielded from even
this limited opportunity for supervisory observation.

The group worker's performance is more open to observation. Miller (1960) points out that "what goes on between the
worker and the group is directly visible to many people"—to
group members, to other workers, and to supervisors (p. 72).
However, "observations of a worker's activity take place . . . on
an informal not a deliberately planned basis" (p. 75).

While the community worker's activities also seem to be
open to observation, this openness is more apparent than real.
As Brager and Specht (1973) note,

Community organization practice is at once more visible and more
private than casework. Although it takes place in the open forums of
the community, where higher authorities may be present, this is
usually only on ceremonial occasions. Surveillance of the workers' *informal* activities is another matter. The real business of community
workers is less likely to occur within the physical domain of higher
ranking participants than the activities of other workers. Thus the
community worker has ample opportunity, if he wishes, to withhold
or distort information. (p. 240)

Many of the community organizer's activities are highly informal and unstructured. "Whereas casework interviews can be
scheduled and group workers conduct meetings on some scheduled basis, the activities of community workers defy regulation
and schedule. Much time is absorbed with informal telephone

conversations, attending meetings in which they may have no formal role, talking to other professionals and other difficult-to-specify activities" (Brager and Specht 1973, p. 242).

By far the most common source of information used by supervisors in learning about a worker's performance is the written case-record material (supplemented by a verbal report) prepared and presented by the supervisee (Kadushin 1974). Thus, in most instances, the supervisor "observes" the work of the supervisee at second hand, mediated through the supervisee's perception and recording of it.

The traditional, and current, heavy dependence on record material and verbal reports for information regarding workers' performance necessitates some evaluation of these sources. Studies by social workers (Armstrong, Huffman, and Spain 1959; Wilkie 1963) as well as other professionals (Covner 1943; Froehlich 1958; Muslin et al. 1967) indicate that case records present a selective and often distorted view of worker performance. Comparison of process recordings with tape recordings of the same contacts indicated that workers failed to hear and remember significant, recurrent patterns of interaction. Workers do not perceive and report important failings in their approach to the client. This omission is not necessarily intentional falsification of the record in order to make the worker look good, although that does happen. It is, rather, the result of selective perception in the service of the ego's attempt to maintain self-esteem. Forty years ago Elon Moore (1934) wrote an article entitled "How Accurate Are Case Records?" The question, which he answered negatively, is still pertinent today. Supervision based on the written record supplemented by verbal report is supervision based on "retrospective reconstructions which are subject to serious distortions" on the part of the supervisee (Ward 1962, p. 1128).

This difficulty regarding recording is sometimes viewed not as a hindrance but rather as an aid in educational supervision. The "process record may distort the actual events that transpire between therapist and patient but it will more faithfully record the way the therapist sees his experience and wishes to communicate it to the supervisor for the purpose of making particular use of supervision" (Ekstein and Wallerstein 1972, p. 276). The worker then reveals himself to the perceptive supervisor through the nature of his selective perception in the recording. "The assumption is that the supervisor's insight and experience, especially when augmented by discussion with the worker, enable him to fill in the missing pieces" not available in the written record (Leader 1968, p. 288). While Hallowitz (1962) concedes that "all case records inevitably contain some distortions and fail to capture important subtleties in the feelings of the client and the worker," he goes on to say that "it is mainly in the supervisory conferences that these distortions are clarified and subtleties of feelings come to light." The skill of the supervisor in correcting distortion "is analogous to that employed by the worker in the clinical interview" (p. 291). The very omissions and distortions become the content for supervisory teaching and the source of supervisee learning about self. Distorted recording is a form of communication. The supervisor is required, in this view, to be perceptive enough to be aware of the nature of the deficiencies in the recording and to discuss these with the supervisee. The supervisor must also accurately extrapolate from the behavior of the supervisee in the supervisory conference to his likely behavior in the interview with the client. These are very difficult tasks, and it is questionable how often they are successfully accomplished. The one empirical test of this viewpoint indicates that the supervisor usually is not successful in post hoc reconstruction of what actually took place between worker and client (Muslin et al. 1967).

Even if this were a valid procedure for educational supervision, it would be a hazard for evaluation. Valid evaluation requires that we know what the worker actually did, not what he thinks he did or what he says he did. If we apply what we know about human behavior to the supervisee reporting on his own performance, we recognize the inadequacies of such a procedure as a basis for either good teaching or valid evaluation. As a consequence of anxiety, self-defense, inattention, and ignorance of what he should look for, the worker is not aware of much that takes place in the encounter in which he is an active participant; some of what he is aware of he may fail to recall; if he is aware of it and does recall it, he may not report it. The comment by two supervisors of child-psychotherapy trainees is applicable to social workers:

> In supervision of child psychotherapists over the year the authors have become impressed with . . . the unexpected degree to which direct observation of the trainee's psychotherapeutic hours reveals important and often flagrant errors in the trainee's functioning—errors which are somehow missed during supervision which is not supplemented by direct observation. This seems to be the case despite the trainee's attempt to be as honest as possible in talking with his supervisors, his use of the most detailed and complete process notes or his attempt to associate freely about the case without looking at his notes. (Ables and Aug 1972, p. 340)

Direct Observation

In response to these difficulties, various innovations have been proposed to give the supervisor more direct access to the worker's performance. The simplest procedure is direct observation of the interview, either by unobtrusively sitting in on the interview or through a one-way screen. The client's permission is needed, of course, for this and any other procedure that opens the client-worker contact to outside observation.

Kadushin (1956a,b, 1957) tested the feasibility of sitting in on an interview in both a family-service agency and a public-assistance agency. Very few clients objected to the introduction of an observer. Postinterview discussion with both the worker and the client, supplemented by some objective measures of interview contamination attributable to observation, indicated that an unobtrusive observer had little effect on the interview.

Schuster and his colleagues utilized this procedure in the supervision of psychiatric residents. "We decided on a simple direct approach to the matter. We decided to have the supervisor sit with each new patient and the resident, as a third party, relatively inactive and inconspicuous but present. . . . In very few instances did our presence seem to interfere significantly with either the resident or the patient" (Schuster, Sandt, and Thaler 1972, p. 155). Duncan (1963), Kohn (1971), and Leader (1968) have also reported on the successful use of direct observation of worker performance in supervision and training.

The supervisor-observer, sitting in on an interview, can easily move to a new role, that of co-worker or co-therapist (Van Atta 1969a). While observing, the supervisor can participate and thereby demonstrate the skills she is trying to teach. Those reporting on the use of the co-therapy procedure in supervision cite the dangers of too direct imitation of the supervisor by the worker and the fact that the worker may feel unable to participate freely and equally in the interview (Rosen and Bartemeier 1967).

Ryan (1964), who has used this procedure in social work supervision, notes that while supervisees are cautious at first, playing "the part of a passive observer during most of the first interview," by the third interview they are "comfortable enough to become more active and from then on the process is well under way" (p. 473).

When the supervisor moves from passive observation of the worker's performance to active participation as a co-worker, conflicting roles may present a problem. The supervisor is simultaneously a co-worker and a teacher-observer-supervisor. Problems of control of the proceedings, initiative in making interventions, and clear acceptance of shared responsibility need to be worked out. In one report of supervisor-supervisee co-therapy responsibility for a group, the ending of the sessions illustrated this conflict. The end of the group meetings was "almost always initiated by the senior co-therapist nodding to the [psychiatric] resident co-therapist who then follows the senior therapist's initiative in standing up and leaving the room" (Anderson, Pine, and Mee-lee 1972, p. 193).

Co-therapy not only provides the supervisee with an opportunity for direct observation of the work of a skilled practitioner, but also a stimulating basis for joint discussions. "The supervisory conference takes on new meaning as the [supervisor] evaluates for the [supervisee's] benefit not only the [super-visee's] performance, but also his own" (Ryan 1964, p. 473). The co-therapy experience is most productive if prepared for carefully and if followed, as soon as possible, by a joint discussion of the experience.

A modification of the co-therapy arrangement is alternate therapy. Supervisor and supervisee share the responsibility for service. For one session the supervisee meets with the individual client or group while the supervisor acts as an observer through a one-way mirror; the following session the responsibilities are reversed (Jarvis and Esty 1968). Although this pattern risks discontinuity in the worker-client relationship, client confusion and resentment, rivalry between supervisor and supervisee in the relationship with clients, and the clients' manipulation of one worker against the other, these difficulties did not seem to develop to any serious extent when the procedure was used.

The one-way-vision screen permits observation without the risk, or necessity, of participation and minimizes the observer intrusion on the interview or group session (Fleischmann 1955). The supervisor can see and hear the interview without himself being seen or heard. Peer-group observation of the interview or group session is also possible. One-way viewing requires a special room, and it has its own hazards. Gruenberg, Liston, and Wayne (1969) note that "the physical setting of the one-way mirror arrangement has been less than conducive to continuous alertness in the supervisor. The darkened room is more often conducive to languor than attentiveness" (p. 96).

Observation Via Tapes

Dependence on retrospective written and verbal reports of the worker-client interaction means that the experience as it actually occurred is lost forever. Similarly, direct interview observation and observation through a one-way screen leave no record for retrieval, study, and discussion. To meet this deficiency some attempts have been made to obtain movie recordings of interviews. The expense, technical difficulties, and delay in making the recording available have inhibited such efforts. Far more feasible, and hence more frequently used, are audio-tape records of interviews. They allow retrieval of the vocal-verbal components of interaction even if visual, nonverbal aspects are missing. The development of videotape has made possible the retrieval of both visual and aural cues.

As quality, convenience, ease of operation, and stability of performance of the available equipment increase, and as bulk and expense (beyond initial outlay) decrease, the use of such procedures is becoming widespread in human service professions generally, despite its current limited use in social work. The importance of such technical aids for supervision is that their use enables us to "reenact the unobservable."

Video taping is done through an unobtrusive port from an adjoining control room containing the equipment. The lens "sees" through a one-way mirror. The simplest procedure is to turn the equipment on at the beginning of the interaction and off at the end. However, in agencies with more elaborate equipment, additional cameras are used, and wide-angle shots, zoom closeups, superimpositions, and split-screen images are edited by personnel in the control room to determine what actually goes on the final tape. One of the disadvantages in the use of these procedures for supervision is that the supervisor has to develop some technical competence—the minimum requirement being a knowledge of how to turn the equipment on and off. Group meetings and conferences require special wide-angle cameras and omnidirectional or multiple microphones.

The client is informed in advance of the taping, and a signed release is obtained. The client also is given the option of specifying that the tape be erased after use in supervision. Video taping through camera ports in the wall rather than inside the interview or conference room is designed primarily to reduce distraction, not to hide the fact of taping from the clients.

Video and audio taping provide considerable advantages for teaching and evaluation besides the more complete, reliable, and vivid information regarding the worker's performance.

The availability of recordings "retrieves" the client for the supervisory conference. The supervisor who knows the client
only from the supervisee's written record and verbal reports
may have difficulty in holding the client as the focus of attention of the conference. The client is a disembodied, dehuman-
ized abstraction. Audio or video tape makes the client's presence immediate and vivid.

Audio and video tapes allow the supervisor to discuss the
client in a way which makes more of what he says acceptable to
the supervisee. To be told is not as effective as to be shown. But
to see for ourselves, which tapes make possible, is perhaps the
most insightful method of learning (Hirsh and Freed 1970,
p. 46). The supervisee, through tape replay, faces himself in his
performance rather than the supervisor's definition of him. One
rather cocksure resident denied feeling much anxiety in the interview situation. On a replay of his videotape, however, he saw
himself light cigarettes and eagerly puff away at them during
several tense moments during the hour. In the discussion of his
behavior, he was able to recall the tension and consider the possibilities of its origin (Hirsh and Freed 1970, p. 45).

The disjunction between a supervisee's mental image of his
behavior and the actuality becomes undeniably clear on tape
replay. One student said, "You get an idea of what you really
look like and project to the [client] but often this is not what
you intended" (Suess 1970, p. 275). The experience of self-
discovery which follows video playback has been aptly described as "self-awakedness." One worker said, "I discovered
by watching the tape that I was too halting in my speech and
that there was not enough continuity in what I was saying.
Without video tape it might have taken months for a [super-
visor] to convince me of this" (Benschoter, Eaton, and Smith
1965, p. 1160).

Audio-visual playback permits considerable self-learning. It
thus encourages the development of self-supervision and independence from supervision. The supervisee has the "opportunity of distinguishing between the model he has of his own
behavior and the reality of his behavior" (Gruenberg, Liston,

and Wayne 1969, p. 49). He has a chance for a second look at what he did, an opportunity to "integrate multi-level messages" he might have missed in the heat of the interaction. Playback provides a less pressured, more neutral opportunity to detect missed interventions or formulate what might have been more appropriate ones. As a supervisor said in pointing to the advantages for self-instruction in video tape, "Sometimes there is no need to point out a mistake. The tape speaks for itself" (Benschoter, Eaton, and Smith 1965, p. 1160).

As a participant-observer in the interview, group meeting, or conference, the supervisee can devote only part of his time and energy to self-observation and introspective self-analysis. He must devote most of his time and energy to focusing on client needs and client reactions. Furthermore, much of his behavior is beyond self-observation. He cannot see himself smile, grimace, arch his eyebrows, or frown. Retrieving the interaction on tape, the supervisee can give his undivided attention to the role of self-observer. Video tape comes close to implementing Robert Burns' wish,

O would the gift the Gods would gee us
To see ourselves as others see us.

The supervisee can play the tape when he is more relaxed and less emotionally involved, and can therefore examine his behavior somewhat more objectively. At the same time, repeating his contact with the full imagery of the event as it took place tends to evoke some of the same feelings that he felt then. (The tape allows the supervisee-observer to relive the experience with some of the associated affect.)

Viewing themselves on video tape or listening to themselves on audio tape may be ego supportive for supervisees. For many, their self-image is reinforced positively by what they see and hear. Supervisees said, in response to the playback experience, "I look better, sound better than I thought" ; "I did better than I realized." Adjectives used to describe themselves, elicited after playback, were similar to, and as positive, as those elicited before playback (Walz and Johnston 1963, p. 233). The direction of the limited change that had taken place was toward a more objective view of their performance. It was a humbling rather than a humiliating experience. Without supervisory intervention, but as a consequence of the playback alone, supervisees' perception of their work tended to become more congruent with the supervisor's perceptions (Walz and Johnston 1963, p. 235). Seeing oneself engaged in behaving competently, intervening in ways that are helpful, tends to reinforce such behavior. Replay not only helps correct errors, it helps to reinforce learning.

The nature of tape technology permits considerable flexibility in how it might be used in supervision. The opportunity for repeated replaying of the interactional event permits supervisor and supervisee to focus exclusively on a single aspect each time. At one time they can focus on the client; another time they can focus on the worker. The same one or two minutes of interaction can be played repeatedly to focus on worker-client interchange. Shutting off the sound on video tape permits exclusive concentration on nonverbal behavior; shutting off the visual image permits exclusive attention to verbal content.

Tapes do not diminish the desirability of supervision even though they do provide the supervisee with a rich opportunity for critical, retrospective self-examination of his work. Seeing and hearing this material in the presence of a supervisor who asks the right provocative questions and calls attention to what otherwise might be missed, provides the supervisee with greater opportunities for learning. The procedure has been institutionalized in counselor training by Norman Kagan and his associates (Kagan, Krathwohl, and Miller 1963) in what they term Interpersonal Process Recall (I.P.R.). The supervisee watches a playback of his video-taped interview in the presence of a trained counselor. The counselor encourages the supervisee, through sensitive questioning, to describe the feelings he experienced during the interview, to translate body movements, to reconstruct the thinking that led him to do and say the particular things he did and said at specific points in the interview.

Self-defensive activity by the supervisee is just as probable

in playback observation as during the interview itself. The use
of tapes is optimally productive only when there is a supervisor
available who can gently, but insistently, call attention to what
the supervisee would rather not hear or see. Mark Twain once
said that "you can't depend on your eyes when your imagination is out of focus." The supervisor, watching or listening to
the tape alongside the supervisee, helps keep imagination in
focus.

Video tapes are employed in group supervision as a stimulus for discussion. Chodoff (1972) played tapes of interviews in
group supervisory meetings, stopping the tape at various points
in an interview to elicit comments from supervisees as to how
they would have handled the situation at that point if they were
the interviewer and to speculate on what would happen next in
the interview.

Supervisor evaluation feedback is likely to have greater effect under conditions of high visibility of worker performance.
Any assessment is likely to be easily dismissed by the worker if
she has little confidence in the supervisor's evaluation because
of limited opportunity to observe performance. Taped material
can be used in evaluation to demonstrate, or validate, patterns
of changing performance over a period of time. An interview, or
group session, taped at one point in time can be compared with
a similar interview or group session taped several months or a
year later.

Tapes can also be used, as records are currently, to induct
new staff. A library of audio and video tapes can be developed
which give the new worker a clear and vivid idea of the work
the agency does.

There are some disadvantages, however, in the use of audio
and video tapes. Conscious of the fact that their entire performance is being recorded, with no possibility of change or revi-
sion, the supervisees may be somewhat more guarded and less
spontaneous in their behavior. They may tend to take more
seriously La Rochefoucauld's maxim, "It is better to remain
silent and be thought a fool, than to speak and remove all
doubt." The worker is more likely than the client to feel anx-

ious, "since the therapist can feel himself being examined while the [client] sees himself as being helped" (Kornfeld and Kolb 1964, p. 457). For most supervisees, the gains from taping their performance appear to offset the risks. Itzin (1960) found that supervisees who taped their interviews for supervision were very much in favor of the procedure. They felt it introduced a desirable objectivity into supervision and helped them overcome evasions, distortions, and other defenses manifested in written reports of their work. One supervisee said, "I feel certain that the supervisor was able to pin down my problems quite early—and understood me much better than he could have had I been able to hide behind process recording" (p. 198). Another commented, "It gave [the supervisor] a much more accurate account of what went on during the interview. When reporting happenings we tend to flavor them with our own thoughts, feelings and needs. I fail to see how it could be otherwise. He knew what we were doing rather than what we said we were doing" (p. 198). One student said, "I can read a thousand books on theory but when I actually saw what was happening it was a great awakening" (Ryan 1969, p. 128).

One of the principal advantages of the use of tapes for supervision is, at the same time, one of its principal disadvantages. Audio and video tapes are complete and indiscriminate. The supervisor faces an embarrassment of riches and may be overwhelmed by the detail available. The problem is clearly exemplified by a detailed analysis of the first five minutes of a tape-recorded psychotherapeutic interview, which yielded a book of over 350 pages exclusively devoted to an analysis of what took place during this limited period (Pittenger, Hockett, and Danehy 1960). A video tape would, of course, have made available even more material; a similarly detailed analysis of the first five minutes of a video-taped interview would have resulted in a much larger book. Perhaps because enough is enough and beyond the point of satiation further additions have little significant incremental effect, some of the studies comparing audio-tape supervision with video-tape supervision show audio tape, with more limited cues available, to be equally effective (English and Jelenevsky 1971). It is possible to avoid the danger of being overwhelmed, however, by selecting limited sections for viewing, judiciously sampling the interaction, and taking an "audio-visual biopsy."

In response to the fact that listening to supervisee tapes is both time-consuming and possibly overwhelming, Hewer (1974) has devised a recording form as a supervisor aid. The form, adaptable for social work, provides the supervisor with a procedure for organizing his response in listening to tapes. The disadvantage of increased demand on supervisory time in "observing" through one or another of these devices is compensated for by the savings in time otherwise spent in reading records or listening to a lengthy rehashing of the worker-client contact.

Taping procedures present a possibly hazardous challenge to the supervisor. If the supervisor can observe the supervisee's performance through use of these procedures, the supervisee can likewise have access to the supervisor's performance. There is an implied invitation to have the supervisor conduct an interview or lead a group so that the supervisee can observe how it should be done. The supervisee who is dependent solely on hearing the supervisor talk about social work has to extrapolate from the supervisor's behavior in the conference how he might actually behave with clients. The role model available to the supervisee is large imaginary. Direct observation of the supervisor in action would make available a more vivid, authentic, and realistic role model for emulation.

Supervisors as well as supervisees can profit from taping and reviewing their work. There is no reported use of such procedures in social work, but supervisors in education have tape recorded their conferences for self-study. Goldhammer (1969) says:

Procedurally the most useful device we have found for self-supervision is to tape record supervision conferences and, along with whatever notes are taken in the process, to use such tapes as an object of analysis. (p. 274) . . . Although it is possible to perform a post mortem without having tape recorded the supervision, it is generally clear that to do so is more difficult, less effecient and less trustworthy than with the analysis of tapes. (p. 278)

There is a persistent question of the distortion of the worker-client interaction resulting from the use of all observational procedures, and the threat to confidentiality. We inevitably face such risks. The requirement that the interview be written up for supervisory discussion breaches confidentiality and is an intrusion on the interview itself. The client's confidences are shared with the supervisor (and sometimes other staff) without his full knowledge and permission. Note-taking to aid recall tends to have an intrusive effect. For the supervisee the interview room is always inhabited by the image of the supervisor. Often the supervisee says or does something in response to what the supervisor might say or feel about it rather than in response to the needs of the client. What is done is done for the benefit of the supervisor to whom the event will be reported. Consequently, even the most benign, least contaminating procedure has intrusive effects.

Reports by psychologists, psychiatrists, and social workers who have used audio and video tape in recording individual or group interviews are almost unanimous in testifying that no serious distortions of interaction had taken place. With considerable consistency, professionals state that very few clients object to the use of these devices; that whatever inhibiting effects these devices have on client communication are transient; that clients are less disturbed than the workers, who are anxious about exposing their performance so openly to the evaluation of others; and that workers take longer to adapt comfortably to this situation than do clients.

The subjective reports of those who have used audio or video tape for service, research, and supervision are consistently supported by systematic research on the effects of such procedures. Some years ago Kogan (1950) found that the use of an audio tape recorder had no significant intrusive effect on social casework interviews. Subsequent studies (Harper and

Hudson 1952; Lamb and Mahl 1956; Poling 1968; Roberts and Renzaglia 1965) confirm this conclusion.

That is not to say that such procedures have no effects. Any change makes for some change. The important question is whether the effects are significant, whether the intrusive consequences are sufficiently deleterious to offset the clear advantages in the use of tapes. The answer clearly seems to be that there are no serious deleterious effects.

The use of tapes cannot be careless or indiscriminate. There are some clients for whom the effects are greater than for others (Gelso 1972; Gelso and Tanney 1972; Van Atta 1969b), and particularly with paranoid clients these procedures would be contraindicated. Niland and co-workers (1971) have observed some of the inhibitory consequences of the use of tape recordings; they emphasize the need for sensitivity to the supervisee's "index of readiness" to utilize audio and video recording.

Supervision During the Interview

Even if the supervisor can observe the work of the supervisee more fully and directly, she is still denied the possibility of teaching at the moment when such intervention is likely to be most effective. Whether she sits in on the interview, observers through a one-way mirror, or listens to and sees the work of the supervisee on audio and video tape, her discussion of the worker's performance is retrospective. It comes after the interview, at a point in time removed from the most intense affective involvement of the worker in the problem situation, when he might be most amenable to teaching. The advantages of immediacy and heightened receptivity to suggestion while under stress are lost. Consequently there have been a number of attempts to use modern technology to permit the supervisor to supervise while the worker is actually engaged in an interview.

A miniaturized transmitter used by the supervisor and a receiving apparatus worn as a small, unobtrusive, lightweight, behind-the-ear hearing aid, allow the supervisor to com-

municate with the supervisee during the course of the interview or group meeting. Watching and listening behind a one-
way mirror or through a video camera pickup, the supervisor
can make suggestions which only the supervisee can hear. The
communication is in the nature of a space-limited broadcast,
and there are no wires impeding the movements of the supervisee.

Korner and Brown (1952) first reported the use of such a
procedure over twenty years ago, calling it "the mechanical
third ear." Ward (1960, 1962) and Boylston and Tuma (1972)
have reported on the use of this device in psychiatric training in
medical schools; Montalvo (1973) detailed use of a similar procedure in a child guidance clinic.

By 1975, devices for such explicit purposes in supervision
were being sold commercially and were electronically very sophisticated. One company that sells a variety of such instruments for "direct use in therapy and training" in psychiatry,
psychology, social work, and counseling and guidance, adver-
tises it as a "Bug-in-the-Ear—a private prompting device, an
electronic aid in training." "The supervisor can point out errors
in psychotherapeutic technique at the moment they are being
committed and redirect the course of therapy into more productive channels. The trainee can immediately see the appropriateness of the supervisor's guidance and is not left to speculate
about what really would have happened if he had done things
differently" (Farrall Instrument Company n.d.). Appealing to
the behaviorally oriented supervisor, the brochure claims that
the "Bug-in-the-Ear is a most excellent reinforcer. Worn unobtrusively by the individual whose behavior is to be modified,
verbal reinforcements can be administered instantaneously
whenever an appropriate behavior arises. Thus the reinforcement comes immediately following the desired behavior and
therefore can be expected to be maximally effective."

For a beginning worker, such a device may help lower "his
initial encounter anxiety, thus allowing him more freedom to
focus on the patient's anxieties. The fact that a supervisor is immediately available, provides significant support so that the

therapist is able to be more relaxed, spontaneous and communicative" (Boylston and Tuma 1972, p. 93).

The supervisor can call attention to nonverbal communication which is often missed, to the latent meaning of communication to which the worker fails to respond, to significant areas for exploration that have been ignored. As Montalvo (1973) notes, "This arrangement assumes that you do not have to wait until the damage is done to attempt to repair events" (p. 345). Becoming aware of these considerations on the spot promotes immediate learning and helps to offer the client more effective service. Boylston and Tuma (1972) illustrate the use of the device. A nine-year-old was very late for his interview, and the therapist was annoyed and upset. When the boy came in,

> he was obviously anxious. He looked at the therapist and stated that the therapist looked different—his hair was "all messed up." Misunderstanding the communication, the therapist commented on his hair. When it was pointed out to the therapist (via the bug) that the boy recognized his more curt voice, the therapist was able to comment on the boy's fear that perhaps the therapist was angry at him for being late. The interpretation of the boy's fears of the therapist's anger led to the patient's being able to relax and promoted further psychotherapeutic intervention. (p. 94)

Clients rarely ask about the hearing aid, "maybe because the earpiece has achieved the status of eyeglasses, which are rarely looked upon with suspicion" (Korner and Brown 1952, p. 83). If a client asks, however, he is told frankly about the use of the device. There is nothing in the reports which suggests that use of the hearing aid has a deleterious effect as far as the client is concerned.

Korner and Brown (1952) report that students felt that "the third-ear experience was worthwhile—were appreciative of the help received through immediate supervision and agreed it was an excellent learning experience" (p. 84). Ward (1962) comments that "to our surprise we found this electronic device to be remarkably ego-syntonic. . . . During the past two years we have systematically surveyed student reaction to direct electronic preceptering and find that about 80 percent of the students react favorably to it" (p. 1129).

Certain dangers associated with the use of the device are clearly recognized. These include the possibility of confusing and disconcerting the worker by too frequent interventions, the possibility of addictive dependence on outside help, the possibility of interference with the worker's autonomy and his opportunity for developing his own individual style. To meet these disadvantages, the approach suggested by those who have used the device is for the supervisor to "broadcast" only during silences or when the worker is making notes; to limit such interventions to clearly important points in the interaction, when the worker is seriously in error or in difficulty; and to make suggestions that are phrased in general terms, "leaving the actual dialogue and action pattern" to the students. "Most trainees point to the fact that the real value for them lies in interpretations of general themes in the psychotherapy process rather than in specific interpretive remarks" (Boylston and Tuma 1972, p. 95).

Observing Worker Performance—a Recapitulation

Case-record material supplemented by the supervisee's verbal report has served a long and useful purpose in social work supervision despite its deficiencies. There is nothing to suggest that it should be discarded. There is much to indicate that it does require selective supplementation through more frequent use of the other procedures discussed in this chapter. Despite their availability and clear utility in meeting some of the problems of supervision, social workers, by and large, have made very limited use of such procedures. In contrast, a study of clinical-psychology training conducted some 20 years ago reported that "use of some form of observing or recording devices in the supervision of interns seems to be a fairly standard procedure" (American Psychological Association 1954, p. 762). A recent questionnaire study indicated that 60 percent of the clinical-psychology internship programs responding used television as part of the training (Zimny et al. 1972). There is no material available on the use of video tapes in the supervision of psychologists in agency practice.

Admittedly, the use of video tape does require large initial expense for an agency, consultation in the selection of equipment from the bewildering array available, and some technical knowledge in the use of the equipment. These considerations may act as deterrents. However, audio tape equipment of high quality requires little expense, minimal knowledge for use, is light and unobtrusive, and its use is familiar to most clients. Observation through one-way mirrors and through sitting in on an occasional interview requires even less imposition. There seems little justification for the neglect of these various methods for direct supervisory access to worker performance.

The Problem of Interminable Supervision

The innovative procedures I have been discussing are all intended to provide the supervisor with more open, more complete access to the worker's performance. Another series of innovations has been proposed in response to the serious controversy regarding the continued need for supervision of professionally competent workers. In 1950 the Census Bureau questioned the advisability of listing social work as a profession, "since its members apparently never arrived at a place where they were responsible and accountable for their own acts" (Stevens and Hutchinson 1956, p. 51). Kennedy and Keitner (1970) note that "there is no other profession where self-determination applies to the client and not to the worker" (p. 51).

The literature reverberates with charges that supervision "perpetuates dependency," "inhibits self-development," "violates worker's right to autonomy," and "detracts from professional status." Reynolds, in 1936, complained of supervision as cultivating "perpetual childhood" in workers: "Much of the time, one must admit, supervision is a necessary evil and it becomes more evil as it becomes less necessary" (p. 103). Judd, Kohn, and Shulman (1962) write that, through supervision,

"workers are caught up in a stage of interminable dependency,
. . . that the close, personalized relationship in individual supervision, characteristic of social work, contributes to infantilizing
the worker" (p. 96).

Over 35 years ago, social workers were arguing that "as
soon as the worker has passed his probationary period, his internship, and is ready to assume full responsibility, he needs to
be made independent in all matters of case work procedure and
held fully accountable for the results he obtains in these cases"
(C.D. 1938, p. 15). By the late 1960s the concern with the harmful personal consequences of prolonged supervision was reinforced by other, quite different considerations. The civil rights
movement, women's liberation, gay activism, the student revolt,
and the Zeitgeist of the counter-culture both reflect and support
a general orientation that views encroachment on personal free-
doms as progressively more suspect and unacceptable. Supervision on the job—any job—has come under examination as part
of this general change in ideological climate. The greater concern with "job conditions" in recent union contract negotiations
includes a reevaluation of the justifications for supervisory controls.

Mandell (1973) notes that the "equality revolution," which
tends toward a reduction in social distance between all professionals and clients, reinforces the already strong press toward
an equalization of the supervisor-supervisee relationship. It had
always been inappropriate for a person aspiring to full professional status to have his autonomy limited by subordination to a
supervisor. Now it is not only professionally inappropriate but
also violates the tenets of equalitarian participatory democracy.

In addition to these general considerations, the 1960s wit-
nessed some changes in social work that fed into the controversy. During this period, rapidly expanding enrollments in
the rapidly rising number of graduate programs in social work
resulted in the availability of an increasingly large number of
professionally trained social workers. As a consequence, the
concern with the professional status of social work has intensified. Since prolonged supervision is supposedly antithetical to

achievement of full recognition of social work as a profession, status considerations amplified the demand for change. At the same time, a diametrically contradictory trend resulted in the same demand. Developing opposition to the professionalization of social work argued for a deemphasis of supervision since the supervisor had nothing much of value to teach in any case (Specht 1972).

The discussion regarding autonomy and freedom from supervision, previously debated with reference to the M.S.W. worker, has received recent additional impetus with the legitimation of the Bachelor in Social Work as the first professional degree. Some standard-setting documents indicate that the practice of such professionals should be "under supervision" or "using social work supervision" or with supervision "readily and consistently available." The need for supervision of such workers is, however, clearly rejected by others who regard this as an infringement on the autonomy of the worker in his self-directing, self-responsible practice and a derogation of his competence.

Most of the assertions with regard to "interminable" supervision are perhaps just that—assertions based on limited evidence. Although there are early complaints about "interminable" supervision, real concern does not appear to have developed until the early 1950s, when reports by Babcock (1951) and Schour (1951) indicated that some social workers were personally troubled about prolonged supervision. Babcock, a psychiatrist, treated some 60 social workers, some of whom complained of dissatisfaction with unduly prolonged supervision.

Beyond this clinical material, there is little factual data available which would permit us to know how many social workers are supervised for how long, and whether supervision is, in fact, "interminable" for any sizable number of professionally trained workers. There are contrary complaints that trained social workers move into supervisory and administrative positions too soon after graduation, that it is atypical for a trained social worker to be employed in direct practice and being supervised five years after graduation. Such claims (or boasts) are made even more frequently for the trained group worker and community organizer. The fact that most entry-level positions in supervision require only one or two years of post–master's degree experience would imply that few professionally qualified practitioners are themselves supervised by the time they reach their sixth year of practice.

It is not altogether true that graduate social workers with practice experience are the only professionals who are supervised. Professionally accredited teachers, engineers, and nurses continue to be responsible to supervisory personnel after years of practice. A study of professionals in industry shows that "industrial laboratories tend not to grant autonomy to scientists regardless of their academic training until after they have proved themselves over a period of time" (Abrahamson 1967, p. 107). Furthermore, the highly independent professions of medicine and law are facing increasing supervision as more of their members find employment in organizational settings. The determining factor seems to be the complexity of the organizational context in which the professional is employed.

The charge of interminable supervision may be factually dubious and yet psychologically correct. This paradox results from the lack of any formalized procedure for termination of supervision. The physician is supervised for a prolonged period after graduation, but there is a clearly understood and accepted date of termination for the period of internship. The social work profession might well consider adopting a formal, institutionalized procedure for termination of educational supervision after a given period.

Studies of attitudes of both supervisors and supervisees regarding this question indicate considerable agreement about the desirability of diminishing supervision with the worker's increasing competence. An N.A.S.W. Chapter study of opinions on supervision found "that most social workers believed supervision should change gradually and flexibly according to the needs of the person supervised, from a phase of direction and teaching to one of more permissive consultation." However, "not one suggested that supervisors should not have administrative responsibilities" (Cruser 1958, p. 25).

In a study of a random sample of some 400 supervisees, most of whom were professionally trained, 75 percent indicated that "as the worker develops professional competence, supervision should change to a consultation relationship to be used when and how the supervisee decides." Only 5 percent of the respondents felt that "supervision should continue on the same basis since professional development is a continuous process." Responses from 470 supervisors were almost identical (Kadushin 1974).

There have been cogent defenses of extended supervision (Eisenberg 1956a, b; Levy 1960). Eisenberg (1956a) points to the continuing supportive needs of the supervisee: "It would be an extraordinary worker who did not, at times, experience some burden and some guilt, some anger and some despair— even a mature and experienced practitioner. . . . In all of this the supervisor stands as helper of the caseworker for the agency; the worker is not alone" (p. 49). The argument is also made that supervision of even the most experienced worker is necessary because help is always needed in objectifying the complex interpersonal relationships in which the worker is involved. However, others might note that while the availability of such objectivity and support is a functional necessity even for the most experienced worker, these can be made available through consultation initiated by the worker when he feels a need for assistance, rather than through supervision.

There is further disagreement about the time needed to achieve freedom from supervision and what aspects of supervision might need to continue to operate. Despite efforts to clarify the criteria of readiness for worker emancipation from supervision (Henry 1955; Lindenberg 1957), they are still very ambiguous. Time in practice is often given as a criterion, but the recommendations vary from one year in practice following graduation from a school of social work (Stevens and Hutchinson 1956, p. 52) to three years (Leader 1957, p. 464) to "four to six years" (Hollis 1964, p. 272). Others regard time in practice as an artificial criterion that denies individual differences in the tempo at which workers move toward readiness for independent practice.

The principal dissatisfaction with continued supervision seems to lie with prolonging educational supervision. Continuing obligatory educational supervision suggests that the worker does not know enough, is not fully competent, is incapable of autonomous practice. As Toren (1972) says, "trained social workers are willing to concede administrative authority to their supervisors as part of the limitations imposed by the organizational framework; however, they resent and resist the teaching function of the supervisor which they perceive as encroaching upon their professional judgment, responsibility and competence" (p. 79).

In contrast to the opposition to continuing educational supervision, there is readier acceptance of the necessity for continued administrative supervision. One of the earliest advocates of freedom from supervision believed that since social workers "work in agencies that are accountable for the performance of each staff member," autonomous practice would still require "that agencies continue to maintain structural channels for enabling staff to be most effectively accountable to administration" (Henry 1955, p. 40). As Leyendecker (1960) notes, freedom from authority of others in autonomous practice does "not seem to be truly applicable to the operation of a social agency requiring, as it does, an organizational structure in which responsibility and accountability are clearly defined and allocated" (p. 56). The recognition that someone in the hierarchical agency structure must continue to perform the functions of administrative supervision has been echoed and reechoed by those who have advocated greater independence from supervision (Aptekar 1959, p. 9; Austin 1961, p. 189; Leader 1957, p. 407; Lindenberg 1957, p. 43).

Even if all workers were well trained, were objectively self-critical, and had developed a level of self-awareness that eliminated the need for educational supervision, even if all

workers were so highly motivated, so self-assured, so rich in
inner resources that they felt no need for supervisory support,
administrative supervision would continue to be necessary as
long as the workers were employees of an agency.

Other professions, including medicine, have adopted similar procedures in dealing with the conflict between professional
autonomy and the need for conformity to organizational requirements (Goss 1961; W. Moore 1970). In organizations such as
hospitals and clinics, a distinction is made between supervision
concerned with administrative detail, the maintenance of orderly routines in the interest of the collectivity, such as scheduling, assignments, coordination of work, allocation of space
and organizational resources, and supervision concerned with
the content and procedure of the physician's actual work with
the patient. Compliance with supervisory directives is expected
with regard to administrative detail. While advice may be offered by supervisory personnel with regard to the physician's
professional activity, the ultimate decision remains with the
physician in contact with the patient.

In moving toward greater worker autonomy, the social work
supervisor retains her administrative responsibilities vis-à-vis
the supervisee, and the hierarchical relationship remains essentially the same. With regard to the educational component, however, the supervisee moves from supervision which is required
to consultation optionally sought at the initiative of the worker.
The spirit of the contact changes accordingly. The supervisor
accepts the worker as a colleague of nearly equal status as far as
knowledge of, and skill in, practice is concerned.

Innovations Toward Worker Autonomy

There is a general recognition of the need for a structured approach to granting the experienced professional worker freedom
from educational supervision; what innovations have been reported in social work which seek to achieve this goal?

I noted in chapter 6 that group supervision can offer the

worker a greater measure of autonomy than that permitted through individual supervision. Peer-group supervision is an extension of this procedure in the direction of still greater independence. As distinguished from group supervision, peer-group supervision invests the peer group with control of group meetings; the supervisor, if he sits in at all, is just another member of the group. It has been defined as a process by which a group of professionals in the same agency "meet regularly to review cases and treatment approaches without a leader, share expertise and take responsibility for their own and each other's professional development and for maintaining standards of [agency] service" (Hare and Frankena 1972, p. 527). In such peer supervision, more properly termed peer consultation, each member of the group feels a responsibility for the practice of the others and for helping them to improve their practice. What a worker does with the suggestions and advice offered by his peers is his own responsibility.

Peer group supervision symbolizes the capacity for greater independence of the worker; it also allows greater spontaneity and freedom in the absence of an authority figure. Nonetheless it presents its own difficulties. Rivalry for leadership and control is often present (Brugger, Ceasor, and Martz 1962), and unless the group is composed of workers with somewhat equal education and experience some staff members may be reluctant to participate, feeling that they cannot learn much from "peers" who know less than they do.

One report of peer-group supervision indicated that the "major disadvantage . . . for the [agency] was the difficulty of administrative decision making in the area of salary increments and professional advancement." The author suggested that this could be handled by a "core supervisor being exposed to the individual [supervisee's] work at stated intervals by means of direct observations and case reviews" (Hare and Frankena 1972, p. 529).

Peer consultation can be organized in the context of the individual conference. For example, Fizdale (1958) discusses a worker in her agency who had done considerable interviewing of both partners together in marital counseling cases. She had, therefore, developed a special skill in handling these "joint" interviews and had special knowledge about when they can be productive. It is quite usual for any staff member to consult with her about the value of a joint interview in a particular case or to get her help in preparing for such an interview or in reviewing the results. (p. 446)

(The process of peer-consultation can result in some feedback which makes its operation time-limited. The system works best with a group of peers of equal competence and status in the group, who consult with one another.) In such reciprocal consultation, while all members incur obligations as consultees, they repay these obligations when they act in the role of consultants. The peer-consultant who is repeatedly asked for advice is faced with a diminishing gain and increasing cost. "As he is increasingly often asked for advice, the value [utility] of the respect implicit in being once more consulted by his colleagues declines, and the cost of the time needed for consultation increases for him. Hence he would become more and more reluctant to give further advice" (Blau 1963, p. 137). The less competent worker, who is more frequently asking for advice, incurs an ever greater obligation to the other consultant-peers, which he finds difficult to discharge. He wears out his welcome and attempts to make restitution by becoming more deferential. The more often he asks for consultation, the more threatening it becomes for his status in the group. At some point it becomes more painful to ask than to go without the necessary help. Either that or he turns to a less competent peer whom he had not previously consulted and to whom he is not, consequently, obligated.

Other proposals for dealing with the negative reactions to continuing supervision concern alterations in the administrative arrangements or administrative relationships in supervision. Wax (1963) reports on one agency's use of "time limited" supervision for master's-degree social workers, permitting them to move toward independent practice within a period of two years in the agency. Supervision is followed by formal and informal peer consultation, and "social pressure from the colleague group replaces the pressure of the parent surrogate supervisor" (p. 41). Even here, however, since the worker "remains accountable for the quality and quantity of his work," there is a continuing need for administrative supervision.

/ Suggestions for changes in the administrative structure involve a redistribution of power and responsibility so that a greater measure of both is given to worker peer-groups (Kahle 1969; Rice 1973; Weber and Polm 1974). Instead of an agency whose administrative structure is sharply pyramidal—large numbers of workers at the base, supervised by a more limited number of middle managers, topped by an administrator—the suggested shape is pyramidal-rectangular. Instead of an agency with a hierarchical orientation, the suggested orientation is more equalitarian.

Intensified implementation of participatory management procedures tends to enhance the autonomy of the worker. Deliberate efforts have been made in some agencies to actively involve direct-service workers in the determination of significant policy decisions and in formulation of operating procedures (Fallon 1974; Weber and Polm 1974).

/ Participatory management is one way of attempting to debureaucratize the agency and reallocate power. Other efforts at debureaucratization, or at least diluted hierarchy, have involved attempts to "eliminate" supervision by redistributing supervisory responsibilities to training specialists, to staff-performance specialists (responsible for evaluation), to operation and program specialists, and to the workers themselves. The reports of such efforts indicate increases in worker autonomy but tend to show problems related to equitable task allocation and the development of other dissatisfactions not previously experienced (Weber and Polm 1974).

One agency has experimented with giving workers greater control over the supervisory process by instituting a contract system (Fox 1974). The supervisee negotiates a contract with the supervisor, specifying the kinds of things he feels he needs to learn within a specific period of time. Similar efforts have involved application of the principles of management by objectives (M.B.O.) to supervision (Wiehe 1973; Raider 1975).

Another innovation involved team service delivery (Brieland, Briggs, and Leuenberger 1973; Rowley and Faux 1966). A team of workers, working together as a unit, is given responsibility for supervision. The "supervisor" is merely one of the team members, although somewhat more equal than others. He acts as a consultant, coordinator, and resource person to team members and, when necessary, as team leader. However, the responsibility for work assignments, monitoring quantity and quality of team members' work, and meeting educational needs of team members is invested in the group. This approach takes group supervision one step farther as a procedure for augmenting worker autonomy. It gives administrative mandate to the peer group to perform the main functions previously performed by the supervisor. The team can, as a team, engage in much significant decision-making, but the imperatives of organizational life still have to be implemented. Final decisions have to be validated by the supervisor, who has ultimate administrative responsibility for team performance.

The problems of organizational coordination and communication may even be intensified with team service delivery, making the functions of supervision especially important. Since different members of the team may be involved with the same family at different times, this approach requires having up-to-date record and reporting material available. It also requires constant coordination to see that team members are not falling over each other in offering service to the family.

Watson (1973) proposes an eclectic approach to counter the "restrictive, infantilizing" effects of "traditional supervision." He suggests that a variety of supervisory procedures be available—individual tutorial, case consultation, supervisory group, peer group, tandem and team supervision—to be used differentially as needed. Having experimented with a variety of approaches to supervision in the large voluntary child-welfare agency with which he is associated, Watson notes that whatever system is used needs to be supplemented

to provide externally those elements that are missing or not emphasized. For instance, in those models in which the teaching component
is secondary (such as the team) the agency must make available additional formal teaching opportunities to the staff served by such a
model. In those systems in which accountability is not part of the
primary unit of contact (such as the peer group model) there must be a
designated representative of agency administration to whom group
members are accountable and formal procedures must be established
to make sure this administrative function is performed. (Watson 1973,
p. 87)

Watson thus confirms the fact that while the functions of supervision can be redistributed and reassigned in a variety of different ways, to a variety of different people in the agency, these
functions ultimately need to be performed if the agency is to get
its work done effectively.

No information is available which would enable us to know
how many agencies have adopted any of these proposed
changes or what percentage of social work supervisees is currently being supervised in accordance with such innovative
procedures. My guess is that relatively few workers are affected. This may be only partially in response to inertia and the
normal resistance to change encountered by any innovation. It
may also be a consequence of the fact that some of the proposed
innovations present difficult problems in implementation and
the fact that their application is feasible only if certain conditions are met.

Generally, the reports of peer supervision and consultation
describe workers who were professionally trained, had considerable practice experience and, in addition, often had advanced
training. Agency administration had confidence that the workers
were sufficiently competent, committed, and self-disciplined to
operate autonomously without harm to clients.

Agencies reporting successful efforts to reduce or eliminate
supervision recognize that these innovative efforts were made
possible by virtue of special staff and structural qualities. Stevens and Hutchinson (1956), reporting on their substitution of
consultation for supervision for workers with one year of agency

experience, say "we recognize that the plan as we are using it is geared to an agency where all members are professionally trained and experienced. Our agency is small. . . . There are fewer rules and regulations necessary in an agency such as this" (p. 54). Kahle (1969) reported on a successful use of the team-unit approach and said that the "modified pyramidal-collegial structure, with its emphasis on unit supervision, is possible only when the majority of the staff have high-level skills" (p. 25). The success of peer-oriented supervisory procedure is largely predicated on mutual trust and regard, a sense of colleagueship and a commitment to help rather than compete— conditions not easy to achieve. It may be that these and similar considerations explain, in part, the slow pace of adoption of the suggested changes.

Recent studies (Kavanagh 1975) tend to suggest that the issue of worker autonomy versus organizational demands, as manifested through supervision, is more complicated than first appears. Workers do not uniformly prefer maximum autonomy, and they balance freedom for self-actualization with other considerations. While there is strong preference for a supervisor who individualizes the worker and acts democratically and considerately, there is a recognition of the need for structure and a desire for flexible direction and supportive guidance.

These seemingly contradictory tendencies are less conflicting when we recognize that a situation which encourages maximum freedom for everyone increases the uncertainty with which each worker has to contend and that constant participation in decision-making is an exhausting exercise.

The desire for professional autonomy and the current demand for greater professional accountability to client and community may be forces pushing in opposite directions. To satisfy the demands of the professional may result in slighting the needs of client and community. Not only are the more traditional professions moving currently in the direction of established procedures in social work, as evidenced by a greater receptivity to the need for and desirability of a cadre of supervisory personnel, but also the limits of professional autonomy in

general are now being openly questioned. Daniels (1974) notes
that the available research raises doubt about whether/

autonomy is indeed vital for the performances of high level professional service. . . . Comparisons in transmittal of health care services
where physicians are supervised and where they are not, provided
some suggestive evidence. Some successes in utilization indicate that
controlled surveillance and supervision by peers and also other health
care practitioners and consumers can result in better quality of medical
care economically practiced. (p. 55)

This research points to a growing question about the effectiveness of accountability procedures in other professions, their
guarantee of service competence and protection of client needs.
(Such critical assessments of the effects of emphasis on professional autonomy in other fields might make social workers question the desirability of following such precedents.)

After studying professional accountability in social work
and other professions, Ruzek (1974) concluded by asking,
"Should social workers attempt to develop an accountability
system resembling the accountability systems in the established
professions such as law and medicine? We think not. For such
systems are seldom effective from the client's perspective. In
fact they serve to insulate the professional and protect them
from their clients rather than to protect clients from professionals, and there is no reason to believe that such a system
would be more effective in social work" (p. 240).

(There are contradictory trends regarding increasing the autonomy of the work force and debureaucratization of organizations.)There is considerable interest and experimentation in industrial organizations, both here and abroad, with increasing
worker input in organizational decision-making, more widely
distributing decision-making power, increasing worker autonomy and participation in management (Hunnius, Garson,
and Case 1973; Jenkins 1974). At the same time there are increasingly insistent demands for accountability and more explicit review of professional decision-making. The two contradictory trends exist side by side but apply to different groups in

the work force. The pressure for greater organizational demo-cratization applies most appropriately to industrial workers and white collar workers who have had far less control over their work situation than they desired or could effectively use. Expansion of worker power in this sector is understandable. Professionals, however, have always had a considerable amount of autonomy. Currently the concern is with limiting the possible abuse of this autonomy by requiring more organizational structure and more explicit peer-group review by accountability procedures. Social workers, while appealing to the trend developing out of problems in industrial organizations, are more likely to be affected by the trend relating to professional organizations.

Administrative and Educational Supervision— the Problem of Separation

A problem that has received considerable attention and debate in the literature on social work supervision is the desirability of separating the administrative and educational functions of supervision. Such a change is designed to reduce the conflict between teaching and evaluation; to reduce the excessive concentration of power in the hands of the person (generally the supervisor) who is simultaneously responsible for both these significant functions; to reduce the burden which responsibility for both these functions imposes on the supervisor, making effectual implementation of each difficult.

The argument for separation of the two functions is also based on the contention that the knowledge, skills, and aptitudes required for competent administration are different from those required for effective teaching. Combining the two functions means that the supervisor would have to be a good administrator as well as a good teacher. Separation permits specialization in performance of these different tasks.

Originally advocated by Austin (1956, 1960, 1961), the suggestion for separation of functions receives support from Devis (1965), Hanlan (1972), and Schwartz and Sample (1972).

They suggest that while both responsibilities are complementary they are also antithetical. The bureaucratic review, control, and evaluation functions of supervision establish a relationship between supervisor and supervisee that makes difficult, if not impossible, the development of the desirable teacher-learner relationship. Conversely, the question is raised whether the requirements of receptivity and psychological freedom necessary for the good learning situation do not conflict with the exercise of authority in administrative supervision. Toren (1969) notes this: "The personal-expressive relationship of teacher-learner infringes upon the maintenance of bureaucratic controls by the supervisor" (p. 174).

In their study of supervision in public welfare, Schwartz and Sample (1972) found supervisors to be excessively burdened by the demands of both functions:

> In the public assistance agencies the staff development functions of the supervisor tend to be honored more in the breach than in the observance. Among the reasons for this failure are the inability of some supervisors to carry out this function because of the press of administrative work; their lack of knowledge, skills, or personal aptitude; or other incapacities for staff development. A specialized in-service training and staff development program represents one kind of response by public assistance agencies to the need to supplement and strengthen supervisors' contributions in this area. (p. 168)

Here the need for specialized competence for effective discharge of the responsibilities of educational supervision is explicitly raised.

As a solution to these difficulties, both Austin and Schwartz recommend assignment of a supervisee to different supervisors for administrative supervision and educational supervision. In response I might point out that contamination of the educational relationship by the administrative relationship is faced in all of education. Every educator in every educational institution faces the problem of establishing an effective teacher-learner relationship while carrying the burden of evaluating the work of the learner. There is no substantial empirical evidence that learning seriously suffers as a result, nor is there any good evidence that learning substantially improves when the educator is absolved of the responsibility for evaluating and grading.

A certain level of anxiety is conducive to learning. Consequently the anxiety that relates to evaluation may be necessary, rather than antithetical, to learning. Nor would separating educational and administrative supervision eliminate anxiety. It may eliminate the anxiety of the formal aspects of evaluation. However, the worker would still be anxious about the personal, informal evaluation of her work by the educational supervisor who had no formal administrative-evaluation responsibilities.

The recommended cure may create greater problems than the supposed disease. The learning needs of the individual worker can be best discerned by the administrative supervisor who is responsible for careful review of the worker's performance. That person is in the most advantageous position to provide the necessary corrective feedback that advances learning. Control over selection and assignment of work responsibilities toward attainment of learning objectives also rests with the administrative supervisor. Consequently it would seem desirable that the administrative supervisor also be responsible for educational supervision.

Although the literature of social work supervision continues to debate the problem, it does not seem to be much of a problem for supervisors. Kledaras (1971) studied role conflict in supervision among 40 supervisors who "indicated that teaching and administration did not pose conflicting demands on their job" (p. 145). Olyan (1972) asked 228 supervisors from a variety of settings to respond to the statement that "the administrative and educational components of a supervisor's job are too much for any one person to do effectively." Fully three-quarters of the supervisors either disagreed or disagreed strongly with the statement (p. 153). In another study, 74 percent of 470 supervisors polled indicated that they felt no conflict between the two responsibilities (Kadushin 1974). An earlier study, which asked a similar question, found that 78 percent of the supervisors saw no conflict (Cruser 1958).

A recent study of 1660 workers in 31 social welfare and re-habilitation agencies showed that 56 percent of the supervisees and 66 percent of the supervisors who were asked about this matter felt that administrative supervision and educational supervision should not be separated. Seventy-seven percent of the supervisors felt that they could do an "adequate job when [they try] to coach and train workers and at the same time take care of routine supervision" (Olmstead and Christensen 1973, p. 205). However, the researchers note that, while the majority opinion is against separation, "enough people experience difficulty in performing the dual roles, for serious thought to be given to the question of whether supervisory effectiveness might not be enhanced if training and supervision were separated, despite the long tradition to the contrary in social work" (p. 206).

A Perspective

Focusing on the problems tends to obscure the very real contribution made by supervision to the effective operation of social work agencies and the general satisfaction with current supervisory procedures. A nationwide sample of approximately 400 professionally trained supervisees anonymously answered the following question: "In general, how satisfied do you feel with the relationship you now have with your supervisor?" Responses were in terms of a five-point scale ranging from "I am extremely satisfied" to "I am extremely dissatisfied." Some 28 percent of the respondents indicated extreme satisfaction and an additional 32 percent indicated that they were "fairly satisfied"—for a total of 60 percent of respondents expressing a reasonable degree of satisfaction in the supervisory experience. Only 15 percent were "fairly dissatisfied" or "extremely dissatisfied" (Kadushin 1974).

Olmstead and Christensen's study of 1660 workers throughout the country showed that, overall, 77 percent were "satisfied" with the supervision they were receiving. The fact that 78 percent of the respondents answered "no" to the question "would you prefer a different type of supervision than you get?" further confirms the generally positive attitude of these workers toward supervision (1973, p. 205). Other studies available also tend to indicate considerable satisfaction with social work supervision (Galambos and Wiggens 1970, p. 18; Greenleigh Associates 1960, p. 132; Scott 1969, p. 95).

I recognize that the studies of personnel turnover cited in chapter 1 indicate that dissatisfaction with supervision was a factor contributing to the decision to leave the agency. Perhaps the different study results are derived from quite different populations—those who stayed in the agency and those who left. The personnel turnover studies do not, however, invalidate the fact that a high percentage of professionally trained workers who remain with an agency are satisfied with the supervision they receive.

Burns (1958) calls attention to the possibilities of exaggerating the extent of dissatisfaction with supervision. In summarizing her history of social supervision, she notes that

despite the evident and intense dissatisfaction with supervision as it has been practiced, it would be easy to overestimate the extent of the problem. Scrutiny of the literature reveals that the negative response to traditional supervisory practice has been evoked, for the most part, in those private agencies where the social work job has been one of relatively low volume, where staff members have been professionally trained, where there has been less turn-over of personnel, and where consultation with other disciplines has been available. Agencies handling a large volume of work, with personnel less well trained, with heavy work loads and less available consultation service, apparently have not found the same problem. The extent of the dissatisfaction, therefore, has been limited. Its limitation does not decry its importance. (p. 162)

Despite some dissatisfaction, agency supervision is, for the most part, doing the job it is charged with doing.

Olmstead and Christensen's nationwide study concluded that good supervision is an important determinant of agency effectiveness. "The data are conclusive. High agency scores on the supervision variable were accompanied by greater employee satisfaction, better individual performance, less absenteeism, better agency performance and higher agency competence" (1973, p. 304). Consequently, greater time and attention need to be devoted to improving current supervisory practice. Many of the complaints about supervision are not the result of problems in supervision as such, but rather of the improper application of supervisory procedures.

The functions of supervision can be performed in a manner that respects the integrity of the worker, permitting areas of worker autonomy in an atmosphere of trust and shared concern. The functions can be implemented in a manner that provides assistance as well as assessment and facilitates the optimum performance of the worker while holding her accountable for her performance.

It is not supervision as such that encourages "infantilizing dependency," but rather poor supervision; it is not supervision as such that restricts and inhibits worker autonomy, but rather poor supervision. The profession might seriously consider, as a partial solution to the problems posed by supervision, a more active program of explicit, formal training for social work supervision in order to increase the number of better supervisors doing good supervision.

There is some research support for the contention that workers supervised by more professionally competent supervisors were less critical of supervision than those workers who experienced less adequate supervision (Scott 1965, p. 81). Supervisors who hold an M.S.W. degree appear to be more effective than non-M.S.W. supervisors in enabling their supervisees to use their knowledge and skills. In testing students entering a graduate school of social work after having worked in the field, Torre (1974) found that "the professional background of the supervisors" was one of only two factors related to how well the students performed. Students who, as workers, had been supervised by professionally trained supervisors did statistically better than those who had been supervised by non-M.S.W. supervisors.

A detailed study of supervision in a county department of public welfare showed that professionally oriented supervisors were seen as less likely to adhere closely to agency rules and policies and to be generally more permissive and non-autocratic in their relations with workers. Professionally oriented supervisors were also more likely to be described by their subordinates as self-confident and willing to back workers in conflicts with clients; they were less likely to be described as impatient or as reluctant to make decisions which were theirs to make than the less professionally oriented supervisors. In summary, the data suggests that . . . those supervisors with more graduate training adhered more closely to the professional model of the supervisor—that of permissive educator who allows caseworkers a greater measure of autonomy. It is also important to note that caseworkers in the county agency apparently preferred the style of supervision offered by the more professionally oriented supervisors. (Scott 1969, pp. 99–100, reprinted with permission of Macmillan Publishing Co.)

Further data "contain at least the suggestion that professionally oriented supervisors were the more effective group in motivating workers to perform as measured by agency criteria" (ibid., p. 101).

Ultimately, however, even with the best of training and the most adequate preparation, supervisors cannot resolve some of the persistent difficulties of supervision. The most significant problems of supervision reflect the significant problems of the profession. They cannot be solved in supervision, by supervisors, but need to be solved by the profession.

Good supervision requires a clear conception of the profession's objectives. Only the profession itself can supply this, and the answer is currently open to debate. At this point the profession of social work seems to have little functional specificity, its claims are pluralistic and diffuse, its objectives are ambiguous, and its image is blurred. Traditionally accepted goals have been challenged, underlying assumptions have been questioned, previously accredited practice is discounted as ineffective or misdirected. In recognition of this reality, the Publications Committee of N.A.S.W. called attention in 1974 to the need for another Milford Conference. That historic conference, held in 1929, was a successful effort to develop a consensus on the definition of social work, its function and purpose. In indicting the need for another such conference in the 1970s, the Publications Committee noted that at this time "there appears to be no agreement within the social work profession on a common conceptual framework for viewing social work functions and practice."

The supervisory cadre lacks the needed support which derives from membership in, and affiliation with, a clearly defined profession whose objectives and functions are sharply specified and whose hegemony over some significant social problem areas has clear community acceptance and legitimation. On the contrary, the conscientious supervisor finds his task made more difficult by the conceptual heterogeneity, if not the conceptual disarray, which currently characterizes the approach to social work objectives and functions and by the community's ambivalent sanction of social work.

Good supervision further requires an effective practice technology, and only the profession and allied sciences can supply it. Good supervision requires a consensually accepted practice theory and adequate procedures for measuring outcomes, and only the profession can supply them. In many respects the essential problems of supervision derive from the unsolved questions facing the profession. What Mosher and Purpel (1972) say about supervision in education is equally applicable to social work.

The difficulty of defining supervision in relation to education . . . stems, in large part, from unresolved theoretical problems about teaching. Quite simply, we lack sufficient understanding of the process of teaching. Our theories of learning are inadequate, the criteria for measuring teaching effectiveness are imprecise and deep disagreement exists about what knowledge . . . is most valuable to teach. There is no generally agreed-upon definition of what teaching is or how to measure its effects. When we have achieved more understanding of what and how to teach and with what special effects on students, we will be much less vague about the supervision of these processes. (p. 3)

Social work supervision essentially faces the same dilemmas. Some of the more significant sins of supervision are those imposed on supervision by the profession.

(The present situation is a transitional crisis.)It has the advantage of making the problems faced by the profession clear and explicit. Determined efforts are being made to resolve these issues, and the result is likely to be a more unified, strengthened profession with a clearer conception of its direction. Social work supervisors will profit from the change and can effectively contribute to achieving it.

Summary

The lack of direct access to supervisees' performance is a problem for supervisors. Workers' reports of their activities often suffer from significant omissions and distortions. Procedures such as direct observation, audio and video tapes, and co-therapy supervision are being used in response to this problem. Tapes provide the supervisor with a complete, reliable view of the worker's performance and provide the worker with the opportunity for self-supervision.

Peer supervision and time-limited supervision have been proposed in response to the problem of prolonged supervision. There is agreement that the supervisory relationship should yield to consultation, although some administrative supervision will continue to be required.

The antithetical components of administrative and educational supervision are not a problem for most supervisors but are sufficiently troublesome that active consideration has been given to separating these responsibilities.

A variety of procedures are being tried to debureaucratize the agency and redistribute managerial decision-making power. These include team service delivery, participatory management, and a supervisory contract system.

Studies show that most supervisees express satisfaction with the supervision they are receiving and that supervisors do a more effective job as a result of formal training.

bibliography

Ables, Billie S., and Aug, Robert G. 1972. "Pitfalls Encountered by Beginning Child Psychotherapists." *Psychotherapy: Theory, Research, and Practice* 9: 340–45.

Abrahamson, Arthur C. 1959. *Group Methods in Supervision and Staff Development.* New York, Harper.

Abrahamson, Mark. 1967. *The Professional in the Organization.* Chicago, Rand McNally.

Agel, Jerome. 1971. *Radical Therapist.* New York, Ballantine.

Aiken, Wilbur J., Smits, Stanley S., and Lollar, Donald J. 1972. "Leadership Behavior and Job Satisfaction in State Rehabilitation Agencies." *Personnel Psychology* 25: 65–73.

Alexander, Leslie B. 1972. "Social Work's Freudian Deluge: Myth or Reality." *Social Service Review* 46: 517–38.

Amacher, Kloh-Ann. 1971. "Explorations into the Dynamics of Learning in Field Work." D.S.W. dissertation, Smith College School of Social Work.

American Psychological Association. 1954. "Internship in Clinical Psychology." *American Psychologist* 9: 760–64.

Anderson, Bruce N., Pine, Irving, and Mee-lee, Denis. 1972. "Resident Training in Co-Therapy Groups." *International Journal of Psychotherapy* 22: 192–98.

Apaka, Tusencko, K., Hirsch, Sidney, and Kleidman, Sylvia. 1967. "Establishing Group Supervision in a Hospital Social Work Department." *Social Work* 12: 54–60.

Aptekar, Herbert H. 1959. "The Continued Education of Experienced Workers." *Child Welfare* 38: 7–12.

Arlow, Jacob A. 1963. "The Supervisory Situation." *Journal of the American Psychoanalytic Association* 11: 576–94.

Armstrong, Margaret, Huffman, Margaret, and Spain, Marianne. 1959.

"The Use of Process and Tape Recordings as Tools in Learning Casework." M.A. Thesis, State University of Iowa.

Arndt, Hilda. 1973. "Effective Supervision in a Public Welfare Setting." *Public Welfare* 31: 50–54.

Austin, Lucille N. 1956. "An Evaluation of Supervision." *Social Casework* 37: 375–82.

Austin, Lucille. 1960. "Supervision in Social Work." *Social Work Year Book, 1960,* pp. 579–86.

Austin, Lucille. 1961. "The Changing Role of the Supervisor." *Smith College Studies in Social Work* 31: 179–95.

Ayers, Alice Q. 1973. "Neighborhood Services: People Caring for People." *Social Casework* 54: 195–214.

Babcock, Charlotte G. 1951. "Social Work as Work." *Social Casework* 25: 415–22.

Bandler, Bernard. 1973. "Interprofessional Collaboration in Training in Mental Health," *American Journal of Orthopsychiatry* 43: 97–107.

Barker, Robert L. 1972. "Conclusion: Research Findings Related to the Education of Baccalaureate Social Workers." In *Manpower Research on the Utilization of Baccalaureate Social Workers: Implications for Education,* ed. Robert L. Barker and Thomas L. Briggs, pp. 89–96. Washington, D.C., U.S. Govt. Printing Office.

Barnard, Chester. 1938. *The Functions of the Executive.* Cambridge, Mass., Harvard Univ. Press.

Barr, Sherman. 1967. "Some Observations on the Practice of Indigenous Non-Professionals." In *Personnel in Anti-poverty Programs: Implications for Social Work Education,* pp. 51–62. New York, Council on Social Work Education.

Bar-Yosef, Rivka, and Schild, Erling. 1966. "Pressure and Defenses in Bureaucratic Rules." *American Journal of Sociology* 71: 665–73.

Bauman, William F. 1972. "Games Counselor Trainees Play: Dealing with Trainee Resistance." *Counselor Education and Supervision* 12: 251–57.

Beiser, Helen. 1966. "Self-Listening during Supervision of Psychotherapy." *Archives of General Psychiatry* 15: 135–39.

Bell, Joanne I. n.d. *Staff Development and Practice Supervision: Criteria and Guidelines for Determining Their Appropriate Function.* Washington, D.C., U.S. Department of Health, Education and Welfare, Social and Rehabilitation Service, Assistance Payments Administration.

Bennis, Warren. 1966. *Beyond Bureaucracy: Essays on the Development and Evolution of Human Organizations.* New York, McGraw.

Benschoter, R. A., Eaton, M. T., and Smith, D. 1965. "Use of Videotape to Provide Individual Instruction in Techniques of Psychotherapy." *Journal of Medical Education* 40: 1159–61.

Berengarten, Sidney. 1957. "Identifying Learning Patterns of Individual Students: An Exploratory Study." *Social Service Review* 31: 407–17.

Berliner, Arthur. 1971. "Some Pitfalls in Administrative Behavior." *Social Casework* 52: 562–66.

Billingsley, Andrew. 1964a. "Bureaucratic and Professional Orientation Patterns in Social Casework." *Social Service Review* 38: 400–407.

Billingsley, Andrew. 1964b. *The Role of the Social Worker in a Child Protective Agency: A Comparative Analysis.* Boston, Mass. Society for Prevention of Cruelty to Children.

Birnbaum, Martin L., and Jones, Chester H. 1967. "Activities of the Social Work Aides." *Social Casework* 48: 626–32.

Bishop, Maxine H. 1969. *Dynamic Supervision: Problems and Opportunities.* New York, American Management Association.

Blackey, Eileen. 1957. *Group Leadership in Staff Training.* Bureau of Public Assistance, H.E.W. Report no. 29. Washington, D.C., U.S. Govt. Printing Office.

Blake, R. R., and Mouton, S. S. 1961. *The Managerial Grid.* Houston, Gulf.

Blane, Stephen M. 1968. "Immediate Effect of Supervisory Experiences on Counselor Candidates." *Counselor Education & Supervision* 8: 39–44.

Blau, Peter M. 1960. "Orientation toward Clients in a Public Welfare Agency." *Administrative Science Quarterly* 5: 341–61.

Blau, Peter M. 1963. *The Dynamics of Bureaucracy.* Rev. ed. Chicago, Univ. of Chicago Press.

Blau, Peter M., and Scott, Richard W. 1962. *Formal Organizations.* San Francisco, Chandler Pub.

Bloom, Leonard, and Herman, Cherie. 1958. "A Problem of Relationship in Supervision." *Journal of Social Casework* 39: 402–6.

Boylston, William H., and Tuma, June M. 1972. "Training of Mental Health Professionals Through the Use of the 'Bug in the Ear.'" *American Journal of Psychiatry* 129: 92–95.

Brackett, Jeffrey. 1904. *Education and Supervision in Social Work.* New York, Macmillan.

Brager, George, and Michael, John A. 1969. "The Sex Distribution in Social Work: Causes and Consequences." *Social Casework* 50: 595–601.

Brager, George A., and Specht, Harry. 1973. *Community Organizing.* New York, Columbia Univ. Press.

Briar, Scott. 1966. "Family Services." In *Five Fields of Social Services: Reviews of the Literature,* ed. Henry Maas, pp. 9–50. New York, National Association of Social Workers.

Briar, Scott. 1971. "Family Services and Casework." In *Research in the Social Services: A Five Year Review,* ed. Henry Maas, pp. 108–25. New York, National Association of Social Workers.

Brieland, Donald. 1959. *An Experimental Study of Adoptive Parents at Intake.* New York, Child Welfare League of America.

Brieland, Donald, Briggs, Thomas L., and Leuenberger, Paul. 1973. *The Team Model of Social Work Practice.* Syracuse, N.Y., Syracuse Univ. School of Social Work.

Briggs, Thomas. 1973. "Social Work Manpower: Development and Dilemmas of the 1970's." In *Educating MSW Students to Work with Other Social Welfare Personnel,* ed. Margaret Purvine, pp. 4–31. New York, Council on Social Work Education.

Brown, Edwin G. 1970. "Selection of Adoptive Parents: A Videotape Study." Ph.D. dissertation, School of Social Service Administration, University of Chicago.

Bruck, Max. 1963. "The Relationship Between Student Anxiety, Self-Awareness and Self-Concept and Competence in Casework." *Social Casework* 44: 125–31.

Brugger, T., Ceasor, G., Frank, A., and Martz, S. 1962. "Peer Supervision as a Method of Learning Psychotherapy." *Comprehensive Psychiatry* 3: 47–53.

Bruner, Jerome S. 1963. *The Process of Education.* New York, Random House, Vintage.

Bruner, Jerome S. 1971. *Toward a Theory of Instruction.* Cambridge, Mass., Harvard Univ. Press.

Budner, Stanley, Chazin, Robert M., and Young, Howard. 1973. "The Indigenous Nonprofessional in a Multiservice Center." *Social Casework* 54: 354–59.

Burke, Donald, and Wilcox, Douglas S. 1971. "Basis of Supervisory Power and Subordinate Job Satisfactions." *Canadian Journal of Behavioral Science* 3: 184–93.

Burns, Mary E. 1958. "The Historical Development of the Process of Casework Supervision as Seen in the Professional Literature of Social Work." Ph.D. dissertation, School of Social Service Administration, University of Chicago.

"Casework Notebook: Dynamic Aspects of Role of Supervisor." 1939. *Social Work Today* 6: 41–42.

C. D. 1938. "The Role of the Casework Supervisor Re-Examined." *Social Work Techniques* 3: 12–16.

Chafetz, Janet S. 1972. "Women in Social Work." *Social Work* 17 (5): 12–18.

Chatterjee, Pranab. 1972. "Commitment to Work Among Public Welfare Workers." *Public Welfare* 30: 53–58.

Chodoff, Paul. 1972. "Supervision of Psychotherapy with Videotape: Pros and Cons." *American Journal of Psychiatry* 128: 819–23.

Cohen, Ruth. 1972. "Student Training in a Geriatric Center." In *Issues in Human Services*, ed. Florence W. Kaslow and associates, pp. 168–84. San Francisco, Jossey-Bass.

Colorado State Department of Public Welfare. 1967. *Report on Review of First Line Supervision*. Denver.

Conyngton, Mary. 1909. *How to Help: A Manual of Practical Charity Designed for the Use of Nonprofessional Workers Among the Poor*. New York, Macmillan.

Covner, B. S. 1943. "Studies in the Phonographic Recorders of Verbal Material: III. The Completeness and Accuracy of Counselor Interview Reports." *Journal of General Psychology* 30: 181–203.

Creecy, Robert F. 1971. *Training and Supervising Case Aides*. Madison, Wis., School of Social Work, Univ. of Wisconsin.

Cruser, Robert W. 1958. "Opinions on Supervision: A Chapter Study." *Social Work* 3: 18–25.

Cudabeck, Dorothea. 1968. "Aides Need Theory." *New Careers* no. 11.

Cudabeck, Dorothea. 1970. "Training and Education of New Careerists in Public Welfare." *Public Welfare* 28: 214–21.

Daniels, Arlene K. 1974. "How Free Should Professions Be?" In *The Professions and Their Prospects*, ed. Eliot Friedson, pp. 39–56. Beverly Hills, Calif., Sage Publications.

Davidson, Terrence N., and Emmer, Edmund T. 1966. "Immediate Effect of Supportive and Nonsupportive Supervisor Behavior on Counselor Candidates' Focus of Concern." *Counselor Education and Supervision* 6: 27–31.

Dawson, John B. 1926. "The Case Supervisor in a Family Agency." *Family* 6: 293–95.

De la Torre, Jorge. 1974. "Use and Misuse of Cliches in Clinical Supervision." *Archives of General Psychiatry* 31: 302–6.

Devine, Edward. 1901. *The Practice of Charity*. New York, Handbook for Practical Workers.

Devis, Donald A. 1965. "Teaching and Administrative Funtions in Supervision." *Social Work* 46: 83–89.

Dimock, Hedley S., and Trecker, Harleigh B. 1949. *The Supervisor of Group Work and Recreation*. New York, Association Press.

Doehrman, Margery J. 1972. "Parallel Processes in Supervision and Psychotherapy." Ph.D. dissertation, University of Michigan.

Dornbusch, Sanford M., and Scott, Richard W. 1975. *Evaluation and the Exercise of Authority*. San Francisco, Jossey-Bass.

Duncan, Mina G. 1963. "An Experiment in Applying New Methods in Field Work." *Social Casework* 44: 179–84.

Educational Testing Service. 1973. *Summary of Research Proposals Submitted to ACSW.* Princeton, N.J.

Eisenberg, Sidney. 1956a. *Supervision in the Changing Field of Social Work.* Philadelphia, Jewish Family Service of Philadelphia.

Eisenberg, Sidney. 1956b. "Supervision as an Agency Need." *Social Casework* 37: 233–37.

Ekstein, Rudolf, and Wallerstein, Robert S. 1972. *The Teaching and Learning of Psychotherapy.* 2d ed. New York, International Universities Press.

Emerson, Richard M. 1962. "Power-Dependence Relations." *American Sociological Review* 27: 31–41.

Engel, Gloria J. 1970. "Professional Autonomy and Bureaucratic Organization." *Administrative Science Qarterly* 15: 12–21.

English, R. William, and Jelenevsky, Serge. 1971. "Counselor Behavior as Judged under Audio, Visual, and Audiovisual Communication Conditions." *Journal of Counseling Psychology* 18: 509–13.

Epstein, Irwin. 1970. "Professionalization, Professionalism and Social Worker Radicalism." *Journal of Health and Social Behavior* 11: 67–77.

Etzioni, Amitai. 1961. *A Comparative Analysis of Complex Organizations.* New York, Free Press.

Fallon, Kenneth P. 1974. "Participatory Mangement: An Alternative in Human Service Delivery Systems." *Child Welfare* 53: 555–62.

Family Service Association of America. 1957. *A Guide to Classification of Professional Positions and Evaluation Outlines in a Family Service Agency.* New York.

Family Service Association of America. 1969. *Social Work Assistants in Family Service Agencies: Reports from FSAA Personnel Committee.* New York.

Farrall Instrument Co. n.d. "Bug-in-the-Ear" advertising brochure. Grand Island, Nebr., Farrall Instrument Co.

Feldman, Yonata, Sponitz, Hyman, and Nagelberg, Leo. 1953. "One Aspect of Casework Training through Supervision." *Social Casework* 34: 150–56.

Feldstein, Donald. 1968. *Community College and Other Associate Degree Programs for Social Welfare Areas.* New York, Council on Social Work Education.

Ferrar, Marcella, and Hemmy, Mary L. 1963. "Use of Nonprofessional Staff in Work with the Aged." *Social Work* 8 (3): 44–50.

Fiedler, Fred E. 1967. *A Theory of Leadership Effectiveness.* New York, McGraw.

Fields, Mrs. James T. 1885. *How to Help the Poor*. Boston, Houghton.

Fizdale, Ruth. 1958. "Peer Group Supervision." *Social Casework* 39: 443–50.

Fleischmann, O. 1955. "A Method of Teaching Psychotherapy: One-Way-Vision Room Technique." *Bulletin of the Menninger Clinic* 19: 160–72.

Fleming, Joan, and Benedek, Therese. 1966. *Psychoanalytic Supervision*. New York, Grune.

Foren, Robert, and Bailey, Royston. 1968. *Authority in Social Casework*. New York, Pergamon.

Fox, Raymond. 1974. "Supervision by Contract." *Social Casework* 55: 247–51.

Frank, Irving H., and Quinlan, Paul M. 1973. "Exit–No Exit." In *The Helping Professions in the World of Action,* ed. Ira Goldenberg, pp. 93–108. Lexington, Mass., Lexington Books, Heath.

Freidson, Eliot, and Rhea, Buford. 1965. "Knowledge and Judgment in Professional Evaluations." *Administrative Science Quarterly* 10: 107–24.

French, John R. P., Jr., and Raven, Bertram. 1960. "The Bases of Social Power." In *Group Dynamics*, ed. D. Cartwright and A. Zander, pp. 607–23. Evanston, Ill., Row, Peterson.

Friesen, Deloss D., and Dunning, G. B. 1973. "Peer Evaluation and Practicuum Supervision." *Counselor Education and Supervision* 13: 229–35.

Froehlich, Clifford P. 1958. "The Completeness and Accuracy of Counseling Interview Reports." *Journal of General Psychology* 58: 81–96.

Galambos, Eva C., and Wiggens, Xenia R. 1970. *After Graduation: Experiences of College Graduates in Locating and Working in Social Welfare Positions*. Atlanta, Southern Regional Education Board.

Galm, Sharon. 1972. *Issues in Welfare Administration: Welfare—An Administrative Nightmare*. Subcommittee on Fiscal Policy of the Joint Economic Committee, U.S. Congress. Washington, D.C., U.S. Govt. Printing Office.

Gartner, Alan. 1971. *Paraprofessionals and Their Performance: A Survey of Education, Health and Social Service Programs*. New York, Praeger.

Geer, Blanche. 1966. "Occupational Commitment and the Teaching Profession." *School Review* 74: 31–47.

Gelso, Charles H. 1972. "Inhibition due to Recording and Clients Evaluation of Counseling." *Psychological Reports* 31: 67577.

Gelso, Charles, and Tanney, Mary F. 1972. "Client Personality as a Mediator of the Effects of Recording." *Counselor Education and Supervision* 12: 109–14.

Getzels, Jacob W., and Guba, E. G. 1957. "Social Behavior and Administrative Process." *School Review* 65: 423–41.

Gitterman, Alex. 1972. "Comparison of Educational Models and Their Influence on Supervision." In *Issues in Human Services,* ed. Florence W. Kaslow and associates, pp. 18–38. San Francisco, Jossey-Bass.

Gladstone, Bernard. 1967. *Supervisory Practice and Social Service in the Neighborhood Center.* New York, United Neighborhood Homes.

Glendenning, John M. 1923. "Supervision through Conferences on Specific Cases." *Family* 4: 7–10.

Gockel, Galen L. 1967. "Social Work as a Career Choice." In *Manpower and Social Welfare: Research Perspectives* ed. Edward Schwartz, pp. 89–98. New York, National Association of Social Workers.

Goffman, Erving. 1952. "On Cooling the Mark Out: Some Aspects of Adaptation to Failure," *Psychiatry* 15: 451–63.

Goffman, Erving. 1959. *The Presentation of Self in Everyday Life.* Garden City, N.Y. Doubleday, Anchor Books.

Goin, Marcia K., and Kline, Frank M. 1974. "Supervision Observed." *Journal of Nervous and Mental Disease,* 158: 208–13.

Goldberg, Gertrude. 1967. "Nonprofessional Helpers: The Visiting Homemakers." In *Community Action against Poverty,* ed. George A. Brager and Francis A. Purcell, pp. 175–207. New Haven, College and Univ. Press.

Goldhammer, Robert. 1969. *Clinical Supervision: Special Methods for the Supervision of Teachers.* New York, Holt.

Goldstein, Arnold P., Heller, Kenneth, and Sechrest, Lee B. 1966. *Psychotherapy and the Psychology of Behavior Change.* New York, Wiley.

Gooding, Judson. 1972. *The Job Revolution.* New York, Collier Books.

Gordon, Jesse E. 1965. "Project Cause, the Federal Antipoverty Program and Some Implications of Subprofessional Training." *American Psychologist* 20: 334–43.

Goss, Mary W. E. 1961. "Influence and Authority among Physicians in an Outpatient Clinic." *American Sociological Review* 26: 39–50.

Gottesfeld, Harry, Rhee, Chongick, and Parker, Glenn. 1970. "A Study of the Role of Paraprofessionals in Community Mental Health." *Community Mental Health Journal* 6: 285–91.

Gould, Karolyn R., Smith, James, and Masi, Terri. 1971. *Career Mobility for Paraprofessionals in Human Service Agencies.* Washington, D.C., U.S. Department of Labor, Manpower Administration.

Gouldner, Alvin. 1954. *Patterns of Industrial Democracy.* New York, Free Press.

Green, A. D. 1966. "The Professional Social Worker in the Bureaucracy." *Social Service Review* 40: 71–83.

Green, Solomon, H. 1972. "Educational Assessments of Student Learning through Practice in Field Instruction." *Social Work Education Reporter* 20: 48–54.

Greenleigh Associates. 1960. *Addenda to Facts, Fallacies and Future: A Study of the AFDC Program, Cook County, Ill.* New York, Greenleigh Associates.

Grossbard, Hyman. 1954. "Methodology for Developing Self-Awareness." *Social Casework* 35: 380–85.

Grosser, Charles. 1969. "Manpower Development Program." In *Nonprofessionals: The Human Services*, ed. Charles Grosser, William E. Henry, and James G. Kelly, pp. 116–48. San Francisco, Jossey-Bass.

Gruenberg, Peter B., Liston, Edward H., Jr., and Wayne, George J. 1969. "Intensive Supervision of Psychotherapy with Videotape Recording." *American Journal of Psychotherapy* 23: 95–105.

Gurteen, Humphrey S. 1882. *A Handbook of Charity Organizations.* Buffalo, N.Y., privately published.

Hadley, John M., True, John E., and Kepes, Sherwin Y. 1970. "An Experiment in the Education of the Preprofessional Mental Health Worker: the Purdue Program." *Community Mental Health Journal* 6: 31–39.

Hage, Jerald, and Aiken, Michael. 1967. "Relationship of Centralization to Other Structural Properties." *Administrative Science Quarterly* 12: 72–91.

Hall, Richard H. 1968. "Professionalization and Bureaucratization." *American Sociological Review* 33: 92–104.

Hallowitz, David. 1962. "The Supervisor as Practitioner." *Social Casework* 43: 287–92.

Hallowitz, Emanuel. 1969. "Use of Nonprofessional Staff: Issues and Strategies." In *Human Services and Social Work Responsibility*, ed. Willard C. Richan, pp. 165–77. New York, National Association of Social Workers.

Hamachek, Joan N. 1971. "Effects of Individual Supervision on Selected Affective and Cognitive Characteristics of Counselors-in-Training: A Pilot Study." Ph.D. dissertation, Michigan State University.

Handler, Joel, and Hollingsworth, Ellen Jane. 1971. *The Deserving Poor.* Chicago, Markham Pub.

Hanlan, Archie. 1972. "Changing Functions and Structures." In *Issues in Human Services*, ed. Florence W. Kaslow and associates, pp. 39–50. San Francisco, Jossey-Bass.

Hardcastle, D. A. 1971. "The Indigenous Nonprofessional in the Social Service Bureaucracy: A Critical Examination." *Social Work* 16: 56–64.

Hare, Rachel T., and Frankena, Susan T. 1972. "Peer Group Supervision." *American Journal of Orthopsychiatry* 42: 527–29.

Haring, Barbara. 1974. *Workload Measurement in Child Welfare: A Report of CWLA Member Agencies, Activities, and Interests*. New York, Child Welfare League of America.

Harper, Robert A., and Hudson, John W. 1952. "The Use of Recordings in Marriage Counseling: A Preliminary Empirical Investigation." *Marriage and Family Living* 14: 332–34.

Harshbarger, Dwight. 1973. "The Individual and the Social Order: Notes on the Management of Heresy and Deviance in Complex Organizations." *Human Relations* 26: 251–70.

Hathway, Marion. 1943. "Utilizing Available and New Personnel." *Compass* 24: 41–42.

Hawthorne, Lillian. 1975. "Games Supervisors Play." *Social Work* 20: 179–83.

H. C. D. 1949. "Through Supervision with Gun and Camera: The Personal Account of a Beginning Supervisor." *Social Work Journal* 30: 161–63.

Henry, Charlotte S. 1955. "Criteria for Determining Readiness of Staff to Function without Supervision." In *Administration, Supervision and Consultation*, pp. 34–45. New York, Family Service Association of America.

Henry, William E., Sims, John H., and Spray, Lee S. 1971. *The Fifth Profession*. San Francisco, Jossey-Bass.

Heraud, Brian. 1970. *Sociology and Social Work*. New York, Pergamon Press.

Herzberg, Frederick, Mausner, B., and Snyderman, B. B. 1959. *The Motivation to Work*. 2d ed. New York, Wiley.

Hewer, Vivian. 1974. "An Aid to Supervision in Practicuum." *Journal of Counseling Psychology*, 21: 66–70.

Hirsh, Herman, and Freed, Herbert. 1970. "Pattern Sensitization in Psychotherapy Supervision by Means of Video Tape Recording." In *Videotape Technique in Psychiatric Training and Treatment*, ed., Milton M. Berger. New York, Bruner-Mazel.

Hollis, Florence. 1964. *Casework, a Psycho-Social Therapy*. New York, Random House.

Holtzman, Reva Fine. 1966. "Major Teaching Methods in Field Instruction in Casework." D.S.W. dissertation, Columbia University School of Social Work.

Hunnius, Gerry, Garson, G. David, and Case, John. 1973. *Workers'*

Control: A Reader on Labor and Social Change. New York, Random House, Vintage.

Hurvitz, Nathan. 1973. "Psychotherapy as a Means of Social Control." *Journal of Consulting and Clinical Psychology* 40: 232–39.

Itzin, Frank. 1960. "The Use of Tape Recording in Field Work." *Social Casework* 41: 197–202.

Jacobs, Jerry. 1969. "Symbolic Bureaucracy: A Case Study of a Social Welfare Agency." *Social Forces* 47: 413–22.

Jarvis, Paul E., and Esty, Jonathan F. 1968. "The Alternative-Therapist-Observer Technique in Group Therapy Training." *International Journal of Group Psychotherapy* 18: 95–99.

Jay, Anthony. 1967. *Management and Machiavelli.* New York, Bantam Books.

Jenkins, David. 1974. *Job Power: Blue and White Collar Democracy.* Baltimore, Penguin.

Jewish Community Center. 1949. "Principles and Practices of Supervision in the Jewish Center." *Jewish Center Worker*, p. 44.

Jones, Betty L. 1966. "Nonprofessional Workers in Professional Foster Family Agencies." *Child Welfare* 45: 313–25.

Judd, Jadwiga, Kohn, Regina E., and Shulman, Gerda L. 1962. "Group Supervision: A Vehicle for Professional Development." *Social Work* 7(1): 96–102.

Kadushin, Alfred. 1956a. "Interview Observation as a Teaching Device." *Social Casework* 37: 334–41.

Kadushin, Alfred. 1956b. "The Effects of Interview Observation on the Interviewer." *Journal of Counseling Psychology* 3: 130–35.

Kadushin, Alfred. 1957. "The Effect on the Client of Interview Observation at Intake." *Social Service Review* 31: 22–38.

Kadushin, Alfred. 1968. "Games People Play in Supervision." *Social Work* 13 (3): 23–32.

Kadushin, Alfred. 1973. *Supervisor-Supervisee: A Questionnaire Study.* Madison, Wis., School of Social Work, Univ. of Wisconsin.

Kadushin, Alfred. 1974. "Supervisor-Supervisee: A Survey." *Social Work* 19: 288–98.

Kagan, Morris. 1963. "The Field Intructor's Evaluation of Student Performance: Between Fact and Fiction." *Social Worker* 3: 15–26.

Kagan, Norman, Krathwohl, David R., and Miller, Ralph. 1963. "Stimulated Recall in Therapy Using Video-Tape: A Case Study." *Journal of Counseling Psychology* 10: 237–43.

Kahle, Joseph H. 1969. "Structuring and Administering a Modern Voluntary Agency." *Social Work* 14 (4): 21–28.

Kahn, Robert L. 1964. *Organizational Stress.* New York, Wiley.

Kallejian, Verne, Brown, Paula, and Wechsler, Irving. 1954. "The Impact of Interpersonal Relations on Ratings of Performance." *Public Personnel Review* 15: 166–70.

Kaslow, Florence W. 1972. "Group Supervision." In *Issues in Human Services*, ed. Florence W. Kaslow and associates, pp. 115–41. San Francisco, Jossey-Bass.

Katan, Yosef. 1974. "The Utilization of Indigenous Workers in Human Service Organizations." In *Human Service Organizations*, ed. Yeheskel Hasenfeld and Richard A. English, pp. 448–67. Ann Arbor, Mich., Univ. of Michigan Press.

Katz, Fred E. 1968. *Autonomy and Organization.* New York, Random House.

Kaufman, Herbert. 1960. *The Forest Ranger.* Baltimore, Johns Hopkins Univ. Press.

Kaufman, Herbert. 1973. *Administrative Feedback: Monitoring Subordinate Behavior,* Washington, D.C., Brookings Institution.

Kavanagh, Michael J. 1975. "Expected Supervisor Behavior, Interpersonal Trust and Environmental Preferences: Some Relationships Based on a Dyadic Model of Supervision." *Organizational Behavior and Human Performance* 13: 17–30.

Kennedy, Miriam, and Keitner, Lydia. 1970. "What is Supervision: The Need for a Redefinition." *Social Worker* 38: 51–52.

Kermish, Irving, and Kushin, Frank. 1969. " 'Why High Turnover?' Social Work Staff Losses in a County Welfare Agency." *Public Welfare* 27: 134–37.

Kettner, Peter M. 1973. "Some Factors Affecting Use of Professional Knowledge and Skill by the Social Worker in Public Welfare Agencies." D.S.W. dissertation, University of Southern California, School of Social Work.

Kledarias, Constantine G. 1971. "A Study of Role Conflict in Supervision." D.S.W. dissertation, Catholic University of America.

Kogan, Leonard S. 1950. "The Electrical Recording of Social Casework Interviews." *Social Casework* 31: 371–78.

Kohn, Regina. 1971. "Differential Use of Observed Interview in Student Training." *Social Work Education Reporter* 19: 45–46.

Korner, Ija N., and Brown, William H. 1952. "The Mechanical Third Ear." *Journal of Consulting Psychology* 16: 81–84.

Kornfeld, D. S., and Kolb, L. C. 1964. "The Use of Closed Circuit Television in the Teaching of Psychiatry." *Journal of Nervous and Mental Diseases* 138: 452–59.

Kornhauser, William. 1962. *Scientists in Industry: Conflict and Accommodation.* Berkeley, Univ. of California Press.

Kramer, Phillip. 1972. "The Indigenous Worker: Hometowner, Striver, or Activist." *Social Work* 17: 43–49.

Lamb, Richard, and Mahl, George. 1956. "Manifest Reactions of Patients and Interviewers to the Use of Sound Recording in the Psychiatric Interview." *American Journal of Psychiatry* 112: 733–35.

Lanning, Wayne L. 1971. "A Study of the Relation between Group and Individual Counseling Supervision and Three Relationship Measures." *Journal of Counseling Psychology* 18: 401–6.

Lawler, Edward S., and Hage, Gerald. n.d. "Intra-organizational Powerlessness among Social Workers: A Test of the Professional-Bureaucratic Conflict." Unpublished paper, Madison, Wis., University of Wisconsin.

Lazerson, Alan M. 1972. "The Learning Alliance and its Relation to Psychiatric Teaching." *Psychiatry in Medicine* 3: 81–91.

Leader, Arthur L. 1957. "New Directions in Supervision." *Social Casework* 38: 462–68.

Leader, Arthur L. 1968. "Supervision and Consultations through Observed Interviewing." *Social Casework* 49: 288–93.

Lee, Porter. 1923. "A Study of Social Treatment." *Family* 4: 191–99.

Leon, Edwina T. 1973. "The MSW as Supervisor of Paraprofessionals." In *Educating MSW Students to Work with Other Social Welfare Personnel*, ed. Margaret Purvine, pp. 38–48. New York, Council on Social Work Education.

Levinson, Perry, and Schiller, Jeffrey. 1966. "Role Analysis of the Indigenous Nonprofessional." *Social Work* 11: 95–101.

Levy, Charles S. 1960. "In Defense of Supervision." *Journal of Jewish Communal Service* 37: 194–201.

Levy, Gerald. 1970. "Acute Workers in a Welfare Bureaucracy." In *Social Problems and Social Policy*, ed. Deborah Offenbacher and Constance Poster, pp. 168–75. New York, Appleton.

Leyendecker, Gertrude. 1959. "A Critique of Current Trends in Supervision." In *Casework Papers, National Conference on Social Welfare, 1959.* New York, Family Service Association of America.

Lieberman, S. 1956. "The Effects of Change in Roles on the Attitudes of Role Occupants." *Human Relations* 9: 385–402.

Likert, Rensis. 1967. *The Human Organization: Its Management and Value.* New York, McGraw.

Linden, Evelyn. 1972. "Working with Aides." In *Day Care Aides: A Guide for In-Service Training.* Rev. ed. New York, National Federation of Settlements and Neighborhood Centers.

Lindenberg, R. 1957. "Changing Traditional Patterns of Supervision." *Social Work* 2: 42–46.

Lindenberg, Sidney. 1939. *Supervision in Social Group Work.* New York, Association Press.

Litwak, Eugene. 1964. "Models of Bureaucracy Which Permit Conflict." *American Journal of Sociology* 67: 177–84.

Lowenberg, Frank M. 1972. *Time and Quality in Graduate Social Work Education: Report of the Special Committee to Study the Length of Graduate Social Work Education.* New York, Council on Social Work Education.

Lutz, Werner A. 1956. *Student Evaluation: Workshop Report,* 1956 Annual Program Meeting of the CSWE, Buffalo, N.Y. New York, Council on Social Work Education.

McCune, Shirley D. 1966. "An Exploratory Study of the Measured Behavioral Styles of Students in Five Schools of Social Work." Ph.D. dissertation, School of Social Service, Catholic University of America.

MacGuffie, Robert, Janzen, Frederick V., and McPhee, William M. 1970. "The Expression and Perception of Feelings between Students and Supervisors in a Practicuum Setting." *Counselor Education and Supervision* 10: 263–71.

Mandell, Betty. 1973. "The 'Equality' Revolution and Supervision." *Journal of Education for Social Work* 9: 43–54.

Marcus, Grace. 1927. "How Casework Training May Be Adapted to Meet Workers' Personal Problems." In *Proceedings of the National Conference of Social Work, 1927.* Chicago, Univ. of Chicago Press.

Marcus, Philip M. 1961. "Supervision and Group Process." *Human Organization* 20: 15–19.

Marohn, Richard C. 1969. "The Similarity of Therapy and Supervisory Themes." *International Journal of Group Psychotherapy* 19: 176–84.

Matarazzo, Ruth G. 1971. "Research on the Teaching and Learning of Psychotherapeutic Skills." In *Handbook of Psychotherapy and Behavior Change,* ed. Allen E. Bergin and Sol Y. Garfield, pp. 895–924. New York, Wiley.

Mattinson, Janet. 1975. *The Reflection Process in Casework Supervision.* Washington, D.C., National Association of Social Workers.

Mayer, John E., and Rosenblatt, Aaron. 1973a. "Sources of Stress among Student Practitioners in Social Work: A Sociological Review." Paper read at the annual meeting, Council on Social Work Education, San Francisco, January 1973.

Mayer, John E., and Rosenblatt, Aaron. 1973b. "Strains between Social Work Students and Their Supervisors: A Preliminary Report." Paper read at the National Conference on Social Welfare, Atlantic City, N.J., May 1973.

Mayer, John E., and Rosenblatt, Aaron. 1974. "Sources of Stress among Student Practitioners in Social Work: A Sociological View." *Journal of Education for Social Work* 10: 56–66.

Mayer, John E., and Rosenblatt, Aaron. 1975. "Objectionable Supervisory Styles: Students' Views." *Social Work* 20: 184–89.

Mayer, Morris, and Matsushima, Joh. 1969. "Training for Child Care Work: A Report on a National Conference." *Child Welfare* 48: 525–32.

Mayhand, Edna, and Grusky, Oscar. 1972. "A Preliminary Experiment on the Effects of Black Supervision on White and Black Subordinates." *Journal of Black Studies* 2: 461–70.

Mechanic, David. 1964. "Sources of Power of Lower Participants in Complex Organizations." In *New Perspectives in Organizational Research,* ed. W. W. Cooper, M. W. Shelly, and H. J. Leavitt, pp. 136–49. New York, Wiley.

Melichercik, John. 1973. "Social Work Education and Social Work Practice." *Social Worker* 41: 22–27.

Merton, Robert. 1957. *Social Theory and Social Structure.* Rev. ed. New York, Free Press.

Meyer, Carol H. 1966. *Staff Development in Public Welfare Agencies.* New York, Columbia Univ. Press.

Meyer, Henry J. 1969. "Sociological Comments." In *Nonprofessionals: The Human Services,* ed. Charles Grosser, William E. Henry, and James G. Kelly, pp. 40–56. San Francisco, Jossey-Bass.

Miller, C. Dean, and Oetting, E. R. 1966. "Students React to Supervision." *Counselor Education and Supervision* 6: 73–74.

Miller, Irving. 1960. "Distinctive Characteristics of Supervision in Group Work." *Social Work* 5 (1): 69–76.

Miller, Ronald, and Podell, Lawrence. 1970. *Role Conflict in Public Social Services.* New York, State of New York Office of Community Affairs, Division of Research and Innovation.

Miller, Samuel O. 1970. "Components of Job Satisfaction for Beginning Social Workers." Mimeographed. School of Social Work, Western Michigan University, Kalamazoo.

Montalvo, Braulio. 1973. "Aspects of Live Supervision." *Family Process* 12: 343–59.

Moore, Elon H. 1934. "How Accurate Are Base Records." *Social Forces,* 12: 501.

Moore, Stewart. 1970. "Group Supervision: Forerunner or Trend Reflector: Part I—Trends and Duties in Group Supervision." *Social Worker* 38: 16–20.

Moore, Stewart. 1971. "Group Supervision: Forerunner or Trend Reflector: Part II—Advantages and Disadvantages." *Social Worker* 39: 3–7.

Moore, Wilbert E. 1970. *The Professions: Rules and Roles.* New York, Russell Sage.

Morill, Richard G. 1968. "Group Identity, Marginality, and the Non-professional." *Archives of General Psychiatry* 19: 404–12.

Mosher, Ralph L., and Purpel, David E. 1972. *Supervision: The Reluctant Profession*. Boston, Houghton.

Mueller, William S., and Kell, Bill L. 1972. *Coping with Conflict: Supervisory Counselors and Psychotherapists*. New York, Appleton.

Muslin, Hyman L., Burstein, Alvin G., Gedo, John E., and Sadow, Leo. 1967. "Research on the Supervisory Process. I. Supervisor's Appraisal of the Interview Data." *Archives of General Psychiatry* 16: 427–31.

Nader, Ralph, Petkas, Peter J., and Blackwell, Kate, eds. 1974. *Whistle Blowing: Report of the Conference on Professional Responsibility*. New York, Grossman Publishers.

Nathanson, Theresa. 1962. "Self-Awareness in the Educative Process." *Social Casework* 43: 31–38.

National Association of Social Workers. n.d. *Reference for Candidates for Admission to the Academy of Certified Social Workers*. Washington, D.C., Academy of Certified Social Workers, National Association of Social Workers.

National Association of Social Workers. 1971. *NASW Standards for Social Work Personnel Practices: Professional Standards*. Washington, D.C.

National Social Welfare Assembly. 1961. *Salaries and Working Conditions of Social Welfare Manpower, 1960*. New York.

Neleigh, Janice R., Newman, Frederick L., Malone, C. Elizabeth, and Sears, William F. 1971. *Training Nonprofessional Community Project Leaders*. Community Mental Health Monograph Series, No. 6. New York, Behavioral Publications.

Nelsen, Judith C. 1973. "Early Communication Between Field Instructors and Casework Students." D.S.W. dissertation, Columbia University School of Social Work.

Nelsen, Judith C. 1974. "Relationship Communication in Early Fieldwork Conferences. Part I–II." *Social Casework* 55: 237–43.

Newman, Edward, and Delaplaine, John W. 1974. *Social Work Manpower in the Seventies*. Washington, D.C., Linton, Mields, and Coston.

New York State, Office of the Comptroller. 1973. *Audit Report on Personnel Non-Productivity, New York City Department of Social Services*. Report no. NYC-24-73. New York: Office of the State Comptroller, Division of Audits and Accounts.

Niland, Thomas M., Duling, John, Allen, Jada, and Panther, Edward. 1971. "Student Counselors' Perception of Videotaping." *Counselor Education and Supervision*. 11: 97–101.

Normandia, Carmen. 1967. "Characteristics and Role of Indigenous Worker." In *Personnel in Anti-Poverty Programs: Implications for Social Work Education*, pp. 63–66. New York, Council on Social Work Education.

Olmstead, Joseph A. 1973. *Organizational Structure and Climate: Implications for Agencies*, National Study of Social Welfare and Rehabilitation Workers, Work and Organizational Contexts, Working Paper no. 2. Washington, D.C., U.S. Govt. Printing Office.

Olmstead, Joseph, and Christensen, Harold E. 1973. *Effects of Agency Work Contexts: An Intensive Field Study*. Research Report no. 2. Washington, D.C., Department of Health, Education, and Welfare, Social and Rehabilitation Service.

Olyan, Sidney D. 1972. "An Explanatory Study of Supervision in Jewish Community Centers as Compared to Other Welfare Settings." Ph.D. dissertation. University of Pittsburgh.

Orchard, Bernice. 1965. "The Use of Authority in Supervision." *Public Welfare* 23: 32–40.

Paige, Clara P. 1927. "Supervising Casework in a District Office." *Family* 8: 307–9.

Patti, Rino J. 1974a. "Organizational Resistance and Change: The View from Below." *Social Service Review* 48: 367–83.

Patti, Rino J. 1974b. "Limitations and Prospects of Internal Advocacy." *Social Casework* 55: 537–45.

Patti, Rino J., and Resnick, Herman. 1972. "Changing the Agency from Within." *Social Work* 17 (4): 48–57.

Payne, Paul A., Winter, Donna E., and Bell, Glenn E. 1972. "Effects of Supervisor Style on the Learning of Empathy in a Supervision Analogue." *Counselor Education and Supervision* 11: 262–69.

Peabody, Robert L. 1964. *Organizational Authority: Superior-Subordinate Relationships in Three Public Service Organizations*. New York, Atherton.

Pearl, Arthur, and Riessman, Frank. 1965. *New Concerns for the Poor*. New York, Free Press.

Pelz, Donald. 1952. "Influence: A Key to Effective Leadership in the First Line Supervisor." *Personnel* 29: 209–17.

Perlman, Helen H. 1947. "Content in Basic Social Casework." *Social Service Review* 21: 76–84.

Perlman, Helen H. 1950. "Teaching Casework by the Discussion Method." *Social Service Review* 24: 334–46.

Peters, Charles, and Branch, Taylor. 1972. *Blowing the Whistle: Dissent in the Public Interest*. New York, Praeger.

Pettes, Dorothy E. 1967. *Supervision in Social Work*. London, George Allen.

Pittenger, Robert E., Hockett, Charles F., and Danehy, John J. 1960. *The First Five Minutes: A Sample of Microscopic Interview Analyses.* Ithaca, N.Y., Martineau.

Piven, Herman, and Pappenfort, Donald. 1960. "Strain between Administrator and Worker: A View from the Field of Corrections." *Social Work* 5: 37–45.

Podell, Lawrence. 1967. "Examination Grades and New Workers." *Welfare in Review* 5: 37–45.

Pointer, Avis Y., and Fishman, Jacob R. 1968. *New Careers: Entry Level Training for the Human Service Aide.* Washington, D.C., New Careers Development Program, University Research Corp.

Poling, E. G. 1968. "Video Tape Recordings in Counseling Practicuum. I. Environmental Considerations." *Counselor Education and Supervision* 8: 348–56.

Popper, Hermine I. 1968. "A Foot on the Ladder." In *Up From Poverty,* ed. Frank Riessman and Hermine I. Popper, pp. 37–54. New York, Harper.

Presthus, Robert. 1962. *The Organizational Society.* New York, Knopf.

Pretzer, Clarence A., chairman. 1929. "Significant Facts Regarding the Turnover of Case Workers in Family Welfare Agencies during 1927 and 1928." *Family* 10: 163–73.

Pruger, Robert, and Specht, Harry. 1968. "Establishing New Careers Programs: Organizational Barriers and Strategies." *Social Work* 13 (4): 21–32.

Purvis, Lurline C. 1972. "Self-Awareness: A Proposal for Supervision." *Journal of Contemporary Psychotherapy* 4: 107–12.

Raider, Melvyn C. 1975. "An Evaluation of Management by Objectives." *Social Casework* 56: 79–83.

Rapoport, Lydia. 1954. "The Use of Supervision as a Tool in Professional Development." *British Journal of Psychiatric Social Work* 2: 66–74.

Reich, Charles A. 1970. *The Greening of America.* New York, Random House.

Reid, William S. 1967. "Social Work and Motherhood: Competitors for Womenpower." *Personnel Information: NASW* 10: 44–47.

Reiff, Robert, and Riessman, Frank. 1965. *The Indigenous Nonprofessional: A Strategy of Change in Community Action and Community Mental Health Programs.* Community Mental Health Journal, Monograph No. 1.

Reynolds, Bertha C. 1936. "Art of Supervision." *Family* 17: 103–7.

Reynolds, Bertha C. 1942. *Learning and Teaching in the Practice of Social Work.* New York, Farrar.

Rice, Robert. 1973. "Organizing to Innovate in Social Work." *Social Casework* 54: 20–26.

Richan, Willard. 1961. "A Theoretical Scheme for Determining Roles of Professional and Nonprofessional Personnel." *Social Work* 6: 22–28.

Richan, Willard C. 1972. "Indigenous Paraprofessional Staff." In *Issues in Human Services*, ed. Florence W. Kaslow and associates, pp. 51–71. San Francisco, Jossey-Bass.

Richards, Steven A., and Jaffee, Cabot L. 1972. "Blacks Supervising Whites: A Study of Interracial Difficulties in Working Together in a Simulated Organization." *Journal of Applied Psychology* 56: 234–40.

Richmond, Mary. 1897. "The Need for a Training School in Applied Philanthropy." In *Proceedings of the National Conference of Social Welfare, 1897.*

Richmond, Mary. 1899. *Friendly Visiting Among the Poor: A Handbook for Charity Workers.* New York, Macmillan.

Riessman, Frank. 1967. "Strategies and Suggestions for Training Nonprofessionals." *Community Mental Health Journal* 3: 103–10.

Riessman, Frank. 1972. "The Crises in New Careers." *New Human Services Newsletter* no. 11, p. 2.

Riessman, Frank, and Goldfarb, Jean. 1964. "Role Playing and the Poor." *Group Psychotherapy* 17: 36–48.

Riessman, Frank, and Popper, Hermine I., eds. 1968. *Up from Poverty.* New York, Harper.

Rigdon, Dorothy. 1972. *The Subprofessional and the Poor: A Conference Report.* Jacksonville, Fla., Department of Health and Rehabilitation Services.

Rioch, M. J. 1966. "Changing Concepts in the Training of Therapists." *Journal of Consulting Psychology* 30: 290–92.

Roberts, Ralph R., and Renzaglia, G. A. 1965. "The Influence of Tape Recording on Counseling." *Journal of Counseling Psychology* 12: 10–15.

Robinson, Virginia. 1936. *Supervision in Social Casework*, Chapel Hill, N.C., Univ. of North Carolina Press.

Robinson, Virginia P. 1949. *The Dynamics of Supervision under Functional Controls.* Philadelphia, Univ. of Pennsylvania Press.

Rose, Sheldon. 1970. "A Behavioral Model for Field Instruction and Supervision." Mimeographed. Madison, Wis., School of Social Work, University of Wisconsin.

Rose, Sheldon D., Lowenstein, Jane, and Fellin, Phillip. 1969. "Measuring Student Perception of Field Instruction." In *Current Patterns in Field Instruction in Graduate Social Work Education*, ed.

Betty L. Jones, pp. 125–34. New York, Council on Social Work Education.

Rosen, Harold, and Bartemeier, Leo H. 1967. "The Psychiatric Resident as Participant Therapist." *American Journal of Psychiatry* 123: 1371–78.

Rosenberg, Morris. 1957. *Occupations and Values.* New York, Free Press.

Rothman, Beulah. 1973. "Perspectives on Learning and Taching in Continuing Education." *Journal of Education for Social Work* 9: 39–52.

Rothman, Jack. 1974. *Planning and Organizing for Social Change: Action Principles from Social Science Research.* New York, Columbia Univ. Press.

Rowley, Carl M., and Faux, Eugene. 1966. "The Team Approach to Supervision." *Mental Hygiene* 50: 60–65.

Royster, Eugene C. 1972. "Black Supervisors: Problems of Race and Role." In *Issues in Human Services,* ed. Florence W. Kaslow and associates, pp. 72–84. San Francisco, Jossey-Bass.

Ruzek, Sheryl K. 1974. "Making Social Work Accountable." In *The Professions and Their Prospects,* ed. Eliot Freidson, pp. 217–41. Beverly Hills, Calif., Sage Publications.

Ryan, C. 1969. "Video Aids in Practicuum Supervision." *Counselor Education and Supervision* 8: 125–29.

Ryan, Francis. 1964. "Joint Interviewing by Field Intructor and Student." *Social Casework* 45: 471–74.

Sales, Esther, and Navarre, Elizabeth. 1970. *Individual and Group Supervision in Field Instruction: A Research Report.* Ann Arbor, Mich., School of Social Work, University of Michigan.

Schein, Edgar H. 1970. *Organizational Psychology.* 2d ed. Englewood Cliffs, N.J., Prentice-Hall.

Schindler, Ruben. 1972. "The Community and Social Service Programs: A Report of a National Survey." In *Community and Social Service Education in The Community College: Issues and Characteristics.* New York, Council on Social Work Education.

Schmidt, Frances, and Perry, Martha. 1940. "Values and Limitations of the Evaluation Process. I: As Seen by the Supervisor. II: As Seen by the Worker." In *Proceedings of the National Conference of Social Work,* pp. 629–47. New York, Columbia Univ. Press.

Schour, Esther. 1951. "Helping Social Workers Handle Work Stresses." *Social Casework* 25: 423–28.

Schubert, Margaret. 1960. "Field Work Performance: Repetition of a Study." *Social Service Review* 34: 286–99.

Schultz, Virginia M. 1970. "Employment Trends of Recent Graduates." *Personnel Information* 16: 15.

Schuster, Daniel B., Sandt, John J., and Thaler, Otto F. 1972. *Clinical Supervision of the Psychiatric Resident.* New York, Brunner/Mazel.

Schwartz, Edward E., and Sample, William C. 1972. *The Midway Office: An Experiment in the Organization of Work Groups.* New York, National Association of Social Workers.

Scott, W. Richard. 1965. "Reactions to Supervision in a Heteronomous Professional Organization." *Administrative Science Quarterly* 10: 65–81.

Scott, W. Richard. 1969. "Professional Employees in a Bureaucratic Structure." In *The Semiprofessions and Their Organization,* ed. Amitai Etzioni, pp. 82–140. New York, Free Press.

Searles, Harold F. 1955. "The Informational Value of the Supervisor's Emotional Experiences." *Psychiatry* 18: 135–46.

Simon, Herbert A. 1957. *Administrative Behavior: A Study of Decision-Making Processes in Administrative Organization.* 2d ed. New York, Free Press.

Simpson, Richard L., and Simpson, Ida H. 1969. "Women and Bureaucracy in the Semiprofessions." In *The Semiprofessions and Their Organization,* ed. Amitai Etzioni, pp. 196–265. New York, Free Press.

Smith, Donald M. 1972. "Group Supervision: An Experience." *Social Work Today* (London) 3: 13–15.

Smith, Zilpha D. 1884. "Volunteer Visiting, The Organization Necessary to Make it Effective." In *Proceedings of The National Conference of Charities and Corrections.* Boston, Geo. H. Ellis.

Smith, Zilpha D. 1887. "How to Get and Keep Visitors." In *Proceedings of the National Conference of Charities and Corrections,* pp. 156–62. Boston, Geo. H. Ellis.

Smith, Zilpha D. 1901a. "Friendly Visitors." *Charities* 7: 159–60.

Smith, Zilpha D. 1901b. "How to Win and How to Train Charity Visitors." *Charities* 7: 46–47.

Sobey, Francine. 1970. *The Nonprofessional Revolution in Mental Health.* New York, Columbia Univ. Press.

Specht, Harry. 1972. "The Deprofessionalization of Social Work." *Social Work* 17(2): 3–15.

Spellman, Dorothea. 1946. "Improving the Quality of Social Group Work Practice through Individual Supervisory Conferences." In *Toward Professional Standards.* New York, Association Press.

Spergel, Irving. 1966. *Street Gang Work: Theory and Practice.* Reading, Mass., Addison-Wesley.

Steggert, Frank X. 1970. "Organization Theory: Bureaucratic Influences and the Social Welfare Task." In *Social Work Administration: A Resource Book*, ed. Harry A. Schatz, pp. 43–56. New York, Council on Social Work Education.

Stein, Herman D. 1961. "Administrative Implications of Bureaucratic Theory." *Social Work* 6 (3): 14–21.

Stein, Herman. 1965. "Administration." In *Encyclopedia of Social Work*, ed. Robert Morris. New York, National Association of Social Workers.

Stelling, Joan, and Bucher, Rue. 1973. "Vocabularies of Realism in Professional Socialization." *Social Science and Medicine* 7: 661–75.

Stevens, Ruth N., and Hutchinson, Fred A. 1956. "A New Concept of Supervision is Tested." *Social Work* 1 (3): 50–55.

Stewart, Rosemary. 1972. *The Reality of Organizations*. New York, Doubleday, Anchor.

Stiles, Evelyn. 1963. "Supervision in Perspective." *Social Casework* 44: 19–25.

Stodgill, R. M., and Coons, A. E. 1957. *Leader Behavior: Its Description and Measurement*. Columbus, Ohio, Bureau of Business Research, Ohio State Univ.

Strauss, Anselm L. 1964. *Psychiatric Ideologies and Institutions*. New York, Free Press.

Studt, Elliot. 1954. "An Outline for Study of Social Authority Factors in Casework." *Social Casework* 35: 231–38.

Studt, Elliot. 1959. "Worker Client Authority Relationships in Social Work." *Social Work* 4: 18–28.

Suess, James F. 1970. "Self-confrontation of Videotaped Psychotherapy as a Teaching Device for Psychiatric Students." *Journal of Medical Education* 45: 271–82.

Switzer, Elaine. 1973. "Chicago Settlement, 1972: An Overview." *Social Service Review* 47: 581–92.

Tannenbaum, Arnold A. 1968. *Control in Organizatons*. New York, McGraw.

Teare, Robert J., Gatewood, Robert D., Feild, Hubert S., and Williams, Thomas D. 1974. *Overview Study of Employment of Paraprofessionals*. National Study of Social Welfare and Rehabilitation Workers, Work and Organizational Contexts, Research Report no. 3. Washington D.C., U.S. Government Printing Office.

Toren, Nina. 1969. "Semiprofessionalism and Social Work: A Theoretical Perspective." In *The Semiprofessions and Their Organization*, ed. Amitai Etzioni, pp. 141–95. New York, Free Press.

Toren, Nina. 1972. *Social Work: The Case of a Semiprofession*. Beverly Hills, Sage Publications.

Torre, Elizabeth. 1974. "Student Performance in Solving Social Work Problems and Work Experience Prior to Entering the MSW Program." *Journal of Education for Social Work* 10: 114–17.

Towle, Charlotte. 1945. *Common Human Needs*. Washington, D.C., U.S. Govt. Printing Office.

Towle, Charlotte. 1954. *The Learner in Education for the Professions: As Seen in Education for Social Work*. Chicago, Univ. of Chicago Press.

Towle, Charlotte. 1962. "Role of Supervision in the Union of Cause and Function in Social Work." *Social Service Review* 36: 396–411.

Tropman, John E. 1968. "The Married Professional Social Worker." *Journal of Marriage and the Family* 30: 661–65.

Tyler, Ralph W. 1971. *Basic Principles of Curriculum and Instruction*. Chicago, Univ. of Chicago Press.

U.S. Civil Service Commission. 1955. *Leadership and Supervision: A Survey of Research Findings*. U.S. Civil Service Commission, Personnel Management Series no. 9. Washington, D.C.

U.S. Department of Health, Education and Welfare, Social Rehabilitation Service. 1975. *Public Welfare Personnel Annual Statistical Data: June 1973*. Washington, D.C., National Center for Social Statistics.

Van Atta, Ralph E. 1969a. "Co-Therapy as a Supervisory Process." *Psychotherapy: Theory, Research and Practice* 6: 137–39.

Van Atta, R. E. 1969b. "Excitory and Inhibitory Effect of Various Modes of Observation in Counseling." *Journal of Counseling Psychology* 16: 433–39.

Vinter, Robert D. 1959. "The Social Structure of Service." In *Issues in American Social Work*, ed. Alfred J. Kahn, pp. 242–69. New York, Columbia Univ. Press.

Walker, Sydnor H. 1928. *Social Work and the Training of Social Workers*. Chapel Hill, N.C., Univ. of North Carolina Press.

Walton, Mary. 1967. "Rats in The Crib, Roaches in The Food." *Village Voice*, May 11.

Walz, G. R., and Johnston, J. A. 1963. "Counselors Look at Themselves on Video Tape." *Journal of Counseling Psychology* 10: 232–36.

Walz, Thomas. 1971. "A New Breed of Social Workers: Fact or Fantasy." *Public Welfare* 29: 19–23.

Ward, C. H. 1960. "An Electronic Aide for Teaching Interviewing Techniques." *Archives of General Psychiatry* 3: 357–58.

Ward, C. H. 1962. "Electronic Preceptoring in Teaching Beginning Psychotherapy." *Journal of Medical Education* 37: 1128–29.

Warren, D. I. 1968. "Power, Visibility and Conformity in Formal Organizations." *American Sociological Review* 6: 951–70.

Wasserman, Harry. 1970. "Early Careers of Professional Social Workers in a Public Child Welfare Agency." *Social Work* 15 (3): 93–101.

Wasserman, Harry. 1971. "The Professional Social Worker in a Bureaucracy." *Social Work* 16 (1): 89–95.

Watson, Kenneth W. 1973. "Differential Supervision." *Social Work* 18 (6): 80–88.

Wax, John. 1963. "Time-Limited Supervision." *Social Work* 8 (3): 37–43.

Weber, Max. 1946. *Essays in Sociology,* trans. and ed. H. H. Gerth and C. Wright Mills. New York, Oxford Univ. Press.

Weber, Shirley, and Polm, Donald. 1974. "Participatory Management in Public Welfare." *Social Casework* 55: 297–306.

Weinberg, Gladys. 1960. "Dynamics and Content of Group Supervision." *Child Welfare* 39: 1–6.

Weissman, Harold H. 1973. *Overcoming Mismanagement in the Human Service Professions.* San Francisco, Jossey-Bass.

Wiehe, Vernon. 1973. "Management by Objectives in a Family Service Agency." *Social Casework* 54: 142–46.

Wilkie, Charlotte H. 1963. "A Study of Distortions in Recording Interviews." *Social Work* 8: 31–36.

Williamson, Margaret. 1961. *Supervision: New Patterns and Processes.* New York, Association Press.

Wilson, Gertrude, and Ryland, Gladys. 1949. *Social Group Work Practice.* Boston, Houghton.

Wolpe, Joseph. 1972a. "Supervision Transcripts: I, Fear of Success." *Journal of Behavior Therapy and Experimental Psychiatry* 3: 107–10.

Wolpe, Joseph. 1972b. "Supervision Transcripts: II, Problems of a Novice." *Journal of Behavior Therapy and Experimental Psychiatry* 3: 199–203.

Wolpe, Joseph. 1972c. "Supervision Transcripts: III, Some Problems in a Claustrophobic Case." *Journal of Behavior Therapy and Experimental Psychiatry* 3: 301–5.

Wolpe, Joseph. 1973a. "Supervision Transcripts: IV, Planning Therapeutic Tactics." *Journal of Behavioral Therapy and Experimental Psychiatry* 4: 41–46.

Wolpe, Joseph. 1973b. "Supervision Transcripts: VII, Neglecting the Case History and Other Elementary Errors." *Journal of Behavior Therapy and Experimental Psychiatry* 4: 365–70.

Woodcock, G. D. C. 1967. "A Study of Beginning Supervision." *British Journal of Psychiatric Social Work* 9: 66–74.

Work in America. 1973. Report of a special task force to the Secretary of Health, Education and Welfare. Cambridge, Mass., MIT Press.

Yelaja, Shankar A., ed. 1971. *Authority and Social Work: Concept and Use.* Toronto, Univ. of Toronto Press.

Zimny, George H., Brown, Joseph E., Ellis, Joanna J., and Sorenson, James C. 1972. "Use of Television in the Clinical Internship Programs." *Professional Psychology* 3: 271–76.

index